Confessing History

CONFESSING HISTORY

*Explorations in Christian Faith
and the Historian's Vocation*

Edited by

JOHN FEA, JAY GREEN, AND ERIC MILLER

Univerity of Notre Dame Press • *Notre Dame, Indiana*

Library of Congress Cataloging-in-Publication Data

Confessing history : explorations in Christian faith and the historian's
vocation / edited by John Fea, Jay Green, and Eric Miller.
p. cm.
Includes bibliographical references and index.
ISBN-13: 978-0-268-02903-6 (pbk. : alk. paper)
ISBN-10: 0-268-02903-2 (pbk. : alk. paper)
1. History—Religious aspects—Christianity.
2. Christian historians—Intellectual life.
I. Fea, John. II. Green, Jay (Jay D.) III. Miller, Eric, 1966–
BR115.H5C59 2010
261.5—dc22   2010024242

To John D. Woodbridge, Christian historian

Contents

PREFACE

One of the richest and most compelling theological concepts in the Christian tradition is that of *calling*. The Hebrew Scriptures and New Testament bear witness to the ways in which God calls his people into covenant relationship, to repentance, to holiness, and to special service in the Kingdom. Christian notions of calling, of vocation, also encompass the divine ordination of all lawful work into which men and women may serve, and the theological import of work itself. Especially with the latter meaning in view, the contributors to this volume have gathered here to ask what the vocation of historian might mean for those who are also followers of Christ. What implications do Christian faith and practice have for living out one's calling as an historian? And to what extent does one's calling as a Christian disciple speak to the nature, quality, or goals of one's work as scholar, teacher, adviser, writer, community member, or social commentator? Written from several different theological and professional points of view, the essays contained in this book constitute a free-ranging conversation about the vocation of the historian and its place in both the personal lives of Christian disciples and Christ's Kingdom at large.

In one sense, the preceding description of this volume seems simple and straightforward. But we know that a book of this stripe violates many of the standing and long-cherished conventions of professional history on at least two levels. First, most practicing historians still unofficially believe that matters of personal conviction and identity act as pollutants in the time-honored quest to tell true stories about the past. After more than twenty-five years of postmodern theory and forty years of identity politics, the historian's craft as practiced in the trenches remains a conventionally scientific one in its tone and temper. It's one thing to have personal identities and convictions; it's quite another to put these matters on display or to profess them as motivations for one's work.

On a second, deeper level, expressing the very humanness of the historian's craft is sure to elicit even greater suspicion when the stated identities and beliefs in question are religious in nature. We each undertook Ph.D. studies in the mid-1990s, a period that will undoubtedly be remembered for generating a kind of postmodern-inspired glasnost toward religious viewpoints in the academy. As devout believers interested in exploring the theological significance of our work as historians, we took courage from the bold discussions of "religious advocacy" and the "outrageous idea of Christian Scholarship" that were so widely heralded during our years of graduate training.[1] But after a decade of murderous religious fanaticism and an American president whose reputation for intellectual incuriosity and reckless foreign policy are regularly attributed to his Christian beliefs, academic tolerance toward religious categories may be reaching its limits. Rather than granting that religious commitment must be a shill for a theocratic conspiracy or the seed of anti-intellectual bigotry, we urge readers to judge the essays that follow on their own merits and, moreover, to consider the possibility that explorations of faith and scholarship have something meaningful to contribute to the wider academic conversation.

Historians of the Reformed theological heritage were the vanguard in making connections between history (and scholarship more broadly) and Christian faith, and have subsequently shaped most contemporary discussions on the relationship between Christianity and the historian's task. These scholars, led by George Marsden, Ronald Wells, and Mark Noll, have argued that the theological presuppositions (or background commitments) of all historians will variously inform their understandings of the past, and studying the past becomes distinctly Christian as faith and scholarship are thoughtfully integrated with one another.[2] While this position has been enormously fruitful, and the editors of this volume remain sympathetic with it, our book seeks to expand this conversation in significant ways.

Using vocation as our organizing principle has freed our contributors to think more broadly about the variety of ways that historians might be called by God to conceive of and conduct their work. The

Reformed integrative strategy has tended to give exclusive attention to the ideational implications of the historian's "worldview" for historical research and writing. While this important dimension of Christian faith is by no means ignored in the essays that follow, the broader appeal of vocation enables authors to focus also on the different way historians connect their faith to their callings as in the varied roles they play: as teachers, church members, cultural critics, public citizens, and professional members of the academy. Such explorations consider the multi-layered identities of the historian, the place of moral inquiry in historical study, the social responsibilities of the historian in contemporary society, and the personal tensions that sometimes express themselves among callings to the academy, to the state, to their families, and to their churches.

In the undertow of Christian scholarship over the past twenty-five years, a number of voices have risen in protest to the ways that the Reformed paradigm has purportedly eclipsed alternate ways of thinking about the relationship between Christianity and academic life.[3] The vocational emphasis of this volume acknowledges these concerns, and serves to open the conversation to explorations of history as conceived among a variety of Reformed and non-Reformed Christian traditions. We believe this broadened conversation is evident in the essays that follow. Since no two Christian traditions interpret the meaning of vocation in exactly the same way, its broad application among a variety of theological and ecclesiastical traditions makes it an uncommonly fertile gathering place for thinking about the implications of Christianity for a faith-oriented life in history. We are only moderately interested in fostering the standing criticism of Reformed strategies, but we hope that the various Catholic, Lutheran, Episcopalian, and broadly evangelical, as well as Presbyterian and Dutch Calvinist, voices in this volume will illustrate that the conversation about Christian scholarship in history is a richly divergent one.

While it is true that notions of calling among all contributors to this volume have been, to one degree or another, shaped by both our respective local churches and our academic institutions, it is important that we here explicitly recognize a strategic hybrid institution that has played no small role in bringing us into conversation with one another.

The Conference on Faith and History (CFH) is an interdenominational academic organization founded in 1968 for the purpose of providing fellowship, a venue for scholarship, and a space for conversation among Christians interested in exploring the relationship between faith and history. Over the past ten years, the editors and many contributors to this volume have been privileged to provide leadership in the CFH, offering some focus to the organization's contemporary purpose and direction. Relationships forged as part of the CFH inform much of what follows in this volume. Even though a book like this tends to highlight the vocational importance of the college classroom, the historical archive, and the local church, we think it is safe to assert that many of us might have remained toiling in these vineyards alone were it not for the genuine sense of community that we found at biennial CFH meetings and in the pages of its journal, *Fides et Historia*.

Another not-so-silent partner in this venture is the Lilly Endowment. We believe that our focus on the relationship between Christian faith and the historian's vocation is particularly pertinent at this moment in light of the recent efforts by Lilly to encourage exploration of this theme on hundreds of church-related college campuses throughout the United States. The volume editors all work at church-related institutions that have been recipients of the two-million-dollar Lilly Christian Vocation Grant, and we have each taken leadership roles in engaging these issues at our respective institutions. John served a two-year postdoctoral fellowship with the Lilly Fellows Program in Arts and Humanities at Valparaiso University, a program devoted to Christian thinking on these issues. Eric and Jay played direct roles in writing grants and shaping Lilly-funded programs at Covenant College and Geneva College. A significant number of contributors have likewise played major roles in carrying forward Lilly-sponsored programs at their schools. We are grateful to the Lilly Foundation for their investment in church-related higher education.

These initiatives have provided great energy on our campuses, enabling us to think more deeply about these questions in ways that have enriched the teaching, the life of the mind, and the collective sense of God's calling at many of the schools represented here. In many ways, we see this volume as an effort to help this national conversation on vocation and church-related higher education move from a general institutional focus toward more particular expressions within the disciplines. We appreciate the generous support of Lilly that has made this volume possible both conceptually and quite literally.

We feel honored to have gathered the gifted historian teacher-scholars represented in this volume, all of whom have spent considerable time in their careers thinking critically and creatively about the relationship between Christian faith and the historian's vocation. Whether in their personal reflections on life in the discipline, their complex discussions of theory and method, or the prophetic challenges they offer to our spheres of service, we believe the essays contained in this volume are worthy tributes to the calling of the Christian historian. But an even greater tribute to this calling will be the lively conversations among our colleagues and students that we hope these essays inspire.

PUTTING TOGETHER a volume of this nature is not easy, and there are many people and organizations we want to thank. First, we want to thank all of the authors in this volume for taking the time to reflect on how their Christian faith informs what they do as scholars and teachers. Some of these essays were presented at the twenty-fourth biennial meeting of the Conference of Faith and History, held in 2004 at Hope College in Holland, Michigan. We served as conference organizers for that meeting and thus appreciate the leadership of the Conference on Faith and History for supporting our vision for the conference. This book was partially subsidized by Lilly Vocation Grants from Covenant College, Geneva College, and Messiah College.

At the University of Notre Dame Press, our editor, Chuck Van Hof, believed in this project from the start and helped to shepherd it through the review process. Matthew Dowd, manuscript editor extraordinaire, made this a better book.

Three former students deserve credit for bringing this book to completion. Jeremy McClellan and Jeremy Fox, both of Covenant College, offered valuable comments based upon their reading of these essays in draft form. Cali McCullough, a recent graduate of Messiah College, put aside some of her own planning for a career in history to help us prepare the book for publication. Katherine Garland, a history major at Messiah College, provided a careful read of the page proofs.

We spent a lot of time thinking and talking about this book project on our breaks from grading Advanced Placement United States history exams. We thus thank our wives—Joy Fea, Beth Ann Green, and Denise Miller—for patiently enduring our absences during our weeks in San Antonio.

Some material in this book has previously appeared elsewhere. We wish to thank the editors of *Fides et Historia* for permission to reprint the essays by Mark Schwehn, Thomas Albert Howard, William Katerberg, and Douglas A. Sweeney, and the editors of *The Cresset* for permission to reprint the essay by John Fea. We also appreciate receiving leave to reproduce the poem "The Reader," which appears in Mark Schwehn's essay and is copyrighted by Houghton Mifflin Harcourt.

This book is dedicated to John D. Woodbridge, a Christian scholar and teacher who has inspired us to think about our careers as historians in terms of the Christian understanding of "calling."

Notes

1. Bruce Kuklick and D. G. Hart, eds., *Religious Advocacy and American History* (Grand Rapids, Mich.: Eerdmans, 1997); George Marsden, *The Outrageous Idea of Christian Scholarship* (New York: Oxford University Press, 1997).

2. See Ronald Wells, ed., *History and the Christian Historian* (Grand Rapids, Mich.: Eerdmans, 1998), passim.

3. Douglas Jacobsen and Rhonda Hustedt Jacobsen, *Scholarship and Christian Faith: Enlarging the Conversation* (New York: Oxford University Press, 2004).

CONFESSING HISTORY

Introduction

A TRADITION RENEWED?

The Challenge of a Generation

ERIC MILLER

THE COMMANDING POSITION OF THE ACADEMY IN
contemporary life is as brute a fact as future historians will ever un-
earth. At present, millions of people, young and old, are inching their
way through curricular labyrinths of all kinds, seeking the hope a high
school diploma no longer affords. Tens of thousands of professors, in
sync with the standards of their respective guilds, work to construct in
these students an outlook and "skill set" that will advance a panoply
of political, economic, and moral ends. And thousands of administrators, aided by vast support staffs, busy themselves directing traffic. The
alumni spill out and scatter annually in massive numbers, equipped to
do the nation's—and the world's—work.

In the main, it is work that has become secularized—another truism
of our times. Accountants, teachers, engineers, nurses, programmers,
lab technicians, attorneys: all proceed from the academy fluent in the
language of the modern world, their religious beliefs properly closeted,
their gaze steady on the job at hand. For the overwhelming majority,
this is mere necessity, the dollar holding steady as the currency of the
age. The cost of its transmission from employer to employee is usually
a significant degree of self-conscious, duly cultivated secularity—not a

1

mandated absence of religious devotion so much as the required presence of procedural norms that make religious language problematic.

Given this, our linguistically straitened circumstance, is it now advisable, or even desirable, for historians of Christian persuasion to practice their craft in a manner that decisively reflects their vision of the world—one that, it should go without saying, may well be in substantial conflict with the ethos and program of the times? This book seeks to make a strong affirmative response to this complicated question.

Or, rather, it joins earlier affirmative responses, seeking both to buttress and challenge them. If, as Eugene Genovese has argued, a tradition consists in "the embodiment of 'givens' that must constantly be fought for, recovered in each generation, and adjusted to new conditions," this book humbly but spiritedly joins a long tradition of writings in which Christian scholars have in diverging eras sought to probe and articulate the ways in which life on earth might be playing out beneath the eye and at the hand of the God of Christian faith.[1] It is well to state at the outset, though, that in this volume we write less as reformers than as explorers, seeking the generational renewal Genovese describes. Through the discovery of new or neglected pathways we pursue a scholarly and vocational end that, in the past century, has been appealing and elusive at once.[2]

John Henry Newman, as the university in the mid-nineteenth century was emerging in its current form, captured with timely brilliance the impulse to secure and advance a distinctively Christian approach to the modern academic disciplines. Newman emphatically urged Christian scholars to counter the modern tide with institutional and disciplinary practices that remained both true to Christian faith and conversant with the rapidly changing intellectual ethos of the age. "Admit a God," he reminded his auditors, "and you introduce among the subjects of your knowledge, a fact encompassing, closing in upon, absorbing, every other fact conceivable. How can we investigate any part of any order of knowledge, and stop short of that which enters into every order? All true principles run over with it, all phenomena converge to it; it is truly the First and the Last."[3] In the decades since, countless Christian scholars have granted Newman's theological premise and embraced his institutional vision, while at the same time struggling to discern how to go about this holy work in a manner consonant with both their creedal confession and their academic professions.

Over the past century many organizations have arisen to advance Newman's project, ranging from whole colleges to small associations. The Conference on Faith and History (CFH) is perhaps a typical example of the latter, a scholarly society launched in 1968 by (mainly) American evangelical Protestants seeking a space for Christian reflection on the discipline of history as well as a place that would sponsor research and writing on religious history in general. In a modest way, it has helped to provide a center for much recent response among Christian historians (including many of the contributors to this volume) to the Newmanian challenge, especially through its journal *Fides et Historia*.

Given that the CFH's organizational launch took place amidst what was the high tide of modernist, scientific influence on the historical profession, the early efforts of the conference, predictably, reflected the moment: the materialist and empirical strictures that governed historical method and narrative proved to be the starting point, and often the end point, for many if not most of the historians associated with the conference. George M. Marsden, then an historian at Calvin College, summarized the practice of many when, in a postscript to his landmark 1980 volume *Fundamentalism and American Culture, 1870–1925*, he both affirmed the superintendence of the Christian God of human history and disavowed any attempt to set forth an understanding of the particular ways such superintendence was taking place. Theologians may be charged with the task of discerning the ways of God, wrote Marsden, but this should not be confused with the historian's task—even the believing historian's task. Historians of faith are as unable to plot the ways of God with men as unbelievers, he contended; examining the past with mere earth-bound vision, all humans are limited to making judgments based on "observable cultural forces."[4]

With this declaration Marsden articulated the consensus of a generation. To be sure, Marsden and those who reflected his approach continued to claim the possibility of a strong connection between a Christian historian's faith and her work as an historian. Historians of faith, Marsden suggested in a later volume, may usefully employ what he termed "background faith commitments" to guide their work.[5]

Calvinists, on this view, might tend to take a dimmer view of human affairs and possibilities than, say, left-liberal secularists, which their researches and narratives should accordingly reflect. But when trying to explore or explain the past, be it the development of the Western university or the Third Reich, all historians, regardless of creed, are left with the same epistemological limitations: the ability to make judgments based only upon "observable cultural forces" and the need to translate whatever theological assumptions the historian might have into suitably secular modes of narrative and analysis.

Not surprisingly, given this framework, Marsden's scholarship (reflective of his generational cohort at its best) has met little significant resistance within the world of academic history. His introductory or concluding sections of his books, where he has confessed his Christian vantage, may make some readers squirm, but his colleagues have tended to find his actual history writing compelling, fitting comfortably within the broad consensus of the profession, as his Bancroft Prize–winning biography of Jonathan Edwards attests.[6]

But does this approach square with the radical program for Christian scholarship as advanced, in touchstone fashion, by Newman? Beginning in the 1990s a younger generation of Christian scholars began to call into question what one of them dubbed, in a plenary address at a biennial meeting of the CFH, the "Marsden settlement."[7] Another charged, matter-of-factly, that most Christian historians had "only rarely questioned the most basic rules of modern scholarship."[8] If it did not quite amount to a revolt, this kind of challenge reflected more than mere intergenerational restlessness. The long quest for a truly Christian practice of history was taking a new turn.[9]

The general circumstance of Christian scholarship had been altered substantially by the late 1990s. The historian James Turner and sociologist Alan Wolfe each published essays that took stock of the enlarging evangelical presence within the academy in the previous two decades. Turner, a colleague of Marsden at the University of Notre Dame and a Roman Catholic, noted in a 1999 *Commonweal* essay the theological dimensions of what he described as "an intellectual renaissance within American evangelicalism," one that had "gone far beyond theology to establish a visible evangelical presence in literary scholarship, psychology, history, philosophy, and other fields." For Turner, the intellectual roots of this renaissance extended deeply into the Roman Catholic, Anglican, and, above all, Dutch Calvinist traditions, which for him seemed to explain both its promise and its limitations: "the new evangelical intellectuals pray as evangelicals," he observed, "but think as Calvinists, or Anglicans, or sometimes even Catholics."[10]

The CFH certainly reflected this enlarging influence and shifting composition of evangelical intellectual life. At the behest of scholars and mentors such as Marsden, and aided by the advent of new communication technologies such as e-mail and the internet, younger scholars emerging from varying quadrants of American evangelicalism had begun to find vital resources for their work and faith outside of their native traditions, and, consequently, had discovered intellectual companions from other Christian communions as well.[11] In a presidential address at the 2000 biennial meeting, William Vance Trollinger, reflecting the new ethos, challenged the conference to more aggressively pursue participants from beyond the boundaries of evangelical Protestantism. The next meeting accordingly opened with an address by a young Catholic historian, Christopher Shannon—who used the opportunity to decry the existing consensus on the Christian practice of history and press for what he conceived of as a more radically Christian approach to history.[12]

For his part, Alan Wolfe focused his essay, published in the fall of 2000 in the *Atlantic Monthly*, on what he described as "a determined effort by evangelical-Christian institutions to create a life of the mind."[13] Renaissances require funding, historians know, and Wolfe noted the critical part that major foundations, including the Pew Charitable Trusts and the Lilly Endowment, had played in sponsoring research, helping to launch publications, and fostering scholarly networks. But, in an appraisal surprisingly positive and sharply critical at once, he chastised evangelical scholars for their tendency to withdraw from the academic mainstream, charging that self-consciously Christian academics too often succumbed to an inclination to "marginalize themselves." The achievement of numerous evangelical scholars (including historians Marsden, Mark A. Noll, and Nathan Hatch) in the broader academy notwithstanding, Wolfe was troubled by what he saw as an inclination to revert to form—a narrow, provincial form. "To succeed in the university and therefore in America, evangelicals will have to put their defensiveness to one side," Wolfe intoned, and respectfully but confidently join the fray.[14]

But why, precisely, should they take that route? This was one of the main questions the younger generation was asking. Their deepening immersion into varying Christian intellectual traditions, as noted by Turner, was leading an increasing number of them not only to reexamine their own evangelical heritage but also to call into question the soundness of the modern university itself—which Wolfe persisted in holding up as the standard by which all scholars, evangelicals and otherwise, should be measured. Many of these Christian scholars, by rooting themselves and their work in creedally defined institutions, were not retreating from serious thought so much as seeking to achieve the very thing Turner, Wolfe, and others—including Noll in his impassioned 1994 polemic *The Scandal of the Evangelical Mind*—had applauded and advocated: the formation of a more sturdy, rich, and distinctively Christian intellectual life, a project that Wolfe's academy, whatever its virtues, had not made it a point to nurture.[15]

One way to grasp the dimensions of the movement to which Wolfe and Turner were both responding is to see it in light of the vast phenomenon we still seem to be able to only call, dumbly, "postmodernity," with its spectacular array of manifestations. From the post–Cold War triumph of global capitalism to the intensifying of cultural pluralism to the (near universal) collapse of belief in universal rationality to the revolutions in communications technology, postmodernity could not but create space for a vigorous rethinking of any variety of modern dogmatisms, whether political, institutional, epistemological, or ecclesiastical. The enormous literature devoted to understanding, explaining, and judging postmodernity that scholars of Christian persuasion from across the disciplines have produced is just one testament of the seismic dimensions of this historic shift on American intellectual life.[16]

The contributors to this present volume write very much as participant-observers in this milieu and moment, and are drawn together through a variety of interweaving networks, the CFH being only one among many. The editors, for instance, after studying church history together at Trinity Evangelical Divinity School (Deerfield, Illinois) in the early 1990s, each pursued Ph.D.s in American history in different graduate programs and went on to accept teaching positions in colleges belonging to the Council for Christian Colleges and Universities (CCCU). As graduate students in the 1990s we participated in conferences, both Christian and secular, exchanged ideas and experiences in (then novel) internet discussion groups, and with many other friends puzzled over the complex questions, illumined by the likes of Turner, Wolfe, Marsden, and Noll, surrounding our own vocational directions.

One experience during these years stands out as particularly emblematic and revealing. In the spring of 1997 two of us attended at Wheaton College in Illinois a conference titled "Reviving the Christian Mind." A Pew-sponsored follow-up to Noll's *Scandal of the Evangelical Mind*, the conference sought to render judgment on the current state of the "Christian Mind" project, gather disparate and often isolated scholars, and point toward new directions for the whole movement. Attendance far exceeded expectations. Reactions were mixed.

A retrospective peek at an internet discussion that took place immediately following the conference reveals the tensions, hopes, and fissures in the project, and the ways in which it was bounding well beyond existing lines of demarcation. The forum was a then-active listserv for Christian historians (but open to anyone interested), going by a name only a techie could love, "HISTEC-2," run out of Baylor University. This particular discussion centered on what one conference participant, a Notre Dame graduate student studying with Marsden, called, in a telling phrase, the "Christians in the academy conundrum."[17] The phrase served as shorthand for a host of troubling questions: How were young evangelical scholars to proceed now that they were engaged in and committed—psychologically, financially, intellectually, and more—to academic vocations? What would count as success? How reliable were their guides? And how uncertain was the future they would face as "Christian scholars"?

A former Noll student and current professor of religion at the University of Manitoba voiced the disappointment of many with the conference. It had featured, he thought, "too many 'consensus' papers from middle-aged, mainstream scholarly successes," and "not enough marginal, provocative papers."[18] Does "More Money + More Specialized Research = Revived Christian Mind," wondered a graduate student from the University of Iowa. This he took to be a central message of the conference, despite the fact that, in his opinion, the "general intellectual decline" in *all* sectors of contemporary American society—not just in evangelicalism—had actually "been accompanied by the rise of the modern research university and an exponentially increasing volume of specialized scholarship." And if the problem with the lack of a rich and sturdy intellectual life among American evangelicals reflected the poverty of their particular religious traditions, as Noll had charged, where at the conference was serious attention given to the church?[19]

The usual center-periphery tensions were acute in these overlapping academic and ecclesiastical circles. Was being peripheral to the secular academy itself a noble and worthy end? Or was moving from periphery to the center the ideal, as the celebratory aura around the conference's stars implied? And what about the periphery-center problem *within* the world of self-consciously Christian scholarship? To what extent did it endanger the whole project? In the judgment of one salty veteran of the scene, an "elitism that matches that in the secular world" was "developing more and more in evangelical scholarship." "The big dogs are so busy trying to escape what they perceive as marginalization that they in turn marginalize a lot of thoughtful and able people in evangelical circles who did not have the good fortune (and that is exactly what it is) to land a top flight academic position. I am not persuaded," he concluded, that "this problem particularly bothers evangelical academic leaders."[20]

Above all, a longing for something more, something beyond the mainstream status quo, whether the Christian or the secular version, seemed to fuel the reflections. A recent University of Chicago Ph.D. and professor at a small midwestern Reformed college admitted that he found it "difficult to accept the ease with [which] some colleagues at Christian colleges seem to regard the status, respectability, power and glory . . . that comes with 'making it'" in the academic mainstream. He found himself instead "struggling to figure out if the 'foolishness' of the Gospel . . . offers any insights into what a Christian intellectual might look like." His students, he recognized, were in the main aliens to the world of prestige and success. How was he to proceed? "Can I be a teaching servant, empty myself of my own pride and ambition and combine scholarship and teaching under the shadow of the Cross?" he asked. "I don't want to redeem scholarship for evangelicalism, or to compete with Stanford, or gain respect from my secular peers. I think I'm doing the work of the Kingdom, in a small and unremarkable way, here in a marginal place."[21]

One young, untenured historian who chose not to attend the conference explained why, capturing poignantly a variety of disaffection shared by many. The "loneliness," the "mild alienation" he felt as a Christian at his own mainstream liberal arts college, he wrote, "is matched only by the loneliness I have come to feel at such conferences." Speaking to "those of us who think that Noll/Marsden/Hatch/et al. may define the center, but certainly not the circumference of Christian scholarship," he went on to share an alternate vision of a Christian scholarly community, touching on questions ranging from historical method to the ideal shape of a scholarly conference. Moving past—far past—the established conventions seemed to him not only good, but necessary.[22]

This book, emerging from experiences such as these (and reflected upon autobiographically in many of the essays that follow), is charged, sometimes dramatically, other times subtly, with the hope, the frustration, the fear, and the yearning that have so freighted this movement and this moment. It is fair to say that the questions that lurk behind most of the essays boil down to these: Is something beyond the current consensus, as represented, for instance, in the work of George Marsden, possible? Is the mainstream historical profession truly the locus of the deepest wisdom and brightest hope for the practice of history? Have our lives as professional historians—and as middle-class professionals—become so straitjacketed that resistance to the status quo is futile? And what within the present moment holds most promise for the advance of a deeply Christian practice of history, whether through writing or teaching? The responses that follow are as varied, heated, and earnest as the times and places from which they emerge. We can only hope Newman is smiling upon them.

IDENTITY, THEORY, COMMUNITIES

Three essays follow these opening reflections that speak with poignancy to that preeminently postmodern category and concern, identity. Crucially, for our purposes, each essay centers on deeply personal reckonings with the standards, practices, and ideals of the historical profession, and with the broad historical circumstance of American intellectual life itself. Mark R. Schwehn, Provost of Valparaiso University and a leading voice in the ongoing conversation on religion and higher learning, narrates his own emergence in the 1960s as an historian struggling to achieve a more full embrace of the Christian faith within an academy that was then highly, even narrowly, secular. His mature conclusions about the relationship between his faith and the practice of history rest within the current practices of the profession, and so represent something of a touchstone for this collection: a perspective other contributors will affirm and reject to varying degrees. "The context of justification, the proper social location for the appraisal of my work as an historian," contends Schwehn, "is the profession itself, not the church, not the church-related university, and not a band of believers who claim epistemic privilege on the basis of religious affiliation."

Una M. Cadegan, while with Schwehn advocating peaceable and productive relations with the historical profession, explores its blindspots and not-so-predictable prejudices through the telling of her own entrance into the academy as a Roman Catholic. "Whether you believe in the Incarnation affects how you read evidence," she concludes, while remaining uncertain about where this frank historiographical and biographical reality should lead Christian historians. For Beth Barton Schweiger, the fact of the Incarnation leads to a fundamental redefining of knowledge itself, so that charity, rather than power, guides the historian's pursuit—a posture she finds at odds with the profession's tendency to nurture, along with much that is good and necessary, a vocational identity that diminishes the sympathy and self-sacrifice that love requires. "If 'knowledge as power' is to be replaced by a pastoral imagination, it will be necessary to learn some new habits," she suggests. "Truthfulness is made possible by truthful people. How can historians become people who can rightly see the dead?"

If "identity" has provided fertile ground for many distinctively post-modern forms of reflection, "theory" has certainly produced a similar yield, and is, in fact, responsible for fostering much historical research and writing on matters of identity. The second part of the book forces a confrontation with a pivotal question, one the profession's ideological and philosophic strictures make risky to ask: How should an explicitly religious identity affect and shape the historian's understanding of theory and method? Addressed somewhat obliquely in the preceding section, this question anchors these six essays.

With his observation that "the swooning of the modernist academic paradigm" has opened up increased rhetorical space for "moral reflection" in the practice of history, Thomas Albert Howard speaks for many in this volume. Nudging historians away from what he sees as the "overweening moral indignation" of much recent historical writing, he makes a case for a more thoughtful and measured form of intellectual engagement. "As historians, we all find ourselves epistemologists now," he contends, "but the ties with philosophy should be thickened." His inquiry into the relationship between the intellectual virtue of prudence and the doing of history provides an illuminating example of how recent turns in the discipline of ethics might enlarge the historian's vocational reach.

William Katerberg's sizing up of the past three decades of theoretical debate on such fundamental matters as objectivity, neutrality, knowledge, and truth leads him to recommend that historians reconceive their vocation in a way decidedly consonant with Howard's vision. Rather than maintaining the (now) traditional guise of the objective scholar, he suggests, historians—and, more to the point, the historical profession—should embrace and reward what he calls "useful scholarship": history researched, written, and taught in service of "living traditions." "If a century of historical scholarship and four decades of theoretical debate reveal anything," he writes, "it is that the search for objective scientific knowledge has not provided a stable foundation on which truth claims, moral decisions, and political projects can be based." Such a foundation the historical profession might yet provide—if it can bring itself to jettison the very dead weight of modernist notions of objectivity and professionalism.

Michael Kugler's contention is that, in the end, even the alleged source of such hopes for objectivity, the eighteenth-century Enlightenment, was not nearly so in thrall to this noble dream as is commonly held. Examining the work of eighteenth-century historians, he finds that they welcomed the literary, even fictive elements many of today's theorists understand as elemental in the doing of history, and that these seminal thinkers saw history as ineluctably in service of particular moral and political programs; "history as ethical reflection," Kugler notes, "was critical to the Enlightenment's 'science of human nature.'" Christian historians, by following these earlier historians, may speak more effectively to the particular communities of discourse functioning within the Christian tradition, and beyond.

It is to this tradition and its various communions and communities that the next two essayists devote their attention. Bradley J. Gundlach explores how the "moral insights" of even self-consciously secular thinkers can be theologically measured and historiographically appropriated by Christian historians in their work. Indeed, he regards such assimilation as not simply a good but also a gift, one of providential proportions—"a proper kind of providentialist history" upon which all Christian communities should rely for their ongoing health and vitality. For his part, Christopher Shannon, in panoramic fashion, provides the most radical call in this volume for Christian historians to reject the prevailing modes and means of doing history for the sake of the faith. "The problem with so much of the debate" among Christian historians, suggests Shannon, "is less that it has failed to offer a distinctly Christian historical practice, but that it assumes current secular historical practice to be, despite an undue secular bias, just fine, thank you very much." He thus takes perhaps the farthest point possible from Schwehn's position on the matter. Christians who participate in the forms of scholarship sanctioned by the academy are actually taking part in what he decries as "the legitimation of the modern secular world," with its all-consuming end of "maximizing the freedom of the individual." He provides the beginnings of an alternate vision, in which the understanding yielded only by belief shapes decisively our historical practices. The section concludes with James B. LaGrand's sharp critique of such views. With a posture far closer to Schwehn's, LaGrand calls readers to consider the perils of what he provocatively calls "preaching through history," urging continued respectful affiliation with the mainstream historical profession.

The concrete, particular historical practices that so concern Christopher Shannon provide the central theme and focus for the final part, "Communities." If identity and theory have been dominant concerns of contemporary historians, a new or perhaps simply different awareness of "community" has framed and shaded these preoccupations, as such influential books as Alasdair MacIntyre's *After Virtue*, Robert Bellah's *Habits of the Heart*, and Michael Sandel's *Democracy's Discontent* bear witness. In a world fragmenting under the aegis of global capitalism, yet also bound together by the same set of forces, people of all ethnicities, classes, and faiths have struggled to understand what "community" is and how it might be attained in these fracturing times.[23]

John Fea and Lendol Calder, in the opening chapters of this part, shed light on the little noticed fact that professional historians mainly do their work as members of particular communities, communities of learning. Through a story about his teaching of "HIS 324: Civil War America" at CCCU-member Messiah College, Fea shows how the wrenching, consequential turns the country took in the mid-nineteenth century made for sparkling classroom discussion and debate on matters of moral and political importance. Moreover, the "interpretive challenge" of foregrounding "faith commitments" in the classroom actually, Fea believes, enhanced the experience, rather than diminished it; the "reflective religious faith" of the students propelled the class in surprising, unanticipated ways.

It is precisely this sort of experience that Calder seeks to elevate and enliven through his essay, bearing the identity-threatening title "For Teachers to Live, Professors Must Die." Driven by love, history professors must come to see their classrooms as the site of encounter with other human beings, rather than a sphere for demonstrating professional expertise. Through a gripping historical narrative that functions as something of a parable, Calder suggests just what is at stake in the persisting failure of the professorate to grasp the human, historical dimensions of the lives they are supposed to "teach." His warning is simple and stark: "The first obligation of college teachers—before knowledge, before passion, before obedience to a particular vocation—is not to be stupid about love's requirements."

Jay Green takes a more analytic look at the ways in which historians might improve their use of analogies in their roles as members of political communities. Because, as he puts it, "the most common way modern people relate to the past is by appeals to historical analogy," Green points toward a more studied, self-conscious way of conceiving of analogies, one that removes the "conceptual barriers between genuine historical awareness and moral inquiry about present realities" that sloppy analogical thinking creates. He thus presents yet another perspective on how understanding history as a form of moral inquiry can enlarge the historian's vocational presence.

The final two essays of part 3 seek to reconnect Christian historians more faithfully to their own two inalienable communities: the church and the profession itself. Robert Tracy McKenzie notes that in the burgeoning literature emerging from the past three decades of faith-and-history discussions, there has been, oddly, little written on how historians might serve the church rather than simply (or mainly) the academy. Urging historians to resist the "years of acculturation in an elitist academic establishment that produces historians increasingly aloof from the society they claim to serve," he proposes concrete ways that historians can participate *as historians* in their particular congregations. Douglas Sweeney closes the section by taking us back into the academy itself, a world, he writes, that is "full of fragile egos, insecurities, uncertainties, and fears, to say nothing of most of the ordinary forms of human suffering." With a deft theological exposition of the doctrines of calling and priesthood, Sweeney encourages believing historians to draw near to their colleagues as friends. Our calling, he writes, is to "practice scholarship as ministry, a form of priestly service intended to bless the larger world."

Wilfred M. McClay draws our conversation to a graceful close with a sharp, careful reading of three twentieth-century historical thinkers—Herbert Butterfield, Christopher Dawson, and Reinhold Niebuhr—whose varied responses to the modern moment might, he suggests, help Christian historians keep their eyes trained on why their vocation matters. "Progress in history," McClay writes, "has turned from a complacent march into a tense tightrope walk." In an age suffering great uncertainty about the direction of history and the very definition of human being, Christian historians must seize upon the "epistemological advantages of Christian commitment" to render the past with all of the conviction, ingenuity, and intelligence at hand.

Such writing and teaching amounts, of course, to confession. And that confessing is above all the gamble Christian historians must take.

CONFESSING HISTORY: PROSPECT

Do these essays, in the end, provide evidence of a new consensus emerging within this circle of historical thinking and practice, one that will change—is already changing—the way we do history? Or do we have instead what earlier critics of the project have charged: yet more talk about how we *might* practice history differently, but little if anything that will lead to narratives, analyses, and practices that differ substantially from that which takes place beneath the auspices of the American Historical Association?[24]

Although its manifestations vary, I believe that, if not a new consensus, at least a common inclination has emerged over the past two decades, an inclination both generational and philosophical at root and with the promise of altering actual practice at many levels. The modern search for explications of causality and agency through the analysis of "observable cultural forces" has proven to be an inadequate approach to the past for many in this generation of Christian historians, and, accordingly, an unsatisfying means to the fulfillment of our vocations. We seek instead to clothe history in rumination, conjecture, meditation, and judgment, all rooted in Christian visions of reality and all in the service of fostering moral intelligence and spiritual vigor in the communities we serve. Moreover, rather than turning to leading theorists of the modern academic disciplines alone for guidance, we find ourselves in consequential and intimate conversation with the work of theologians and philosophers, joining a tradition of reflection with ancient roots and one that continues strongly to this day, with or without the historical profession. Jay Green casts this overarching vision and hope with succinct force. For those harking toward this hope, "real theological language, strengthened by a biblical framework with real authority, would powerfully invade and transform our very real and critical pursuits of historical understanding." Christian historians would weave into their thinking and practices "the vivid texture of their confessions, the rich heritage of their traditions, and the immense learning of modern theology."[25]

Of course, moving beyond the profession's ideological and methodological strictures would almost certainly require a willingness to move beyond the profession itself, at least in part, and at least for a time. Far from being self-destructive, though, this exodus might in the end prove to be a boon: it could free us to devote our energies and resources to speaking not to a very established and fairly intransigent academic profession, but rather to each other. We might, in other words, find ourselves participating more fully in a commonwealth of Christian scholars, a land with a geography and polity, and with a set of ideals, symbols, and standards, at fruitful variance with the academic mainstream.

To be sure, the risks in this sort of movement are considerable. At its best, the world of mainstream academe continues to hold forth and maintain a stringent and demanding scholarly ethos. Only the naïve would assume that such truly necessary standards and resources, reflective of a historically powerful tradition, could be easily transferred to an institutionally distinct (and financially poorer) academic world. And the creative tension between diverging worldviews and traditions that scholarly excellence—of whatever philosophic orientation—has always required is far more difficult to maintain than the default tendencies of either total withdrawal from or submission to the dominant culture.

But in view of our truest purposes, Christian scholars have no choice but to pursue this alternate pathway. If we are to fulfill our callings to bless the church and the world, we must devote ourselves to the costly process of rerooting our thinking about the ways of God, his creatures, and his creation in the rich soil of deep, expansive Christian reflection. Noll and company are undoubtedly right: the "Christian mind" is indeed necessary for the ongoing vitality of Christianity itself, and for something like it to exist, distinctly Christian organizations, institutions, and discourses (such as those reflected in this volume) must not simply exist, but *thrive*. What recent history shows us, in no uncertain way, is that to rely on either mere congregational life or the secular academy for this sort of specialized, intensive intellectual and educational labor is to risk continued enormous loss. The ongoing renewal of deep and variegated Christian intellectual traditions demands a different kind of rooting.

In a word, as we remain in committed conversation with those beyond our confessional pale, we must continue to devote energy and wealth to the construction and cultivation of nurseries for Christian thinking and learning: colleges, presses, journals, conferences, societies, foundations, retreat centers, and more. If Christian intellectuals of this generation can seize upon the good inheritance that is theirs, and with it press toward the realizing of this ongoing project, then a tradition, one their faith holds to be of enormous consequence, may be renewed.

Notes

1. Eugene Genovese, *The Southern Tradition: The Achievement and Limitations of an American Conservatism* (Cambridge, Mass.: Harvard University Press, 1994), 4–5.

2. Donald A. Yerxa pithily describes the impasse at which modern attempts to practice history in a distinctively Christian way have arrived in "That Embarrassing Dream: Big Questions and the Limits of History," *Fides et Historia* 39:1 (Winter/Spring 2007): 53–60.

3. John Henry Newman, *The Idea of a University*, ed. Frank M. Turner, Rethinking the Western Tradition series (New Haven: Yale University Press, 1996; orig. pub. New York: Longman, Green, 1899), 29.

4. George M. Marsden, *Fundamentalism and American Culture: The Shaping of Twentieth Century Evangelicalism, 1870–1925* (New York: Oxford University Press, 1980), 230. For a brief critical history of the CFH, see D. G. Hart, "History in Search of Meaning: The Conference on Faith and History," in *History and the Christian Historian*, ed. Ronald A. Wells, 68–87 (Grand Rapids, Mich.: Eerdmans, 1998).

5. George M. Marsden, *The Outrageous Idea of Christian Scholarship* (New York: Oxford University Press, 1997), 48–51.

6. George M. Marsden, *Jonathan Edwards: A Life* (New Haven: Yale University Press, 2003).

7. Christopher Shannon, "Christian History in an Age of Christian Scholarship," paper in possession of the author.

8. William H. Katerberg, "Is There Such a Thing as 'Christian' History?" *Fides et Historia* 34:1 (Winter/Spring 2002): 58.

9. For a report and interpretation of the emergence of this challenge, see Eric Miller, "Reckoning with History: Report from the Conference on Faith and History," *Historically Speaking* 4:3 (February 2003): 26–27.

10. James Turner, "Something To Be Reckoned With," *Commonweal*, January 15, 1999, 11–13.

11. Many of these Protestant intellectuals have, of course, ended up converting to Orthodoxy or Roman Catholicism along the way. On this phenomenon, see Scott McKnight, "From Wheaton To Rome: Why Evangelicals Become Catholic," *Journal of the Evangelical Theological Society* 45:3 (September 2002): 451–72; Jason Byassee, "Going Catholic," *Christian Century*, August 22, 2006, 18–23.

12. Trollinger's address was published as William Vance Trollinger Jr., "Faith, History, and the Conference on Faith and History," *Fides et Historia* 33:1 (Winter/Spring 2001): 1–10. A much modified version of Shannon's plenary address is published in this present volume.

13. Alan Wolfe, "The Opening of the Evangelical Mind," *Atlantic Monthly* (October 2000): 58.

14. Ibid., 76.

15. Mark A. Noll, *The Scandal of the Evangelical Mind* (Grand Rapids, Mich.: Eerdmans, 1994). The aim of spawning a "Christian mind," reflected with vigor in Noll's book, emerged out of the mid-century re-emergence of evangelical Christianity in the aftermath of fundamentalism. Among the books for a wide audience that reflected the concern were Harry Blamires, *The Christian Mind* (London: S.P.C.K., 1963); James Sire, *The Universe Next Door* (Downers Grove, Ill.: InterVarsity Press, 1976); Kenneth A. Myers, *All God's Children and Blue Suede Shoes: Christians and Popular Culture* (Wheaton, IL: Crossway Publishers, 1989); and Os Guinness, *Fit Bodies, Fat Minds: Why Evangelicals Don't Think and What To Do About It* (Grand Rapids, Mich.: Baker Book House, 1994).

16. See, for example, in chronological order: Albert Borgmann, *Crossing the Postmodern Divide* (Chicago: University of Chicago Press, 1992); Roger Lundin, *The Culture of Intepretation: Christian Faith and the Postmodern World* (Grand Rapids, Mich.: Eerdmans, 1993); Brian J. Walsh and Richard Middleton,

Truth Is Stranger Than It Used To Be: Biblical Faith in a Postmodern Age (Downers Grove, Ill.: InterVarsity Press, 1995); Stanley J. Grenz, *A Primer on Postmodernism* (Grand Rapids, Mich.: Eerdmans, 1996); Kevin J. Vanhoozer, *Is there a Meaning in This Text?* (Grand Rapids, Mich.: Zondervan, 1998); Millard Erickson, *Postmodernizing the Faith: Evangelical Responses to Postmodernism* (Grand Rapids, Mich.: Baker Academic, 1998); Douglas Groothuis, *Truth Decay: Defending Christianity Against the Challenges of Postmodernism* (Downers Grove, Ill.: InterVarsity Press, 2000); Myron B. Penner, ed., *Christianity and the Postmodern Turn: Six Views* (Grand Rapids, Mich.: Brazos Press, 2005); Crystal Downing, *How Postmodernism Serves (My) Faith: Questioning Truth in Language, Philosophy, and Art* (Downers Grove, Ill.: InterVarsity Press, 2006); James K. A. Smith, *Who's Afraid of Postmodernism? Taking Foucault, Lyotard, and Derrida to the Church* (Grand Rapids, Mich.: Baker Academic, 2006).

17. Kurt Peterson, 23 April 1997, on HISTEC 2 listserv. A copy of this discussion is in the possession of the author.

18. Ibid., John G. Stackhouse, 23 April 1997.

19. Ibid., Russ Reeves, 24 April 1997.

20. Ibid., Richard V. Pierard, 27 April 1997.

21. Ibid., Mike Kugler, 23 April 1997.

22. Ibid., Lendol Calder, 30 April 1997.

23. Alasdair MacIntyre, *After Virtue: A Study in Moral Theory*, 2nd ed. (Notre Dame, Ind: University of Notre Dame Press, 1984); Robert N. Bellah et al., *Habits of the Heart: Individualism and Commitment in American Life* (Berkeley: University of California Press, 1985); Michael J. Sandel, *Democracy's Discontent: America in Search of a Public Philosophy* (Cambridge, Mass.: Harvard University Press, 1996).

24. Donald Yerxa has sharply but sympathetically summarized this line of criticism in "That Embarrassing Dream."

25. Jay D. Green, "On Peeling Back Ceiling Panels: Theology and the Dilemma of Christian Historiography," *Fides et Historia* 34:1 (Winter/Spring 2002): 35.

Part One

IDENTITY

Chapter One

FAITH SEEKING HISTORICAL UNDERSTANDING

MARK R. SCHWEHN

IN WHAT WAYS MIGHT CHRISTIAN FAITH ENLIVEN, INFORM, and enrich historical understanding? If one regards the teaching and writing of history as a Christian vocation, what difference does that self-understanding make in the actual practice of one's craft? Since I think that the sometimes ineffable connections between our spiritual and our intellectual lives cannot be described in a way that should apply in detail to all of us, I have chosen to address this important matter by way of autobiographical reflection about my own faith seeking historical understanding. We all make our pilgrimages across the sometimes contested terrain occupied by both faith and reason, religious conviction and disciplined inquiry, in our own peculiar ways, depending upon our working theologies, our fields of study, our institutional locations, and the full constellation of our sometimes contending loyalties. The best we can hope for is good company on our pilgrimage, not some neat formula or prescription that will guide each and every one of our distinctive journeys to similar destinations. In that spirit, I offer the following self-critical account of my own pilgrimage as a Christian and a historian thus far.

First, some reminders. . . . Memory is the thread of personal identity, history the thread of public identity. And R. G. Collingwood among others has taught all historians never to equate or confuse the two. Memory is a notoriously self-serving and treacherous instrument, making the past activities of the mind mere spectacle refracted through present longings and interests. History often relies on testimonies borne of memory, but until these testimonies are critically examined and, as Collingwood would put it, reenacted in the historian's own mind, they are only testimonies and never by themselves history. What then shall we call the testimonies of an historian about how he came to think historically and about how his historical thinking was shaped by his Christian faith? Do my memories become history due to the contingent fact that the mind that is recollecting them happens to be the mind of an historian? Collingwood would think not. He would insist that my memories become history if and only if I have evidence for them, not simply because the mind in which the memories are reenacted happens to be the mind of an historian.

I begin with these somewhat abstract and philosophical reflections, not because I propose to take us all on a metaphysical journey, for this would be a cardinal sin among historians who are frequently suspicious of philosophy. Rather, I want to remind us all at the outset that simply to engage in the practice of testimony or confession or autobiographical reflection, simply to plunge into the mysteries of personal continuity, is already to honor a practice whose deepest roots in the West are Christian. I have in mind here of course St. Augustine's *Confessions* and Augustine's own image of the Christian life as one of pilgrimage, a journey whose final destination lies beyond space and time as we know them. To recover even a part of the shape of that journey is therefore both an act of faith, for that process presupposes pattern and continuity before these are actually discovered by the searching mind, and an act of humility, for we soon learn that we cannot know ourselves by ourselves. Only God can catch the human heart and hold it still. And when we come to see this, as we must see it as soon as we try to understand our own stories, we should bring forth praise more than knowledge. Or rather, our self-knowledge, such as it is, must become itself a form of praise.

THE MAKING OF AN HISTORIAN:
AN AUTOBIOGRAPHICAL REFLECTION

With this much as prologue, let me turn now to the endeavor to comprehend the relationship of the Christian faith to the practice of history by way of autobiography. I shall do this in three parts. I will first simply tell the story of how I came to be an historian and of how I chose my subject matter. I will then attempt to reflect upon how my own historical scholarship has been informed and, I hope, enriched by my Christian faith. Finally, I want to enlarge the topic somewhat to the larger question of how Christian faith has sustained the life of my mind, a question that includes but extends well beyond the practice of history.

When I came to Valparaiso University in 1963, I knew I loved to think about things, I knew that I was not called to the ordained ministry as my father and grandfather and great-grandfather had been before me, and I knew that I was not very good at science or math. I was also pretty scared, suffering from the "imposter syndrome," whose major symptom was believing that I had all my life been pretending to be smart and managing to fool a lot of people, and believing as well that I was soon to be found out. I won't write about my fears here, since I still suffer from them. I will instead describe how I developed from someone who was pretty much open to studying anything in the area of the humanities and the social sciences to someone who chose to study history.

I wish I could claim that this development was one of deliberate and carefully self-conscious choice. It was instead one of accident, contingency, and chance, or so it seems to me even now from my own limited, earthly perspective. I finished my first year of college with my imposterhood intact, vaguely bewildered as to why no one had yet discovered the depths of my ignorance, not yet realizing that my teachers were not at all interested in making that kind of discovery, since, among other things, they were even more aware of their ignorance than I was of my own. It would take me many years to learn about the true nature of teaching and learning. But at the beginning of my sophomore year in 1964, I still thought that successful work in college involved concealing ignorance, and I had yet to find myself in the grips of an intellectual passion.

Then it happened. I took a required survey course in U.S. history from a professor who offered to meet with any of us for an extra hour each week if we wanted to do more reading. I'm ashamed to admit—but this is a confession, after all—that I joined this group just to be sure I'd earn a good grade in the course. But I soon became hooked on history. This professor used the extra readings to show us how different historians had offered radically different interpretations of the same events or the same historical periods or the same historical personages. I found this a kind of revelation. When I learned much later that the gospels might be different interpretations of the life of Jesus of Nazareth, this would provoke a crisis of faith. But for that earlier time, since we were talking about historiography and not christology, I felt liberated and excited, not threatened.

This professor for some reason or another liked my work. Since he was a bachelor who had no children of his own, he in a way adopted many of his students. I was one of them. Within weeks he had given me several books (I only learned years later that these were, of course, desk copies). Within months I had taken two more courses from him. By the end of the year, he had taken me out for coffee scores of times, and on one of those occasions he told me that I should someday be a Danforth graduate fellow, since I was a pretty good student, since I wanted to teach someday, and since I was serious and articulate about my religious convictions. I had never heard of Danforth fellows, but three years later I found myself in possession of a Danforth fellowship to Stanford University to study American intellectual history.

I have always thought that had this professor been teaching, say, literature or theology, I would now be a literary critic or a theologian. But perhaps not. For there was another development coincident with this one that shaped my emerging sense of vocation just as deeply. Valparaiso University did not have in those days of the 1960s a particularly strong faculty. Students who wanted a first-rate education could get one at Valparaiso, but as many of us said to one another at the time, you had to take professors, not subjects. In other words, many of us plotted our class schedules not by what we would need for this or that major or minor but by which professors we wanted to have for our teachers. We hoped, not unreasonably, that sooner or later we would discover that some assortment or another of courses would add up to a major or that we could petition some office for a so-called "individualized major." In the 1960s, this strategy worked easily. It would not work so readily today.

In any event, one of the brightest and toughest professors at Valparaiso in those days was a philosopher who had been studying for the ordained ministry when he fell in love first with systematic theology and then with philosophy. After earning a Ph.D. at Harvard, he spent a year at Oxford studying with A. J. Ayer, and he became a resolute logical positivist. I did not know all of this at the time. I did, however, find this professor's introduction to philosophy course the most exciting course I had ever taken. I easily earned an A in the course and only later learned that this professor had an entirely different set of standards for introductory courses than he did for advanced courses. But I became determined to take this professor for everything he taught. So I took him for early modern philosophy in the department's historical sequence. I took him for epistemology. And I finally took him for a course that was the most important one I took at Valparaiso: "Religious Language and the Challenge of Logical Positivism." I should add parenthetically that there were other outstanding philosophy professors in those years, and I soon had a major in that field without realizing it.

And so it came to pass that I spent over two years of my undergraduate life studying with a man who longed to believe with every fiber of his being but who could not bring himself to do so any longer because he believed that the logical positivists had shown conclusively that religious language was meaningless. I read literally scores of very difficult books that tried to show in one way or another how religious language might be shown to satisfy the positivists' verification criterion of meaning. And to this professor's credit, he much preferred students who would argue forcefully and carefully with the positivists to those who quickly became parrots of the party line. For the first time, the life of the mind was not an exercise in puzzle solving. It had taken on a real existential edge. Ideas really mattered in a profoundly personal sense. And I found myself on a crusade of sorts. I was determined to refute positivism for myself, because it had begun to erode what I then took to be the foundations of my own faith, and for my teacher, because I sensed that if I could prove A. J. Ayer wrong, I might save my teacher's soul! This whole endeavor evinced a curious admixture of pride, charity, and salvation through intellectual work. And the endless papers, the scores of all-nighters talking philosophy with the professor and other students, the earnest efforts to find some way to reconcile ideas and values that were finally incommensurable, and the unavailing attempts to reconvert my professor shaped my scholarly life in some obvious ways and some not so obvious ways.

A few years ago, in going through some old papers, I found the essay that I had written as part of my Danforth fellowship application. I was startled to learn that I had somehow during my senior year in college set out the course of study that would preoccupy me at Stanford. Until I found the document, I had always remembered that my dissertation topic had been the result of particular courses I had taken and particular professors I had studied with in graduate school. So much for memory! But there it was in cold print in my Danforth essay: I wanted to study American history, I wrote in 1966, during the period from roughly 1870 through roughly 1920, when many intellectuals had come to grips with the challenges of modern science both to their faith and to their understanding of their work in the humanities and the emerging social sciences. And I had wanted to undertake such a study, I wrote further, in order to sort out my own perplexities about these matters by studying others who had struggled with the same issues at the very beginning of the rise of the modern research university in America.

The book that shaped my thinking in preparing the essay was by H. Stuart Hughes, and it was entitled, *Consciousness and Society: The Reorientation of European Thought, 1890–1930*. Its second chapter was called "The Revolt against Positivism." In other words, I had chosen to carry on the argument I had been having for two years with myself and with my philosophy professor by means of history rather than by means of philosophy. And my project would prove to be self-reflexive in more ways than one. Hughes did not have logical positivism in mind when he wrote about positivism, since he was focused primarily on a period prior to the emergence of the Vienna circle in the 1920s. He defined positivism as the insinuation of the models and the methods of the natural sciences into the discourse of the humanities.[1] I was determined to resist scientism and positivism because I was a Christian. And my resistance would take two forms. First, I would study those who themselves found ways to appreciate and to take full account of the powers of scientific explanation even as they refused, sometimes on religious grounds, to be completely captured by natural-scientific methods and metaphors. But second, I would choose to write history in what was then considered an old-fashioned way, intellectual history whose method was multi-contextual and whose explanatory form was narrative. In other words, I would refuse the temptation to make history another one of the hard social sciences, a field for testing social-scientific "covering laws" on people and societies in the past.

This proved to be a somewhat lonely enterprise in those days. For one thing, my fellow graduate students were all enamored of the new social history, and they were enthusiastically studying family history, undertaking social mobility studies using the latest statistical techniques, or probing into kindred disciplines like demography and ethnography. For another thing, there were no American intellectual historians in the Stanford history department at the time. It was a terrific department, and I learned immense amounts from the likes of David Potter, Carl Degler, Don Fehrenbacher, Allan Matusow, Linda Kerber, and a new arrival named David Kennedy. But I had once more to cobble together an academic program that spoke to my deepest questions. I therefore decided to enroll in the Graduate Program in Humanities at Stanford, a course of study that had to be undertaken in addition to a Ph.D. in a regular field. And I took a lot of European intellectual history with people like Paul Robinson. Perhaps because he was so new and so unfamiliar with the ways of graduate education at Stanford, David Kennedy agreed to be my dissertation advisor even though he was a social and political historian, then finishing his book on Margaret Sanger and the battle for birth control in America, a subject remote from my interests.

My department was very kind to me, maybe overly indulgent. But my primary intellectual companions were my fellow graduate students in the humanities program and the individuals whom I chose to study— Henry Adams and William James. Both of these men had been present at the creation of the modern research university at Harvard. Both were deeply seduced by scientism even as they were at the same time repelled by it. Both made major contributions to their fields of study, Adams in history, James in psychology. Both resisted scientism and positivism from partly religious motives, James moving toward pragmatism and the *Varieties of Religious Experience*, Adams moving away from positivistic history and toward autobiography in *The Education of Henry Adams*. Neither thinker countered positivism by moving back to a lost world. Adams mourned his whole life long the lost world of classical republicanism that had formed him, but he never thought he could return to it. And James remained ever a Darwinian of sorts even as he retained his own father's convictions about the reality of religion. I wound up arguing that modern consciousness was born in these two men at least from the unsettling and unsettled conflicts within them between head and heart, between faith and reason, between their gifts and their experiences, between their own generation and the generation of their fathers and mothers, between some of their most deeply cherished convictions and the imperial claims of modern natural science. And both of them had in different ways reversed the project of St. Augustine in his *Confessions*. In the words of Henry Adams, "Whereas Augustine had worked from multiplicity to unity, I was forced to work from unity to multiplicity."[2] This trajectory would be reenacted in many ways and in many idioms by most of the major intellectuals of the twentieth century.

In other words, I came to see these men as different versions of my old philosophy professor at Valparaiso, who had the will to believe, so to speak, but not, in his judgment at least, the rational warrants for it. And when I came to write my dissertation, I used for the first chapter the typology developed by Isaiah Berlin in his magnificent essay on Tolstoy's view of history called *The Hedgehog and the Fox*. According to this binary classification, the hedgehog sees only one big thing, seeks unity, and longs for some single principle or system or architectural structure in terms of which all things fit together. The fox by contrast sees only the many, irreducibly diverse, incommensurable, and irreconcilable things. Berlin was interested in Tolstoy because the Russian count had the heart of a hedgehog and the eyes of a fox. He longed for unity as fiercely as anyone has ever longed for it, yet he could only see the many. And he was too honest and too intelligent to settle for a quick and easy fix to mend his divided soul. I wondered as I wrote that first chapter and I wonder still whether this phenomenon of the divided soul has become almost characteristic of modern intellectuals in one form or another. And I wondered too whether this peculiar and unstable hybrid of hedgehog and fox might be connected to the simultaneous attraction to and repulsion from the claims and the achievements of modern science.

It should by now be obvious that my own work in history began as a search for kindred spirits, for intellectual companions who were much wiser and more accomplished than I could ever be and who had, like me and like some of my own teachers, sought for most of their lives to reconcile desire with professional duty, belief with the claims of reason, the one with the many. I think I chose history over philosophy because I needed ideas clothed in flesh and blood more than I needed conceptual purity and logical refinement. I needed friends along the way, and I needed them to be on the side of modernity, not opposed to it. So I chose the way of history, and I chose to cast my study in defiantly (at the time) narrative terms, seeking to render an intelligible account over time of the changes in the lives and ideas of two instructive teachers. I took a bit of comfort from what H. Stuart Hughes had written about one of my subjects, Henry Adams. "Adams," Hughes wrote in *Consciousness and Society*, "was so old fashioned that by the end of his life he had become a modern."[3] And through these many years of study, I became more a Christian thinker and teacher who happened to do history than a Christian historian. My work on Adams and James and later on the academic vocation in the era of the secular research university was steeped and dyed every step of the way in my Christian faith. But for better or for worse, neither my subjects nor my methods nor my habits of writing have been dictated by the so-called "state of the art" within my own discipline.

FAITH AND SCHOLARSHIP

To come now to the second part of this exploration, we must ask the following question: Granted that my Christian faith motivated and shaped my scholarship at almost every turn, did my faith *improve* my scholarship, and if so, how? A more generalized form of this question is right now a fairly hot topic, that is, the relationship between one's religious conviction and the cogency or quality or persuasiveness or professional merit of one's scholarship. My fellow American intellectual historian David Hollinger has been both relentless and eloquent in reminding us of the fundamental distinction between contexts of discovery and contexts of justification. In other words, Hollinger would readily agree that my Christianity motivated my choice of a field of study, disposed me toward a particular subject or problem, influenced my habits of historical attention, even shaped my preferred mode of historical explanation. But he would strenuously insist that the value, the persuasiveness, and the intellectual merit of my work should be exclusively determined by the standards of the historical profession, not with reference to my faith.

True, we might argue among ourselves as historians about what counts as good history, what counts as evidence, and what should be the preferred modes of historical explanation. True too that such standards do change over time and always remain contestable. Nevertheless, we dare not allow special pleading based on race, class, gender, national origin, or religion when it comes to assessing the quality of someone's scholarship. And we dare not permit as warrants for historical claims allegations of special divine revelation, appeals to divine providence, or the formal approval of ecclesiastical bodies. The context of justification, the proper social location for the appraisal of my work as an historian, is the profession itself, not the church, not the church-related university, and not a band of believers who claim epistemic privilege on the basis of religious affiliation.

So I must be very careful here by making a distinction myself. I *do* think that my Christian faith has strengthened my work as an historian, and I *do* think that the quality of my work has been in part determined by my faith, but I do *not* think that it would ever be proper, sensible, or rationally defensible to *appeal* to my Christian faith in an attempt to demonstrate or defend the quality of my scholarship. As a contingent fact of my biography, my Christianity did indeed inform both the content and the character of my scholarship. But the quality of that scholarship should only be determined by my professional peers. Those peers may be mistaken in their appraisals of my work, of course, but the way to change inadequate assessments is not to appeal to my biography but to the profession's own standards and its application of them. Perhaps the standards need to be amended. Perhaps the standards are fine, but the application of them has been in some sense in my case defective. Perhaps my peers are just speaking the truth when they find my work short of the mark. The context of justification is about the proper location of these arguments and about the sorts of appeals that should be allowed to count as these arguments proceed.

None of this means, however, that the claims I am about to advance about how my Christian faith in fact improved the quality of my scholarship are false or inappropriate. To show the genesis of something is not to validate it. With this important qualifier in mind, let me briefly describe two respects in which I think my work was and remains consistently strengthened by the practice of my Christian faith. First, I think that my Christian training and the work of the Holy Spirit instilled within me certain virtues like charity and humility that have given to my work as an historian a measure of balance, sympathy, and fairness that it might not otherwise possess. Second, I think that I have been able more easily to resist certain temptations to self-serving explanations and interpretations by my tendency to construe objectivity not as a practice but as an ascetic discipline.

In my 1993 book *Exiles from Eden,* I developed the first of these two points at length, so I shall not belabor the matter here. Suffice it to say that because I was raised to consider *some* written work as sacred, I became habituated to think that when certain texts seemed obscure or wrong-headed or inconsistent, the problem was more likely in me than in the text. In other words, I was disposed toward the intellectual and spiritual virtue of humility. Now of course I know that not all texts are sacred. And I know that many texts really are obscure, biased, inconsistent, or wrong-headed. But I still begin reading most great texts by presuming that the author is wiser than I am, and I seek therefore to balance a hermeneutics of suspicion with a hermeneutics of care or *caritas.* And I do believe that over the years this hermeneutic has served me well. I believe that humility and charity have cognitive value, and that insofar as I live up to the best that is in me, I am a better historian for it, a quality that shows in my work.

The point about objectivity is harder to make in these postmodern times, but just for that reason it is worth the effort. I think that objectivity, properly understood, should refer neither to the notion of unmediated access to reality nor to the view that we could ever become free from bias or purified of distortions or generically human (whatever these achievements might mean). Rather, I think objectivity should refer, and to a larger extent than we realize it has always referred, to what Thomas Haskell calls "the expression in intellectual affairs of the ascetic dimension of life." Though he ignores altogether the significance of the historical connection between asceticism and monasticism, Haskell is right, I think, in understanding ascetic practices like objectivity as "indispensable to the pursuit of truth. The very possibility of historical scholarship as an enterprise distinct from propaganda," Haskell continues,

> requires of its practitioners that vital minimum of ascetic self-discipline that enables a person to do such things as abandon wishful thinking, assimilate bad news, discard pleasing interpretations that cannot pass elementary tests of evidence and logic, and, most important of all, suspend or bracket one's own perceptions long enough to enter sympathetically into the alien and possibly repugnant perspectives of rival thinkers. All of these mental acts—especially coming to grips with a rival's perspective—require *detachment*, an undeniably ascetic capacity to achieve some distance from one's own spontaneous perceptions and convictions, to imagine how the world appears in another's eyes, to experimentally adopt perspectives that do not come naturally—in the last analysis, to develop, as Thomas Nagel would say, a view of the world in which one's own self stands not at the center, but appears merely as one object among many.[4]

So objectivity is the name for that discipline whereby we seek to incorporate as many different perspectives into our thinking and our writing as we can. It is a discipline, I believe, that has Christian roots, and it has without a doubt improved the quality of my scholarship.

Could I have become a humble, charitable, more or less objective historian without being a Christian? Of course I could have! But that would not be the story of my life. And this point cannot be stressed enough. Personal narratives like my own can be instructive, but they cannot and should not be reduced to an illustration of some general and necessary principle or elevated into some kind of moral imperative. Shrewd students of human nature will have by this time noticed that my own story of myself thus far has been quite partial and selective, given the restricted topical focus. My own sense of self and choice of subject were also shaped by matters of gender and race and class. In my denomination, deciding not to be an ordained clergyman would not have been a personal struggle for a woman in the same way it was for me because it never would have been a live option. And my subjects are elite white males like me. There is much more to my story than I have told, and I would do well, at another time and place to practice a little bit of the hermeneutics of suspicion on my own narrative. Remember, however, the question I have been addressing, "How *can* Christian faith sustain enhance the character and quality of historical scholarship?" not how *must* it do so or how *only* Christian faith can do so.

CHRISTIAN FAITH AND THE LIFE OF THE MIND

I turn now to my third and final point that takes us beyond history to the life of the mind or at least to the life of liberal learning. How can Christian faith sustain the life of the mind? Consider the following poem by Richard Wilbur about the fundamental act of liberal learning, the act of reading:

THE READER
She is going back, these days, to the great stories
That charmed her younger mind. A shaded light
Shines on the nape half-shadowed by her curls,
And a page turns now with a scuffing sound.
Onward they come again, the orphans reaching   5
For a first handhold in a stony world,

The young provincials who at last look down
On the city's maze, and will descend into it,
The serious girl, once more, who would live nobly,
The sly one who aspires to marry so,   10
The young man bent on glory, and that other
Who seeks a burden. Knowing as she does
What will become of them in bloody field
Or Tuscan garden, it may be that at times
She sees their first and final selves at once,   15
As a god might to whom all time is now.
Or, having lived so much herself, perhaps
She meets them this time with a wiser eye,
Noting that Julien's calculating head
Is from the first too severed from his heart.   20
But the true wonder of it is that she,
For all that she may know of consequences,
Still turns enchanted to the next bright page
Like some Natasha in the ballroom door—
Caught in the flow of things wherever bound,   25
The blind delight of being, ready still
To enter life on life and see them through.[5]

I have chosen to close with a meditation on this poem for three reasons, all of them having do to with my own life and the life of my own mind as that mind has unfolded within the academy. First of all, I have become over the years a fierce partisan of liberal education, and I know of no other text that gives a better sense of a love of reading or of why we should love to read. Second, between my first works of history and my later works on the academic vocation, I wrote a good deal of literary criticism, I think because I learned along the way that simply to read a text historically is often to miss what is most important about it. And finally the poem makes me challenge in important and relevant ways some of the things I have told you both about my own life and about the writing of history.

Notice these lines: "Knowing as she does / What will become of them in bloody field / Or Tuscan garden, it may be that at times / She sees their first and final selves at once, / As a god might to whom all time is now." Well, yes, the reader of great imaginative literature can taste divinity in just this way, I think. But the historian must resist this temptation when it comes to her subjects. *She* may know from her beginning in 1820 that the Missouri Compromise of that year will lead eventually to the end of civil war in 1861, but she dare not treat her subjects as though *they* knew as much. They could not in principle have known it. As my teacher David Potter once told me, "If historians had a little more foresight and a little less hindsight, they would all be better off by a damned sight."

No, the historian is more like the reader described as the poem continues, "Or, having lived so much herself perhaps / She meets them this time with a wiser eye, / Noting that Julien's calculating head / Is from the first too severed from his heart." This is a reference to the central character of Stendhal's great novel *The Red and the Black*, and it shows how the reader, herself developing over time, will read the world anew depending upon her own experience and location. What once seemed surprising comes eventually to seem inevitable, the end contained in the beginning. Historians are, of course, trained to be aware of their own biases and their own sources of insight into the truth of matters. And as they mature, they do in fact, simply by virtue of that maturity, see much of the world they study more truly. And that is why, to quote another Stanford historian, Gordon Craig, who spoke in an idiom similar to Potter's, "a historian is no damn good until she is forty."

Whatever the case, we are given here two ways of reading lives, leading us to understand the true enchantment of it all. And some of this same enchantment comes from reading our own lives in light of the Christian faith, for with these two ways of reading we are brought again to the world of Augustine's *Confessions* and to some salutary corrections of my own autobiographical narrative as I have thus far presented it. Recall that I have stressed over and over again the contingent and accidental character of my life as it unfolded. This is the way of good history, I think, and it seems true to me from my earthbound perspective. Things *could* have been otherwise. My history professor could have been a theology professor and I might today be a theologian. Then again, as Lee Hardy and others have taught us, we discern our callings, what God summons us to do and to be, through the voices of other human beings whom God puts in our life's way. What looks to us, what must look to us, as human beings and historians as accident, chance, and contingency, looks from the point of view of Him "to whom all time is now" as of a piece. What we discover *ambulando*, along our pilgrimage, was given to us from eternity. And this is the mystery of time and eternity and change and continuity that finally exhausted even the mind of Augustine.

We shall not solve that mystery in this essay. We can say this much, however. Faith may well shape our historical understanding. But that understanding is not all there is. Viewed historically, the connections between my faith and my scholarship are contingencies unfolded over time. Viewed from the perspective of Him, for whom all time is now, these connections are providential. To render the account of my life historically, as I might have done had I not chosen the way of autobiography and had I instead provided evidence for my claims, is to order contingencies chronologically. To render it providentially, as Augustine taught us, is to give praise. For the Christian, Chronos is from everlasting to everlasting contained by Logos. The Logos did of course become flesh and dwelt among us, thus taking on the burdens of history and finally redeeming it. But we Christian historians live between the times, at one and the same time honoring Chronos in our work and the Logos in our alleluias. Thanks be to God.

Notes

1. H. Stuart Hughes, *Consciousness and Society: The Reorientation of European Social Thought, 1890–1920* (New York: Random House, 1958), 37.

2. Henry Adams, *The Education of Henry Adams* (Boston: Houghton Mifflin, 1973), xxvii–xxviii. Though the "Editor's Introduction" was signed by Henry Cabot Lodge, it was actually written by Henry Adams.

3. Hughes, *Consciousness and Society*, 192.

4. Thomas Haskell, "Objectivity Is Not Neutrality: Rhetoric vs. Practice in Peter Novick's *That Noble Dream*," *History and Theory* 4 (May 1990): 131.

5. Richard Wilbur, *Collected Poems, 1943–2004* (New York: Harvest Books, 2006), 5.

Chapter Two

NOT ALL AUTOBIOGRAPHY
IS SCHOLARSHIP

Thinking, as a Catholic, about History

UNA M. CADEGAN

I DO NOT REMEMBER WHEN I FIRST HEARD THE EXPRESSION, "All scholarship is autobiography." I do remember that it made intuitive sense to me. What I took it to mean was that a scholar's project, his or her life's work and its distinguishing perspective, usually has deep roots in personal background and life experience. Like most helpful insights, this one can quickly become reductive. It can be used to dismiss work that deserves attention and evaluation if, in our impeccable judgment, a researcher's perspective is partisan or distorted. Nonetheless, it has long seemed evident to me that knowing something about who the scholars working in a field are is an important part of understanding how that field reflects its subject.

As I began drafting this essay, I set out to discover the source of this expression, and found I could not locate one. It also seems to be a much less common saying than I thought. To the extent that it has a source, it seems to be taken as a variant on the idea that "all history is (auto)biography," which can be found attributed to Nietzsche, Emerson, Macaulay, Carlyle, Disraeli, and Amos Oz. This idea, in its turn, is variously used to mean either that it is impossible to construct a collective account of the past (and, therefore, we remain mired in the inevitably limited and self-interested memories of individuals) or, alternatively, that only individual life histories are interesting enough to sustain any real sense of the past.

So, faced with the evanescence of my central organizing idea, I did what any respectable scholar would do and decided to use it anyhow. Despite its apparent obscurity, it has served me pretty well for almost twenty years. The desire to comprehend within the grand sweep of things a group with which one identifies autobiographically—especially if they have been heretofore overlooked—can produce compelling, evocative scholarship.

My premise in this essay is that the historian of religion who is also a believer has a distinctive need for conscious reflection on this auto-biographical connection. Without conscious reflection, it is too easy to fall into cheerleading on the one hand or score-settling on the other. It is even easier, perhaps, to lapse into self-indulgence—hence the caveat of my title, which is aimed primarily at myself. Thinking about the autobiographical roots of my work as an historian has made me more consciously attentive to doing the work of the historian, as historian, well. Thinking about where that work has taken me not only as an historian but also as a believer has opened up vistas I never would have imagined seeing. I will offer below three examples of how this has happened and is happening yet. The first has to do with the origins of my conscious awareness of the particular task of the believing historian who is a member of a tradition that makes historical claims; the second, with how that self-consciousness, once evoked, continually opens up new dimensions of that original task. The third episode attempts to capture some sense of how this sustained integration—pursuing the scholarly intellectual tasks of the believing historian—has reinvigorated and deepened the belief that helped prompt the intellectual journey.

THE DISENCHANTMENT OF THE WORLD

When I began graduate school, it was my first experience outside Catholic education since kindergarten. I probably should have expected some significant challenge to my worldview, but I was taken almost entirely by surprise. In particular, I found exceedingly strange how exceedingly strange the people around me found the continued practice of religion. It was my first encounter with one of the foundational assumptions of the modern academy—the disenchantment of the world. I could not have put the issue to myself in these terms during those first two years. What I knew then, mostly, was that I felt very odd, and that what was normal and comfortable to me was alien and alienating to many others. This sense of estrangement had a personal dimension, an effect on the relationships I formed over those years, but the dimension important here is how it affected my encounter with the material I was studying. The first time I remember being able to begin to articulate what I was experiencing was in a course on American intellectual history taught by a great historian of American philosophy. We read a line-up of major thinkers I would be intimidated by even today—Jonathan Edwards, Chauncey Wright, Charles Peirce, Josiah Royce, William James, C. I. Lewis, Willard Quine. With each work that we read and discussed, in between my struggles simply to understand the content of what I was reading, I saw what seemed to be an increasingly systematic attempt to explain almost everything without any reference to God. (That this came as a surprise to me in the early 1980s is itself cultural evidence of an interesting sort.) My primary reaction to this attempt was a kind of bafflement—not just at the inability to understand the ideas, but to see why these authors would go to all this trouble. Since God did exist, and that existence did explain so many of these things, why spend time trying to construct an alternative explanation? I was too shy, and too conscious of my own naïveté, to ask questions about this in class. However, in what I now suspect was not a coincidence, the professor in almost every seminar pointed out the places in the text where the author was in fact attempting to leave room for the possibility of religious belief. It still seemed to me to be a waste of effort, but it was an important lesson in what not to assume about a writer's intentions.

When it came time to select a paper topic for the course, I asked if I could write about T. S. Eliot. I knew very little about him, but I did know that he had, after more or less defining the modern as a landscape within which religious belief was impossible, converted to Christianity and spent the rest of his career writing poetry influenced by that perspective. During the secondary research for this paper, I became aware for the first time of the disdain Eliot earned for his conversion and the apparent scholarly consensus about the negative effect on his poetry of his capitulation to meaning. My resulting analysis was pretty painfully ingenuous, though the professor was not nearly as hard on it as it deserved. What helped set me on the course I am still following today, though, was reading Eliot's *Four Quartets* for the first time. I had studied as an undergraduate some of Eliot's shorter important poems, but on picking up the *Four Quartets* all I knew about them was that they were the longest and most important work he wrote after his conversion.

Feeling very scholarly and very artistic at the same time, I lay on the beanbag chair in the living room of my apartment and read the poems out loud. The first, "Burnt Norton," made little impression on me, then or now. But the second, "East Coker," worked its way into my consciousness as no work of art had ever done before. By the time I reached the lines that begin the poem's final stanza, I was having a hard time reading out loud through the tears. I like thinking about the comedy someone like David Lodge or even Muriel Spark could find in this picture, because making fun of it might be the only way to convey how serious an experience it was. "Home is where one starts from. As we grow older / The world becomes stranger, the pattern more complicated / Of dead and living" were words so deeply true to my experience of moving out and away from a working-class upbringing in an industrial town on the Ohio River to graduate study at an Ivy League university that they could easily be weighed down by their own solemnity into trivial cliché. Looking back on this moment and laughing preserves them from that fate and reminds me of what path this experience put me on—or, better, revealed I was already on, and who had walked it before me.

All this is prelude to the conversation that really forms the focus of this first of my three episodes, which occurred during the first semester of my second year of graduate work. If I had been unprepared intellectually and emotionally for my initial encounter with analytic philosophy, I was even less fit to begin an exploration of postmodernist literary theory. I was by this time conscious enough of my own struggle to have a more coherent notion of what was getting in my way. The foreseeable difficulty of reading the dense and difficult prose with any understanding was compounded by my inability to believe that the texts I was reading actually said what they said. It seemed very clear to me that what I was encountering was a worldview, one which presumed as a starting point (without making a case or an argument for the starting point's necessity) the rejection of traditional religious belief and practice in any form. I could not make sense of how to discuss the ideas in these texts without discussing this deep background, but neither the texts themselves nor the seminar discussions seemed to offer an opening. Hoping for some advice on how to address this difficulty, how to make my way into a conversation that interested me but didn't seem to have any room for me, I made an appointment with the seminar professor. Her reaction took me aback. The course, she said, was moving in the direction it was moving, and if I wasn't interested in that direction I was free to drop it. This response was not as heartless as it might seem in cold print, just honest, but the choice was nonetheless that stark. The realization I had in reaction was one of the real turning points of my intellectual life, and I trusted the honesty of this professor enough that I even articulated it at the time. It was always going to be the case that any scholar engaged in historical study who was Christian would have to sort out what it means that Christianity makes claims about events that happened in a certain time and place. I would just have to give things some time and see what I could work out for myself. The instructor responded that the only person she was aware of in the field of literary studies who had maintained a religious perspective and yet earned wide respect as a scholar was Walter Ong. I was at that point only vaguely aware of who Ong was, but looking back I can see now that that moment was when he joined the throng of people who would be my guides and supports through the next stages of the journey, whether or not they ever became aware of their roles.

I left this meeting with something much more valuable than the generic reassurance I had been looking for going into it. I had a new clarity about a central aspect of my intellectual life and my scholarly project. If I was going to become a scholar in the company of these people who so dazzled me even as they were shaking the foundations of my beliefs, and at the same time maintain the religious identity that was too central to who I am to imagine relinquishing it, it was up to me to take responsibility for working out how they could fit together. Clarity about a task does not automatically supply skill or peace of mind in performing it, and I had little of either for the rest of that year. But what I did and do have was an intellectual project that is still preoccupying me, both explicitly and in the background of almost everything else I do as an historian. It is at once the most abstract and dense theological problem—the implications of the Incarnation for understanding human life on earth—and the most pragmatic evidentiary and methodological task.

On the practical end, this self-conscious awareness from early on of the special responsibility believers have for taking into account the historical claims of their traditions has helped me develop two aspects of my work that potentially benefit both church and academy. The first is a continual awareness of the extent to which religion and religious believers were a factor in American history and culture. For a number of reasons, including the significantly increased secular focus of U.S. school curriculums following the school decisions of the 1960s, religion and religious believers receded into the background of U.S. history to an extent that distorted the narrative. Restoring this wide variety of actors to their appropriate place on the historical stage is not primarily an act of devotion or denominational partisanship; in fact, it could be as easily justified as faithful adherence to the Enlightenment value of careful attention to all relevant evidence. Catholics have been especially absent from general accounts of U.S. history—religion is seen as an important dimension of New England settlement, of early-nineteenth-century evangelical expansion, of antislavery activism, but somehow disappears as a category when large numbers of Catholic and Jewish immigrants start arriving in the years following 1830. Labor historians seldom take the predominance of Catholics among the U.S. working class into account in their work, and the history of women's religious congregations is only very recently being taken seriously as a crucial and fascinating dimension of women's history. It can be argued, and fairly well-documented by correlation, that immigration history became a lively subfield at the point when a scholarly generation who were the children and grandchildren of predominantly Catholic immigrants entered the academy. It would be simplistic to the point of offense to argue that scholars can and should only study "people like us." It seems evident, however, that what prompts interest in history on the part of many historians is the impulse to understand how the community that produced them was shaped historically—hence the historian's distinctive variant of "all scholarship is autobiography." If the result of such investigation is to restore to the historical narrative people and events unreasonably overlooked, church and academy both benefit.

There is a second pragmatic consequence of taking on as a contemporary historian this awareness of the historical claims of religious traditions. In a review of Marilynne Robinson's novel *Gilead*, critic Judith Shulevitz wrote in *Slate*, "It was the critics struggling to determine whether a book this religious could also be literature who made me understand why I found it unforgettable. For inspiration Robinson has reached so far into the prehistory of American writing that she bypasses the Enlightenment conviction that art is distinct from religion."[1] Shulevitz diagnoses here a condition of the contemporary novel that provides an important analogy for historians. Because religion has for several historians' generations been inadequately developed as a category of analysis, we are lacking in the tools for dealing with its evidence. We have difficulty distinguishing between theological or devotional language as primary source evidence and as profession of faith. We find it easy to explain away as a by-product of or mask for the intersections of gender, race, and class. Conversely, we try to erase the categorical autonomy of race, gender, and class because their history so often tarnishes what we want to believe about the efficacy of religious belief and religious community. Well-trained historians who are also believers in traditions that make historical claims seem to me to have a particular obligation to help hone the tools that have been left unused for too long. It is an old project, but a new one, too, as Shulevitz also hints in summing up *Gilead* as almost "a prophecy about American literature, . . . pointing us toward a spiritual renewal after decades of ever giddier modernism, postmodernism, and moral indifference. The direction [Robinson] heads us in strikes me as hopeful and fresh, as fresh as the Bible itself, and also slightly terrifying." Perhaps an historian (a very brave, very humble historian) should aim to do something analogous for contemporary historical writing.

ALL SCHOLARSHIP IS AUTOBIOGRAPHY

I am not that historian. But, as I have worked away over the past decade or so, hoeing my own row, I have caught glimpses of some vistas where more talented gardeners might usefully venture.

The main strand of my own research illustrates the notion that all scholarship is autobiography so obviously that I do not need to describe it at length here. I have explored from a number of angles the role of Catholic literary culture in the intellectual and cultural history of twentieth-century U.S. Catholicism, especially as people involved in Catholic literary work found ways to understand and explain themselves as Catholic and American and intellectual. This concern with laying claim to an honest stake in both Catholic tradition and American credibility flowed directly from my graduate school experience of trying to find my feet in the high lonesome spaces of academia without being forced to shed the trappings of the tradition that had formed me intellectually as well as religiously. What I found when I looked in some of the more mundane byways of American Catholic literary life were a lot of people concerned with maintaining the same integration.

Like many historians, as I became more familiar with the period in which I specialized, I was drawn toward understanding more thoroughly the periods that preceded it. This was especially true in my case because the critics and teachers and interpreters of literature whom I was studying constantly invoked the past to illustrate and undergird one of their fundamental premises: that art, literary and otherwise, could no more be separated from religion than could any other aspect of human experience. This impulse was in part defensive—American Catholics, persistently dismayed at the absence of Catholics in the first ranks of American writers, harkened back to the achievement of Dante to exhort their compatriots' efforts in service of the same high integration of religion, art, and culture. I was aware of the extent to which this perspective diverged from standard secular accounts of American literary history. This awareness was sharpened to high relief by the experience of teaching in Florence in the summer of 2000.

A heady experience for any Americanist, these five weeks in "the cradle of the Renaissance" brought together three elements of my training and career in a way that gave rise to preoccupations I've been sorting out ever since. The physical encounter with the material environment of the medieval and Renaissance eras heightens a Catholic historian's sense of the weight and depth and variability of tradition. Skills acquired years before in an ethnographically oriented American Studies graduate program that sought to understand connections among literature and politics, architecture and economy, religion and landscape were recharged and honed by being called on in a new and rich context. Most important, I was in the company of colleagues who knew and loved Florence, who delighted in ensuring that colleagues were able to adapt their disciplines and topics to take best advantage of the site, and who believed fervently in getting students out into the city as often as possible. The experience helped me to see many things differently, but one morning's visit to the Cappella Brancacci gave rise to persisting questions about how—literally and tangibly—we see the past, and altered the focus of my work in some minor but significant ways.

The Cappella Brancacci, in the church of Santa Maria del Carmine, is one of the places in Florence where you can watch the Renaissance happen. Its frescoes of Adam and Eve and of scenes from the life of St. Peter were begun by Masolino, acknowledged master of Gothic painting, and continued by Masaccio, a younger man and the artist credited with reinventing the use of perspective in painting that is one of the hallmarks of Renaissance art. Thanks to an inattentive or generous docent, my colleague and I had an hour in the tiny space instead of the usually allotted ten minutes, and with his help I learned to see the differences in technique that differentiated one painter's work from the other's.

What I did not see was the difference in subject matter or emphasis that, much more than I had consciously realized beforehand, I had been expecting. I had been primed to see what various teachers and sources had told me the Renaissance represented—a turn to this world instead of the next, to identifiable individuals instead of indistinguishable masses of souls, to "man, the measure of all things," as art historian Kenneth Clark titled the episode on the Renaissance in his 1969 BBC television series *Civilisation*, in which he describes the Masaccio frescoes as "the grandest of all testimonies to the dignity of man." I was expecting exhilarating confirmation of this dramatic shift that had ushered in the "disenchanted" world we know today, this moment in which Western civilization stopped seeing God in all things and saw only human beings, the heroic individual.

What I saw instead was a world very much charged with the grandeur of God. The fifteenth-century Florentine setting, rather than diminishing the biblical events in favor of temporal realities, rather than foregrounding the bustle of a world too busy and prosperous to realize it had left God behind, instead seemed to radiate with a conviction that the people and events of apostolic times were still present. Instead of repudiating medieval sacred timelessness, the Renaissance figures mingling with Jesus and Peter and the other apostles seemed to emphasize the presence of the divine in time. In its own idiom, it expressed a confidence as tangible as that of any medieval Coronation of Mary arraying the communion of saints past, present, and future: the confidence that eternal time is now. The eternal inhabits the temporal, the transcendent animates the local. Saint Peter walking down the streets of Florence, healing the son of Theophilus while a crowd of Florentine *cittadini* looks on, could indeed suggest civic pride and this-worldly focus. But it could just as easily be evidence of a conviction that the events of the earliest years of the church were as present, as discernible, in fifteenth-century Florence as they had been in first-century Palestine.

I left the chapel elated, but with my head whirling. Over the rest of that summer and the following year or two, I realized the experience had helped to precipitate what I can best describe as a crisis of authority. Who was I, an Americanist as both teacher and scholar, on a first trip to the continent, to think that this masterpiece of Renaissance art could refute what we are most sure we "know" about the Renaissance? One way to answer this question is to resort to pure autobiography, merely to assert that what I brought with me to the Cappella Brancacci was uniquely my own, and that my only goal in telling this story is to share my experience. Not an unworthy goal (memoir is popular for a reason), though this approach also has a quite respectable scholarly warrant. I came late to this party, I realize. (Most of my epiphanies are like that.) I had learned and had largely been persuaded in graduate school that works of art are created as much by the viewer as by the maker, and that therefore my rendering of the frescoes' meaning was no more or less valuable or worthless than anyone else's. A defensible, even fashionable answer, but unsatisfying and a little lonesome. I am largely persuaded that meaning is contingent, but it is still an object of wonderment to me as well as a tangible catalyst for investigation that we *make things mean*. The processes by which "we," in all our multifarious configurations, go about doing this are discernible and documentable—classic primary source material for historians.

This is easy to say but difficult to do. It would require an entire scholarly career to responsibly examine the construction of the idea of the Renaissance in the United States, and I haven't got one to spare. Nevertheless, within my own mind this particular bell could not be un-rung, and I have over the past several years attempted in limited ways to examine how the idea of the Renaissance appears and functions in the context of my work as a teacher of American Studies and an historian of American Catholic literary culture. What seems inescapable to me is the centrality of one particular data point: that this idea was largely the creation of nineteenth-century, upper-class, Anglo-American Prot-estants.[2] I used to resist stating this conclusion so flatly, because it could seem to convey a tribal glee ("Take back the Renaissance!") that is far from my intention or goal. But the observation has continued to seem germane and fruitful to me, so I have pursued it, trying as much as pos-sible to take the circumstance primarily as data, and to reflect on what it means for twentieth-century American Catholic cultural history that the pervasive American view of the Renaissance was largely formulated by American Protestants, convinced that American society was rightly secular, and that the history of civilization was to a great extent the his-tory of humanity's overcoming of the superstition and authority-ridden docility that for them typified the Middle Ages and the dominance of the Roman church. The Renaissance was the turning point in history because it was for them entwined with the throwing off of the church's domination, especially of learning. The art of the Renaissance had to be proven great, but had to be a human achievement aimed toward human ends.

The emerging cultural importance of the Renaissance in the nineteenth and early twentieth century had two interrelated strands. As a period of artistic, intellectual, and cultural flowering, the Renaissance came to occupy a central place in the historical imagination of key nineteenth-century writers and intellectuals. It was both one of the most important examples of the potential heights of human artistic achievement and, increasingly, a crucial way station in a nationalist history of representative government that originated in ancient Greece and culminated in the American experiment. The Renaissance also entered very literally and materially into American culture with increasing rapidity at the end of the nineteenth century when members of the burgeoning industrial aristocracy began to acquire and imitate its art and architecture as markers of their own cultural arrival. In contrast to an antebellum generation that had cultivated a self-consciously plain style in decorative and fine arts alike, believing it to be in keeping with the egalitarian, democratic ethos of American life, the turn of the century saw American industrial wealth invested in building castles and palazzi as private homes and public museums, furnished with paintings and frescoes and pediments and altarpieces from the churches and convents and monasteries and palaces of countries all over Europe, but most avidly and prestigiously from the Italy of the Renaissance.

These two strands are distinct but intertwined. One decisive connection is that neither the intellectuals nor the inventors can consider the Renaissance a Roman Catholic phenomenon. For the intellectuals, what makes the Renaissance important in the history of thought and politics are the seeds it plants that will grow into enlightenment and revolution: the recovery and translation of classical texts; the beginnings of secular political theory, separable from hierarchy and papal authority; and, as I have already noted, a perceived emphasis on the individual, the human and this-worldly, defined in contrast to the communal, religious order of medieval time. It might seem that the patrons and purchasers, connoisseurs and clients who made the Renaissance central to the American art market would find it more difficult to "de-Catholicize" the Renaissance, given the overwhelmingly religious subject matter of the period. But three factors made doing so not only possible but necessary. Increasing formalism in art and art theory rendered the subject matter of a work of art increasingly irrelevant to evaluating its quality. Simultaneously, Renaissance art was inevitably almost completely physically severed from its original contexts of worship and devotion by the great aestheticizing museum movements of the late nineteenth and early twentieth centuries. One aspect of context did persist, however: because the Catholic Church was the sole (or at least the wealthiest) patron available to sponsor artistic production on the scale the greatness of contemporary artists required, the religious content of Renaissance art could be dismissed as an historical accident, merely a by-product of this circumstance. The disassociation of the Renaissance from Roman Catholicism that resulted from this combination of factors—the definition, indeed, of the Renaissance in opposition to many aspects of Roman Catholicism—made the period and its associations available to the American governing classes of the early twentieth century as a native cultural heritage, a lineage long and deep enough to help undergird the emerging world-historical self-image of the United States.

I have found, as I have given sustained thought to this idea of the Renaissance over the past few years, that I see it with the altered vision that surprised me in the Brancacci Chapel. In ways I was not conscious of before that day, I see as a Catholic historian—as an historian whose skills are shaped by Catholic sensibilities as much as by methodological training, as a Catholic preoccupied with fitting all sorts of evidence into an ever more complex understanding of how we got from there to here. If the Renaissance was about the discovery of the "human" and of "reality,"[3] is there implicit a suggestion that what came before was less "human," less "real"? Fully exploring the implications of these ideas, as I have said, would require an additional scholarly career. But on the modest scale of my own understanding of U.S. Catholic history in the twentieth century, what the contemporary view of the Renaissance leaves out is as suggestive as what it includes. Perhaps its most interesting irony is that Italian art and culture were becoming central to the self-concept of the American upper classes at the same time that actual Italian immigrants were coming to represent something potentially un-American. The exponentially increasing number of immigrants from Italy to the

U.S. in the years around the turn of the twentieth century were at best primitive peasant Catholics and at worst dangerous anarchists. In either case, they were something close to the opposite of the rational, self-controlled, democratic citizen and consumer emerging as the ideal middle-class self in the early years of the twentieth century. The idea of the Renaissance served to buttress a vision of American culture that Italian immigrants—urban, working class, Catholic, much more likely to frequent nickelodeons and vaudeville shows than symphony halls and art museums—circumvented and ornamented and eventually largely disregarded in the years immediately following the First World War.

To be fair, it was in some sense uniquely possible at the beginning of the twentieth century to dissociate the idea of Italy from Roman Catholicism, because at its establishment a half century earlier the Italian state had decisively rejected Vatican control over Italian politics. Italy in this historical moment stood at last with the other nations of Europe in espousing representative secular government and equating hierarchical authority with a primitive past that modern nations and modern individuals needed to reject. The Pope, an anachronistic monarchical figure imprisoned in the Vatican, was both threatening and impotent, insidious and ridiculous. His position confirmed for upper-class Americans who were claiming the Renaissance as their own intellectual, artistic, and cultural heritage that the country in which it had originated had not brought it to fruition. Americans, then, could be its rightful heirs and stewards.

I am intrigued by the likelihood that this idea of the Renaissance was an important component in defining American Catholics out of mainstream U.S. intellectual culture in the early and middle years of the twentieth century. By locating the importance of the Renaissance in values that could be separated from—and, in fact, defined against—Roman Catholicism, and then traced in a clear trajectory that led inexorably to Harvard in 1900, the American intellectual and cultural elite could incorporate the heritage of Europe and of Western civilization into its own self-understanding without having to address Roman Catholicism as anything other than a dying, irrelevant polity. It did not have to be met as an intellectual equal.

Engaging Roman Catholicism as an intellectual tradition in the early twentieth century would have required mending one of the defining breaches in modern intellectual life—that between theology and philosophy. Philosophy had endured in the Western academy as a viable intellectual enterprise; theology, except within divinity schools and seminaries, had been defined out of an increasingly scientized intellectual landscape. To the extent that it remained a legitimate subject for scholarly study, theology was translated into "religion," and disaggregated into component sociological factors such as class, race, gender, region, ethnic identity, and political affiliation, which then could be approached using the methods of social science. But this is the rough equivalent of looking at the frescoes in the Brancacci Chapel and seeing only pigment and form and technique. Among many other things, the doctrine of the Incarnation is an *idea*, and, as with so many other fundamental organizing ideas at the center of complex systems, our view of it literally changes what we see when we look at the past and its traces. In other words, whether you believe in the Incarnation affects how you read evidence. Whether this is a good thing or a bad thing I do not know, but trying to be conscious of it and to communicate honestly about it is, I think, one of the more interesting contemporary intellectual tasks of the believing historian.

Mending the breach between philosophy and theology is not part of an historian's job description (for which I am sure most philosophers and theologians are grateful). But we—that is, believing historians interested in investigating not "religion" but living religious traditions, communities existing inside and outside of time, using the tools of the historian but maintaining a humble sense of their limits—could do a better job than we have done of tracing the causes and consequences of the breach, and asking some pointed questions about what data and evidence it has caused us and our colleagues to overlook. Another Renaissance touchstone is Raphael's 1509 fresco *The School of Athens*, the familiar image of Plato and Aristotle at the center of an array of philosophers, a quintessential celebration of the power and long tradition of human reason. What is virtually forgotten is that the *School of Athens* stands opposite the *Disputa*, or the Disputation of the Holy Sacrament.

At the center of this fresco is the Eucharistic host in a monstrance, sur-rounded by members of the Church Militant and the Church Trium-phant, with an exultant resurrected Christ reigning amidst depictions of the other persons of the Trinity. In other words, in its original context *The School of Athens'* celebration of the power of human reason is and must be complemented and accompanied by the communal, timeless, sacramental celebration of what is beyond reason. The loss of this con-text is strikingly evident even in the original space itself: it is possible to stand and watch tour groups pour into the room, be pointed by their guides toward *The School of Athens* for a few words about the fresco's most famous features, then be ushered out of the door opposite with-out ever turning an eye toward the *Disputa*. Simply turning around and seeing what lies behind us, mindful of what we share with but how we differ from those who have stood in our footsteps before, is a prob-ably inexhaustible method for enriching our sense of past, present, and future.

HISTORY AS SACRAMENT

A sustained reexamination of the visual (and other) evidence of the Renaissance with the integrated mind that keeps philosophy and the-ology as partners reveals many forgotten connections and contexts. It presents, however, perhaps especially to a Catholic historian, a specific temptation, one that I think historians have to resist, even when its lure seems particularly honorable. It illuminates and, I believe, more fully serves the available evidence to see the Renaissance not as the occa-sion of a radical break with a premodern, medieval past, but instead as one episode of a still-continuing drama within which the relationships between church and world, communal and individual, sacred and pro-fane, continually reconfigure. But this very emphasis on continuity can be an opening to the temptation inherent in seeing things *sub specie aeternitatis*: seeing everything worldly in the light of eternity can seem to diminish the importance of examining and understanding and argu-ing about how things change over time. If everything matters ultimately, does anything matter very much in any one moment? Do the things we argue over most vociferously as historians have any resonance at all when we see them in light of tradition, belief, and revelation?

If I thought they did not, I would no longer be an historian. But I have been thinking about what it is, precisely, that helped form in me this sensibility that historical events and actors matter. One very likely answer is the experience of liturgy, the sustained and continually re-vived realization that repetition is an occasion for renewed understanding and depth, not simple reoccurrence. The Eucharist, weekly and daily, has been perhaps the most consistent aspect of my life for nearly forty years. I have been struck in my research on twentieth-century Catholic intellectual life how little Catholics write about the presence and the experience of the sacraments. I am convinced, though, that this lack of explicit reflection is not evidence of the unimportance of the sacraments in Catholic intellectual life. Instead, I think their importance is too dense, too pervasive, and too implicit, too dependent on things beyond and outside of words, to be conveyed easily or, in most cases, effectively. So, in trying to convey how the integration between studying history and living the Christian tradition deepens over time, I need to try to describe my hearing the gospel of the raising of Lazarus proclaimed during the 2006 Lenten season.

It might have been the first time I had ever heard it, the story seemed so strange and powerful to me. That strangeness is a hallmark of John's gospel, and in reflecting on the story I am not trying to dispel the strangeness or explain it away. One aspect of the account did seem to go beyond strange and become troubling, the more I thought about it. Jesus's reply to the initial report of Lazarus's illness is, "This illness is not to end in death, but is for the glory of God, that the Son of God may be glorified through it" (Jn 11:4). He then waits two days before setting off for Bethany, saying to the apostles as they leave, "Our friend Lazarus is asleep, but I am going to awaken him" (11). When the apostles mistake this for the healing sleep of recuperation, Jesus spells it out: "Lazarus has died. And I am glad for you that I was not there, that you may believe. Let us go to him" (14–15). The deception here seems gratuitous; the delay in hastening to Lazarus's deathbed deliberately cruel. The dimness and misunderstanding of the apostles frequently present occasions for Jesus's teaching in John's gospel, and the goal of God's glory and their belief might make their feelings seem puny by comparison. I hope I am not simply trying to evade a hard teaching, though, when I say that this explanation was not satisfying to me. And, as I puzzled through how the story moves from its beginning to its end, I found myself propelled deeply into a new awareness of the grace of thinking historically, of thinking about events as succeeding one another in time, so that what happens next can be something that never happened before.

The story's discomfiting details took on a different resonance when I began to think of its events as really occurring in time. Of course, the gospels, and the gospel of John especially, present post-resurrection understandings of who Jesus is, the result of the experience and reflection of the early Christian communities. But wouldn't a full post-resurrection understanding (if there could be such a thing) need to encompass some existential, visceral awareness of what could possibly be at stake in being in the presence of someone with power over death? Would Jesus himself be hesitating over the implications and consequences of the situation? Pondering why Jesus says this illness is not to end in death—is it possible he himself, in the moment, did not know what that meant? That he himself learned something about his capacity not just to heal but to restore life, to conquer death, in the process of this experience?

Martha confronts Jesus with the hard results of his delay in coming: my brother would not have died. But, she also declares quite straightforwardly her confidence that whatever Jesus asks, God will grant. She meets Jesus's assertion that her brother will rise by affirming her belief in the resurrection on the last day. And, in response to Jesus's reply that he *is* the resurrection, she names him as Messiah. What remains ambiguous here is at what point the raising of Lazarus shifts from then to now, from the eschatological horizon to the present moment. One possibility is that when Martha affirms Jesus as Messiah, and the moment approaches in which all his foreknowledge will come to fruition, the connection between resurrection and eternal life on the one hand, and mortal life, life in time, on the other, takes on an enormity it had not had for him before.

This realization may help illuminate another of the story's great mysteries, the depth of Jesus's emotion. While most translations soften the verb to "perturbed" or "troubled in spirit," commentaries make clear that in the original Greek the word is very strong. And as he takes in the reality of Lazarus's death, it seems, Jesus himself weeps. If he knew that "this illness is not to end in death," and that its point is that God may be glorified, why is his emotion so deep? I cannot pretend to answer this question adequately, but what I have been pondering since hearing this gospel anew is that, at the center of this moment right before the events on which history as we in the West define it pivots, we find human love, and we find the finality of time.

To love other human beings as humans love must be as different from loving as God loves as being human is from being divine. Jesus presumably experienced both together in some way, and maybe this experience is his realization of the possibility, the meaning, the feeling of their sundering. Jesus, as human, could here be mourning Lazarus, but he could also be mourning his own solidarity with all these people, his having to give over the sweetness and comfort of human presence for the alien grandeur of the capacity to defeat death. The three references to Jesus's deep emotions reverberate with the enormity of the moment when that capacity takes effect in human history.

The story highlights the extent to which being human means being a creature in time. For Jesus to love humans as humans, as he loved Martha, Mary, and Lazarus, the beauty of being a creature in time must have been apparent to him, must have been one of the most distinctive aspects of his experience of life on earth. Loving humans as human means also, of course, knowing the inconsolable loss of human presence in time that death brings about, and Jesus himself would not yet have known what that meant as a human being.

What seems clear to me from all of this is that when we press the gospel's focus on the glory of God and the importance of our belief to its crucial moments, we find, not that the ordinary connections and events of human experience diminish in their particularity and importance, but that they are in their very specificity and lovableness the gateways to the ultimate. If this is so, it would seem to have some very concrete implications for how Christians think of themselves as historians. That historians are charged with helping society to think about the way in which human experience unfolds in time means living at the center of this mystery during the most mundane bibliography-compiling, citation-checking, draft-revising historical work. Nothing we do as a scholar or teacher or citizen takes place outside this horizon, apart from this reality of being created in time for a life outside of time. Everything we do that increases a sense of wonder about the smallest detail of this picture is of ultimate importance. A deepening identification with the reality of the past and the humanity of its inhabitants is indispensable and mutually enriching to the practice of a tradition that makes historical claims.

HISTORY AS MYSTERY

Everything I have written here could be simply a gloss on one of the most interesting lines in Flannery O'Connor's letters: "Mystery isn't something that is gradually evaporating. It grows along with knowledge."[4] When I first read O'Connor's letters over twenty years ago, I identified less with her than with the young recipient of this observation, nineteen-year-old Alfred Corn, who had written in the spring of 1962 expressing his anxieties over whether a university education made it impossible to have religious faith. In her reply, O'Connor refutes Corn's apparent speculation about the extent to which the behavior of O'Connor's characters is determined. A determined world, O'Connor makes clear, would be a much less interesting one. In my attempt here to articulate the way by which I have come, so far, in understanding myself and my work as a Catholic historian, I have been reminded that the whole thing is much more mysterious to me now than it was when I started. Not the first time Flannery O'Connor has told me something about myself long before I knew it.

Pleading mystery is a legendary Catholic cop-out, of course, but that does not free the writer from the obligation to be clear about where the boundaries of the mystery lie. Before we come anywhere near standing still in mystic contemplation, we have a lot of work to do. Not that it is a bad thing for reflection on personal experience to yield some pragmatic historical and historiographical questions. If the results of these experiences remained only personal, they would be narcissistic flotsam, not even rising to the level of autobiography. And the tasks that emerge from reconsidering the place of religious traditions in the past century-and-a-half of historical scholarship, while not innovative, are nonetheless radical, in that they ask us to return once again to the roots of the profession, and to speak in some very fundamental ways to the profession as a whole, not only to those who share our beliefs about the world. But, in the end, mystery itself is not, in some sense, mysterious, if by "mysterious" we mean something that tries to keep itself from us, keep us guessing and stumbling. Instead, mystery is very near, always waiting to ambush us, in the most mundane of our tasks, because we deal with the stuff of which the gracious mystery at the heart of the world is made.

NOTES

1. Judith Shulevitz, Review of *Gilead*, by Marilynne Robinson, in "The Year in Culture," *Slate Magazine*, December 30, 2004, available at http://www .slate.com/id/2111569 (last accessed March 13, 2010).

2. Lynne Walhout Hinojosa, *The Renaissance, English Cultural Nationalism, and Modernism, 1860–1920* (New York: Palgrave Macmillan, 2009); Mary Ann Calo, *Bernard Berenson and the Twentieth Century* (Philadelphia: Temple University Press, 1994).

3. Bill Moyers, in *The Power of the Past*, asks of an art historian in the Brancacci Chapel, "This reality, this discovery of reality was new and radical for that time, wasn't it?"

4. Letter from Flannery O'Connor to Alfred Corn, August 12, 1962, in Sally Fitzgerald, ed., *The Habit of Being: Letters of Flannery O'Connor* (New York: Farrar, Straus, Giroux, 1979), 489.

Chapter Three

SEEING THINGS

Knowledge and Love in History

BETH BARTON SCHWEIGER

Jesus looked at him and loved him.

—Mark 10:21

You can know a thing to death and for all purposes be completely ignorant of it.

—Marilynne Robinson, *Gilead*

THERE IS, NICHOLAS BOYLE HAS ARGUED, AN INTIMACY between language, people, and moral meaning that postmodern theory has very nearly robbed from us.[1] Although Boyle writes to defend Christian literary humanism, the relationship he invokes stands as fine a description as any of why I write history. "Intimacy" is the best word I can muster to describe what it is to spend eight hours bent over the diary of a person who has been dead for a hundred and fifty years, trying to trace personality and tone of voice in spidery handwriting that is maddeningly difficult to make out, straining to hear one side of nearly incomprehensible conversations about people and events I can rarely identify. To write history is, for me, to make a relationship with the dead. I try to see people in the archives. I take enormous pleasure in this task of recovery and discovery, and in the creative work that follows as I decide how to tell their story. Like the meeting of characters in fiction, these encounters count as a genuine expansion of my experience, offering a perspective beyond self and the possibility of wisdom.

Yet my pursuit of the dead is a problem. One does not have to be in thrall to theory to wonder if seeing people across the centuries is even possible. What Rowan Williams has called "the sheer dreadful irreducible distance" between people only seems worse in the archive.[2] Some of the great minds of our time have devoted their lives to telling us how much we will never be able to see in dusty manuscripts, arguing that any archive is incomplete and arbitrary, and that language can obscure even more than it reveals.[3] At best, it seems, I might be able to see the dead only as they chose to represent themselves. At worst, I will only see myself reflected in the records they have left behind.

In this essay, I want to briefly explore how the limits on our ability to see and to know the dead bear on a central problem for any Christian who writes history: the necessity of loving them. It seems inescapable that I must love the subjects of my history.[4] I mean love here neither in a sentimental nor idealistic sense. Far from the Pauline "love which bears all things," love for St. Augustine signified enjoyment, "not the name of something that we do, but of a relation in which we stand." As Oliver O'Donovan has explained, in the Augustinian sense, enjoyment "distinguishes between enjoyment and 'use,' where the object is put to the service of some project. Love, whatever actions it gives rise to, is contemplative in itself, rejoicing in the fact that its object is there, not wanting to do anything 'with' it."[5] Love, then, discounts violence against the beloved.

Yet on these terms, my relationship with the subjects of my history seems to defy any understanding of what a loving relationship might be. This is true in two very different senses. How can I love the author of a fragment of poetry? Or a nameless face in a photograph? Or the author of a diary I have worked for years to comprehend? How can I love people whom I have never met? Limited knowledge of the dead is compounded by a second problem, that of the stunning imbalance of power between historian and subject. I can use the people I encounter in the archives without their consent for my own purposes, for my own pleasures, for my own professional gain. The dead can languish without defense in my books; I can even silence them with their own words. My purposes may be honest. But what if they are not? And what if my honest purposes only end by disfiguring my subjects? How can they speak truthfully in my history? How can I be a neighbor to the dead in my books?

In history, the call to love one's neighbor is extended to the dead.[6] For the Christian, knowledge about the past, as any knowledge, should serve the ends of love. Miroslav Volf has exhorted Christians to "remember rightly," by which he means remembering truthfully. The goal of truthful memory, he writes, is "unhindered love of neighbor."[7] My history can take part in God's redemption only if it somehow takes part in his love.

This call for love and truthfulness is extended not only towards the subjects of history, but also towards the historian. A true vocation, Rowan Williams has observed, leaves no place to hide, no room for self-deception. Instead, vocation seeks truthfulness in love. In seeking to know the dead in love, an historian may foster truthfulness in herself. The question at the heart of Christian community, first posed by Christ to the disciples, is "tell me who you think I am."[8] It is a question historians should extend to those we meet in the archives.

Thus, two kinds of truthfulness are at stake in history as vocation: truthfulness about the dead and truthfulness about the historian, and they cannot be separated one from the other. This perspective moves away from the view of history as a tool of reform to concentrate on how the particular habits of history as practice can change the historian and, in turn, shape the histories she writes. Writing history entails more than trying to wrench the world into a shape the historian might believe is warranted. Jacques Maritain condemned "the magical fallacy" that an "artist's proper calling is to change the world according to his or her vision." Virtuous making aims not at the good of humanity but at the good of what is made, Maritain argued. And while history is a craft, not an art, both artisans and artists should recognize that something larger is at stake in the act of making than the will to power. Why should a Christian write history? One answer is to envision history as a spiritual as well as a critical discipline, and to allow those about whom we write and the peculiar intellectual disciplines of our craft to change us. Instead of using the dead to gain leverage over the past or traction in the profession, the discipline of history can be a means of grace in the life of the historian. The writing of history, rightly done, can challenge and change the historian.[9]

Many things might be said about the problem of love in history. Here, I focus on two points. First, the practice of history as vocation should embrace human limitations, including our limited knowledge, as an opportunity rather than a problem. Second, it should eschew the stable habits of professional identity to embrace one that is contingent and open to being formed by those one encounters from the past. Central to this approach is the need to deny knowledge of the past as power and to practice knowledge in love.

In considering the question of vocation and history, I rely on the work of several theologians, among them Rowan Williams, Karl Barth, and Miroslav Volf, who have written eloquently about the importance of historical thinking to the church. The chief task of the history of theology is to build up the church, something a general history cannot claim. Yet these insights can apply more generally to the Christian who writes history as well. I intend this essay as an invitation to further conversation about the relationship between the two tasks.

Between Two Worlds

The possibility of grace in the practice of history is rooted in what Simon Schama has called the historian's "habitually insoluble quandary." The quandary is "how to live in two worlds at once; how to take the broken, mutilated remains of something or someone from the 'enemy lines' of the documented past and restore it to life or give it a decent interment in our own time and place."[10] Gerald R. Strauss has made a similar point. "As historians we live in two worlds, and our dual citizenship brings conflicting loyalties," he writes.[11] "We are stuck as historians with the fundamental dissociation created for us by our double lives in the past and in the present. Our sentiments towards what is chronologically or spatially remote from us—what reaches us only indirectly through artifacts, is essentially inert, and must be put into motion by our imagination—can never be the same as our feelings towards that which is immediate, close, alive to all our senses and very real."[12]

These are remarkable observations, for they evoke the similarity between the work of the historian and the vocation of the Christian: it is to live in two worlds, and to be at home in neither. Unlike Schama and Strauss, I cannot view this status only as a problem to be somehow overcome. It is the familiar habit of my life, this double-mindedness. Christians stand between here and eternity, between the glass darkly and unfettered sight. And however much I may strain against the place in which I find myself, the conflicting loyalties and dissociations my position invokes offers an opportunity rather than a problem to be solved. Human love never begins from full knowledge of the beloved. It is always an act of faith.

Schama and Strauss find two implications in the historian's double life. First, they assert that historians labor under impoverished conditions. Our histories would be better, they imply, if we had more knowledge. More, the historical record is hardly a transparent window into the past; instead, it always distorts what we can see. As in quantum physics, the measuring of a human life necessarily changes it. Indeed, some historical records intentionally veil the subjects that we seek out in them. All of this adds up to scarcity: historians do not have all that is required. And second, the distance between ourselves and our subjects is fraught with peril. The hard work of history is to somehow compensate for, or to bridge, this gap. Both of these ideas—that our incomplete knowledge of the past hinders us, and that our distance from the dead makes them difficult to see—are problems only if we wield knowledge as power in our histories. By contrast, wise and charitable ways of knowing are hindered by neither of these conditions.

Truthful histories depend neither on the size of the archive nor on the historian's proximity to the dead. In an age when my students click a mouse to retrieve an archive that would shame any claims for the library in ancient Alexandria, I find it difficult to believe that we need more information about the dead in order to do them justice. This generation has access to more information about the dead than any that has come before us. What we need are historians who will reflect wisely about what we already know (or what we will learn). The writing of truthful history depends both on the character of the historian and on the purpose of our histories. We must begin by asking, what are our histories for?

Schama's answer, at least in this book, is to gain a sense of communion with the dead. He writes of a character in a novel Henry James left incomplete at his death, an historian named Ralph Pendrel. History was not enough for Pendrel. He wanted to know things that could never be documented, and things for which there could never be *enough* documents. James fixed things for Pendrel with time travel. When Pendrel inherited a house in London, he crossed the threshold and simply walked into 1820. Like Pendrel, Schama mourns the lack of knowledge about the past that leaves historians "forever chasing shadows, painfully aware of their inability ever to reconstruct a world in its completeness, however thorough or revealing their documentation. . . . [W]e are doomed to be forever hailing someone who has just gone around the corner and out of earshot." Even if, Schama concludes, "our flickering glimpses of dead worlds fall far short of ghostly immersion, that perhaps is still enough to be going on with."[13] In this view, genuine knowledge of the past would allow us to commune with the dead. Since that is impossible, historians must settle for incomplete knowledge, a poor substitute for experience. One reviewer suggested that James never finished the novel because he saw the folly of his character's desire for intimacy with the past.[14]

Yet even if the possibility of communion with the dead is rudely dismantled, the desire remains. I have confessed that it is one of the primary reasons I myself go into the archive in the first place. Why is this desire so strong? One answer is that it is driven by a desire to possess and master the dead. "History was a way to live extra lives," Tony Hendra recalled of his adolescent obsession, "to cheat the limits of flesh and blood, to roll the rock back from the tomb and free the resurrected dead."[15] Here he echoes Schama's desire to restore "the broken and mutilated remains" of the dead to life. These astonishing claims demonstrate how knowledge of the past can make us feel like gods. We remain haunted by Bacon's seventeenth-century adage that "knowledge is power," and by the centuries-old illusion of the possibility of universal knowledge, or something very close to it. Where Bacon envisioned knowledge as an instrument (albeit one to benefit humankind rather than individuals), Foucault insisted that the goals of knowledge and power were inseparable: that we control by knowing. In spite of their differences, a universal perspective trumps a particular one in both of these schemes. The notion that more knowledge offers more control is a familiar one. All scholars flirt with this kind of power. We aspire to write books that encompass worlds in order to somehow compensate for the unyielding limits we meet in our own mortality.

There is a strange violence in this pretense to universal comprehension. Rowan Williams has called attention to the relationship between knowing and power, describing knowledge without love as a "terrible threat." Knowing another's secret, we are tempted to use it as a weapon. ("I am not the only one who has to suppress the urge to break eggs or drop cut-glass vases just because I *know* they're fragile.") Curiosity, he writes, can be an "unscrupulous rationalization of the lust for power . . . the diabolical thirst to know without loving, to *substitute* knowing for loving." "Is there anything in human relations more frightening than that?" he asks. The will to power is reflected even in our destructive knowledge of ourselves, which can be a source of self-hatred and loathing. Knowing as power is all the more horrifying because we have been made aware of an alternative. Unlike us, God practices "kind knowing," which shuns power in favor of "knowing by kinship." He has practiced in full the "ecstasy" of love, Williams writes, by going outside of himself and inhabiting us in the person of Christ Jesus.[16]

So what does knowing and loving, knowledge practiced in love rather than as power, demand of a Christian historian? Williams suggests that Christians should practice a "pastoral imagination," which mimics God's own charitable knowing of us. A pastoral imagination views others not in terms of oneself, but in terms of themselves, "trying to sense their experience as they are experiencing it, seeing with their eyes, feeling with their nerves." Knowledge is not power, but a wise charity practiced toward us by the One who knows what it is to be both creator *and* creature.[17]

This impulse is echoed in Karl Barth's call for charity in the history of theology. "History is not a paint-box at the disposal of anyone who thinks he knows something and has a need to make his knowledge more impressive. . . . [H]istory is made up of living men whose work is handed over defenceless to our understanding and appreciation upon their death. Precisely because of this, they have a claim on our courtesy, a claim that their own concerns should be heard and that they should not be used simply as a means to our ends." For Barth, the historian's responsibility to the dead means that "history writing cannot be the proclamation of judgment." This is not naïveté. His severe restraint is rooted in his particular historical task, which is the history of the church. The history of theology, Barth writes, is meant to bear witness to the truth of God, and the responsibility of the historian is that of one Christian to another, "bearing and being borne by each other . . . having to take mutual responsibility for and among the sinners gathered together in Christ." When historians enact the last judgment over other people, they violate the mystery of the body of Christ, he writes.[18]

The question of judgment is at the heart of the problem of knowledge as power.[19] Barth finds himself standing in the midst of the faithful in his history, hedged in by his responsibility to the cloud of witnesses that surround him. For him, this community determines what he can think about the past. "There is no past in the Church, so there is no past in theology," he declares, allowing the history of the church to be a spiritual discipline rather than merely a critical intellectual enterprise. But the problem of knowledge as power is not limited to the historian of theology, as I have argued. While the historian of theology may have a special responsibility to the church, other historians need to consider how Barth's call for charitable restraint should shape their approach to the dead outside of the church.[20] Dietrich Bonhoeffer has argued that judgment, the "forbidden objectification of the other which destroys single-minded love," should be withheld from those outside of the church, too, even in the face of evil in the other. He brooks no compromise on this point. "Neither I am right nor the other person, but God is always right and shall proclaim both his grace and his judgment."[21]

What, then, is the relationship of judgment and critical inquiry for the Christian historian? Does the Christian scholar need to forego the latter entirely to avoid the former? Can or should an historian refrain from judging the dead, and if so, what does it look like? The unsettling nature of this question underscores how central judgment is to contemporary conceptions of history. Barth's charity to his own subjects was rooted in their membership in the church. Yet Barth himself wrestled mightily with nineteenth-century theologians, a tradition that he found singularly distasteful. His struggle produced a double-edged theory of criticism and charity, and his views on the matter are useful for historians who write about matters other than the church.

Barth identified several ways in which history might reflect knowledge as charity rather than power. First, he counsels that we listen attentively to the dead.[22] More than once, he invokes the phrase, "calm, attentive, and open" to describe the ideal stance of the scholar towards the voices of the past. The scholar should strain to hear not only one's favorite voices, he cautions, nor only those deemed most important by tradition, but *all* voices. In this, he describes the writing of history as an almost mystical enterprise in which the historian herself may not realize which voices are most important. Additionally, Barth calls for a listening that is deeply historical. Many of the questions posed by the dead are our questions, he writes, and their answers posed in "a language appropriate to their time . . . just as we in our time . . . are concerned to find a language in which to give our answer." Sometimes their intentions were the same, at others different from our own. Nevertheless, the standard is unyielding. "We must always . . . investigate the particular context and concern of the past and understand this from its own relative centre and not from ours."[23]

In my own field of early American history, an example of the importance of listening can be seen in the recovery in the past half-century of the voices of women, slaves, and Native Americans, a development that has dramatically reshaped and expanded the narrative of the United States. Rather than being mere scholarly fashion, the recovery of these voices confirms the importance of all people to historical understanding. But "all people" includes their oppressors. Here one encounters great difficulties. How, for example, should a Christian listen to an American slaveholder? What should one hear when one does? And what is the appropriate response? A central figure in my course in early nineteenth-century American history is the South Carolinian

James Henry Hammond. An ambitious man, Hammond acquired more than one hundred slaves and thousands of acres at his marriage, making him one of the wealthiest men in the state that he later served in the U.S. Senate and in the governor's mansion. He subsequently fathered several children with the women he owned. Hammond never claimed a devout Christian piety, but he firmly believed that God sanctioned his mastery over his slaves. "Our only safety against the torrent of abolition," he wrote, "is to drive our piling to the rock—the rock of ages—the Bible."[24] Hammond's raw ambition to master all of his dependents—enslaved and free—differed from the goals of another South Carolinian planter, Charles Colcock Jones. Charles Jones was a sincere Christian man, and by any meaningful measure of his day, a benevolent master. He had agonized over slavery in his youth, particularly during his years of study at Andover and Princeton, at one time declaring it unqualifiedly against the laws of God. He eventually silenced his own fears by devoting his life to "the religious instruction of the slaves." If slavery must continue, Jones reasoned, then it must be reformed and brought under the supervision of Christian people. Accordingly, Jones devoted most of his working life to evangelizing slaves on his own and neighboring plantations. He died in 1863 as the Union troops approached his plantation, firm in the conviction of both his sin and of his Savior, an earnest Christian slaveholder to the end.[25]

"From its own relative centre, and not from ours," Barth writes. To consider Hammond and Jones and their slave society on these terms is fraught with difficulties. To see them rightly is not to excuse them or to sentimentalize them or to dismiss them. Barth is not asking for this, I do not think. And yet a kind of paralysis can set in, as it frequently does as I face students who almost gleefully see the specks in the eyes of these men and their peers. Knowledge is not another name for debunking, for stripping things down to their perverse core, which according to the spirit of our age nearly always means the exercise of raw power. C. S. Lewis invites us to look through the window to see the garden, but warns us against seeing through the garden. "The whole point," he writes, "of seeing through something is to see something through it. . . . [T]o 'see through' all things is the same as not to see."[26] Wise and graceful ways of living require more than the deconstruction of power, even of a slaveholder. There is more to see in the lives of Hammond and Jones than merely that.

What, then, can we learn from Christian slaveholders? One possibility is to learn from them to look for the logs in our own eyes. Hammond and Jones were blind to the enslaved human beings who stood before their eyes. They died unwilling to embrace the full wisdom offered in their theology and unable to breach the terrible chasm that opens when one human being claims complete knowledge and power over another. At the very least, Hammond and Jones can teach us how easily blindness comes upon human beings and to ask, to what are *we* blind?

A second way to strip knowledge of its pretensions to power is in the frank acknowledgement of the limits of human understanding and of the craft of history itself. "The one who is all too sure, illegitimately sure . . . cannot and may not notice carefully 'what a wise man thought before us,'" Barth writes.[27] It is by no means the case, he observes, that one's hearing of the voices of the past is initially correct. The Christian scholar should always remain open to revision and correction. Instead of straining against the limitations of history, yearning pointlessly like Schama and Strauss for a universal perspective on the past, the Christian historian should consider that it is precisely the limits of historical knowledge that contain creative possibilities. "What is the world that art takes for granted? It is the world in which perception is always incomplete," Rowan Williams has observed.[28]

While particularity can be a scandal for historians, it ought not be a problem for historians who are Christians. Our desire for a universal perspective on human history, for grand and sweeping syntheses, is not entirely misplaced. The desire to understand is a deeply human good. But as Williams has cautioned, curiosity can open a Pandora's box of power. The assertion of a universal truth about the past is a claim to mastery that too often forces the dead into the procrustean bed of professionalism. Christians know well the beauty and necessity of the particular in human history. "Theology must begin with Jesus Christ, and not with general principles, however better or, at any rate, how illuminating they may appear to be," Karl Barth declares.[29] The incarnation of

Christ encompasses the infinite in a single life, elevating the significance of the particular, the limited, and the specific in a Christian's view of the human past.

Neither the particularity of the past, nor the particularity of our knowledge about any historical subject, is problematic. The making of the history itself holds intrinsic value, and the incompleteness of any history, like the finitude of all human work, points to the infinite perfection of God. For the historian, this incompleteness is apparent in our inability to find a model that will account for the complexity of the past. Any model is incomplete and in some sense false, and the same is true for our historical models. As makers of history, when we confront the finitude of our own work, we can decide "whether the end of the process is unavoidable tragic frustration . . . or a contemplative orientation towards what is never going to be contained, the world in the eyes of God."[30]

Flannery O'Connor chose the latter. Her genius as a fiction writer can be found (in part) in her understanding of limitation as possibility in the art of fiction. Echoing Maritain, O'Connor found the will of God imbedded in the limits of her art, for He established, she argues, "the laws and limitations" of fiction. She was impatient with those who saw the Church as oppressing artists, for she saw limits inherent in her art rather than imposed by the Church. She was equally dismissive of critics who thought she should use her stories to save souls. "For many writers it is easier to assume universal responsibility for souls than it is to produce a work of art," she pithily observed, "and it is considered better to save the world than to save the work." For her part, O'Connor was content with the demands that her art made upon her. In this, she offers a model for all Christian scholars. She understood both the limits of her power and the necessity of submission to the work itself.[31]

So, then, what does history demand of the Christian historian? What are its laws and limitations? Two straightforward limits are the historical record itself and the community in which the historian works.[32] Professional historians pledge to avoid distorting the record, and their work is critically reviewed by their peers. These limits are present regardless of whether the work is written by a Christian or not. Like O'Connor, Christian historians should be working assiduously to save the work rather than the world. Even the distance between us and our subjects can become a kind of advantage, for the historian's distance from the past carries an oddly double meaning. On the one hand, it may be viewed as a problem to be solved, most clearly via the fragile bridge of language. Yet on the other, "historical perspective" is heralded as one of our most powerful tools. Distance does not always need to be bridged. Instead, it offers a critical space for reflection that we believe is necessary for assessing and seeing the past truthfully.[33]

A Christian historian is not free. Limited by the archive, by what the dead chose to say in the first place, and by the laws and limitations of our craft itself, a Christian historian may be a very good historian. But if contemporary definitions of good history turn on judgment and on the practice of knowledge as power, then a history written by a Christian may not necessarily be recognized by her peers as good history. Nor may it be recognized as good history by the church, which has repeatedly demonstrated it has its own ideological fish to fry. The church has gotten a lot of history wrong. So the particular stories that Christian historians tell may not be not be perceived as complete or even as necessary, particularly if their chief characteristic is to practice knowledge as love. But the practice of history as pastoral imagination offers something further: the possibility of extending Christian charity across time. It is the historian's "in between" status, this "already, but not yet" place in which the historian tries to stand, what Schama called the quandary of living in two worlds at once, that makes a pastoral imagination possible.

The Character of the Christian Historian

If histories that treat knowledge as charity rather than power depend neither on the size of the archive nor proximity to the dead, they do depend upon the character of the historian. Quite aside from the question of how our knowledge of the past is limited is another equally important question: who is the historian and how does her identity shape her history? If "knowledge as power" is to be replaced by a pastoral imagination, it will be necessary to learn some new habits. "Christian discourse is not a set of beliefs. . . . [I]t is a constitutive set of skills that requires the transformation of self to rightly see the world," Stanley Hauerwas has argued. Truthfulness is made possible by truthful people. How can historians become people who can rightly see the dead?[34]

The relationship between professional training and history as Christian vocation is a vast and complicated one that I cannot hope to exhaustively explore here. In my experience, they have little in common with one another, although I have spoken with others for whom this is decidedly not true. Regardless, the relationship between the two is important for Christians who practice history to consider.

The temptation to practice any vocation as a profession, particularly when one's vocation *is* a profession, is difficult to avoid. The rigors of professional formation in long years of graduate school can deeply imprint young scholars with many traits that do not set well with a Christian calling: ambition, a harshly critical spirit, cynicism, competition, and arrogance. Others are more valuable, among them: intellectual curiosity, critical inquiry, a wide familiarity with a body of work in a specific discipline, the skills to write strongly and well, and the clarity of thought required to do so. All of the qualities one learns in graduate school shape both the history that one writes and the relationships one develops with colleagues in the discipline. Yet many of these habits should be set aside in favor of the deeper purpose of historical knowledge—one not found on any seminar syllabus—which is to serve the ends of love.

Professional formation thus creates a stable identity that hinders Christian practice. The stable professional identity forged in graduate school denies the unstable (and unsettling) identity that is required to remain open to those we meet in the archive and to the practice of knowledge as love. "Professionalization" is necessarily a process of winnowing out, of narrowing allegiances and priorities in order to conform to the rigid standards of the guild. Miroslav Volf has argued that, in fact, an unstable identity is required for what he calls a "theology of embrace." This unstable identity is formed in the place between distance and belonging.[35] I will return to this point later.

Historians can fall prey to at least two kinds of false stability in their vocation, both of which are predicated on the notion of expertise. First is the notion that we are experts about the dead simply because we are alive and they are not. Historians face an Edenic temptation akin to that offered by the tree of knowledge of good and evil. Historians are beings with potentially infinite foreknowledge of their subjects. As a consequence of the accident of our birth, we unwittingly ate of the forbidden fruit of knowledge. There is no suspense in the lives we study. We will eventually learn how the dead met their end and why. Yet good history always balances precariously between hindsight and the attempt to, as Barth says, understand the past "from its own relative centre and not from ours." Here, knowledge can be a hindrance, stifling the very historical consciousness that historical study requires. Historians have knowledge of the dead that must be denied, or at least set aside, in order to practice a pastoral imagination towards them. In Rowan Williams' terms, knowing the secret of another person's heart can be dangerous. Even first-year history students grasp the possibility that their knowledge is superior to those they study merely because they are alive.

Second, the historian's stable identity as an expert is predicated on long training in graduate school. The identity formed in those harrowing years of intense study and insufficient income through school and the search for a tenure-track job is by the best standards of our time an intensely "professional" identity. And yet, this professionalism is a problem for those Christians who seek to practice history as a vocation.

Professionalism is a problem for the Christian because it practices knowledge as power. Most of those who become scholars have spent their lives looking for an "A," and being rewarded tangibly for their expert use of knowledge in classes and on exam papers. Once in graduate school, knowledge becomes the only tool at hand for most students. Knowledge that is sufficiently demonstrated in seminars, essays, conference papers, and fellowship proposals brings tangible (and powerful) rewards, often in the form of money. Graduate students learn that the hierarchy of the profession is predicated on knowledge, and not all of it is knowledge about the past. The most powerful knowledge for students is knowledge of professional networks that will afford them fellowships, book contracts, or even the highly prized tenure-track job. Intellectual merit is simply not enough. In the end, scholarship is not the purely intellectual pursuit many students expected, although the ancient roots of "professing" remain. Historians like to cast the profession as one in which the value of ideas transcends that of cash and where wisdom is valued above power, but one of the most important lessons of graduate school is that professional history is a bureaucracy like any other. There are careers to be made.[36]

The world of professional history does not reward charity or wisdom. Where is mercy at the American Historical Association? What form does justice take in the job register? Who considers love in the endless array of bloodless panels at professional meetings? The stakes are high for students who have sacrificed income to study for so long and who have backed themselves into a professional identity that is difficult to deny—jobs so few, competition for fellowships so fierce, publishers so hard to please, the drive to make an "A" still very much alive. The language of charity seems to be doing no discernible work in this world.[37] Knowledge practiced as love seems bizarrely impractical. For many the possibility of history as a Christian vocation remains a good thing, but it seems pointless without first achieving history as a profession. How can one do the former without the latter? Many of those who hope to practice history as a vocation rather than a profession run the risk of sanctifying their ambition in the name of God. And so knowledge can become, even for the best-intentioned Christian students, power rather than wisdom and charity.

Miroslav Volf has proposed a model for Christian identity that may be useful to historians who wish to flee careerism and embrace vocation. He offers a vision of a Christian identity "with one foot outside their own culture" and the "other firmly planted within it." Volf counsels Christians to maintain a distance from their culture even while they do not leave it. "Christians are not the insiders who have taken flight to a new 'Christian culture' and become outsiders to their own culture.... [T]hey are distant, and yet they belong." "Both distance and belonging are essential," Volf continues. "Belonging without distance destroys . . . but distance without belonging isolates." Both are violent because they practice exclusion, the first as bigotry, the second as isolation. "Distance from a culture must never degenerate into flight from that culture, but must be a way of living in a culture," Volf writes.[38]

There are many ways that a Christian historian might be distant to the culture of professional history and yet belong to it. I suspect that nearly all of those who are working as historians, particularly those who teach in public universities, have worked out their own means of doing this. But I have found Volf's work helpful on this point. He proposes a "theology of embrace" that centers on the "dynamic and mutually conditioning identities" of those involved. He uses the story of the prodigal son to demonstrate the profoundly "new order" that the father institutes in his embrace of the prodigal. What is useful here is Volf's analysis of the father's ability to embrace the transgressor. "His behavior was governed by one fundamental 'rule': relationship has priority over all rules. . . . Relationship is prior to moral rules" allowing the "will to embrace" to be "independent of the quality of behavior." It is the father's "profound wisdom about the priority of the relationship, and not some sentimental insanity," Volf writes, that explains the father's strange prodigality towards his sons.[39]

It is this "priority of relationship" for the Christian that renders a stable, unchanging professional historical identity unacceptable. The professional identity is, above all, an individualistic identity. Scholars are fiercely independent, and the long lists of those they thank in their acknowledgements sometimes suggest they doth protest too much. Scholars work alone, even in crowded library reading rooms. They leave family and community thousands of miles behind to find a tenure-track job. They travel long distances, again alone, to spend countless hours in silent archives. Putting relationship first would seem to be a strikingly countercultural value in this professional context.

Just as the father had to set aside culturally prescribed norms of patriarchal behavior in order to foster his relationship with his son, so Christian historians should set aside the often unyielding standards of professional norms in order to foster relationship with their peers, students, and the people in their books. We must unfix the rules and destabilize our identities as "professional" historians in order to take the risks of relationship with all of these people, for it is only in relationship that vocation can triumph over profession, that knowledge can be practiced as love instead of power. Envisioning love in history means relinquishing the security of a stable professional identity, one that nearly always seeks to exercise power, in favor of one that is open to others, whether they be living or dead.

IN THE end, envisioning love in history is to envision love in the here and now. Seeing the dead affords practice in seeing the living. The limits of our understanding of those who are gone are matched by our blindness towards the people across the room. The limits of our wisdom and charity towards the subjects of our books is matched by the limits of self-giving love in our daily lives. Christian theology teaches that we can, and indeed must, see the dead. An historian's encounter with people in the archives must be genuine, not an extended episode of self-absorption. But Christianity also teaches that we should rightly see the living. "There is no past in the Church," Barth declares. The responsibility of the historian is that of "bearing and being borne by each other . . . having to take mutual responsibility for and among the sinners gathered together in Christ." In the end, the Good News is that our broken attempts at loving those around us, either in the archive or down the hallway, in a faded manuscript or on the bus, will finally and fully be redeemed.

NOTES

I am grateful for conversations with Christy Adams, Kurt Berends, Elizabeth Kurtz Lynch, Simon Perry, Thomas Schweiger, and the Tuesday morning theology group of St. Mark's Church, Newnham, during 2004–5.

1. Nicholas Boyle, *Who Are We Now? Christian Humanism and the Global Market from Hegel to Heaney* (Notre Dame, Ind.: University of Notre Dame Press, 1998), 250.

2. Rowan Williams, "Knowing and Loving," in *A Ray of Darkness* (Cambridge, Mass.: Cowley Publications, 1995), 8.

3. Michel Foucault, *Archaeology of Knowledge and the Discourse on Language*, trans. A. M. Sheridan Smith (New York: Pantheon Books, 1972).

4. I am grateful to Simon Perry for helping me to understand what I mean by this.

5. Oliver O'Donovan, *Common Objects of Love: Moral Reflection and the Shaping of Community* (Grand Rapids, Mich.: Eerdmans, 2002), 11–24, quote on 16.

6. Here I am bracketing the question of whether one can encounter an "other" in the past. For the moment, I am content to practice history in the assumption that I can indeed find people in the archive, which seems to me an

important aspect of the Christian doctrine of the communion of saints. I have been persuaded by James K. A. Smith, who sees language as incarnational, and thus revelatory, because of the Incarnation of Christ; see his *Speech and Theology: Language and the Logic of Incarnation* (New York: Routledge, 2002).

7. Miroslav Volf, *The End of Memory: Remembering Rightly in a Violent World* (Grand Rapids, Mich.: Eerdmans, 2006), 65.

8. Williams, "Vocation (1)," *Ray of Darkness*, 150–51.

9. This paraphrases what Sam Wells has set out in a very different context. "The theology that I had hoped would help me to change others had succeeded in changing me"; *Transforming Fate Into Destiny: The Theological Ethics of Stanley Hauerwas* (Carlisle: Paternoster Press, 1998), xiii. Maritain is cited in Rowan Williams, *Grace and Necessity: Reflections on Art and Love* (Harrisburg, Penn.: Morehouse, 2005), 11. For a complete account of his views, see Jacques Maritain, *Art and Scholasticism, With Other Essays*, trans. J. F. Scanlan (New York: Charles Scribner's Sons, 1930). On history as a spiritual discipline, one that can challenge the "assumption that I . . . stand at the centre of all patterns of meaning," see Rowan Williams, *Why Study the Past: The Quest for the Historical Church* (Grand Rapids, Mich.: Eerdmans, 2005), 110.

10. Simon Schama, *Dead Certainties (Unwarranted Speculations)* (New York: Alfred A. Knopf, 1991), 319.

11. Gerald R. Strauss, "The Dilemma of Popular History," *Past & Present* 132 (August 1991): 130–49, quote on 144.

12. William Beik and Gerald R. Strauss, "Debate: The Dilemma of Popular History," *Past and Present* 141 (November 1993): 207–19, quote on 219.

13. Schama, *Dead Certainties*, 320, 326. Henry James's unfinished novel was titled *The Sense of the Past*.

14. Cushing Strout, "Border Crossings: History, Fiction, and Dead Certainties," *History and Theory* 31 (May 1992): 153–62.

15. Tony Hendra, *Father Joe: The Man Who Saved My Soul* (New York: Random House, 2004), 77.

16. Williams, "Knowing and Loving," *Ray of Darkness*, 8–11. Jeremy Begbie's sermon at St. Mark's prompted these thoughts in the first place, and he kindly directed me to Williams' published sermon.

17. Ibid., 10.

18. Karl Barth, "The Task of a History of Modern Protestant Theology," *Protestant Theology in the Nineteenth Century: Its Background and History* (Grand Rapids, Mich.: Eerdmans, 2002), 3, 8–9.

19. The question of judgment seems to me to be a more pressing problem for historians of the modern period, who more often pursue a politically informed "usable past" than scholars of earlier periods.

20. Barth, "Task of a History," 3. Where Barth sees the history of theology as "bearing witness to the truth of God," in my view, histories written by Christians reveal only what humankind has made of God. The anthropologist Mary Douglas has described how perception of God is mediated by society. "When people are citing theology—the reformer's theology, for example—they have in mind some sort of ideal society which would make sense of that theology." Quoted in Paul Baumann, "Anthropology With a Difference: Mary Douglas at 80," *Commonweal* 128:14 (August 17, 2001): 19. See also Mary Douglas, *Natural Symbols: Explorations in Cosmology* (Harmondsworth: Penguin, 1973).

21. Dietrich Bonhoeffer, *The Cost of Discipleship* (New York: Macmillan Publishing Company, 1963), 204–5.

22. Barth's call to hear the dead echoes his larger point that faith comes by hearing, by revelation.

23. Barth, "Task of a History," 3–15.

24. Quoted in Drew Gilpin Faust, *James Henry Hammond and the Old South: A Design for Mastery* (Baton Rouge: Louisiana State University Press, 1982), 279–80.

25. Erskine Clarke, *Dwelling Place: A Plantation Epic* (New Haven: Yale University Press, 2005).

26. C. S. Lewis, *The Abolition of Man* (New York: Macmillan, 1965), 91.

27. Barth, "Task of a History," 5.

28. Williams, *Grace and Necessity*, 135.

29. Karl Barth, *Church Dogmatics: A Selection* (New York: Harper & Row Publishers, 1962), 87–88.

30. Williams, *Grace and Necessity*, 21.

31. Flannery O'Connor, "The Church and the Fiction Writer," in *Collected Works* (New York: Library of America, 1988), 807, 812, and 810.

32. William Cronon, "A Place for Stories: Nature, History, and Narrative," *Journal of American History* 78 (March 1992): 1347–76. Cronon names a third limit on narrative that is relevant primarily to environmental historians, those imposed by the natural world.

33. Martha Nussbaum has made a similar point about philosophy's role in reflection; *Love's Knowledge: Essays on Philosophy and Literature* (New York: Oxford University Press, 1990), 283.

34. Stanley Hauerwas, "Positioning: In the Church and the University but not of Either," in *Dispatches from the Front: Theological Engagements with the Secular* (Durham, N.C.: Duke University Press, 1994), 7, 10.

35. Miroslav Volf, *Exclusion and Embrace: A Theological Exploration of Identity, Otherness, and Reconciliation* (Nashville, Tenn.: Abingdon Press, 1996), esp. 156–65.

36. Hannah Arendt has written of what happens in the face of the "curious loss of ideological content" when "the movement itself becomes all important" in reference to the trial of Adolf Eichmann; see her "Holes of Oblivion, From a Letter to Mary McCarthy," September 20, 1963, in *The Portable Hannah Arendt*, ed. Peter Baehr (New York: Penguin Putnam, 2000), 389.

37. Here I borrow the language of Hauerwas, who argues that the doctrine of the Trinity does "no discernible work" for many liberal Protestants; "Positioning," 7.

38. Volf, *Exclusion and Embrace*, 49–50.

39. Ibid., 156–65.

Part Two

THEORY AND METHOD

Chapter Four

VIRTUE ETHICS AND HISTORICAL INQUIRY

The Case of Prudence

THOMAS ALBERT HOWARD

IT HAPPENED IN 1824 IN THE UNLIKELY PLACE OF A PREFACE to a book entitled *Histories of the Latin and Germanic Nations from 1494 to 1514*. In this preface, the young Leopold von Ranke wrote, "History has been assigned the high office of judging the past, of instructing the present for the benefit of future ages. To such high offices this work does *not* aspire: it wants only to show what actually happened (*wie es eigentlich gewesen*)."[1]

While debate continues as to what Ranke meant by these ubiquitously invoked words, it's fair to say that they have at least come to symbolize a fundamental break with an older humanist tradition, harkening back at least to Cicero, that saw a firm and natural connection between knowledge of the past and "instructing the present," between history and ethical reasoning, between Clio and moral philosophy. Of course, in many sectors of society, this tradition continues apace: there's something commonsensical about it. Ask any undergraduate why they're taking a history class and one is likely to hear something invariably resembling George Santayana's quip that "those who cannot remember the past are condemned to repeat it."

However, since the rise of the modern research university in the nineteenth century and the concomitant professionalization of history as an academic discipline, historians have generally shied away from moral and philosophical reflection, not to mention from attentiveness to the moral formation of students. To obtain scientific and professional validation, the pursuit of objectivity became the goal, the high road to intellectual respectability and disciplinary autonomy. "The strict presentation of the facts, contingent and unattractive though they may be," wrote Ranke in the same preface, "is the supreme law." Philosophy, moral reasoning, ethics—these were animals of a different sort, and crossbreeding was to be discouraged. Instead, attention to the particular, shorn of moral evaluation; exhaustive research; source criticism; peer review among one's own kind; individual expertise; and increasing specialization became the means to reach the "supreme law" of objective representation.[2]

Specialized expertise in particular emerged as the gold standard for serious historical work. "Due to the enormous expansion of [historical] science," wrote the young Jacob Burckhardt in 1840 while a student in Ranke's seminar in Berlin, "one is obliged to limit oneself to some definite subject and pursue it single-mindedly."[3] The goal of historical study, like the objective of modern scholarship generally, the historian Heinrich von Sybel wrote in 1874, is that

> the student gain a clear consciousness of the aim of science and the operations by which science reaches this aim. It is necessary for the student to go himself through these operations with regard to one subject, . . . to follow up some problems to their last consequences—up to the point where he can say that there is nobody in this world who, on this point and on this subject, can teach him any more; a point where he can say here he stands safe and firm on his own feet, and decides entirely by his own judgment.[4]

This imperative toward specialized expertise, if I may generalize, spread like prairie fire in research universities in the transatlantic world in the late nineteenth century, incinerating in the process the older, Ciceronian-humanist tradition of *historia magistra vitae*, which coupled history and moral philosophy. Professional historians today are descended from the first squatters on this scorched plain.

To be sure, the swooning of the modernist academic paradigm in recent decades and the postmodern turn in intellectual affairs has altered the rhetorical environment in which professional historiography operates.[5] Even so, a reflex against moral reflection remains entrenched in the profession. We're adept at analyzing the events that, say, led to World War II, but who among us *really* has the mental furniture to try to explain if a combatant's entry was just or unjust—or if war and justice mix at all? How would peers in a graduate seminar react if a student concluded, upon finishing a critical biography of Churchill, that she had been deeply moved and drawn personal lessons on wise leadership? Or, what if a student asked to write a dissertation on how activists in the civil rights movement exhibited the classical virtue of fortitude or the theological virtue of hope?

Even if my points are granted, one might reasonably counter that the problem with the academy today is not that there's too little moralizing, but too much of it. After we've been roused from the "noble dream" of objectivity, ideological disarray and none-too-thinly-veiled political programs have become the order of the day in historical scholarship and in the classroom.[6] Pulling for the "right" groups in history and expressing moral indignation at the "wrong" ones have supplanted a nobler universalist, Enlightenment vision. Cooler heads have not prevailed.

Fair enough. But arguably nothing clouds moral perspicuity as much as overweening moral indignation, especially if it flows from an a priori scheme of historical righteousness in which the friends and enemies of progress have been divided in advance. Thus, I would hesitate to characterize the present moment as conducive to serious and sustained moral reflection; more evidence suggests the triumph of the ideological and the political, something to which the myriad forces we call postmodernism have undoubtedly contributed.

But postmodernism has its sunnier side. Only a doctrinaire defender of Enlightenment universalism would gainsay the fact that recent currents in historiography have opened the door for more diverse perspectives, and thus to sensitivity of how social and cultural locations shape knowledge, historical or otherwise. Black, female, Native

American, Hispanic, and, indeed, Christian voices have "more room at the table" these days; and the conversation is the richer for it—if at times cacophonous. The postmodern imperative of diversity, let's call it, has also had the salutary effect of making historians more attentive to epistemology and thus forged a link, over Ranke's posthumous disapproval, between history and philosophy. The project of "Christian scholarship" in particular—typified, most notably, by George Marsden—has pioneered the way in this endeavor, making religious scholars of various outlooks reflect on the cultural, social, and theological assumptions that give rise to and shape intellectual projects, theirs and others.[7]

As historians, we all find ourselves epistemologists now. But the ties with philosophy should be thickened. Epistemology is one important point of contact. Ethics is another. Thinking more deliberately, with a more informed philosophical and theological vocabulary, about ethics in our historical work is a worthy task in itself and one that could help restore (at least in some appropriate settings such as church-related liberal arts colleges) a humanist sense of history as an intellectual endeavor committed both to accurate representation and serious moral reflection, to knowledge of the past and wise living in the present. Such an endeavor does not mean simply "passing judgment" on historical actors and actions; and it should not be conflated with shoehorning one's insights into conformity with prevailing definitions of social justice.

Alas, it is exquisitely more vague and indeterminate. Even as we seek to preserve the best elements in the post-Rankean enterprise, it requires that the historical knower forsake wraithlike detachment for the examined life. It entails regarding historical knowing as means of learning to live thoughtfully, wisely, and well. It means learning to feel what Augustine described as a "bewildering passion" after reading Cicero's lost text, *Hortensius*. "To love wisdom itself," the bishop of Hippo wrote, "whatever it might be, and to search for it, pursue it, hold it, and embrace it firmly. . . . [This] excited me and set me burning with fire."[8]

Fortunately, ours is a particularly favorable moment for historians to think more seriously about ethics and its relationship to historical scholarship and teaching. One of the most promising developments in ethical theory in recent decades has been the ascendency of a body of work known as "virtue ethics." Defying simple ideological and religious classification, thinkers as diverse as G. E. M. Anscombe, Philippa Foot, Josef Pieper, Peter Geach, Alasdair MacIntyre, Martha Nussbaum, Stanley Hauerwas, Linda Zagsebski, and Gilbert Meilaender have contributed to this development. Theirs is a diverse, contradictory, and evolving body of work. It is also one that historians ignore at their peril.[9]

In general terms, virtue ethics may be thought of as a third-way alternative to two dominant schools of twentieth-century normative ethics: the so-called Kantian or deontological school and that of consequentialism. The former seeks to define rationally defensible rules of moral action, irrespective of the moral agent's time, place, and historical circumstance. The latter weighs the rightness or wrongness of actions on the basis of their perceived outcomes and effects on society. The former descends from eighteenth-century Prussia, the latter from nineteenth-century Britain, particularly the utilitarian thought of Bentham and Mill, which sought to maximize the well-being of the many. The two schools by no means exhaust contemporary possibilities of ethical reasoning, but they've been the biggest players in a field in which virtue ethics has sought, quite effectively, to constitute a meaningful alternative. In contrast to both schools, virtue ethics places particular stress on the inner state of the moral actor, the predisposition of the individual or the community to act in virtuous patterns on the basis of cultivated knowledge about what constitutes human excellence or flourishing (in the Aristotelian sense of *eudaimonia*). With consequentialists, virtue ethicists are concerned about the social outcomes of actions, but they place more emphasis on the intellectual and behavioral disposition, the developed ethical habits, of the moral agent. With Kantian-deontologists, virtue ethicists are not moral relativists, but they are more skeptical that ethics can be rationally codified once and for all; experience, common sense, and the complexity of things human—they would argue—suggest the difficulty of this desirable enterprise. What is more, the crucial and formative role of particular traditions and histories, as Alasdair MacIntyre has taught, cannot be factored out when evaluating the normative claims of ethical discourses.[10]

In the Christian intellectual tradition, virtue ethics has a venerable history, but one that in the Enlightenment's aftermath must be (at least for many of us) rebuilt from the ruins. Not surprisingly, the tradition draws from both classical and scriptural sources, from Athens and Jerusalem. Aristotle's *Nichomachean Ethics* and Cicero's glosses on this text are perhaps the most important classical sources, developed most compellingly and influentially by Thomas Aquinas—albeit by no means ignored by later, anti-scholastic humanists, whether Catholic or Protestant.[11] The wisdom literature of the Old Testament and the Pauline epistles are the most important scriptural sources. From these sources, we derive the conventional list of the traditional seven virtues: the classical or cardinal virtues of prudence, justice, courage, and temperance; and the Christian or theological virtues of faith, hope, and love (cf. 1 Cor 13). While we would do well not to see this an exhaustive list, many wise heads have judged it an able template for the Christian life. Dante in his *Commedia*, for example, encounters the seven virtues, allegorized as heavenly nymphs, just before the appearance of Beatrice, the symbol of divine love.[12] In more recent times, the neo-Thomist philosopher Josef Pieper has eloquently articulated the template of the virtues:

> First: the Christian is one who, in *faith*, becomes aware of the reality of the triune God. Second: the Christian strives, in *hope*, for the total fulfillment of his being in eternal life. Third: the Christian directs himself, in the divine virtue of *love*, to an affirmation of God and neighbor that surpasses the power of any natural love. Fourth: the Christian is *prudent*; namely, he does not allow his view on reality to be controlled by . . . his will, but rather he makes . . . [his] will dependent upon the truth of real things. Fifth: the Christian is *just*; that is, he is able to live "with the other" in truth. . . . Sixth, the Christian is *brave*, that is, he is prepared to suffer injury and, if need be, death for the truth. . . . Seventh: the Christian is *temperate*; namely, he does not permit his . . . desire for pleasure to become destructive and inimical to his being.[13]

While the template *in toto* is often forgotten or misconstrued, we certainly recognize the individual virtues contained within it. It is not uncommon among Christian scholars, in fact, to hear the enterprise of historical scholarship and teaching legitimized on the basis of some of these virtues. Two that immediately come to mind are justice and love.

As Christians we are duty-bound to love our neighbors, but we cannot do so, particularly in a culturally diverse society, unless we know something of their history and background. Ergo, we must study history. Or: as Christians we must be concerned that justice exists in this world. To achieve justice though, whether in the Middle East, Sudan, the former Yugoslavia, or here at home, we must know the story behind ongoing conflicts, hatreds, prejudices, and the peoples therein involved. Ergo, we must study history. These represent excellent means of legitimizing historical inquiry, and this essay has no designs to call them into question.

And yet in contemporary discussions, one particularly important virtue is noticeably given short shrift, pushed to the side, almost fallen out of memory. I refer to the virtue of prudence, *prudentia*. This is a particularly noteworthy development, because in classical Christian ethics, prudence occupied a singular and important position; it was regarded as "the mother and mold" of the other cardinal virtues and the indispensable ally of the theological virtues. Today the word, if it is used at all, is more likely to be understood as caution, timorousness, small-mindedness—perhaps not even as a virtue at all, but as an instinct toward self-preservation incompatible with more ambitious schemes of social justice and charity, and certainly at odds with the distinctly modern demi-virtues of authenticity and self-actualization.[14] "To the contemporary mind," as Pieper has written, "the concept of the good rather excludes than includes prudence."[15]

In the remainder of this chapter, I advance a countervailing case, persuaded that an informed discourse about prudence is valuable for the work of the historian, the Christian historian in particular. Retrieving prudence from the amnesia that the contemporary church often exhibits toward its own intellectual resources serves two goals. First, as a classical virtue, but one with powerful resonance in Christian scripture (particularly Old Testament wisdom literature), prudence can be rendered complementary to both natural law and revelation-based traditions of ethical-theological reflection. As such, it has the potential to help bridge the divide between Christian and non-Christian conceptions of historical knowing—a divide all too evident when a Christian historian approaches the past through the prism of providentialist or

Kuyperian-presuppositionalist (that is, "Christian worldview") reasoning. Second, while prudence is an "intellectual virtue" (in Aristotle's definition), a matter of knowledge, it has historically implied appropriate moral behavior and action in the world. It seeks to link knowledge, ethics, and right action. Thus understood, prudence offers some promise to repair the breach, bequeathed to us by Ranke's legacy, between historical knowing and moral philosophy; it holds out some promise of restoring the idea of *historia magistra vitae*, history as the teacher of life, history as the love of wisdom, in contrast to both modernist historiography (the ideal of objectivity animated by an institutional imperative of relentless topical specialization) and postmodernist historiography (the inertia of this imperative bereft of the original ideal).

However, as salutary as prudence might be for historical thought, the knowledge that it fosters, I would submit, is ultimately, *sub species aeternitatis*, one of disconsolation. Even as it seeks to guide one to moral reflection and action, prudence discloses to Clio the tragic and ironic character of human affairs, the *tristitia saeculi* (the "sadness of the world"), reminding us that our best efforts take place within, and are themselves not immune to, the pervasiveness of human concupiscence and fraudulence. For the Christian at least, prudence therefore underscores the penultimate and provisional character of all human efforts of moral action and social amelioration. But in doing so, it suggests the necessity of another virtue: that of hope—but a hope in which the immanent must always be viewed against an eschatological horizon.[16]

But now it merits asking why prudence was considered the foundation, the mother, of the other virtues. Why would Aquinas write, *Omnis virtus moralis debet esse prudens*, all virtue is necessarily prudent?[17] The reason is fairly straightforward and it has to do with the fact that prudence entails a sober-minded view of reality, an accurate, unsentimental measure of how the world and human nature *are*. It is a matter of being, of ontology, of predicating all good actions and understandings on *how being is,* how human reality is in fact constituted. In his discussion of prudence, Josef Pieper puts it this way:

> All duty is based upon being. Reality is the basis of ethics. Goodness is the standard of reality. Whoever wants to know and do the

good must direct his gaze toward the objective world of being, not toward his own sentiment or toward arbitrarily established "ideals" and "models." He must look away from his own deed and look upon reality. The "soundness" of justice, of fortitude, of temperance, of fear of the Lord and of virtue in general is in the fact that they are *appropriate to objective reality, both natural and supernatural.* Conformity to reality is the principle of both [intellectual] soundness and [ethical] goodness. The precedence of prudence indicates that the realization of goodness presumes knowledge of reality.[18]

Objective knowledge of reality? *Wie es eigentlich gewesen?* How things actually were—and are. It would sound as though we have stumbled back upon Ranke's dictum. In a certain respect we have. However, prudence is not content with knowledge alone, of beholding human reality; rather it seeks to render accurate knowledge relevant to good action and human flourishing. In the words of Pieper again:

Prudence . . . [seeks to] transform . . . knowledge of reality into the accomplishment of the good. It encompasses the humility of silence, i.e., unbiased understanding, memory's faithfulness to being, the art of letting things speak for themselves, the alert composure before the unexpected. Prudence means hesitant seriousness . . . , the filter of reflection, and *yet also the daring courage for definitive resolution.*[19]

Parts of this definition suggest a prescription for sound historical scholarship. "The humility of silence"—listening attentively to historical texts and documents for every nuance and shade of meaning. "Unbiased understanding"—striving to constrain one's own assumptions and prejudices from distorting the truth. "Memory's faithfulness to being"—validating the importance of individual and collective memory in our constructions of the past. "The art of letting things speak for themselves"—bringing to life actual historical voices. And "alert composure before the unexpected"—readiness to alter or abandon one's own thesis about the past in light of new discoveries and countervailing evidence.

Together, these sentiments do in fact resonate with Ranke's dictum and thus with the modern historical enterprise. And where there is overlap, Rankean aims should certainly be embraced. But, again, prudence transcends representation alone; it countenances no absolute divide between history and moral philosophy, between knowledge about the past and instructing the present. This dimension of the virtue is amplified by considering two of Pieper's pregnant phrases—prudence as "hesitant seriousness" (*zögernden Ernst*) and "definitive resolution" (*Endgültigkeit des Beschließens*)[20]—and two of his concomitant definitions of imprudence: "irresoluteness" (*Unschlüssigkeit*) and "thoughtlessness" (*Unbesonnenheit*).[21]

Beginning with "definitive resolution" and "irresolution," one should simply note, what is a truism for Christians, that we live in a moral universe and there are no sidelines. Moral reflection and resolution are existential imperatives. By virtue of the very nature of things, we, *even historians*, are actors in this universe and thus we would do well to recognize that our historical constructions—in books, in articles, in the classroom, in casual conversations—always have relevance to the present, whether in making policy, in designing laws, in shaping institutions, in molding public opinion, and, not least, in ordering the moral lives of self and others. We are not, and can never be, in Nietzsche's felicitious phrase, "spoiled idlers in the garden of knowledge" but are always already participants in "life"—a wonderful, tragic, complex, hopeful moral life.[22]

For this reason, I am persuaded that one commonplace approach to historical instruction is especially problematic. It goes something like this: we should present students with all sides of a particular issue and then let students decide for themselves. If one were to define this as the penultimate goal of historical learning, I might agree. But it cannot stand as the ultimate. Instead, I think it's our obligation to press students even further, to engage and not trivialize their moral imaginations, to kindle their capacities of moral reasoning, to escort ethical reflection, with lavish pomp and circumstance, from its post-Rankean exile right back into the heart of the history classroom. What moral options would a Polish Catholic bishop have vis-à-vis secret police agents during the Cold War? Did Dietrich Bonhoeffer obey a moral

injunction in supporting Hitler's assassination? Do reenactors of historical battles unwittingly glorify war? Why is there a Holocaust museum in Washington, D.C., and *not* one dedicated to the institution
of American slavery? Does the conservatism of Edmund Burke provide cover for the persistence of unjust institutions and practices? Can
progressive mantras like toleration and equality often mask a ruthless
quest for institutional and political power? What are the *right, the most
compelling, the most searchingly honest,* answers to these questions? We
are not "trespassing" into philosophy, but treating our students (and
ourselves) as moral agents, when we ask them at least to broach and
wrestle with the normative questions that historical inquiry inevitably
raises.

Indeed, while not discounting the tremendous difficulties involved,
prudence counsels answers—or at least attempted answers—to these
questions and countless more that history and life bring before us. Irresoluteness as a manifestation of imprudence, by contrast, leads to
deliberation and judgment tumbling uselessly into futility, into moral
paralysis or jaded amoral sophistication, instead of into the finality of a
decision, a right way of being, thinking, or acting in the world. "[T]he
true 'praise' of prudence," writes Pieper, "lies in decision which is directed straight toward application in action."[23]

But if irresoluteness is one aspect of imprudence, thoughtlessness
is another. In personal and public life, this simply means acting on the
basis of little or no knowledge, without deliberation, having failed to
reach a sound judgment or having taken the shortcut of oversimplifica-
tion. In historical thought, it means a refusal to acknowledge the full
complexity of the past; it means cajoling the past to serve one's own
political agendas and personal predilections, to construct narratives of
history that promote one's own desired future, instead of allowing penetrating cognition of the past to assist in understanding, and acting in,
one's actual present. As such, it bespeaks a type of intellectual inconti-
nence, desire overcoming reason, more than outright fraud or deceit.
Now one might draw some comfort from this, for at least in Dante's
scheme of hell, the practitioner of this vice would wind up in the upper
circles of the damned among the carnal and the gluttonous, and not in
the lower circles among the willfully deceitful.

Better yet, if the historian, though thoughtless, were nonetheless penitent and found herself at the bottom of purgatory, instead of the gates of hell, she would find guidance. It would not come from the poet Virgil, however, but rather—of all people—from a frumpy Englishman named Herbert Butterfield. Indeed, Butterfield's classic *The Whig Interpretation of History* (1931) remains among our ablest guides for historical thinking in general and for encouraging the "hesitant seriousness" that Pieper identifies as a trait of prudence.[24] Butterfield's work (perhaps more by implication that explication) reminds us that historical-cum-ethical knowing, though indeed necessary as I have argued, is also difficult, that knowing the past always proceeds through a tangled web of motivations, beliefs, impersonal forces, individuals, institutions, and possible outcomes. Nonetheless, the historian's proper business is fidelity to the past in its vexing, unabridged complexity. Attentiveness to this complexity, by extension, is the prerequisite for hesitant seriousness, the probing moral thoughtfulness that prudence demands and right action requires. Put differently, prudence applied to historical thought has a dual, dialectical quality: a fixed insistence on the necessity of moral reasoning, but also a recognition that such reasoning can be exceedingly, sometimes unfathomably, complicated. Absolute moral clarity is an elusive quarry; often the best we can do is render the truly obscure merely difficult. This should not paralyze thought and action; it should chasten it.

This point merits underscoring because the principal "optical illusion" or "fallacy" of the historical knower, as Butterfield contends, is epistemological overconfidence, a penchant to read past and present events to confirm a desired future and to validate oneself or one's group as a mouthpiece in the service of this future. In his day, Butterfield was worried by how liberal Protestant historians of the nineteenth century, "Whig" historians, had tended to reduce the Reformation to "the birthplace of modern political liberty" instead of regarding it, as sixteenth-century contemporaries experienced it, as a period of social disquiet, religious division, and personal and political tragedy. Other examples of this fallacy are well-nigh endless. Marx's reduction of the past to conflicting economic interests advancing toward a classless society is probably the best known example of recent times. Leopold von Ranke's own gravitation to the nation-state as the engine of historical advancement none-too-subtly dovetailed with his ideas of Prussian-German greatness and of Germany's historical destiny in central Europe. The historical fruit of Marxism in the twentieth century and the legacy of nineteenth-century nationalist historiographies should remind us that "history" does not just judge other arenas of human endeavor, but stands under its own perpetually receding potential for praise or indictment.

The antidote to this "Whig fallacy," Butterfield suggests, lies in acts of "imaginative sympathy" with the past, which attempt, however imperfectly, to recapture the past in its complexity. "Perhaps the greatest of all the lessons of history," Butterfield writes,

> is this demonstration of the complexity of human change and the unpredictable character of the ultimate consequences of any given act or decision of men; and on the face of it this is a lesson that can only be learned in detail. . . . The fallacy of the Whig historian lies in the way in which he takes . . . [a] short cut through complexity.[25]

In the ethical and moral arena, the complexity of history reveals some hard truths—truths that call into question our desire for simple narratives or cheap moralizing, as well as our impatient longing to believe that the line dividing good and evil cuts through classes and types of people and not, as Solzhenitsyn taught us, between every human heart. It reveals, as Hannah Arendt has instructed, that unspeakable crimes occupy not only the extremity of human experience, but the ordinary and banal.[26] It reveals that slave owners could simultaneously be capable of extraordinary acts of friendship, charity, and devotion to family. It reveals, as the tortures at Abu Ghraib prison in Iraq make clear, that well-meaning Americans can quite easily commit acts of stupendous inhumanity. It reveals that noble causes are often dogged with sinister interests and that ignoble ones cannot suppress the fact that those involved still bear the *imago Dei*.

What is more, attentiveness to the complexity of the past can highlight the imponderably difficult nature of assessing moral development and progress. In the seventh circle of hell, to draw again from Dante, the Florentine poet places blasphemers, sodomites, and usurers together.

Today, blasphemy is recognized as an act of free expression, sodomy is protected by the rights of privacy, and usury, well, that's simply the way of the modern world. The path from Dante's day to ours then is a long and complex one, but the historian—the prudent, Christian historian—should make efforts to understand the twists and turns along the way, open to capacious, nuanced historical comprehension without neglecting moral engagement.

But, as I've indicated, ethical judgment should not simply be passed "upon" history, for encountering the past always has the discomfiting potential to encourage moral scrutiny of our present. If upon reading Dante, the student finds the medieval world simply quaint, strange, or outdated, the historian has not done her job. It is only when one profoundly understands why the sodomites, blasphemers, and usurers in that seventh circle of hell *must* forever be tormented on a sandy plain "as great flakes of flame fell slowly / as snow falls on the Alps on a windless day" that one obtains the full illuminating, unsettling freight of historical understanding, which in turn helps allow for the hesitant seriousness to live wisely and well in the present.

So again, ethically engaging the past through the vehicle of prudence is quite different from pronouncing grandiose moral judgments on history. For we possess no temporal perch immunized from the need of self-scrutiny. Thus, just as our age must understand and size up another, so the age we evaluate deserves a fair chance to size up ours. Dante's world and ours meet on an equal plain, as it were, in a spirit of mutual criticism and admiration, each asking and answering the other. The student who only asks (of the past) comes up short, but so too does the student who only answers (for his age), for a repository of virtue lies neither in our present nor wholly in the past.

Thus, the asking and answering will always have a provisional, makeshift, or ambiguous character. The historian, to an extent, is always winging it. But winging it and wisdom are by no means sorry bedfellows, for in the act of historical-moral reasoning, the virtue of prudence, of appraising the simultaneous necessity and difficulty of moral understanding and action, makes its character known. "The asking and the answering are bound to be ambiguous," Robert Penn Warren has written on a similar point, for [historical] experience carries no labels. But there is a discipline of the mind and heart, a discipline both humbling and enlarging, in the imaginative consideration of possibilities in the face of the . . . irrevocable past. The asking and the answering which history provokes may help us to understand, even to frame, the logic of experience to which we shall submit. History cannot give us a program for the future, but it can give us a fuller understanding of ourselves, and of our common humanity, so that we can better face the future.[27]

On this point (and indulging in one final reference to Dante), I should note that in the *Inferno* some of the damned, strangely, possess foreknowledge of the future but no knowledge of the present. "You seem to see in advance all time's intent," Dante says to the Florentine heretic Farinata degli Uberti, "but you seem to lack all knowledge of the present." There's a lesson in this for any historian who believes she may easily forsake prudence for prophecy, who refuses to tell how history was but expounds on how it has to be, who forsakes time for "time's intent." Dante's sinners are poised for yet further calamity: the corruption of the good of the intellect assured to the damned. For when time shall be no more, "when the Portal of the Future is swung to," their intellects are stranded in unreality, permanently voided of rational capacity.[28]

We would do well then to live and act wisely in the present with a steady glance upon the past, which, after all, is all we mortals have to set against our own age. Overweening efforts to predict and pronounce upon the future—whether in the inevitability of a classless society, in the inexorable laws of progress, in the Hegelian triumph of reason, in the proclamation of America's destiny, in the master narrative of secularization, in the modernist epic of science and technology, in the coming age of this, and the dawning century of that—are bound, finally, to get one into trouble and disappoint. And if such efforts do not void the intellect entirely for all eternity, we might at least agree that they risk discrediting it in the present age.

All of this, of course, does not mean that a brighter future should not be hoped for and worked toward, a future of goodness and virtue in fact, of faith, hope, and love; of temperance, courage, justice, and, indeed, prudence. But desirability should never be equated with inevitability, even probability. Conforming to putative "laws of history" should never obscure the messier necessity of individual moral agency in history—even the agency of the inquiring historian. In this indeterminate business, prudence thus counsels the fragility of goodness and the banality of evil, and works to strengthen the former and expose the latter. Historical understanding attentive to the ethical can be a powerful ally in both efforts.

NOTES

An earlier version of this chapter appeared in the journal *Fides et Historia* 37/38 (2006): 23–34. I thank the editors of this journal for allowing me to reprint material here. I am also grateful to Robert Sweetman (Institute of Christian Studies, Toronto) and Gillis Harp (Grove City College, Pennsylvania) for their comments on this essay when it was originally presented as a paper at the Conference on Faith and History, Hope College, October 13–16, 2004. The editors of the present volume also helped strengthen my arguments.

1. Leopold von Ranke, *Geschichte der romanischen und germanischen Völker von 1494 bis 1514*, 2nd ed. (Leipzig, 1874), vii.

2. Ranke's legacy, to be sure, is vast and its interpretations conflicted. The influence of positivism in the late nineteenth century, arguably more so than Ranke himself, allowed for Ranke's words to be understand as a prescription for strict value neutrality in scholarship. For an entry into the literature on Ranke's influence, see Georg Iggers and James Powell, eds., *Leopold von Ranke and the Shaping of the Historical Discipline* (Syracuse: Syracuse University Press, 1990).

3. Jacob Burckhardt, *Briefe*, vol. 1, ed. Max Burckhardt (Basel: Benno Schwabe, 1949), 233–34.

4. Heinrich von Sybel, *Die deutschen Universitäten, ihre Leistungen und Bedürfnisse* (Bonn, 1874), 18.

5. Georg Iggers, *Historiography in the Twentieth Century: From Scientific Objectivity to the Postmodern Challenge* (Hanover, N.H.: Wesleyan University Press, 1997).

6. Peter Novick, *That Noble Dream: The "Objectivity Question" and the American Historical Profession* (Cambridge: Cambridge University Press, 1988).

7. George M. Marsden, *The Outrageous Idea of Christian Scholarship* (New York: Oxford University Press, 1997).

8. Augustine, *Confessions* (New York: Penguin, 1961), 59.

9. See Jean Porter, "Virtue Ethics," in *The Cambridge Companion to Christian Ethics*, ed. Robin Gill, 96–111 (Cambridge: Cambridge University Press, 2000), and Gregory Trianosky, "What is Virtue Ethics all About?" *American Philosophical Quarterly* 27 (October 1990): 335–44. The renewed interest in virtue in modern ethical theory is generally held to have begun with G. E. M. Anscombe's seminal article "Modern Moral Philosophy" published in the journal *Ethics* in 1954. It is reprinted in Anscombe, *Ethics, Religion, and Politics* (Minneapolis: University of Minnesota Press, 1981), 26–42.

10. To be sure, this begs some larger normative questions beyond the scope of this chapter. See Alasdair MacIntyre, *Three Rival Versions of Moral Enquiry* (Notre Dame, Ind.: University of Notre Dame Press, 1988).

11. On the importance of Aristotelian ethics in Protestant thought, one would do well to consider the reformer Philipp Melanchthon. See Philipp Melanchthon, *Orations on Philosophy and Education*, ed. Sachiko Kusukawa, trans. Christine F. Salazar (Cambridge: Cambridge University Press, 1999).

12. See canto 29 of the *Purgatorio*.

13. Josef Pieper, *Kleines Lesebuch von den Tugenden des menschlichen Herzens* (Ostfildern: Schwabenverlag, 1988), 20–21; translations of Pieper are mine.

14. See Charles Taylor, *The Ethics of Authenticity* (Cambridge, Mass.: Harvard University Press, 1992).

15. Josef Pieper, *The Four Cardinal Virtues: Prudence, Justice, Fortitude, Temperance* (Notre Dame, Ind.: University of Notre Dame Press, 1966), 5. The widely consulted Macmillan's *Encyclopedia of Philosophy* (1967), revealingly, has no entry on prudence.

16. On the virtue of hope, see Josef Pieper, *Faith, Hope, Love* (San Francisco: Ignatius Press, 1997), 87–138.

17. On Thomas Aquinas's treatment of prudence, see *Summa Theologiae* II-II, 47–56. Cf. Daniel Mark Nelson, *The Priority of Prudence: Virtue and Natural Law in Thomas Aquinas and the Implications for Modern Ethics* (University Park: Pennsylvania State University Press, 1992), and James E. Keenan, "The Virtue of Prudence," in *The Ethics of Aquinas*, ed. Stephen J. Pope, 259–71 (Washington, D.C.: Georgetown University Press, 2002).

18. Pieper, *Kleines Lesebuch*, 21–22 (emphasis added).

19. Pieper, *Kleines Lesebuch*, 26–27 (emphasis added).

20. Pieper, *Kleines Lesebuch*, 26.

21. Pieper, *Four Cardinal Virtues*, 13. Cf. Josef Pieper, *Das Viergespann: Klugheit, Gerechtigkeit, Tapferkeit, Mass* (Munich: Kösel-Verlag, 1964), 26–27.

22. Friedrich Nietzsche, *On the Advantage and Disadvantage of History for Life*, trans. Peter Preuss (Indianapolis: Hackett, 1980), 7.

23. Pieper, *Four Cardinal Virtues*, 13.

24. It might reasonably be supposed that this work of Butterfield's is a classic in the "Rankean" tradition of disavowing moral interpolations from the historian, and that Butterfield's later work, *Christianity and History* (1949), makes more room for moral evaluation. (The latter, it should be noted, was written after the Nazi debacle.) A strong case can be made for this. However, with respect to the delimited sphere of moral inquiry I seek to recover for historical reflection (particularly *prudential reasoning as an aspect of virtue ethics*), I actually think that Butterfield's *Whig Interpretation* is more valuable than *Christianity and History*, even though the latter seems to allow for the moral judgments that the former calls into question. See chapter 3 ("Judgments in History") in Butterfield, *Christianity and History* (London: Collins, 1949), 67–91.

25. Herbert Butterfield, The *Whig Interpretation of History* (New York: W. W. Norton, 1965), 21–22.

26. Hannah Arendt, *Eichmann in Jerusalem: A Report on the Banality of Evil* (New York: Viking Press, 1963).

27. Robert Penn Warren, *The Legacy of the Civil War* (Lincoln: University of Nebraska Press, 1998), 100.

28. See canto 10 of the *Inferno*.

Chapter Five

The "Objectivity Question" and the Historian's Vocation

WILLIAM KATERBERG

MORE THAN MOST SCHOLARS, HISTORIANS HAVE EXPERIENCED their disciplinary identity as one in crisis, or at least flux. Aspiring to the modern priesthood of science, they have felt the burden of being viewed as a peculiar form of literature or a propaganda arm of the political system. How else to explain the most common rhetorical move of the historian? That is, the claim that unlike those who look to the past for pecuniary reasons, historians study it for its "own sake." Politicians use the past to legitimize policies, wars, and moral campaigns. Film makers use it to sell tickets. Even sociologists exploit it as raw material to produce grand theories. But historians study the past on its own terms, as objectively as possible, and for no other reason than its inherent interest. But in claiming this "own sake" vocational purity, do we protest too much? And do we sell ourselves short? In his classic study, *That Noble Dream*, Peter Novick told the story of the American historical profession in terms of the ritually familiar "objectivity question."[1] His narrative suggests that historians address their identity crisis in epistemological terms. What is scientific knowledge? Is historiography a science? And what are the challenges to historiography in achieving the scientific ideal of objectivity?

This essay argues that historians have approached their dilemmas of identity from the wrong standpoint. The central issues are not epistemological but vocational. Instead of appealing to the "purposelessness" of history and idealizing the study of the past for its "own sake," historians should redefine their vocation in terms of history being useful for life. This is not a radical suggestion, but returns historiography to its roots. As Frederick Jackson Turner, a "founding father" of the American Historical Association, said in 1891: "Each age writes the history of the past anew with reference to the conditions uppermost in its own time." Turner nodded to the fact-oriented, scientific claims of the emerging discipline, but it was not the point. Only the "antiquarian strives to bring back the past" for its own sake, he said. The "historian strives to show the present to itself by revealing its origin from the past. The goal of the antiquarian is the dead past; the goal of the historian is the living present." Quoting Johann Gustav Droysen, he concluded: "History is the 'Know Thyself' of humanity—the self-consciousness of mankind."[2] Such a calling does not invalidate studying the past for its own sake, and out of sheer interest, nor reduce history to utilitarian public service. But gathering accurate knowledge about the past and understanding why things happened is merely the means. The defining goal of history should be the service of life. This essay begins by addressing the current state of the "objectivity question." Then, it turns to the historian's vocation in order to move past the increasingly stultifying debate over objectivity.

HISTORY AND THEORY AT AN IMPASSE

Although some observers—fearfully or gleefully—claim that modern historical study is in crisis, it is more accurate to say that debates over objectivity, methodology, and theory are at an impasse.[3] Histororiography is at an impasse, not in crisis, because despite decades of debate the day-to-day teaching and scholarship of most historians has not changed in any essential way. The corporate influence on universities, declining funding for scholarship, the rising cost of journals and books, and shrinking library budgets aside, historians continue to churn out detailed monographs and synthetic studies, as well as reproduce themselves in the form of history majors and graduate students, and maintain the institutions of the historical profession. The substance of theoretical debates seldom touches their work in a direct way, regardless of the sound and fury. Scholars who focus on theoretical issues are simply another discrete subdiscipline, churning out their own monographs, and their work only rarely contaminates that of historians outside of intellectual and cultural history.[4] And yet the debates themselves point to problems significant enough that perhaps there should be a true profession-wide crisis.

For much of the twentieth century, historians debated the possibility of objectivity, given the personal and political subjectivity of the historian.[5] These debates have grown in sophistication with discussions of the sociology of knowledge, notably Thomas Kuhn's idea of "paradigm shifts," and the social history of ideas.[6] Is it still possible to take seriously modern ideals of scientific objectivity, in which heroic scientists transcend their time, culture, and place and see the world from the outside, as if from a god's-eye viewpoint? It is noteworthy that in recent decades the project of defending objectivity, or some other notion of stable, reliable knowledge, has turned to emphasizing a pragmatic social understanding of objectivity in which the professional institutions and methods of the discipline provide checks and balances that keep scholarship honest, and the diverse, contentious, and (ideally) democratic community of scholars judges which scholarship is reliable, even if controversial, and which is unreliable. This pragmatic "objectivity" is grounded institutionally, culturally, socially, and indeed politically, and is not heroically transcendent or individually autonomous. The knowledge produced thus is "universally" valid only insofar as it is judged so by a diverse community of scholars in a given time. And it is stable and reliable, rather than completely relative, because some points of view are ruled out of bounds. But this "workable" approach to knowledge and truth is always provisional and, even more, is always "political," as a product of intellectual communities and institutions that need to legitimate and reproduce themselves.[7] In short, it is intersubjective rather than objective.

The "linguistic turn" has raised a related set of challenges.[8] Does language correspond to the real world? If used precisely, is it transparent? Or does language in some sense (also) construct or create reality? This is not to say that the material world does not exist, or that it does not have an impact on us and we on it, except via language.[9] The question is whether we are able to experience the "real world"—to understand it and make decisions about how to act in it—except via the conceptual tools that language makes possible. At issue here is not only the unstable, changing, multifarious character of language, and the aporias in translating between languages, even between variations in the same language in different regions, communities, and eras. More to the point is the work that words do. Do they refer to something "out there," or do they have meaning only in relation to other words? Even if they do refer to something out there, because people "mean" them to do so, do they not also carry interpretive concepts and meaning with them? Can words merely point to something, or do words by their nature, intent, and use also convey interpretative significance? In short, are even our most basic experiences always already interpreted?

From this perspective, truth and facts are not "out there" but rather are *statements* about what is out there, and historians ought not to conflate the two. Narratives raise similar questions. Can narratives merely describe something, or do they by nature interpret and explain? Given the choices that storytellers must make about where to start and end a story, what to include or exclude, what conflict or process will be the central engine of the plot, which characters to make primary and which marginal, and so on, narratives cannot help but interpret and explain, historical narratives included. The significance of language and narrative as an issue is hard to overstate. It reinforces the point about the culturally and historically rooted, interpretative, and thus contingent quality of knowledge and truth. More than that, it suggests that objectivity would not be possible even if historians, as individuals or in communities, could shed their subjective commitments and biases. By their nature, language and narrative do not permit transparency and mere description.[10] These insights comport well with a Christian emphasis on human finitude and the recognition that, while all truth is God's truth, any human understanding or statement of truth is finite, perspectival, and partial.[11] This "linguistic turn" is especially significant for historians, who study something that is gone, something that exists only in documents and other traces left behind that must be interpreted. Is language a prison-house from which historians cannot escape? Can they get to the experiences of people in the past—that is, to the past itself? Or can historians, in practice, only interpret the traces that have been left behind? And, more hopefully, whatever their limitations, do language and narrative also make meaning possible?

As the social history of ideas and studies of language and narrative indicate, the classic historical problem of objectivity is thus structural rather than merely individual. Of course individual persons exist, but the modern, idealized "individual," who is autonomous and able to transcend historical circumstances, does not. Individuality and critical reason are shaped by and, to a significant degree, are products of the evolving social and cultural circumstances in which people live, as proponents of a pragmatic understanding of objectivity contend. If this is so, then is the idea of objectivity still meaningful, even if made more modest with notions of provisional knowledge and workable truth? Or do such "modest" changes subvert the original understanding of objectivity beyond recognition? Should the term thus be abandoned as an ideological construction or empty slogan? Is the ideal of pure science, unsullied by interests and purposes other than studying the thing itself, no longer workable? If not, if science is always caught up to one significant degree or another in the interests and aspirations of the society that produced it, what does this mean for the historical profession?

In terms of theoretical positions, I am suggesting, the divide is not a deep one between those who argue that historians can continue to work as they always have, albeit with more care to take into account the limits of historical knowledge, and those who contend that the profession must change in some fundamental ways. Most scholars agree that the insights associated with social history, the sociology of knowledge, and the linguistic-narrative turn are important and must be taken into account. And most agree that classic modern ideals of historical science and objectivity are flawed in their ahistorical naïveté. Some postmodern critics claim that history is merely a literary genre. Nonetheless, even historians who are radical on these issues, and contend that there is a fictional quality to history, usually insist that unlike pure fiction narrative choices in historiography have evidentiary limits and are not wholly arbitrary, in that for historiography to be a distinctive project it must have some sort of referential quality, however problematic and provisional.[12] The two sides of the theoretical divide really are debating the details of intersubjectivity and the relative reliability of historical knowledge. But, if the theoretical divide is not unbridgeable, scholars' perceptions of how to respond to it, and their sense of its consequences for the profession and the relationship between academic historical study and other approaches to the past, reveals a deeper divide.[13]

When pushed—when their work is compared to historical films and novels, heritage sites, historical reenactments, history channels on cable TV, and popular nonfiction, or when the politics of the profession are compared to a politician's use of the past—historians continue to fall back on the reassuringly familiar rhetoric of objectivity and their professional expertise. (I catch myself doing it all the time.) Unlike these others, we say, our work is not self-interested, not propaganda, not done to make money, and not for the sake of the present, but for its own sake and for the sake of the past. It also is common to hear dismissals of these others on the grounds that their work is not reliable—because it was not produced by a scholar who has earned a Ph.D., but by a huckster or amateur.[14] In short, when pushed most historians instinctively return to the familiar rhetoric and clichés of objectivity. Even when an historian explores something from the past to shed light on a contemporary issue—as in a book by John Patrick Diggins that uses Abraham Lincoln's free soil liberalism to address present-day American dilemmas—it often is dismissed. "Diggins thinks of himself as an intellectual historian," Gordon Wood said derisively, "but in fact he is not a historian at all. He is a cultural critic who uses history" to call people today "to come to terms with the nature of their society." Such a project may be legitimate, Wood allowed, but *by definition* it is not history. History must always and only can be "an accumulated science, gradually gathering truth through the steady and plodding efforts of countless practitioners turning out countless monographs"; those, like Diggins, "who cut loose from this faith do so at the peril of their discipline."[15]

It was not always so. Until recently, according to David Harlan, "history was one of our primary forms of moral reflection," as eminent scholars held up "a mirror to our common past." They encouraged their readers, as fellow citizens, to consider, "This is what we value and want, and don't yet have. This is how we mean to live and do not yet live."[16] The practice of historical cultural criticism has not entirely disappeared, of course, but it has been overwhelmed by the technical sophistication and specialization of historiography, a trend to which theorists have contributed, even as they critique the scientific pretensions of traditional modern historiography. The trend is a part of the logic of history as an academic discipline. In graduate training, in searching for a job and earning tenure, and in promotions and grants, historiography as expert knowledge is rewarded and history done in the service of public life is discouraged.[17] Historians may agree that true objectivity is not possible, may claim the civic benefits of studying the past, and may even be comfortable with present-day concerns influencing the questions that they ask. But only rarely do questions about the use and meaning of history shape the thousands of books, dissertations, and essays that they produce in a direct, defining, determinate, and substantial way. The past is in effect still, to be studied for its own sake, not that of the living. Professionalism thus exerts a powerful undertow against useful scholarship.

Women's history provides a good example. It boldly proclaimed an activist agenda in the 1960s: historiography that would inspire contemporary women, intellectual labor tied to social and political change. Practitioners began by searching the past to provide present-day feminists with inspiring models. In the 1970s, they critiqued the oppression of women, historicized mainstream conventions of proper womanhood, and looked to ordinary women to reconstruct a culture of common womanhood. In response, in the 1980s, minority scholars showed how race, religion, class, and sexual orientation divided women. What did slave women have in common with white mistresses? What did sisterhood mean when native-born Protestant women slandered immigrant Catholic women as an immoral threat to the nation? The work of a generation of scholars had uncovered diverse, conflicting women's experiences. Ironically, by historicizing ideals of femininity and sexuality, scholars had subverted the idea of a universal, essential womanhood that spanned culture, geography, and time. Their work thus contributed to a diverse, if sometimes divided and engaging movement. And yet, over time, despite their commitment to politics and emancipation, feminist scholars too increasingly became caught up in the technical and methodological debates of the academy, and their work frequently alienated them from nonscholars. In the long run, all too often activism gave way to academic professionalization.[18]

This example suggests something fundamental about the contradictory ideals of modern historiography. On the one hand, in the spirit of modern science and rationality, historians have aspired to objective, disinterested knowledge in which the knowing subject (the scholar) remains separate from her or his object of study. Accordingly, they have long asserted that distance from the past makes objective knowledge possible and have cast suspicion on those who pursue mere contemporary history.[19] Properly, knowledge is to be accumulated for its own sake. On the other hand, when asked why study history, historians usually have pointed to the need for people to have ties to the past for the sake of vigorous citizenship, coherent cultural identities, and the spiritual evolution of humanity. The first of these purposes demands a separation from the past, which is a lifeless object held up for scrutiny. But the second calls for continuity with the past and for participation in living traditions. The ostensible resolution to this incongruity is the hierarchy of knowledge assumed in modern scientific thought, in which verifiable facts are deemed the foundation for truth claims and moral decision-making. Empirical knowledge is the starting point, and on this ground interpretation and application follow. Historical scholarship thus privileges and prioritizes factual knowledge and relegates to secondary and derivative status questions of meaning, moral decision-making, aesthetics, and political activity.[20] Ironically, historians are far more rigorously purist than other "scientists" in their pursuit of research for its own sake and their almost total neglect of useful history. As Howard Zinn has noted, in the physical sciences the bulk of research is application-oriented, and "pure" research is the exception.[21] By contrast, whatever the ritualized nostrums about the value of history that they may invoke on occasion, historians typically leave it to their readers to figure out the significance of the past for the present and the future.

But the irony runs deeper still. If a century of historical scholarship and four decades of theoretical debate reveal anything, it is that the search for objective scientific knowledge has not provided a stable foundation on which truth claims, moral decisions, and political projects can be based. Instead, whatever provisional stability there is in historical knowledge, it is dependent on the credibility of the diverse and (ideally) democratic intellectual institutions and communities that produced it. In other words, truth, facts, and life cannot be disentangled.[22] As the case of women's history suggests, moreover, the pursuit of technical scholarship has overwhelmed and subverted the pursuit of history in the service of humanity. The crisis in contemporary historiography thus is threefold: unresolved theoretical debates; mainstream historians who as a matter of practice ignore these debates; and a neglect of the useful, life-serving purpose of history (even though the scientific ideal that fosters this neglect has long been fragmenting). One way through these dilemmas is to shift the focus of historical and theoretical debates from methodology and the possibility of producing stable knowledge to the purpose and meaning of historical study. In short, a shift from epistemology to vocation. If history is in the midst of a crisis, it is a crisis of vocation, not a crisis of epistemology.

MEANING AND PURPOSE IN HISTORY

At first glance, the notion that focusing on the meaning and purpose of history can move the profession past its theoretical and methodological impasse seems foolish. If most historians ignore hard questions of theory or cannot agree on how to address them, the problems only get worse when it comes to the use of history. The sound and fury is louder still and much more public, and the possibility of consensus is more distant, as historians fight not only with each other but with government officials, think tanks, parents, the entertainment and tourist industries, veterans' groups, and so on, over textbooks, curriculum, popular films, museum displays, and heritage sites. Historians normally try to keep their scholarship free of overt politics and other nonscholarly entanglements, but they are citizens and members of various kinds of communities, and sometimes they use their scholarly authority to address public issues.

These public issues often seem to come down to a battle between academic history and public memory.[23] David Blight has depicted such conflicts clearly in his study of the Civil War and American memory: "*History*—what trained historians do—is a reasoned reconstruction of the past," he argues. "It tends to be critical and skeptical of human motive, and therefore more secular than what people commonly refer to as memory. *Memory*, however, is often treated as a sacred text of potentially absolute meanings and stories, possessed as the heritage or identity of a community." If history is studied, memory is owned. At the confluence of historical study and public memory is a powerful, sometimes destructive, sometimes uplifting "turbulence," Blight observes.[24] Such a strict distinction between history and memory cannot easily be sustained, however, whatever professional and psychological stake historians have in trying to do so.[25] Typically, both sides of a given conflict will appeal to scholarship and objective facts, defend civic values and definitions of their national community, and depict their opponents as agenda driven. Both sides will be both critical and constructive in their approach to the past and its connections to civic or national communities in the present. Both will promote their own sacred meanings and stories and attack those of the other side. Finally, academic historians can be found on both sides of almost any given public issue; and heritage producers sometimes do engage in sophisticated, critical historical analysis.

But if the distinction between the two "streams of historical consciousness" is ambiguous and needs to be subverted, the conflicts themselves are real enough. A brief example makes the point. In nation after nation, pundits and politicians have explained contemporary political divisions by citing the failure of historians to write compelling national histories.[26] They often attack social history, in which each subnational community must have its story told, allegedly at the expense of traditional national-political histories that tell citizens what they have in common. Moreover, critics complain, scholars spend more time criticizing national failures than praising noble ideals and heroic accomplishments. *Who Killed Canadian History?* by J. L. Granatstein, and "Privatizing the Mind: The Sundering of Canadian History, the Sundering of Canada," by Michael Bliss, are good examples. The response to such criticism is striking. Defenders of social history appeal to facts and the value of research done for its own sake, and thus defend the integrity of the past and their own scholarship. But they also emphasize the value for contemporary public life of critical, multicultural history. "It is important that English-Canadian students understand Quebec's historical sense of uniqueness; it is also important that they appreciate the sense of community, the experiences of oppression, and the desire for political redress of other Canadian groups," several historians insisted in a response to Bliss. "The tragedy is not that . . . students are inundated with this, but rather that they are offered so *few* opportunities to discover these issues. An understanding of ourselves as a 'nation' or indeed as many nations within one, will not come by propping up an older national history . . . which is built on the suppression of women's, native and other voices. It might come, however, from a better understanding of our diverse experiences and histories." Only a historiography that gives full attention to regional conflicts and to diverse ethno-cultural groups can lead to a more just, peaceable society in Canada today.[27] At issue here are not matters of fact so much as ethics and conviction. What does a good society look like, and how do its values shape historical narratives, present-day politics, and hopes for the future? Conflicts over these normative and historical issues have played themselves out in the United States and Canada in recent years in battles over school history standards, plans at the Smithsonian to do an exhibit on the Enola Gay and the use of the atomic bomb on Japan, and a National Film Board documentary on the Canadian air force and the bombing of German cities in World War II.[28]

The point is simple. It is difficult to make strict categorical distinctions between history and memory, history and heritage, scholarship and advocacy, and the academic realm and public life. As critics of academia emphasize, and defenders occasionally recognize (in historiographic essays or public controversies), scholarship carries political implications, even when individual scholars do not consciously work with such convictions or goals in mind. The point that follows is more complex. In courses that fill basic core requirements—such as Western or world history, or national surveys—historians often explain the relevance of history for community memories and good citizenship. Teachers also do so when asked to justify the time and money spent on historical study by parents and taxpayers. And, when drawn into public controversy over a specific issue, historians (like other scholars) will use their research or call on their professional credibility to exercise influence. But in their *scholarship* itself, by and large, and in their judgments about the relative worth of a scholar as a member of the profession, they prefer to keep scholarship and public life strictly separate. Technical scholarship is rewarded, and work that addresses the public in general is not. (An influential historian like Richard Hofstadter might not get tenure today!) As noted earlier, the modern assumption is that moral decision-making follows from objective knowledge and reliable facts. But does this two-step process work? Remember that today even its defenders usually agree that objectivity is possible only in a socially and politically contextualized, provisional sense, which makes it not so much "objectivity" as socially self-critical intersubjectivity. Yet, paradoxically, scholars still try to maintain a wall of separation between their scholarship and the public, and thus render their political commitments and moral vision all but invisible. In short, their work is shaped by their social-political values (and is not objective in the classic sense of the term) but without in turn shaping public life. Is it a surprise that many observers are cynical about the professional claims historical scholars make to objectivity, and wonder about the worth of their scholarship?

Howard Zinn has criticized this pattern in *The Politics of History*. From the viewpoint of a radical, he condemns most academic history as mere "private enterprise." History that is written self-consciously to address a moral, social, or political issue can indeed "twist" the truth, he agrees. But "nonconcern" (the "own sake" ideal) can result "in another kind of distortion, in which the ore of history is beaten into neither a ploughshare nor a sword, but is melted down and sold."[29] Such "pure history" is, in effect, an economic commodity. Historians are entrepreneurs whose "profits" are salaries, tenure, promotions, and prestige. Such considerations, while not "excluding either personal activism or socially pertinent scholarship, tend to discourage either."[30] There are exceptions, but in practice scholarship serves a social purpose, if at all, via a trickle-down approach, "which holds that if only you fill the libraries to bursting" eventually something useful will "reach a society desperate for understanding." Against such scholarship, in which the rhetoric of fidelity to the past legitimizes the use of history in the service of professional standing, Zinn urges scholars to acknowledge that accurate facts and the production of reliable knowledge—which most historians define as their essential calling—are not enough, but merely a starting point for the ultimate goal of promoting humane values, a just society, and communities of memory.[31] If such values and the intersubjective social-political contexts of scholarship are what make "workable" objectivity possible, and if historians cannot transcend present-day values and interests, then the question is which ones should they promote and to what effect?

Will scholars influence the societies that shape them? Will their scholarship uphold and defend the status quo or critique and transform it? There is a "relationship between the relative well-being of professors, their isolation in middle class communities, their predictable patterns of sociality, and the tendency to remain distant, both personally and in scholarship, from the political battles of the day," Zinn suggests.[32] Does the pursuit of objective scholarship, in its effect or its non-effect, tend to reinforce and legitimate the prevailing social-political order? Do most scholars have a stake in doing so? (I have in mind my Calvin College–funded TIAA-CREFF retirement plan!) And, is it a wonder that people often view historiography as irrelevant for changing the world in which they live, when scholars claim to be neutral, and as much as possible disguise their moral and political commitments? All scholarship need not have advocacy in mind or be of immediate use, but historians should consider advocacy and utility to be legitimate scholarly professional concerns. It is a matter of balance. Historians should put more effort into applied scholarship, like scholars in the physical sciences, rather than passive-aggressively leaving the politics implicit in their narratives and analysis. And they should address public issues directly, rather than hiding their light under a bushel and only hinting at issues. Advocacy should not ideologically overdetermine the history that they tell. Nevertheless, in the end, while honest accurate analysis, fidelity to one's sources, and reliable knowledge are necessary, they are not enough, and they are not the point.

Such a transformation of the historical profession would not solve the theoretical impasse that I have described by producing a theoretical or political consensus. But it would point historians in another direction, liberating them *as scholars* to take part in public life and serve the humanistic purposes that once defined the liberal arts.[33] It also would legitimate resisting trends in higher education toward "measurable outcomes" that narrow education into job training and skills development. The fetishizing of expertise, professional authority, and objectivity have distorted historiography and theoretical debates, leaving them sterile, and have done so in the interests of a consensus that has never existed among historians, the larger academy, or North American society. A better goal is to legitimate the participation of historians, *as scholars*, in the public conflicts that shape liberal democracies. If faith and learning cannot be segregated, as Christian historians have argued, neither can scholarship and citizenship. It is the community of historians—and the diverse, contentious political and intellectual values and conflicts it embodies—that offer hope for public life, not the promise of professional expertise or neutral facts.

HISTORIOGRAPHY, TIME, AND MEMORY

The case that I am making for shifting the essential goal of historiography from accumulating reliable knowledge to addressing questions of meaning and purpose fits with some aspects of the postmodern turn. If modern thought privileged facts, knowledge, and functional performativity, a key trend signaled by postmodern thought is a return to questions of ethics and morality—that is, to the purposes to which facts, knowledge, and expertise are directed.[34] For the study of history, this would be a return to what Friedrich Nietzsche considered its only legitimate goal: serving life. A "postmodernist" before its time, Nietzsche condemned scientific history as dehumanizing and nihilistic. The "natural relation of an age, a culture, a people to history," he said, is "brought on by hunger, regulated by the degree of need, held within limits by the inherent plastic power" of life. Taken in "excess without hunger, even contrary to need," knowledge does not promote action; rather, it leaves people to drag around "an immense amount of indigestible" facts, like stones in their bellies. From this viewpoint, academic historical knowledge is not a living culture, "but only a kind of knowledge about culture," one that "stops at cultured thought and cultured feelings but leads to no cultured decisions."[35]

Contrary to the ideal of knowledge accumulated for its own sake, Nietzsche argued that history belongs to the living only insofar as they are active and striving, preserving and admiring, or suffering and in need of liberation. "Monumental" history provides models for people to emulate; "antiquarian" history is a matter of revering traditions, giving thanks for existence, and preserving the past for those who will come later; and "critical" history serves life by dragging traditions "to the bar of judgment," interrogating and condemning them.[36] But, even "useful" history can choke life. Monumental history may lead people to fool themselves with "tempting similarities" and forget that in the past which is inconvenient. Antiquarian history degenerates when present-day life no longer animates it and reverencing the past encourages people to hate everything new. Critical history destroys life when it puts a knife to the roots of a people or allows revolutionaries to fool themselves by thinking that they have not inherited the passions, errors, or aberrations of the past.[37] In short, even forms of history intended to serve life can undermine it, if the past is misused or distorted, or becomes a substitute for life. This ideal of history serving life never quite disappeared among historians, but it was overwhelmed by the scientific and professional imperatives of modern scholarship.[38]

Implicit in the ideal of history that serves life is an approach to temporality that contrasts sharply with that employed by modern historians. Historians normally do not think much about how they conceptualize time in their work. Their approach is astronomical-mathematical and linear, in that the units of time they use are defined by the length of planetary days, lunar months, and solar years and provide a linear mathematical line that, in theory, extends infinitely from the past and into future. Whatever their personal beliefs about the Big Bang, providence, and the like, such metahistorical visions rarely come into play in their scholarship. They are treated as historically contingent markers— the birth of Christ, referred to now as the Common Era, reflecting the dominance of the Western calendar—and no longer pave the way for a teleological metanarrative.[39] Modern historians also treat events as unique and unrepeatable (and the flow of time as irreversible), stressing the "decisive differentiation between the present and the past" and their own distance from the past, and view comparisons between distinct periods of time with suspicion.[40] By contrast, Nietzsche saw time as cyclical, repetitive, and recurring. Rejecting notions of development, he emphasized the basic commonalities and enduring dilemmas of the human experience, and called on people to give up progressive illusions and accept the finitude of human existence. Historians are likely to be wary of his treatment of temporality, from a theoretical standpoint, but there is much to learn from him.[41] If events do not repeat themselves, and if we cannot go back in time, there are good reasons for historians to reconsider matters of temporality and the relationship between the past, present, and future, doing so to redefine the way they approach their scholarship.

Perhaps the most basic reason is that in their day-to-day life, people's experience of time is not linear, or at least not only so. Quotidian and joyful memories, as well as traumatic ones, locate people in the past and the present simultaneously. (The past is not dead, it is not even past, as William Faulkner famously put it.) The anticipation of future events, in fear or hope, likewise is not strictly linear. Furthermore, for participants in traditions and members of communities temporality is not linear. For example, Christians recognize their distance from the ancient church, but their belief in the "communion of the saints" spans time and space. Similarly, "imagined communities" of citizens stretch into the past and the future. Despite my best academic efforts to teach them scholarly "distance," my students often use the pronoun "we" and identify with Americans in the past, simultaneously recognizing temporal distance and erasing it. In our own ways, scholars do the same. We typically treat time as linear and distancing when looking at the past itself. But, at the same time, when doing so, we engage in conversations with scholars who wrote in the past, often the distant past. Likewise, when we raise questions or suggest avenues for scholars who will follow us, we anticipate the conversation being carried on in the future. Historiographical debates and our use of secondary sources are not merely about knowledge but involve participating in an imagined community of scholars, even if our participation in that "communion" is implicit (hidden in the footnotes). The ongoing, seemingly never-ending debate in the historical profession about the dilemmas of objectivity and sub-jectivity is a good example. Is it not a case of people engaged in the endless effort of maintaining and (re)defining a living tradition and evolving community? This is not linear temporality. It is about partici-pating in a tradition, being faithful to its origins, and guarding that tra-dition for the future. And, as in any community, the process of defining and maintaining it, and being faithful to it and guarding it, is contested and reveals the internal diversity, tensions, and even contradictions held within the community.

These examples suggest that the border that historians draw instinc-tively between history and heritage is problematic. In its self-conception, especially when defining itself against nonprofessionals, modern his-toriography is based on a "decisive differentiation between the present and the past." Gabrielle Spiegel has made this point clearly in her com-parison of historical time to "liturgical" time. "Like modern medicine," she declared unambiguously, "the practice of history becomes possible only when a corpse is opened to investigation. . . . Historians must draw a line between what is dead (past) and what is not, and therefore they posit death as a total social fact, in contrast to tradition, which figures a lived body of traditional knowledge, passed down in gestures, habits, unspoken but nonetheless real memories, borne by living societies."[42] My claim is that historians do not live up to this ideal in their scholarly practice, which contains its own liturgical, tradition-enacting rituals in relation to the past.[43] More importantly, her vivisection ideal is by itself inadequate. My point is not to wholly delegitimize linear conceptions of time or the ideal of distance. They are basic to historical analysis and narration. But the nonlinear experience of time also is basic to human life and story-telling, and it too must define historiography. To put it differently, historians need to go beyond merely recognizing that time is intersubjective—which most do, as a matter of *theory*—and transform their *practice* of historical scholarship with that recognition in mind.[44]

This is not a small task. Even historians who have redefined objec-tivity in a socially contextualized, intersubjective, pragmatic sense con-tinue to treat the past almost exclusively in linear fashion in their work. That is, they neglect the tradition-enacting, critical-memory function that history (heritage) plays in the communities in which they live. One exception to this pattern is Howard Zinn, in his project to promote a radical historiography. He emphasizes not just distance but also our connections to the past, and has explored the utopian potential of the past.[45] Another exception is Mark Noll, whose work epitomizes the best of modern historiography in his careful effort to be "objective." But in *The Scandal of the Evangelical Mind*, he offered a *cri du couer* to his own tradition, acknowledging its populist power but openly lamenting and condemning its habitual neglect, even scorning, of the intellect. *Scandal* looks to the past to reveal the roots of contemporary problems in American evangelicalism, to find sources of intellectual vigor in evangelicalism and other Christian traditions, and to thus transform and intellectually and spiritually reinvigorate it for the future. The same *cri du couer* animates much of Noll's academic writing, but usually it is hidden and must be read between the lines, as in *America's God*, where he concludes that by the late nineteenth century American theology was unorthodox where profound and superficial where orthodox.[46] While most of Noll's writing is typically academic, *Scandal* exemplifies the potential for critical history to speak from the heart, and speak *directly* to traditions and communities. If we are open to nonlinear approaches to time, history, and heritage, historians can contribute to the transformation of life in the present and future. Such nonlinear openness would encourage us to contribute to public memory, practice prophetic cultural criticism, and shape hopeful visions of the future—overtly, and as an essential part of our scholarship, rather than implicitly in trickle down fashion.

There are many theoretical issues at stake here—such as the differences between premodern, modern, and postmodern experiences of time, and the possibility of "conversations" between people from very different times and cultures. But the significance of how we approach temporality—when we study the past itself, and when we think about how historians and their audiences relate to the past and future—is clear. Questioning strictly linear, modern historical approaches to time and history provides us with ways and reasons to rethink our distance from and relationship to the past. The issue is not theory so much as practice. Historians should as a matter of calling seek to connect their audiences to the past, critically and appreciatively, by questioning and challenging traditions, and "liturgically" restating and redefining those traditions (as well as emphasizing distance from the past and approaching it as dead and gone, as Spiegel advocates). Such a redefinition or broadening of the historian's vocation has the potential to reinvigorate historiography by transcending stale conversations about methodology and the reliability of historical knowledge; by transgressing the border between "history" and "heritage" and turning it into a "frontier"; and by shaping communities of memory, critical public debate, and hopeful visions of the future. History in the service of life becomes possible when scholars recognize, explore, and practice such a dynamic relationship to the past.

CHRISTIAN FAITH AND THE TRANSFORMATION OF THE HISTORIAN'S VOCATION

As I have stressed, the issues here are less theoretical than matters of vocational identity and practice. When pushed, or simply asked, most historians will concede the flawed ideal of objectivity, acknowledge (or complain about) the politics embedded in most scholarship, and embrace something like the pragmatic understanding of "objectivity" (that is, intersubjectivity) that I have described. They also will agree that while the history we write and teach is defined by a linear, astronomical-mathematical approach to time, people's day-to-day experience of time is rhythmic, cyclical, and liturgical as well as linear. My point thus is not theoretical, but practical: despite recognizing these things, when pushed, we continue to do our scholarship as if the ideal of scientific objectivity remained credible. Little has changed in basic historical practice or disciplinary rhetoric. Even if history *is* inseparable from life, and even if history *ought* to serve life, in practice most historians continue to do their work as if life exists only in the cloisters of their profession. The occasional application of historical study and wisdom to life in the classroom, especially in "civilization" courses that meet core requirements, and the occasional foray into issues of public debate are exceptions that prove the rule. It is this practice and the learned instinct of defining legitimate history in "own sake" terms that need to change. Historians should follow scholars like Zinn, Diggins, and Noll in doing useful history, should view it as scholarship, should teach their students to do it well, and should value and reward it in the same way that other academic disciplines reward "applied," life-serving scholarship, rather than dismiss it and warn graduate students and untenured faculty away from it.[47] Indeed, such work ought to be the defining goal—though not the only goal—of historical scholarship.

Christian scholars should lead the way in promoting this redefined and transformed historical practice, precisely in the spirit of the gospels and the most basic calling of the Hebrew and Christian scriptures—to love God with all your heart and to love your neighbor as yourself. As Jim Olthuis has suggested, the default instinct in Western thought has been to focus on questions of epistemology and ontology (as does most of the theoretical literature on integrating faith and history). But the most basic calling of the Bible is not about knowledge or right ideas; it is about love.[48] To Olthuis's insight we might add the biblical phrase, "faith, hope, and love" (from 1 Cor 13). It captures the liturgical treatment of time in the Bible, "faith" standing for memories of God's faithfulness in the past, "hope" for the anticipation of God's fulfillment of his promises in the future, and "love" for the calling to live here and now with these memories and promises in heart and mind. And it is this vision of time that animates the prophetic critique of injustice and impiety in both the Hebrew and Christian testaments.

This shift, from giving priority to "own sake" knowledge to putting the priority on loving intersubjective relationships, is mirrored in postmodern ethical thought, which emphasizes that our relationship with the "other"—the Bible's "stranger" and "alien"—is the defining problem of our time and ought to be the starting point for ethics and thought. Indeed, it is telling that many of the influential theorists making this case have been Jewish (for example, Martin Buber, Emmanuel Levinas, and Jacques Derrida) and have worked self-consciously out of their religious tradition. It is appropriate too that this shift is rooted in the experience of pluralism in a globalizing world, as that experience played a significant role in undermining confidence in the ideal of objectivity.[49]

The rough parallel between postmodern ethical thought and the biblical calling to love your neighbor points to the opportunity, the opening, that Christian scholars have today to redefine the historian's vocation. And it points to the challenge to work as Christians in distinctively Christian communities, in the historical profession, and in a wider public realm that is bewilderingly, wonderfully, and sometimes threateningly diverse.

What would it mean for historians to follow the biblical imperative to love their neighbors, and live in faith, hope, and love (charity), *as historians*? What would it mean for their obligations to the dead, in the past that they study? For their audiences today: the students and communities of readers in the present in which they live? And for the future, to which their lives and work will make a contribution?

My goal here is not to answer these questions, but to legitimize them as the essential questions and the defining concerns for historians to address, *as historians and Christians*. More than that, it is to insist that historians are obligated to address them as an essential part of their vocation and scholarly practice. If human beings live between the past and the future, and if a liturgical temporality and time-spanning communion are essential aspects of human existence, then it is a failure of vocation for historians to neglect such matters. If not historians, then who will bring the wisdom and resources of the study of the past to the experiences and needs of living well and living faithfully in the present and future? Such a vocational obligation need not be met by all historians (Christian or otherwise) in the same way. But it ought to be an essential element of the historical profession as a whole and of the individual vocation of each historian. In diverse ways, history and social studies teachers and public historians already do some of these things. For their part, Christian historians often have insisted on the legitimacy, inevitability, and obligation of integrating faith and history, even in a public scholarly profession in which not all participants share the same faith. If the defining element of Christian faithfulness is loving relationships, not better knowledge, then being good "citizens" in the many and diverse communions and communities in which we live, as historians, is essential to "integrating" history faithfully.[50]

NOTES

1. Peter Novick, *That Noble Dream: The "Objectivity Question" and the American Historical Profession* (New York: Cambridge University Press, 1988).

2. Frederick Jackson Turner, *Rereading Frederick Jackson Turner: "The Significance of the Frontier in American History" and Other Essays* (New Haven: Yale University Press, 1998), 18–19.

3. For an introduction to these debates, see Philip Jenkins, ed., *The Postmodern History Reader* (New York: Routledge, 1997).

4. This assertion is based on personal observations in the various departments in which I have been a graduate student and taught, and my reading of my own fields of research (historiography, religious history, U.S.-Canadian relations, and the North American West).

5. See Novick, *That Noble Dream*, and Georg Iggers, *Historiography in the Twentieth Century: From Scientific Objectivity to the Postmodern Challenge* (Hanover, N.H.: University Press of New England, 1997).

6. See Joyce Appleby et al., *Telling the Truth About History* (New York: W. W. Norton, 1994).

7. See Thomas Haskell, *Objectivity is Not Neutrality* (Baltimore: Johns Hopkins University Press, 1998); and Richard Bernstein, *Beyond Objectivism and Relativism* (Philadelphia: University of Pennsylvania Press, 1983).

8. See "AHR Forum: Intellectual History and the Return of Literature," with essays by David Harlan, David Hollinger, and Allan Megill, *American Historical Review* 94:3 (1989): 581–653; "AHR Forum: The Old History and the New," with essays by Theodore Hamerow, Gertrude Himmelfard, Lawrence Levine, Joan Wallach Scott, and John Toews, *American Historical Review* 94:3 (1989): 654–98; and further discussion by James Kloppenberg, *American Historical Review* 94:4 (1989): 1011–30, and Joyce Appleby, *American Historical Review* 94:5 (1989): 1326–32; Dominick LaCapra, *Rethinking Intellectual History* (Ithaca, N.Y.: Cornell University Press, 1983); and, Elizabeth Hedstrom, "History and the Limits of Interpretation," *Intellectual History Newsletter* 18 (1996): 89–97.

9. Richard Rorty, *Contingency, Irony, and Solidarity* (New York: Cambridge University Press, 1989), 4–5.

10. The literature is voluminous, especially in journals such as *Clio* and *History and Theory*, but also in monographs and edited collections. In addition to material cited above, see Geoffrey Roberts, ed., *The History and Narrative Reader* (New York: Routledge, 2001); and, Brian Fay et al., eds., *History and Theory: Contemporary Readings* (Oxford: Blackwell, 1998).

11. On Christianity and the hermeneutical questions at stake here, see, for example, James K. A. Smith, *Who's Afraid of Postmodernism? Taking Derrida,*

Lyotard, and Foucault to Church (Grand Rapids, Mich.: Baker Academic, 2006); and *The Fall of Interpretation: Philosophical Foundations for a Creational Hermeneutic* (Downers Grove, Ill.: InterVarsity Press, 2000). For my own take, see "Redemptive Horizons, Redemptive Violence, and Hopeful History," *Fides et Historia* 36:1 (2004): 1–14.

12. For example, see Hayden White on the Holocaust. In response to criticism, he has agreed that some ways of emplotting the narrative are not legitimate. There are limits. (The issue is not the individual facts, but the ethical and aesthetic imperatives that limit the number of legitimate ways to tell the story of the Holocaust.) See White, "Historical Emplotment and the Problem of Truth," in Jenkins, *The Postmodern History Reader*, 392–96.

13. This assertion is difficult to demonstrate even in a close reading of a discrete set of texts, let alone for theorists and historians in general. See the debates in parts 3 and 4 of Roberts, *The History and Narrative Reader*, and excerpts from Gabrielle Spiegel, Tony Bennett, and Susan Stanford Friedman in Jenkins, *The Postmodern History Reader*, 180–203, 219–30, 231–36. Also note the points of contention between John Zammito and John E. Toews, on the one hand, and Joan Scott and Dominick LaCapra, on the other, in John E. Toews, "Intellectual History after the Linguistic Turn: The Autonomy of Meaning the Irreducibility of Experience," *American Historical Review* 92:4 (1987): 879–907; John Zammito, "Are We Being Theoretical Yet? The New Historicism, the New Philosophy of History, and 'Practicing Historians,'" *Journal of Modern History* 65:4 (1993): 783–814; Dominick LaCapra, "History, Language, and Reading: Waiting for Crillon," *American Historical Review* 100:3 (June 1995): 799–828. The distance between these positions is exaggerated by polemical rhetoric.

14. This generalization is based on my own experience, but it is deeply rooted in the historical profession. On professionalization and history, see Novick, *That Noble Dream*; Burton J. Bledstein, *The Culture of Professionalism: The Middle Class and the Development of Higher Education in America* (New York: Norton, 1976); and Thomas Haskell, ed., *The Authority of Experts: Studies in History and Theory* (Bloomington: Indiana University Press, 1984).

15. Gordon Wood, "Liberalism and Stubbornness," *The New Republic* 223:18 (October 30, 2000): 40; on John Patrick Diggins, *On Hallowed Ground: Abraham Lincoln and the Foundations of American History* (New Haven: Yale University Press, 2000). The second Wood quote is in David Harlan, *The Degradation of American History* (Chicago: University of Chicago Press, 1997), xxviii.

16. Harlan, *Degradation*, xv; the first quoted phrases are Harlan's words, and the full sentence is his quotation of Michael Walzer, *The Company of Critics: Social Criticism and Commitment in the Twentieth Century* (New York: Basic Books, 1988), 230.

17. I am alluding to Thomas Kuhn's analysis of paradigms of "normal" science and of scientific revolutions. The institutions of the history profession tend to produce a certain kind of scholar, scholarship, and discourse of scholarship. On "normal" historiography, see Robert Berkhofer Jr., *Beyond the Great Story: History as Text and Discourse* (Cambridge, Mass: Harvard/Belknap, 1995); and, Harlan, *Degradation*. Howard Zinn makes the same point as I do here in *The Politics of History*, 2nd ed. (Urbana: University of Illinois Press, 1990).

18. See Harlan, *Degradation*, chap. 3, on women's history in the 1990s. For an overview of women's history, see Margaret Bendroth, "Men, Women, and God: Some Historiographical Issues," in *History and the Christian Historian*, ed. Ron Wells (Grand Rapids, Mich.: Eerdmans, 1998). Also see Nancy Hewitt, "Beyond the Search for Sisterhood: American Women's History in the 1980s," in *Unequal Sisters: A Multi-Cultural Reader in U.S. Women's History*, 2nd ed., ed. Vicky Ruiz and Ellen Carol DuBois (New York: Routledge, 1994); and Jane Roland Martin, *Coming of Age in Academe: Rekindling Women's Hopes and Reforming the Academy* (New York: Routledge, 2000).

19. Distance is the one "bias" that long has seemed compatible with objectivity, presumably because it makes a disinterested, more objective approach to the past possible. But surely it is as much a "perspective," and thus a "mere" perspective, as proximity and closeness. And, surely, being close has advantages in understanding an experience that distance does not.

20. These assumptions are described and critiqued by Hans-Georg Gadamer in *Truth and Method*, 2nd rev. ed., trans. Joel Weinsheimer and Donald G. Marshall (New York: Continuum, 1998), Part II, section II.

21. Zinn, *Politics of History*, 12.

22. Postmodernists and other critics of the science and objectivity often are attacked for promoting relativism. But, as Novick's account of the historical profession in *That Noble Dream* shows, the scientific model has not produced stability—not in historical narratives, the politics of the profession, or the politics of the American nation. As I see it, the onus is now on defenders of the scientific model to prove that "objective" facts can produce stability. The opposite case, that reliable knowledge depends on the diverse and often fractious communities and institutions of the historical profession, and that stability is always provisional, seems more credible. Indeed, this is what defenders of "pragmatic" and "workable" notions of objectivity, knowledge, and truth are saying. It is just that they want to hold onto the rhetorically powerful discourse of "objectivity."

23. Similar conflicts often can be found between scholars and members of other types of communities with cherished memories, such as churches, political parties, and geographical regions.

24. David Blight, *Race and Reunion: The Civil War and American Memory* (Cambridge, Mass.: Harvard University Press, 2001). On the scholarship on

memory, see Kerwin Klein, "On the Emergence of *Memory* in Historical Discourse," *Representations* 69 (Winter 2000): 127–50.

25. On the psychological stake that historians have in maintaining a strict boundary between expert history and popular heritage, see Peter Gay, *The Cultivation of Hatred: The Bourgeois Experience, Victoria to Freud* (New York: Norton, 1993), chap. 6.

26. See Ian McKay, "After Canada: On Amnesia and Apocalypse in the Contemporary Crisis," *Acadiensis* 28:1 (Autumn 1998): 76–97. For a useful comparative survey, see Chris Lorenz, "Comparative Historiography: Problems and Perspectives," *History and Theory* 38:4 (February 1999): 25–39; the same issue includes several articles on specific countries.

27. Linda Kealey et al., "Teaching Canadian History in the 1990s: Whose 'National' History Are We Lamenting?" *Journal of Canadian Studies* 27:2 (Summer 1992): 130; it is in response to Michael Bliss, "Privatizing the Mind: The Sundering of Canadian History, the Sundering of Canada," *Journal of Canadian Studies* 26:4 (Winter 1991–92): 5–17.

28. See Edward T. Linenthal et al., eds., *History Wars: The Enola Gay and Other Battles for America's Past* (New York: Henry Holt & Company, 1996); and Graham Carr, "Rules of Engagement: Public History and the Drama of Legitimation," *Canadian Historical Review* 86 (June 2005): 317–54.

29. Zinn, *Politics of History*, 15.

30. Ibid., 16.

31. Ibid., 18, 20, 295.

32. Ibid., 16, 32.

33. See Bill Readings, *The University in Ruins* (Cambridge, Mass.: Harvard University Press, 1996); and John Michael, *Anxious Intellectuals: Academic Professionals, Public Intellectuals, and Enlightenment Values* (Durham, N.C.: Duke University Press, 2000). From the viewpoint of premodern traditions, see Alasdair MacIntyre, *After Virtue: A Study in Moral Theory*, 2nd ed. (Notre Dame, Ind.: University of Notre Dame Press, 1984).

34. See Zygmunt Bauman, *Postmodern Ethics* (Oxford: Blackwell, 1993); and David Lyon, *Postmodernity*, 2nd ed. (Minneapolis: University of Minnesota Press, 1999). Also note Martin Jay, "Is there a Poststructuralist Ethics?" in *Forcefields* (New York: Routledge, 1993); and MacIntyre, *After Virtue*. Self-consciously "postmodern" and "traditional" thinkers are pursuing a rethinking of ethics and morality in the wake of modernity's failures.

35. Friedrich Nietzsche, *On the Advantage and Disadvantage of History for Life*, trans. Peter Pruess (Indianapolis, Ind.: Hackett Publishing), 23, 24. On the political context, see Christian J. Emden, "Toward a Critical Historicism: History and Politics in Nietzsche's Second 'Untimely Meditation,'" *Modern Intellectual History* 3:1 (April 2006): 1–31.

36. Nietzsche, *On the Advantage*, 14–15, 19, 21.

37. Ibid., 17, 20, 21, 22.

38. For example, see Novick, *That Noble Dream.*

39. See F. C. Haber, "The Darwinian Revolution in the Concept of Time," in *The Study of Time*, ed. Haber et al. (New York: Springer 1972); and Reinhart Koselleck, *Future Past: On the Semantics of Historical Time*, trans. Keith Tribe (Cambridge, Mass.: MIT Press, 1985).

40. Gabrielle M. Spiegel, "Memory and History: Liturgical Time and Historical Time," *History and Theory* 41 (May 2002): 160–61.

41. On Nietzsche, time, and history, see Carl E. Pletsch, "History and Friedrich Nietzsche's Philosophy of Time," *History and Theory* 16 (1977): 30–39.

42. Spiegel, Memory and History," 160–61.

43. Klein does not deal with the secular "piety" of the discipline of history in his essay, "On the Emergence of *Memory* in Historical Discourse," but the definition and defense of modern history writing has always struck me as having a liturgical character and a faith in the dogmas of objectivity, the academy, and science ("dogma" signifying the beliefs that a community holds in common).

44. For example, in his useful and insightful theoretical discussion of history and time, John R. Hall examines how scholars organize linear-chronological time. But he never considers, even in a footnote, the temporality and historicity of the historian, or that of her or his audience. See John R. Hall "The Time of History and the History of Time," *History and Theory* 19:2 (1980): 113–31.

45. See the essays in Zinn, *Politics of History.*

46. Mark Noll, *The Scandal of the Evangelical Mind* (Grand Rapids, Mich.: Eerdmans, 1994), and *America's God: From Jonathan Edwards to Abraham Lincoln* (New York: Oxford University Press, 2002).

47. As the co-editor of a textbook series with Harlan Davidson, I encounter this fear on a regular basis, that books without footnotes, intended for students or general audiences, will not count for tenure, and might be held against a young scholar. This problem is more common at research than teaching institutions, but it signals what the profession values most.

48. See James Olthuis, "Crossing the Threshold: Sojourning Together in the Wild Spaces of Love," *Toronto Journal of Theology* 11:1 (1995): 39–57; and James Olthuis, ed., *Knowing Other-Wise: Epistemology at the Threshold of Spirituality* (New York: Fordham University Press, 1997). For an example of an exception to this pattern, see Perry Bush, "What Would History Look Like If 'Peace and Justice' Really Mattered?" *Fides et Historia* 34:1 (Winter/Spring 2002): 49–56.

49. See Bauman, *Postmodern Ethics*, and Zygmunt Bauman, *Life in Fragments* (London: Blackwell, 1995). On pluralism and objectivity, see Appleby et

al., *Telling the Truth About History*. My position is a postmodern redefining of both Christian humanism and the humanistic spirit of Enlightenment thought, which have been neglected amid the hegemony of scientific-objectivist discourse. See Stephen Toulmin, *Cosmopolis* (Chicago: University of Chicago Press, 1990). In this volume, see Michael Kugler, "Enlightenment History, Objectivity, and the Moral Imagination," which I read (against the grain) as a "postmodern" reclaiming of Enlightenment-era humanism.

50. On public history, see James B. Gardner and Peter S. LaPaglia, eds., *Public History: Essays from the Field*, rev. ed. (Melbourne, Fla.: Krieger Publishing, 2004). For examples in practice, see *The Public Historian* 26:1 (2004), a special issue on environmental history. For my take on integrating Christian faith and history, see William Katerberg, "Is There Such a Thing as 'Christian' History?" *Fides et Historia* 34:1 (2002): 57–66.

Chapter Six

ENLIGHTENMENT HISTORY, OBJECTIVITY, AND THE MORAL IMAGINATION

MICHAEL KUGLER

*The search for objective knowledge, because of its commitment
to a realist picture, is inescapably subject to skepticism and cannot
refute it but must proceed under its shadow. Skepticism, in turn,
is a problem only because of the realist claims of objectivity.*
— Thomas Nagel, *The View from Nowhere*

WELL INTO EUROPE'S SEVENTEENTH CENTURY, THE CLASSICAL
tradition of reading history was bent towards forming a masculine civic
personality. Political, ecclesiastical, and military narratives, mostly, they
offered moral models of tested authenticity. Historians (with the possible exception of Machiavelli) typically exhorted young male readers
to become virtuous Christian citizens. This development of the civic
personality was the exchange of one character—selfish, slothful, greedy,
lustful—for one identified by the impress of duty, moral rectitude, and
spiritual righteousness.

According to Mark Salber Phillips, fiction challenged history with a
new model. Poetry, the stage, and the novel encouraged reading towards

shaping an inner life that competed with reading for instruction in public action.[1] The invocation of sympathy and sentiment suggests how
characteristics previously considered feminine, different from the civic
masculinity of the classical tradition, begin to invade Enlightenment
historical writing.

The reader's enthusiasm for assuming the identity of both the historical and fictional character was renewed by the Protestant emphasis
on conversion, especially since intense individual spiritual scrutiny increasingly came through the reading of conversion narratives. In the
Christian faith the person is fragile, a redeemed sinner in a fallen world.
For Protestants, a soul was reborn in conversion, an event that had to be
narrated. Maintaining one's love and dedication to God, turning every
thought and desire over to Him in obedience, was difficult. The classical
tradition likewise described a fragile person, the citizen struggling to
retain his civic zeal in the face of his republic's political and territorial
successes. In Britain it is possible to follow these two accounts of spiritual and cultural fragility from Bunyan to Defoe to Boswell.

In the seventeenth and eighteenth centuries, European Christians
also had the opportunity to shape their souls through spiritual techniques, techniques increasingly formed under the new empirical epis-
temologies and psychologies.[2] But there was danger in changing one's
moral character. Assuming a new identity meant exchanging a God-
given specific identity and moral and spiritual responsibility for frivolous mask-wearing. The Protestant fear of the stage took on a revived
form in eighteenth-century Britain in the context of the striking effect
of sensory experience discussed by empirical epistemology, and further
worked out by the growing concern over sentiments—concern about
proper education of youth, increasingly female, in a literate, middling
class consumer culture. The public exercise and exhibition of emotion
provoked by plays paralleled similar private experiences of reading.[3]

One of the most striking defenses of the re-creation of historical
sentiment emerged from the Scottish Enlightenment. The influential
Edinburgh jurist and writer, Henry Home (Lord Kames), suggested just
how willing the reader must be to abandon his or her true personality in
order to assume one found in history texts. In his *Elements of Criticism*
(1762) Kames wrote, "The reader's passions are never sensibly moved,

till he be thrown into a kind of reverie; in which state, losing the consciousness of self, and of reading, his present occupation, he conceives every incident as passing in his presence, precisely as if he were an eyewitness."[4] Kames echoed a claim made some years earlier by his friend and relative, David Hume: the present should dissolve within this engagement with a literary past right before the eye of the imagination.[5] Even self-consciousness momentarily vanishes. If moving the passions is the goal, only such a powerful reader-response will do so.

Kames asserted that this was the writer's great and central desire. Nothing should, as Phillips put it, interfere with "the illusion of actuality," techniques eighteenth-century British historians borrowed from the novel, poetry, and the stage.[6] They earnestly wanted to give the reader the air of immediacy and identification with the past actor's interiority. Documents, letters, eyewitness accounts certainly allowed historians like William Robertson and Edward Gibbon to render their claims unimpeachable. To increase this air of actuality they depended upon documents *and* upon accurately portrayed universal human capacities to passion and sentiment, "illusions" yielding the most accurate type of history possible. They might also be the most illustrative of the human capacities to virtue and vice that make moral instruction, true didactic history, possible.[7]

In this light, long-standing attacks on the Enlightenment's supposed arid and abstract "rationalism" just don't persuade.[8] Scholars have made a substantial recovery of Enlightenment fascination with human passions and, in particular, sentiments.[9] Phillips has shown how British Enlightenment historians were also intensely interested in the evocation of the reader's emotions. What has often been credited to Romantic historicism—the compelling claim that historians are primarily responsible to evoke the past through re-creation of character and place, and by encouraging a sympathetic bond between reader and character—was actually a hallmark of the best of Enlightenment British writing. While William Robertson and Edward Gibbon excelled Hume in their commitment to research and careful citation, they made no more claims to neutral objectivity than he.

An exposition like that of Phillips should encourage a fresh reading of the Enlightenment in general. History as ethical reflection was critical to the Enlightenment's "science of human nature." Enlightenment historians, I'll suggest, refused to be objective if that meant the attempt to describe the past without convictions. Rather, they claimed moderation, a coolness of conviction. They maintained it during a committed account of the past conforming not to political or religious party, but a reasoned assessment of the evidence. They could be biased but not in a manner that handicapped their arguments. They were not neutral in a sense with which objectivity is often confused. In our own age, historians as different as Thomas Haskell and David Harlan have asked why we should even try to remain morally neutral storytellers about the past.[10] Committed to high standards of evidence and argument, Hume for instance was eager to encourage public political and religious debates. He wanted to counter older historiographic charges with new and, in his mind, better ones that offered the public a needed balance of accounts about, for instance, England's history. But he was not simply a skeptic. Hume was convinced like other Scottish historians that the historical discipline was part of a broader moral philosophical enterprise, responsible to encourage reflection on virtue and duty among active citizens.[11]

Yet a strong distrust of Enlightenment history endures. Recent postmodern and self-proclaimed Christian accounts of the Enlightenment attack its corrosive skepticism and arrogant claims to foundationalist objectivism.[12] The recent responses seem rooted in or inspired by Max Horkheimer and Theodor Adorno's *Dialectic of the Enlightenment*, distinguished for laying the catastrophes of Western war and genocide at the feet of instrumental, universalist Enlightened reason.[13] Postmodern reactions against the Enlightenment followed up on the seminal *Dialectic*. Michel Foucault attacked the notion of the Enlightenment as a "classical age" in two influential books exposing enlightened reform as rigid rational classification of deviation, resulting in a gentler but more successful type of coercion and control.[14] Following these trails some historians and historically minded political theorists now call for a total revision of the field of history in general by pulling down the Enlightenment legacy.[15] The long-standing Christian antipathy to the Enlightenment legacy and its alleged adherence to foundationalism has recently been buoyed by postmodernism's apparent success.[16]

One definition of narrative includes locating the reflective self in stories of a particular time and place.[17] Enlightenment historians used historical narratives to place themselves and readers in a world of deteriorating intellectual respect for religion. I shall discuss three historians of Protestant background, from Protestant countries (England and Scotland), who expressed disappointment, suspicion, and even hostility towards those religious communities. I'll quickly give examples from their narratives of human religiosity. Using Haskell's distinction between objectivity and neutrality I'll discuss their versions of it. I'll evaluate their accounts in relation to attacks on Enlightenment claims to objectivity, and in light of Christian responses to Enlightenment antireligious bias. Finally, I'll reflect upon the aid anti-religious stories give Christian historians, while trying to emulate the humility prompted by the Gospel narratives.

MORAL IMAGINATION IN THREE ENLIGHTENMENT HISTORIANS

Hume published the first volumes of the *History of England*, narrating the Stuart period, in 1756. Among the controversies he created was his portrayal of the Protestant faith. He already had a well established reputation for religious skepticism from his *Treatise of Human Nature* (1739), the *Enquiry Concerning Human Understanding* (1748), and the *Enquiry Concerning the Principles of Morals* (1751), as well as some of his essays.[18] Hume's apparent complacency over his reputation as a religious skeptic, but even more the power of his skeptical arguments, would eventually prompt close friends like Hugh Blair and Adam Ferguson to seek a "Christian Hume": someone who was Hume's intellectual equal and who could publicly defend the Christian faith.[19] Others like the Reverend Robert Wallace defended Hume's right to voice respectful public skepticism, for not only did liberty protect him and compassion require gentleness, but he provoked Christians to consider their faith propositions and to offer stronger, more compelling ones.[20]

I'll concentrate on a small sample of Hume's historically minded religious skepticism. He was convinced that human affairs are often best characterized as ironic.[21] This was born of his doubts that philosophers could provide precisely rational explanations of human action and equally certain rational accounts of morality. Hume accounted for human affairs under the rubric of the "unintended consequences" of human actions, a sensibility found throughout Scottish social and historical writing.[22] Human affairs were too complex, and human understanding too clouded by passion and ignorance, to warrant more than a moderate confidence in explaining human action. At best even an approximate comprehension of our personal motivation is possible. The wise "anatomist" of human nature, which in Hume's case quite easily becomes an historian, must be on the watch for explanations of human culture that at first seem unlikely. Hume, as Donald Livingston argues, developed a philosophical method from which he concluded that all accounts of morals should be understood and communicated as stories.[23] Recognition of the unintended outcomes of even the most careful and well-planned human action should encourage civic and moral humility.

Moral philosophy requires narration, and the most entertaining and instructive were narrations of the past. History as a discipline and England's history in particular encouraged especially serious moral reflection.[24] One of Hume's most interesting morally charged themes is the irony of cultural progress achieved in large part thanks to the opponents of enlightenment. The best example is his portrayal in *The History of England* of the Puritan's responsibility for the establishment of English civil liberty. Hume was motivated to write the *History* partly as an exercise in historical rhetoric ("style" as he put it), but in large part to answer the Whig and Tory apologists in their battle over the ancient constitution, hoping to offer a third way.[25] The Stuarts were not to blame for the seventeenth-century disputes between monarchy and parliament. "[Though] it is pretended that these doctrines [of absolute monarchy] were more openly inculcated and more strenuously insisted upon during the reign of the Stuarts, they were not then invented; and were only found by the court to be more necessary at that period, by reason of the opposite doctrines which *began* to be promulgated by the puritanical party."[26] Laying the roots of absolute monarchy at the feet of the heroic Protestant Queen Elizabeth, Hume's next surprising move was to suggest that the first "faint dawn of the spirit of liberty among the English" came in 1571, in Parliament's reaction against her authoritarian rule. From what more surprising source could that spirit have sprung than the Puritans? In earlier works Hume had attacked religious fanaticism and the clergy who encouraged it.[27] He complained again in the *History* of the pathetic and exaggerated piety of the Puritans, but in that particular age they provoked a consequence quite unlike their motivations. Their fanatical piety and courage, their immovable confidence in their religious convictions, drove them into an inevitable clash with the hard-liner Elizabeth. In an age, Hume suggested, when MPs had to be bribed to take seats, Puritan zealots sought places with conviction, eventually winning a majority and thereafter ascendance over church and state.[28] "So absolute, indeed, was the authority of the crown that the precious spark of liberty had been kindled, and was preserved, by the Puritans alone; and it was to this sect, whose principles appear so frivolous and habits so ridiculous, that the English owe the whole freedom of their constitution."[29] For the sake of rhetorical effect Hume perhaps knowingly exaggerated the power of that single sectarian cause to generate the "whole" of modern English liberty. But the double irony remains: the most narrow and bigoted of English sects provoked the events that gave the English their modern liberty; the Puritan vision of a narrow, godly commonwealth laid the foundation for the relatively broad religious liberty the British enjoyed in Hume's age.

Hume's ironic account of the historic evolution of religion had begun long before the *History*, in 1748–52, while writing *The Natural History of Religion*. Published after the first volume of the *History of England* in 1757, Hume suggested how a fanatical zeal could oddly enough provoke a beneficial cultural conviction like civic liberty. He then bore down upon theism itself. From his survey of classical sources, he argued that an abstract, rationalist theism evolved out of a superstitious but essentially harmless pantheism. The more strict, rationalist, and systematic the theism, the more absurd its attempts to explain the ways of such a God to humankind. Though often silly, the pantheist's accounts of evil and human suffering were less intellectually and morally offensive, Hume suggested, than those ascribed to a single all-powerful, all-knowing, and merciful God. Theists would find such claims remarkable, for they were the end product of thousands of years of philosophical speculation that had rendered theism respectable. Theists assumed the superiority of their faith to polytheism.[30] Echoing a jibe at least as old as the ancient Greeks, Hume charged religion with originating in fear and ignorance. Theism, and especially theistic attempts at philosophically sophisticated speculation called theology, were more than polytheism the product of fear. Abstract, complex theological speculation did not originate in calm, moderate reflection, but was generated by ignorance, terror, and the human rage for organizing experience into systems. The more rational a religious belief, the more absurd it became. Realizing the tenuous hold of conviction upon such propositions, the theist holds all the more tenaciously to them.[31]

Hume's account of religion and liberty suggested that as long as religious bigotry was balanced against another authoritarian force, like Puritanism against Elizabeth, the struggle over time could yield surprising benefits. But that happy circumstance rarely occurred. Religious bigotry usually opposed liberty; Hume concluded that civilization and the liberty necessary to it was a fragile human blessing. Scotland's enlightenment, he and his contemporaries agreed, had only emerged when narrow Presbyterian zealotry had exhausted its fury in the civil wars, and closer cultural and economic exchange with England expanded the cultural horizons of literate Scots.[32] Throughout his *History of England* Hume avidly sought to entertain readers—to provoke wonder, surprise, intellectual challenge and enjoyment, as well as sympathy for the dead. He had "shed a generous tear for Strafford and Charles I" and hoped to provoke one in his reader.[33]

Hume's attempt at a moderate but affective narrative critical of religious zeal became a provocative benchmark for other historians. Edward Gibbon, considering models for his projected history of the Roman Empire, turned to the *History of England* and *The Natural History of Religion*.[34] Like Hume, Gibbon committed himself to writing history as instructive and entertaining narrative, deeply influenced by reflection on fictional art forms.[35] The infamous chapters 15 and 16 of *The History of the Decline and Fall of the Roman Empire* paralleled Hume's earlier attacks. Hume had targeted in particular Puritan moral rigidity. Gibbon agreed, turning on Christianity in its purest original form. This religion had been so unworldly that to their pagan communities its converts seemed less than fully human, as seen in their devotion to martyrdom.[36] Purity and zeal were themselves intense passions; the early Christians could live up to them for only so long. Despite more elites converting to the Christian faith, the otherworldly teachings of the Christian message were still at odds with the pagan civic culture built upon traditional Roman duties. Gibbon distrusted passionate zeal in all its forms, pagan or Christian. Contrasted to the primitive civil zeal of the early Republic, from Domitian's death to the ascension of Commodus even corrupted Roman ambition produced the "most happy and prosperous" age of human history.[37] Over time Christians systematized their otherworldy beliefs by way of ancient philosophizing—the origins of Christian theology. Those abstract and often (to pagan eyes) nitpicking theological speculations diverted even more energy and resources that could have revitalized the deteriorating imperial administration.[38] For centuries Christians had made poor citizens, whose faith prevented any deep involvement in civic affairs.

Gibbon pressed his polite Christian reader with two ironies from the early history of the church. First, the whole of chapter 15 turns on Gibbon's humble assertion that he will merely treat the secondary evidentiary causes of the growth and development of the Christian church. The primary cause of that growth, "the convincing evidence of the [Christian] doctrine itself, and . . . the ruling providence of its great Author," are outside historical investigation.[39] Then, the early Christians earn a backhanded compliment for their innocent, zealous moral and spiritual purity. A religion holding wealth, prestige, and civil welfare in such contempt (a "criminal" disregard, sniffed Gibbon) would hardly have appealed to a readership among educated, comfortable, and polite Anglicans.[40] But as is typical of the master ironist, Gibbon's praise has its price. Since God must accomplish his ends through human passion and circumstance, only secondary causes can be tested by evidence and argument. Echoing Hume's conclusion to the essay "On Miracles," Gibbon implies that any assertion of the truth of Christianity has no empirical or rational status. Those who believe such claims with zealous certainty are unlikely models of rationality or moderation.

Gibbon summarized the spirit of such claims in his "General Observations on the Fall of the Roman Empire in the West," which follows his account of their final defeat by the barbarians.[41] He is able there to refer back to the earlier chapters, explaining the barbarians' role in Rome's deterioration and fall. In a manner similar to Hume's account of the Puritan role in securing English civil liberty, Gibbon suggests that Constantine's conversion, thereafter protecting and aiding the church, sacralized Christian service to the state. The influence of unworldly Christians throughout the empire would continue to eat away at Roman patriotism and duty, eventually weakening the fabric of the state. The new-found patriotism Christians could offer the empire temporarily revitalized its civic health. Rome's deterioration was too far gone to be halted, but the redirection of Christian energies in service to the Empire delayed its final collapse. Gibbon therefore offered a complex causal account of the role Christianity played in Rome's fall. This in turn prompted him to take up the fragility of civilization, and reflection upon modern Europe's future.

Like Hume, Gibbon evoked a rhetorical coolness.[42] Like Hume he had little patience with theological speculation. Mary Wollstonecraft was also sensitive to the freedom of religious conscience. Her metaphysics of the unified and eternal soul, her published promotion of proper masculinity (opposition to drinking, gambling, and so forth), her call for male-female relations to be fully equal partnerships—all were rooted in her nonconformist Protestant background.[43] She cast part of her feminism from that background, and also from the religious individualism borne of Protestant introspection, which, in turn, was further shaped and fed by the novel. As a feminist she was very sensitive to uses of religion to hinder the participation of women in the public square, to keep them soft, slender creatures complementary to active men, and therefore unfit for anything but sexual attraction, marriage, and child rearing.[44] During the French Revolution she was conscious of religion's role in hindering the advance of civic liberty. In her 1794 *An Historical and Moral View of the French Revolution*, she coupled "superstition" with aristocratic oppression as the two ancient forces arrayed against liberty and progress. She praised Voltaire and Rousseau for their attacks on "a priest-ridden society."[45] Wollstonecraft claimed that sentiment was the force behind this change in the development of ideas of civil liberty. The French suffered under despotism; they pined for liberty. An "empire of tyranny" can perhaps be overturned only by "a revolution in opinion"; the philosophes used entertaining rhetoric and compelling argument to expound the suffering and humiliation of French subjects under the Ancien Regime.[46] Wollstonecraft, like Gibbon and Hume, appealed to the reader's heart from empirical conviction about the operation of the sentiments. In her account, the revolution was possible because the heart's longings and misery drove the imagination to create workable political solutions.

Wollstonecraft's psychology in her earlier *Vindication of the Rights of Women* (1792) bridged the stereotypical gap between Enlightenment and Romantic accounts of the personality. She claimed there that the capacity for sensibility was indistinguishable from the self, and that the source of sympathy and benevolence, the "heart," could be trained to care more immediately and deeply.[47] While she was convinced that reason must impose its mastery over the passions, they should cooperate: "the passions unfold reason."[48] Reason is of itself constrained until engaged by the active passions. Constant and cool, reason should guide the passions. The heart however directs reason towards its proper objects of affection. Her history of the revolution depicts a role for the imagination and sentiments in historical writing and reading recalling Kames. The imagination contemplates recollected sensations, provoking natural sentiments. The imagination generates these shapes or "characters," which emerge as "reveries"—the same word used thirty years earlier by Kames.[49] Suffering drives the understanding to find solutions; the tyrannical French monarchy, aristocracy, and church imposed such suffering on the citizenry that their conception of civic liberty was as much an object of passionate desire as it was a political program.

Wollstonecraft narrated a developing French love of liberty and search for reform in a manner very similar to her own story of oppression by men and her search for gender equality. This is most apparent in the epistolary account of her 1795 tour of Scandinavia. She wrote of traveling in a very old region still dominated by "feudal" oppression and ignorance, but also a country marked by a very old and relatively unimproved wilderness. Wollstonecraft deeply sympathized with that region and its people, suggesting that the world still required reforms progressing in Britain and in France before the Terror.[50]

By 1794 Wollstonecraft's estrangement from her lover, Gilbert Imlay, and travel as a single mother intensified her frustration over the apparent failure of the revolution. The radicals' betrayal of French democracy exposed the tenacity of despotism in Scandinavia, the tyranny of men over women, and her imprisonment in a failed relationship. Wollstonecraft narrates her pilgrimage to self-consciousness; narrating liberty carries the writer and reader through the path to enlightenment. The heart is prompted to express itself by experience, and over time acquires memory, trains the sentiments, and provokes reason to profundity and clarity.[51] Scandinavia's agedness prompted moral reflection—the tombs of dead kings, ancient rocky seascapes, the unchanged brutality of men over their wives. She feared personal annihilation after death; she scorned the church's power over an ignorant, oppressed populace.[52] Only the cultivated mind could generate and populate a stimulated imagination; therefore careful historical reflection was necessary to the well-informed and formed imagination.[53]

Wollstonecraft's interior history became almost inseparable from her account of the French Revolution and the progress of revolution across Europe.[54] Her life's tensions and interior struggles mirrored those she saw in Europe. She oscillated from confidence to pessimism about her personal happiness, symptoms paralleled in her portrait of revolutionary Europe. The French Revolution first provoked optimism, and later autobiographical accounts of betrayal and dismay.

The work is filled with affective scenes of identification with the dead or oppressed, of place and idea useful in moral reflection, often of somber kind. She believed that the original noble ideals of the revolution had been betrayed, reaching some conclusions not unlike those of her great opponent Edmund Burke. Still she sought a middle ground of gradual, active political reform that was not simply the creature of a political culture's natural evolution (as Burke argued) out of its religious and aristocratic traditions.[55]

What then did these historians share? They narrated pasts partly as stories of their own place in a religious world they found corrupt, bigoted, and hypocritically intertwined with state authority. If narrative suggests a community, in these cases their stories implied an enlightened "Republic of Letters," an alternative community (or even "civil society") to the church.[56] They cast their subjects in ironic Enlightenment historical narratives. They borrowed this turn from Greeks and Romans (Thucydides, Tacitus) who also suggested that civilization was frail. Liberty was a precious cultural commodity and historically in short supply, none of which seems the typical stereotype of Enlightenment rationalist optimism. Hume purposefully wounded English pride in their Constitution. Though they might enjoy an unrivaled civic liberty, the English could take little or no direct credit for its creation. Gibbon's history is often melancholic, with the shadow of Rome's future fall shrouding decision and event. For Wollstonecraft, gender relations had driven women with no political power to exploit sexual attraction to their advantage. Males who enjoyed civic authority ironically were ruled by their wives, fulfilling the ancient claim that slavery corrupts the master as well. She seemed at times in her history of the revolution to make a similar claim about the French. Ancien Regime exploitation had provoked the third estate into an extreme passion for liberty, expressed in democratic excess and violence. All, especially Wollstonecraft, used affecting scenes, prompts of melancholy, and the enjoyment of surprise at ironic turns that not only entertained readers but provided them moral instruction within reflection. The historian wove scenes of suffering into his or her narrative so that the reader had regular opportunities to exercise his or her sentiments. In so doing the moral imagination was enlivened and trained. Such readers might possibly also become better citizens, prodded into civic action by the sight of needy fellow citizens.

From Narrative History to Hope

I've intended this account partly to challenge simplistic attacks against Enlightenment arrogance, universalist assumptions, and the tendency of modernity to build programs of management and control based on those assumptions.[57] Philosophe arrogance and moralism, as unattractive and unwarranted as it is, did not lead to modernist authoritarianism.

The historians I have discussed wrote partly to create "reality effects" for their readers. Their portraits of the past would move, surprise, and provoke, even at times outrage their readers. In this form history starts to look a bit more like fiction. Fiction mimics our experience or our convictions about what experience should mean. Satire, comedy, tragedy, and irony may yet convey a true moral claim about human life. Fiction's entertaining power can certainly come in part from its ability to allow us an escape from our experience or convictions (to inhabit someone else's choices, outcomes, especially if quite different from our own—a subversive or less ordinary life), as much as from its mimetic quality. But artists of fiction seeking true stories are as constrained by integrity about source and authentic recounting as the historian. They and their readers debate the actions of a character consistent with the story's established boundaries, serving a function very similar to historical context. They seek "reality effects" as much as the historian; but they do so differently and self-consciously as participants in a different genre of literature. Historians generally share the conviction they must faithfully represent sources of information outside their own imagination, and in turn demand accountability for that from one another. The historians I've discussed crafted "affecting" portraits of the dead because they sought to enlarge the sympathies, to train the sentiments, of their readers—a critical element in moral instruction.[58] In the eighteenth century, fiction and history appeared to be subgroups of moral philosophy broadly conceived. In those cases it was no insult or epistemological concession for history to admit a cousinship with fiction.[59]

Claiming that history uses "reality effects" partly for purposes of making moral claims upon the reader is to concede two important charges of postmodernist critics of "normal" history.[60] But attempts to divide history from fiction according to commitments to "truth," "facts," and so on, probably fail to sort out the issue of narrative. As I suggested above, fiction is often as committed to the truth as history. The strong reactions against such claims by Richard Evans and others have only encouraged further attacks on modern history's foundationalist assumptions.[61] But just because history and fiction share storytelling, are they indistinguishable? A historical character is the author of her actions within the story in a way that isn't possible for a fictional figure inside his own.[62] As Allan Megill has suggested, the "literary" quality (non-neutral verbal craft associated with "literature") of historical writing can be distinguished from a "fictive" quality (explanatory organization, such as causal accounts and typologization, which offer a cleaner portrait of a messier real world). The "deep ontological point" here is that "the historical object itself is a 'fictive' creation, something constituted *as object* by the mind of the historian and his or her readers. Yet this is not to assert that 'there is no *there* there'; it *is* to assert that the historian makes the particular historical objects presented in his or her work."[63] Realism and accuracy may equally impinge on the fiction writer and the historian, but the measure of historical accuracy remains the possibility of a third-party evaluation of that accuracy, by reference to evidence not invented by any of the historians involved in the discussion of what happened "way back when." Analytical research methods for reaching a defensible, moderate objectivity are necessary to help us figure out what happened in "the way back when" and to help us give the past a proper context—in other words, to establish the past's meaning.[64] Historians with such different points of view as Harlan, Haskell, and Robert Berkhofer Jr., still agree that history deserves its full due as a narrative art, while demanding of one another adherence to those very methods that together make up the virtue of scholarly integrity. If so, it seems possible to accept history's status as a member of the moral philosophical arts, while still arguing with one another over evidence and distorting bias.

For some time Alasdair MacIntyre has argued that only in narratives associated with "communities of discourse" (the phrase belongs to Robert Wuthnow) could compelling moral accounts be offered. Such communities share intellectual, educational, and religious traditions and convictions.[65] The Christian tradition offers such a community of discourse; it also draws from narratives of interiority. Portraits of the inner states of historical actors prompt moral reflection and also, hopefully, conversation both inside and outside the academy. How might this emphasis on writing from within a community of discourse be encouraged and challenged by the narrative and didactic character of the Christian Gospels? Harlan has suggested putting one's moral "take" up front to make it explicit in historical narratives.[66] From a different side, recent discussions of the Gospels as historical narratives offer models for how Christians might follow such a suggestion. William Placher argues that the Gospels model a form of narrative where story-telling is dialogic and relational, implying that such a dialogue requires making one's point of view sharp enough to provoke a reply.[67] On the subject of the Resurrection, Rowan Williams asserts that the Gospels themselves avoid a "master narrative," other than asserting that it took place; diversity of account and viewpoint suggests that God tolerates if not encourages continuing dialogue when we cannot decide with certainty "what happened." Humans cannot master through critical research or imagination even the central event of Christian history.[68] Modeled on the dialectical, unmasterable Gospel stories, we can conceive a historical narrative that is reasonably objective and faithful to a Christian tradition. Yet the unmasterable nature of the *most* important story in our lives is humbling; if we can tell but not master *this* story, we don't have to be discouraged if we cannot master the other stories we struggle to tell well. Telling a story where our faith and calling meet, a story that finally evades our grasp, can be frustratingly, beneficially, humbling.

In turn humility should encourage us to make careful, measured theological claims, and from such claims to reason carefully about the world. I would contend that Jesus's attacks on organized religion and ritual can press us to consider the human tendency to turn worship and theology into mastery of talk about God and of ourselves. There, we are no longer creatures dependent upon a loving God but managers of religious experience and religious morality. I fear that as a consequence we are confident enough to turn this managerial training upon the world at large.

The Enlightenment historians help us reflect upon religious mastery. Their attacks on religion and religious accounts of human experience formed part of a broader perspective on the development of civilization, often critical to an account of "progress." The advance of liberty of inquiry and speech, the search for and publication of dependable knowledge about nature, the shift away from Ancien Regime authorities and towards the accountability of all political power to public opinion or civil society, depended upon stripping religion of its political and judicial authority.[69] However, "progress" as a description and goal varied significantly from writer to writer. Baron D'Holbach's slash-and-burn tactics against religion found few supporters among contemporaries, including such a self-conscious pagan as Hume. Whereas a younger Voltaire was willing to tolerate religion for its role (properly limited in authority, of course) in meliorating the violent passions of the masses, a Scot like Hugh Blair argued that "Christ's religion was one of refined feeling, not dogma," and "Christianity was essentially a religion of feeling."[70] If we follow the Enlightenment movement state by state, we'll find more organizations and communities of writers led by clerics and active churchmen and women than not.[71]

We would still read these historians critically; we certainly don't have to follow their exaggerations or swallow their stereotypes of religious life, positive or negative. But I think they can give us a hand in a world where fundamentalism and fanaticism not only appear in the forms of intolerant and uncompromised terror, but in democracies shaping the public conversation of political life into Manichean accounts of civic difference. Nuanced, full accounts of public affairs, let alone one's opponents in debate, are tossed aside because they don't encourage the rallying of a united party. Religion is a useful ally to political ideology, for it has long defended tradition and what qualifies as "the natural"—sexuality, the physical world, human institutions, whatever we group under the God-created state of affairs that we recognize and understand. Too much is at stake, we're told; it's us or them. And they can't be trusted. Surely, as Thucydides wrote, cool discussion of complex issues is taken as lack of courage; intolerant arrogance becomes the only acceptable mark of courage and conviction (*The History of the Peloponnesian War*, 3:82, 2-4). Truly, the best are full of doubt and the worst have a furious certainty. We intellectuals, like the Enlightenment historians, are skilled at ironic observation. Irony, one of the great literary motifs of the Enlightenment historians, also encourages humility when applied to religious subjects. Yet irony isn't enough.[72] Even outrage isn't enough, and when I talk with students about fascism, terrorism, or genocide, when I talk with students about the checkered history of our own faith, I struggle to find words beyond irony and outrage. Toward telling hopeful stories, perhaps? It's time to begin self-consciously constructing a reasonable account of trust and hope that extends from the Christian gospel and through to our historiographic methods and stories.[73] Provoked by the love of Jesus and born in a hopeful story of redemption and the coming kingdom, yet informed of religion's oft-played supporting role in authoritarianism and violence, telling stories that expose our convictions, but skeptical enough to be on the watch, I would like to find a way to redeem some Enlightenment historical sensibility, and still move beyond it.

Notes

1. Mark Salber Phillips, *Society and Sentiment: Genres of Historical Writing in Britain, 1740–1820* (Princeton: Princeton University Press, 2000).

2. See Michel Foucault in, especially, "Technologies of the Self" and "The Political Technology of Individuals," in *Technologies of the Self: A Seminar with Michel Foucault*, ed. Luther H. Martin, Huck Gutman, and Patrick H. Hutton, 16–49 and 145–62 (Amherst: University of Massachusetts Press, 1988); and *The History of Sexuality*, vol. 2, *The Use of Pleasure*, and vol. 3, *The Care of the Self*, trans. Robert Hurley (New York: Vintage Books, 1985 and 1986). See also my article, "The Cross, the Powers, and Enlightenment Techniques of the Self," *Fides et Historia* 36:1 (2004): 15–29.

3. The reformers of male manners thought this inner transformation appropriate and necessary. See G. J. Barker-Benfield, *The Culture of Sensibility: Sex and Society in Eighteenth-Century Britain* (Chicago: University of Chicago Press, 1992).

4. Henry Home, *Elements of Criticism*, ed. Peter Jones, 2 vols. (Indianapolis: Liberty Fund, 2005; orig. pub. London: A. Miller, and Edinburgh: A. Kincaid & J. Bell, 1762), 1:69.

5. David Hume, "Of the Study of History" (1741), in *Essays Moral, Political, and Literary*, ed. Eugene F. Miller (Indianapolis: Liberty Classics, 1985), 565–66.

6. Phillips, *Society and Sentiment*, 109. For Roland Barthes' important discussion of a similar theme, see "The Reality Effect," in *French Literary Theory Today*, ed. Tzvetan Todorov, trans. R. Carter, 11–17 (Cambridge: Cambridge University Press, 1982), and "The Discourse of History," trans. Stephan Bann, in *Comparative Criticism: A Yearbook*, ed. E. S. Shaffer, 3–20 (Cambridge: Cambridge University Press, 1981).

7. In this way Adam Smith and others argued that the most sentimental, most accurate, and therefore the most instructive historians were the ancients, particularly Tacitus; Phillips, *Society and Sentiment*, 82–87.

8. In his 1926 classic *The Art of History*, J. B. Black suggested that, based on an infamous passage from Hume's *Enquiry Concerning Human Understanding*, the Scot considered human nature simply a repeating decimal in the historian's calculations of the past's dimensions; *The Art of History: A Study of Four Great Historians of the Eighteenth Century* (New York: F. S. Crofts, 1965), 95–98. For the distinction between Enlightenment and historicist perspectives, see Hayden White, *Metahistory: The Historical Imagination in Nineteenth-Century Europe* (Baltimore: Johns Hopkins University Press, 1979), 70–80.

9. This took forms as different as Voltaire's love of a natural world that could provoke powerful emotion, the Edinburgh elite's championing of the pathetic heroic sentiments of Macpherson's Ossian, or even Helvetius's mechanistic accounts of humans as primarily passionate creatures. The best work, like Ernst Cassirer's *The Philosophy of the Enlightenment* (Boston: Beacon Press, 1955), never bought into this exaggeration. Among the recent discussions is R. S. Ridgway, *Voltaire and Sensibility* (Montreal: McGill-Queen's University Press, 1973), and *Ossian Revisited*, ed. Howard Gaskell (Edinburgh: Edinburgh University Press, 1991). Karen O'Brien has discussed how the great Enlightenment historians carefully wielded literary craftsmanship to create the *story* of the Republic of Letters in her *Narratives of Enlightenment: Cosmopolitan History from Voltaire to Gibbon* (Cambridge: Cambridge University Press, 1997).

10. Thomas Haskell, "Objectivity is Not Neutrality: Rhetoric versus Practice in Peter Novick's *That Noble Dream*," *History and Theory* 29 (1990): 129–57; David Harlan, *The Degradation of American History* (Chicago: University of Chicago Press, 1997).

11. David Allan, *Virtue, Learning and the Scottish Enlightenment: Ideas of Scholarship in Early Modern History* (Edinburgh: Edinburgh University Press, 1993), chaps. 3 and 4.

12. Of course the attack on Enlightenment rationality had precedent in the eighteenth century itself. On the counter-Enlightenment, see Isaiah Berlin, "The Counter-Enlightenment" and "Herder and the Enlightenment," in *The Proper Study of Mankind: An Anthology of Essays*, ed. Henry Hardy and Roger Hausheer (New York: Farrar, Straus and Giroux, 1998), and "Joseph de Maistre and the Origins of Fascism," in *The Crooked Timber of Humanity*, ed. Henry Hardy (London: John Murray, 1990); and Darrin M. McMahon, *Enemies of the Enlightenment: The French Counter-Enlightenment and the Making of Modernity* (Oxford: Oxford University Press, 2001).

13. Max Horkheimer and Theodor Adorno, *Dialectic of Enlightenment: Philosophical Fragments*, ed. Gunzelin Schmid Noerr, trans. Edmund Jephcott (Stanford: Stanford University Press, 2002).

14. Michel Foucault, *Madness and Civilization: A History of Insanity in the Age of Reason*, trans. Richard Howard (New York: Vintage Books, 1973), and

Discipline and Punish: The Birth of the Prison, trans. Alan Sheridan (New York: Vintage Books, 1979).

15. Keith Jenkins, *Why History? Ethics and Postmodernity* (New York: Routledge, 1999); John Gray, *Enlightenment's Wake: Politics and Culture at the Close of the Modern Age* (New York: Routledge, 1995). Overviews of this subject are everywhere, but I've been helped by two: Robert F. Berkhofer Jr., *Beyond the Great Story: History as Text and Discourse* (Cambridge, Mass.: Belknap Press, 1997); and Madan Sarup, *An Introductory Guide to Post-Structuralism and Post-modernism*, 2nd ed. (Athens: University of Georgia Press, 1993).

16. Three recent collections of essays take up the subject and form a use-ful introduction: Norman Geras and Robert Wokler, eds., *The Enlightenment and Modernity* (New York: St. Martin's Press, 2000); Keith Michael Baker and Peter Hans Reill, eds., *What's Left of Enlightenment? A Postmodern Question* (Stanford: Stanford University Press, 2001); and Daniel Gordon, ed., *Postmodernism and the Enlightenment: New Perspectives on Eighteenth-Century French Intellectual History* (New York: Routledge, 2001). Alasdair MacIntyre's work is foundational for anti-Enlightenment Christian scholars: *After Virtue: A Study in Moral Theory*, 3rd ed. (Notre Dame, Ind.: University of Notre Dame Press, 2007); *Whose Justice? Which Rationality?* (Notre Dame, Ind.: University of Notre Dame Press, 1988). Christian rejoinders to the Enlightenment (usually partnering in some manner with what they take to be postmodernism) can be found in the following: N.T. Wright, *The Challenge of Jesus: Rediscovering Who Jesus Was and Is* (Downers Grove, Ill.: Intervarsity, 1999), 100–101, 193–94; George Marsden, *The Outrageous Idea of Christian Scholarship* (Oxford: Oxford University Press, 1998), 89, 109–11; Leslie Newbigin, *Foolishness to the Greeks: The Gospel and Western Culture* (Grand Rapids, Mich.: Eerdmans, 1986), chap. 2; David K. Naugle, *Worldview: The History of a Concept* (Grand Rapids, Mich.: Eerdmans, 2002), 254, 299–300, 305–6, 312–13, 316, 333; C. Stephen Evans, *The Historical Christ and the Jesus of Faith: The Incarnational Narrative as History* (Oxford: Clarendon Press, 1996); Brian J. Walsh and J. Richard Middleton, *The Transforming Vision: Shaping a Christian World View* (Downers Grove, Ill.: Intervarsity, 1984), chap. 8; Steven Garber, *The Fabric of Faithfulness: Weaving Together Belief and Behavior during the University Years* (Downers Grove, Ill.: Intervarsity, 1996), 50–59, 80, 93; Stanley J. Grenz, *A Primer on Postmodernism* (Grand Rapids, Mich.: Eerdmans, 1996), chaps. 3 and 4. For the Enlighten-ment (and thus wrongheaded) origins of modern biblical scholarship, and the terrible harm it has done for Christian faith, see Luke Timothy Johnson, "The Humanity of Jesus," in *The Jesus Controversy: Perspectives in Conflict*, ed. John Dominic Crossan, Luke Timothy Johnson, and Werner H. Kelber (Harrisburg, Pa.: Trinity Press, 1999).

17. Lewis P. Hinchman and Sandra K Hinchman, "Introduction: Toward a Definition of Narrative," in *Memory, Identity, Community: The Idea of Narrative in the Human Sciences* (Albany: State University of New York Press, 1997), xv.

18. His reputation for religious skepticism had prevented his election to Edinburgh's Chair of Moral Philosophy in 1746. See Ernest Campbell Mossner, *The Life of David Hume*, 2nd ed. (Oxford: Clarendon Press, 1980), chap. 12; Richard Sher, "Professors of Virtue: The Social History of the Edinburgh Moral Philosophy Chair in the Eighteenth Century," in *Studies in the Philosophy of the Scottish Enlightenment*, ed. M. A. Stewart (Oxford: Clarendon Press, 1990).

19. One example: "I am told that Dr Beaty, or his party, give out that he has not only refuted but killed D. Hume. I should be very glad of the first, but sorry for the other"; Adam Ferguson to Adam Smith, September 2, 1773, in *The Correspondence of Adam Ferguson*, ed. Vincenzo Merolle, 2 vols. (Brookfield, Vt.: William Pickering, 1995), 1:97.

20. "The Necessity or Expediency of the Churches Inquiring into the Writings of David Hume Esquire . . ." (1756), written (but unpublished) during the General Assembly proceedings to consider excommunicating Hume. Edinburgh University Library La.II.97[2], especially fols. 19, 50–72. See also his "A Letter from a Moderate Freethinker to David Hume Esquire Concerning the Profession of the Clergy," Edinburgh University Library, La.II.97[1].

21. For Hume as an ironist, see White, *Metahistory*, 54–59; Peter Jones, *Hume's Sentiments: Their Ciceronian and French Context* (Edinburgh: Edinburgh University Press, 1982), and Phillips, *Society and Sentiment*, 65–71.

22. An introduction to this issue and some of the literature is Ronald Hamowy's *The Scottish Enlightenment and the Theory of Spontaneous Order* (Carbondale: Southern Illinois University Press, 1987).

23. David Livingston, *Hume's Philosophy of Common Life* (Chicago: University of Chicago Press, 1985), 218.

24. Of England's late medieval history Hume wrote: "Nor is the spectacle altogether unentertaining and uninstructive, which the history of those times presents to us. The view of human manners, in all their variety of appearances, is both profitable and agreeable; and if the aspect in some periods seems horrid and deformed, we may thence learn to cherish with the greater anxiety that science and civility, which has so close a connexion with virtue and humanity, and which, as it is a sovereign antidote against superstition, is also the most effectual remedy against vice and disorders of every kind"; *The History of England from the Invasion of Julius Caesar to the Revolution in 1688*, 6 vols. (Indianapolis: Liberty Fund, 1983), 2:518–19. Hume wrote his *History* out of chronological order, and the above reflection, which concludes his account of the reign of Richard III, was actually the last he wrote.

25. "I am convinced that the History of England has never yet been written, not only for style, which is notorious to all the world, but also for matter; such is the ignorance and partiality of all our historians"; Hume to James Oswald, in *The Letters of David Hume*, ed. J. Y. T. Grieg, 2 vols. (Oxford: Clarendon Press, 1932), 1:179.

26. Hume, *History of England*, Appendix to James I, 5:127, italics Hume's.

27. See "Of Superstition and Enthusiasm" (1741) and "Of National Characters" (1748), both in Miller, *Essays*, but for the latter see 199–201, note 3.

28. Hume, *The History of England*, 4:65–67. The Puritans were "actuated by that zeal which belongs to innovators, and by the courage which enthusiasm inspires"; 4:146.

29. Ibid., 4:145–46.

30. Hume, *Natural History of Religion*, in *Principal Writings on Religion Including Dialogues Concerning Natural Religion and The Natural History of Religion*, ed. J. C. A. Gaskin (Oxford: Oxford University Press, 1993), chap. 1.

31. Ibid., 153, 166, 172–73.

32. See Alexander Wedderburn's anonymous introduction to the first edition of the *Edinburgh Review* (1755); John Ramsay of Ochtertyre's memoirs, Ochtertyre Manuscripts, National Library of Scotland, ms. 1638, fols. 653–55; ms. 1639, fols. 753–55.

33. On this theme, as well as Hume's moderate language, ironic sensibilities, and moral convictions as an historian, see Leo Braudy, *Narrative Form in History and Fiction: Hume, Fielding, and Gibbon* (Princeton: Princeton University Press, 1970), chap. 3. O'Brien discusses Hume with similar interests; for his sentimental character portraits, see *Narratives of Enlightenment*, 63–70.

34. David Womersley, "Introduction," in Edward Gibbon, *The History of the Decline and Fall of the Roman Empire*, 3 vols. (New York: Penguin, 1995), 1:xxxvii.

35. Braudy, *Narrative Form*, chap. 5; O'Brien, *Narratives of Enlightenment*, chap. 6.

36. Gibbon, *Decline and Fall*, 1:546.

37. Ibid., 1:103. In fact, Gibbon likely found the early Roman Republicans as zealously puritanical, in a pagan civic manner, as the early Christians were spiritually and morally. See his comparison of the two where he asserts that poverty "guards" zealous virtues; 1:478.

38. Ibid., 1:790–95, 823–29; summarized in 2:511; for Gibbon's sense of the tedium of the debate, see 1:766–89, summed up on 785; for its brutality, 1:823–4.

39. Ibid., 1:446–47.

40. Those ancient men Gibbon most admired as intellectual contemporaries—especially Tacitus, Plutarch, Epictetus, and Marcus Aurelius—were

unfortunate enough to remain unconvinced of the truths of primitive Christianity; ibid., 1:482. He then concludes, "the lower we depress the temporal condition of the first Christians, the more reason we shall find to admire their merit and success. It is incumbent on us diligently to remember, that the kingdom of Heaven was promised to the poor in spirit, and that minds afflicted by calamity and the contempt of mankind, cheerfully listen to that divine promise of future happiness; while, on the contrary, the fortunate are satisfied with the possession of this world, and the wise abuse in doubt and dispute their vain superiority of reason and knowledge"; 1:510.

41. Ibid., 3:508–16.

42. But his scorn for Christian obscurantism and outrage at religious injustice are hard to miss. For sharper examples and for Gibbon's clever, harsh attacks on some of his clerical critics, see his 1779 *A Vindication of Some Passages in the Fifteenth and Sixteenth Chapters of the History of the Decline and Fall of the Roman Empire*, in *Decline and Fall*, vol. 3, Appendix 3.

43. Janet Todd, *Mary Wollstonecraft: A Revolutionary Life* (New York: Columbia University Press, 2003), 59–61, 149–50.

44. Mary Wollstonecraft, *Vindication of the Rights of Women*, in Wollstonecraft, *Political Writings*, ed. Janet Todd (Toronto: University of Toronto Press, 1993).

45. Wollstonecraft, *An Historical and Moral View of the French Revolution*, in *Political Writings*, 300–303.

46. "But the irresistible energy of the moral and political sentiments of half a century, at last kindled into a glaze the illuminating rays of truth, which, throwing a new light on the mental powers of man, and giving a fresh spring to his reasoning faculties, completely undermined the strong holds of priest craft and hypocrisy"; ibid., 303–4.

47. Wollstonecraft, *Vindication*, 143.

48. Ibid., 83.

49. Wollstonecraft, *Historical and Moral View*, 311.

50. Wollstonecraft, *A Short Residence in Sweden, Norway, and Denmark*, in Wollstonecraft and William Godwin, *A Short Residence in Sweden and Memoirs of the Author of The Rights of Woman*, ed. Richard Holmes (New York: Penguin, 1987), 131, 150.

51. "We reason deeply, when we forcibly feel"; ibid., 171.

52. Ibid., letters 1 and 7, and pages 112, 118–21, 131.

53. Ibid., 123.

54. She was not alone in this; the same can be said of men as different as Edmund Burke, as well as Adam Ferguson and, later, Thomas Carlyle.

55. Wollstonecraft, *A Short Residence*, Appendix.

56. Hinchman and Hinchman, "Introduction," xxiii. On the Republic of Letters and civil society as alterative community, see Dena Goodman, *The Republic of Letters: A Cultural History of the French Enlightenment* (Ithaca: Cornell University Press, 1994).

57. Historians have recently begun responding to these critiques. Along with the essay collections cited in note 16, see Robert Wokler, "The Enlightenment Project and its Critics," *Poznan Studies in the Philosophy of the Sciences and the Humanities* 58 (1997): 13–30.

58. For a Christian dimension applied to Hume's commitment to enlarging his audience's moral sympathies, see Shirley Mullen, "David Hume and a Christian Perspective on History: Insights from an Unlikely Ally," *Fides et Historia* 35:2 (Summer/Fall, 2003): 55.

59. Phillips, *Society and Sentiment*, 114–28; Braudy, *Narrative Form*. On the larger issue of history as chronologically a subgroup of fiction, see Nancy Partner, "Historicity in an Age of Reality-Fictions," in *A New Philosophy of History*, ed. Frank Ankersmit and Hans Kellner (Chicago: University of Chicago Press, 1995).

60. Berkhofer, *Beyond the Great Story*; Harlan, *Degradation of American History*; Hayden V. White, *The Content of the Form: Narrative Discourse and Historical Representation* (Baltimore: Johns Hopkins University Press, 1987).

61. Richard Evans, *In Defense of History* (New York: W. W. Norton, 1999); Keith Jenkins, *Why History?* chap. 4.

62. MacIntyre, *After Virtue*, chap. 15, but esp. page 215, where he also calls human life "enacted dramatic narratives."

63. Allan Megill, "'Grand Narrative' and the Discipline of History," in Ankersmit and Kellner, *A New Philosophy of History*, 171–72, italics Megill's.

64. Raymond Martin, "Objectivity and Meaning in Historical Studies: Toward a Post-Analytic View," *History and Theory* 32:1 (February 1993): 43, 50.

65. MacIntyre, *After Virtue*, and *Whose Justice? Which Rationality?* He argues that Aristotle, Aquinas, and Scots like Francis Hutcheson and Adam Ferguson did this; however, Hume and Smith wrote from a different community of discourse, that of the cosmopolitan Republic of Letters. As a result they portrayed humans as independent individuals in no need of such a traditionalist, intellectually narrow community. In *Society and Sentiment*, Phillips has made this claim about eighteenth-century historical writing too difficult to maintain. However, there is still a great deal of value in MacIntyre's account of a philosophical basis for narrative and community.

66. See Harlan, *Degradation of American History*. For a critical discussion of full disclosure, see Berkhofer, *Beyond the Great Story*, chap. 6.

67. William Placher, *Narratives of a Vulnerable God: Christ, Theology and Scripture* (Knoxville: Westminster John Knox Press, 1994), and *The*

Domestication of Transcendence: How Modern Thinking about God Went Wrong (Knoxville: Westminster John Knox Press, 1996). Erich Auerbach suggested that the Gospel narratives were aggressive, closed worlds, demanding that the reader fully buy into its boundaries and rules; *Mimesis: The Representation of Reality in Western Literature*, trans. Willard R. Trask (Princeton: Princeton University Press, 1953), chap. 2.

68. Rowan Williams, *The Resurrection: Interpreting the Easter Gospel*, 2nd ed. (Cleveland: Pilgrim Press, 2002), chap. 5.

69. R. R. Palmer, *Catholics and Unbelievers in Eighteenth-century France* (Princeton: Princeton University Press, 1939); see also McMahon, *Enemies of the Enlightenment*.

70. John Dwyer, *Virtuous Discourse: Sensibility and Community in Late-Eighteenth Century Scotland* (Edinburgh: J. Donald Publishers, 1987), 59, 61.

71. In significant ways the European Enlightenment was a cultural movement led by Christians of various theological stripes, from within institutions that identified themselves as Christian. See Richard Sher, *Church and University in the Scottish Enlightenment* (Princeton: Princeton University Press, 1985); Martin Klauber, *Between Reformed Scholasticism and Pan-Protestantism: Jean-Alphonse Turretin (1671–1737) and Enlightened Orthodoxy at the Academy of Geneva* (Selinsgrove: Susquehanna University Press, 1994); in general, Roy Porter and Mikulas Tiech, eds., *The Enlightenment in National Context* (Cambridge: Cambridge University Press, 1981).

72. White, *Metahistory*, 434; Michael Roth, "The Ironist's Cage," in *The Ironist's Cage: Memory, Trauma, and the Construction of History* (New York: Columbia University Press, 1995), 160–61.

73. I've started here: Jürgen Moltmann, *Theology of Hope: On the Ground and Implications of a Christian Eschatology*, trans. James W. Leitch (Minneapolis: Fortress Press, 1993); Jacques Ellul, *Hope in Time of Abandonment*, trans. C. Edward Hopkin (New York: Seabury Press, 1972); Miroslav Volf and William Katerberg, eds., *The Future of Hope: Christian Tradition Amid Modernity and Postmodernity* (Grand Rapids, Mich.: Eerdmans, 2003). For a small model of thinking in theological story that takes history and contemporary circumstances seriously, see William T. Cavanaugh, "The World in a Wafer: A Geography of the Eucharist as Resistance to Globalization," *Modern Theology* 15:2 (April 1999): 181–96.

Chapter Seven

ON ASSIMILATING THE
MORAL INSIGHTS OF THE
SECULAR ACADEMY

BRADLEY J. GUNDLACH

INTRODUCTION, BY WAY OF AUTOBIOGRAPHY

All of us as Christian historians are also in a sense secular historians. We
have all trained in the secular academy, and we take a lot of the secular
academy with us. We take methods, emphases of study, key books that
shaped us in graduate school. We take an appreciation for insights originating in ideologies and methodologies that we may have previously
regarded simply as enemy territory. And often we so internalize our
training that our mentor or committee seems always to be sitting on our
shoulder, judging our writing and lecturing.

I can say personally that I've found it important to be reconciled to
my graduate school past—in my case, my years as a Ph.D. student at the
University of Rochester. Those years were the most difficult of my life,
and for a good while I seriously doubted the value of my training. Some
of my doubts sprang from "program envy": a worry that others got a
better Ph.D. than I did. Did they have a more congenial cohort of fellow
students, closer relationships with their mentors, better books assigned
them, better research and job opportunities? A good number of my wor-
ries were matters of self-doubt: perhaps I hadn't taken in as much as I

should have, hadn't worked hard enough. And beyond these personal issues were systemic concerns. I worried that graduate training had alienated me from something I used to love, as history became a duty and a
burden in the daily "Grad Grind" (the psychologically unhelpful title of
our graduate student rag). Friends outside the university—thankfully I
made a point of finding such—observed that historical study was making me incapable of decision, as I instinctively treated every question
as an open one requiring more thought. Was graduate school making
me value scholarly prowess more than goodness, kindness, faithfulness?
And particularly, was the pose of cultural critic making me incapable of
living and enjoying life as it is in my time and place, cultivating in me
a pervasive sourness about society in general and people in particular?
Coming to the Ph.D. program from a seminary M.A., I assumed that
these two phases of my training were fundamentally antagonistic. It
didn't help that the director of graduate studies had an enormous poster
of Karl Marx on the wall behind his desk, frowning down on me over
his shoulder.

Recently, however, I have had the opportunity to teach much more
from the center of my training—in American cultural and intellectual
history under Christopher Lasch and Robert Westbrook—and have
been refreshed by the rediscovery that my graduate training really was
valuable and really did point me not just to good material and good
scholarly habits, but also to penetrating insights into the moral system
of our contemporary American culture. These insights help frame my
sense of calling as an historian to exercise a critical function, criticizing not only American cultural and societal failures but also the ways
in which American evangelical culture participates in those failures.
Which raises the question: if I find it valuable to appropriate values and
moral insights from the secular academy, am I somehow compromising
the distinctively Christian moral vision of the good life?

A comment of B. B. Warfield's got me thinking about the notion of
assimilation in the sphere of ideas and agendas. Writing about evolutionary theory, Warfield said, "We may be sure that the old faith will be
able not merely to live with, but to assimilate to itself all facts."[1] Warfield
did not mean that we should adapt Christianity to modern ideas; that

was the error of theological modernism. Rather, he meant that Christianity must adapt new facts for use in its venerable edifice, so that they are *incorporated into it* as valuable building blocks.

Warfield based this image on his particular understanding of "theological encyclopedia," the relation of various branches of knowledge to the project of theology, and the relation of various kinds of theology to the grand synthesis of it all: systematic theology.[2] With his interest in system-building, Warfield had in mind facts (and a nineteenth-century notion of "facts" at that) rather than moral visions or moral agendas. But I still find his imagery of assimilation promising for the question at hand. Surely Warfield's metaphor smacks of a pretty old-fashioned Christian triumphalism, and Calvinists of Warfield's stripe have been criticized for it[3]—but I'd point out that in assimilating material from outside the Christian tradition, Christians are after all letting their system be affected by it. They are making their Christian view dependent, in a sense, on such materials. To adopt a biological reading of the metaphor, when an organism assimilates something, it digests it and uses the useful parts for its own growth. You are what you eat. Thus there is a kind of dialectic of dependence and dominance, if you will, in such an idea of assimilation.

To bring this down to a specific case, as a Christian I find the social and cultural criticism of such scholars as Christopher Lasch, Philip Rieff, Jackson Lears, Alasdair MacIntyre, and Robert Bellah to be very appealing—not just for their tracing the historical roots and extensive ramifications of the consumerism, individualism, emotivism, and therapeutic ethos that beset our culture today (that is, not only for their historical data)—but for their moral vision of what modernity (especially the capitalist order and overweening confidence in scientific control) has cost us individually and communally in terms of the good life.[4] I find that their call to face-to-face community, to commitment and mutual responsibility, to rootedness and the recognition of limits, resonates with properly Christian values. It also, very importantly, provides a valuable critique of the extent to which American evangelicalism has accommodated—has assimilated itself *to*—some of the more insidious nasties of modernity. I want in this chapter to describe this two-edged value of their moral agenda, to reflect on its virtues and limitations, and especially then to reflect on the very idea of assimilating a moral agenda of the secular academy.

The Moral Vision of Bellah, Lears, and Lasch

To simplify and focus this project, I will treat the moral agenda of three of the scholars I named above: Robert Bellah, Jackson Lears, and Christopher Lasch. I see their insights and vision to be basically of one piece, yet to display a certain progression, in the order in which I have listed them, from useful observations about American moral culture and generalizations about its relation to Christianity (Bellah), to an exploration of specifically religious longings and their role in twentieth-century cultural developments (Lears), to an intensive probing of the similarities and differences between religious and secular moral visions (Lasch).

Bellah's prizewinning *Habits of the Heart: Individualism and Commitment in American Life* found its way onto many a pastor's bookshelf because of its analysis of American individualisms and its exposure of the ways individualism cuts against commitment and community. With a team of co-writers Bellah warns against the prevalent individualism that defines "personality, achievement, and the purpose of human life in ways that leave the individual suspended in glorious, but terrifying isolation."[5] In the course of two centuries modern individualism has become the "first language" of American culture, a first language that proves inadequate as a basis of moral discourse. Americans need to draw on traditions other than this shared language of individualism in order to articulate our actual commitments or to critique the culture that too often undercuts community.

Bellah identifies three central strands of American moral vision: the biblical, the republican, and the modern individualist traditions. The last named subdivides into two overlapping phases: the pursuit of individual gain in career, at the expense of relationships and personal commitments (utilitarian individualism, exemplified by Ben Franklin), and the pursuit of self-fulfillment through the cultivation of private life (expressive individualism, exemplified by Walt Whitman and mediated to the twentieth century by the therapeutic language of psychology). The former called forth the latter—expressive individualism is a reaction against and compensation for the crass materialism and the repressive and mechanistic work patterns of the utilitarian, capitalistic economic order. Contemporary American society, then, is defined by the figures of the Manager, concerned only with efficiency and profitability, and the Therapist, who helps the individual to maximize personal satisfaction in the realm of private life. Our lives are thus profoundly divided—and worse, even in the private sphere of personal fulfillment our "center is the autonomous individual, presumed able to choose the roles he will play and the commitments he will make, not on the basis of higher truths but according to the criterion of life-effectiveness as the individual judges it."[6] What communities we do build, then, have a highly contingent quality: they are mere "lifestyle enclaves" based on affinities of values and needs, rather than real communities that make legitimate demands on us and that involve our getting along despite our differences.

Jackson Lears's *No Place of Grace: Antimodernism and the Transformation of American Culture, 1880–1920* explores that world of expressive individualism in rich historical detail, focusing on overt expressions of revulsion at the spirit-desolating effects of industrialized, scientized modernity. Lears takes his title from a poem by T. S. Eliot called "Ash Wednesday." There is, Eliot writes,

> No place of grace for those who avoid the face
> No time to rejoice for those who walk among noise and deny
> the voice.

The din of industrialism and the denials of positivism are inescapable realities; there is no turning back to a simpler time—and yet Lears's cast of antimodernists laments the loss of what Peter Berger called a sacred canopy of meaning. Lears elaborates in a compelling narrative this "antimodern ambivalence," clearly expressed in the lives of cultural elites, but—and here's the clincher—now well established in the common culture. The "weightlessness," gnawing sense of ennui, and nervous prostration experienced privately by many late-nineteenth-century elites bear witness to "a pattern of evasive banality" in the modern culture of industrial America. Antimoderns turned to therapy, the Arts and Crafts movement, militarism and the strenuous life, Eastern mysticism—anything to act as a substitute for the authentic religious experience now rendered either impossible by science or trivial by liberal Protestantism. In seeking raw, enlivening experiences (aesthetic contact with the sublime, craftsmanly contact with wholistic production, Teddy Roosevelt–style vigorous engagement) or in becoming mere "tourists of the supernatural," antimoderns tried to recapture the *experience* of meaning without actually inhabiting it. Religion gave certain psychological rewards as a byproduct of the religious life; now antimoderns sought the byproduct as the end in itself. He who would save his life shall lose it. This attempt at ersatz fulfillment, Lears points out, is at the heart of the therapeutic ethos all around us today.

Christopher Lasch, in *The True and Only Heaven: Progress and Its Critics*, ventures as a sympathetic outsider to write about providence, grace, and eschatology in the Christian tradition and to sift essentially Christian notions from modern substitutes for, or perversions of, them. Under the stress of scientism and the Adam Smith–inspired "moral rehabilitation of desire," he argues, a rich and morally substantial tradition was eclipsed by the idea of "progress"—a radically different notion altogether, but one that has been misread as a secularized version of Christian hope. Lasch cites Reinhold Niebuhr to affirm that the Kingdom of God was neither to be the end of the world nor an ideal for future society but rather "a community of the faithful living under the judgment inherent in the evanescence of earthly affairs and more particularly in the 'doom of threatened societies.'" The Christian view of history and providence did not, could not smoothly transition by "secularization" into the promethean nineteenth-century confidence in endless progress. In the Christian vision, "History mattered because it was under divine judgment, not because it led inevitably to the promised land." And prophecy, the heart of Christian moral vision, "put less emphasis on the millennium to come than on the present duty to live with faith and hope, in a world that often seemed to give no encouragement to either."[7]

Lasch stands as a secular historian keenly attuned to the distinction between the truly sacred and the poor substitutes modernity has offered in its stead. In his final book, *The Revolt of the Elites*, he heaps scorn on Allan Bloom's *The Closing of the American Mind* for its hope in the university as a sacred institution. Quoting Philip Rieff, "The worst way to defend culture is by deifying it." Like Lears, Lasch sees the all-important issue of priority in religion: "Culture may well depend on religion," he writes, "but religion has no meaning if it is seen merely as the prop of culture." When the end becomes the means to some other end, it loses its sacred character and forfeits its peculiar power.[8]

Flowing from this essentially Niebuhrian attention to judgment, humility, and the idolatry that results from their neglect, Lasch goes on in his many writings to recommend a chastened vision for human society and the good life, one defined by face-to-face relations, an acceptance of limits, and an appreciation of the givenness of life. He advocates what he calls "plain style" in academic writing, so that no highbrow/lowbrow distinction might intrude to sever the public from the intellectual. He affirms the wisdom and responsibility of the family as over against social-science experts, and looks to the lower middle class, that much despised target of radical criticism, as the best hope for American culture. He combines what Stuart Weaver calls a puritan and a populist impulse,[9] forging not only a sturdy cultural critique, but an alternative call to the good life.

In Lasch, then, we find a secular historian who lays open for us the distinctive character of traditional Christianity's moral vision of history, for which no mundane goods or goal can serve as substitute. We find a thinker deeply appreciative of the earthly goods of life but aware of the impossibility of their ever replacing the sacred. It is no wonder that when he died in 1994, Father Richard John Neuhaus's journal *First Things* carried an admiring obituary that declared Christopher Lasch not far from the kingdom.[10]

Assimilating the Bellah-Lears-Lasch Agenda

Of course a great deal more ought to be said even to attempt an encapsulation of the thought of these three, but I hope I have sketched enough of it to illustrate the point of this chapter—that we may find plenty of promising moral vision in the work of the secular academy. Positively, we may find in Bellah, Lears, and Lasch a real resonance with Christian concerns—and therefore many useful materials for the Christian to appropriate into an expressly Christian framework. Their critique invites us to indict American culture's banality, its poor substitutes for what religion provides. They expose the spiritual bankruptcy of positivism, with its naïve faith in progress and confidence in the sufficiency of science to solve human problems, pointing out specifically how the modern secular utopia proved a fraud. They identify the therapeutic ethos that substitutes medical for moral or religious standards of value.[11] They criticize the idea that the needs of the self are the elemental building blocks of the needs of society, and the consequent pretense that there need be no contest between selfish goods and social goods.

Identifying in the history of our socioeconomic order the causes of these cultural missteps, and taking note of the communal requirements that sustain belief in lasting truths and values, the Bellah-Lears-Lasch critique also invites us to uncover ways in which American evangelicalism tends to be bound up in the same problems as secular America, insofar as it remains committed to some of the worst aspects of modernity. For Lears these include imperialistic violence and unrestrained corporate expansion. Bellah prompts us to ask, Are evangelical churches mere "lifestyle enclaves"? Are we offering the gospel to people for its utility in a selfish quest for fulfillment? A great many more such questions await our consideration.

On the other hand, in assimilating this moral vision we should recognize its limits and consider how to incorporate the good into a Christian frame. There is a certain pathos to the recognition on the part of secular people that their secularity violates human needs. Lasch, especially, writes in the tradition of Joseph Wood Krutch (*The Modern Temper*) and Walter Lippmann (*Preface to Morals*), two figures who in the late 1920s articulated the emptiness that secularity brought, yet felt they had no alternative but to try to reconstruct morals without the sacred canopy of meaning. Eric Miller has recently lamented the ultimate futility of Laschian jeremiads, which lack the power to reverse the trends.[12]

Stephen Carter said recently, "The fact is that there are some arguments that simply lose their power or are drained of their passion when they're translated into a merely secular mode."[13] Perhaps in assimilating these moral agendas we should revert frankly to moral and biblical language. Lasch—even with his evident moral concern for family life, meaningful community, and the recognition of human evil—is typical of secular writers in wanting to avoid the moralizing tone of a Robert Bork (*Slouching Towards Gomorrah*) or of the proverbial Mrs. Grundy. Casting social evils in individual moral terms amounts, he believes, to blaming sin for them, and where does that get us? It allegedly shuts down inquiry into conditions (social, economic, industrial) that have caused our societal problems. Again, casting social ills in moral terms may result in blaming the victims, as in the case of prostitution or ghetto poverty. Duly noting that concern, though, can we not say that pride and selfishness, not just "expressive individualism," are at work in American culture? Reintroducing overtly moral terminology, and the specifically Christian sense of such terms, infuses the argument with a power that rises above the demythologized world that Lasch and others still occupy. Uncovering "expressive individualism" and a "therapeutic ethos"—even when recognized as poor substitutes for religion—still leaves them in the realm of historical construct, the product of social, economic, and intellectual conditions. We are still bound in a world of change and semblance, power and construct, intended and unintended consequences of human choices, never rising to issues of goodness and truth.

I have urged us to employ a distinctively Christian moral vision of the good life, one that benefits from secular insights but rises above them. What might that vision of the good life entail? Following Lasch, Lears, and Bellah, the good life involves a recognition of limits, countering our culture's mania for control and manipulation, its faith in unbounded progress through technological mastery. And beyond a recognition, a Christian should add an *acceptance* of limits as not just there, but as *given*, built by God into our world and our selves. The limits created by God are not barriers to fulfillment, but *gifts*, the embracing of which is good and healthy. There are other limits, too, resulting from our fall into sin; thus acceptance of limits will involve a due sense of guilt, a lamentation for our fallen state. When a Christian recognizes and accepts the limits of our created and fallen state, it is an act not of merely Stoic resignation, but of trust in God the Father who orders all things well and in Christ the Redeemer who delivers us from sin. Christian resignation, unlike Stoic resignation, is relational.

Beyond these considerations of individual consciousness, and again enlarging upon Lasch, Lears, and Bellah, a Christian moral vision includes the goal of shared community. Our splintered, mobile society sadly lacks the experience of long-standing relationships, shared memory, a sense of place and belonging that spans generations. An important dimension of the good life is found in such things. The limitation of our physical being (that is, our embodiment, our being here and not there) is not a bad thing, but a good, to be received with joy as God's intention. All earthly goods are not just to be used, but to be received and savored (in their proper place) with a heart of thanksgiving to God, accompanied by a pervading awareness that life itself, and certainly the good things in life, are gifts of a just, merciful, loving God.

Without this larger Christian frame, both thought and lived, the moral vision of the best cultural critics leaves us starving for the bread of life.[14] The earthly communities we build, even traditional ones with some modicum of permanence, cannot match our longings. We need community in Christ; we must seek to live out the good life in commitment to each other in the Kingdom of God, and we must realize that we will not get there this side of heaven. As Augustine explained in *On Christian Doctrine*, the intrinsic value of earthly goods is always only partial; all our loves must pass through the earthly good to find their end in God.[15]

To return to academic discourse, historians must carefully sift the descriptive from the normative to do our spadework well—but in the end we must return to the pouring of the concrete, the building of walls, the framing of the edifice of *meaning* for our present. As keepers of the public memory, "wise ones of the tribe," we still carry that duty.[16]

Outsiders Helping Insiders

How shall we interpret the helpfulness of these voices from outside the Christian fold, voices which prove so valuable in opening our eyes to ourselves and to our own tradition in a way that insiders usually miss? Outsiders often see things that insiders cannot, precisely because of their status as outsiders. They bring a fresh, somewhat disinterested perspective, freed from the blinders that exclusive discourse among insiders can produce. Alexis de Tocqueville and Harriet Martineau, famous nineteenth-century observers of American society, spring immediately to mind. And more valuable still are outsiders who have spent considerable effort understanding the inside, sympathizing with it. Jan Shipps's reflections on "outside insiders" and "inside outsiders" are very useful here. A Methodist whose scholarly career has focused on the history of Mormonism, Shipps urges historians of religious traditions other than their own to get to know the people and immerse themselves in the language (popular and theological) of the tradition they are studying. Even in the scholarly analytical mode they must be careful not to "fail to credit fully the importance of believers' commitments" to doctrine, worship, and the activity of the supernatural in their midst.[17] She suggests, then, a way for outsiders to cross into the insider mindset enough to exercise a truly sympathetic understanding while retaining the advantages of outside perspective, such as approaching a hotly contested issue with the relative open-mindedness of an uninvolved party, identifying the real issue in a long-standing squabble that has cut such a deep channel for itself that participants cannot imagine it flowing by another route, or simply recognizing that accepted terms of engagement have in some way missed the main point. Lasch, especially, in his intensive inquiry into the differences between Christian views of history and secular confidence in progress, functions as valuable "inside-outsider" to American Christians, even as his wide reading and debt to radical analysis enable him, an American himself, to function as an "outside-insider" offering fresh perspective on American culture.[18]

And this is part of God's providence for us, I believe. To appropriate such insights from outsiders, I suggest, is to engage in a proper kind of providentialist history. There has been a lot of talk lately about providentialist history, as when evangelicals express concern over the "methodological naturalism" they perceive in the work of George Marsden, Mark Noll, and others. "Providentialist history," these folks say, means the recognition, in published historical work, of supernatural intrusion into the historical process. The favorite example is the Great Awakening—will we write accounts of it that see God as a primary agent in the revival, or treat it only in terms of human, this-worldly causes such as deferred marriage, the psychological strain of the fading of Puritanism, and savvy marketing techniques? But to call the recognition of distinctively supernatural activity "providentialist" is rather a skewing of the theological notion of providence. Providence is God's workaday activity in the processes of the world—to be distinguished from creation on the one hand and miracle on the other. It is, in a nineteenth-century phrase, "the method of the divine government." To a providentialist, history written in terms of natural causes—which might better be called by their older philosophical and theological name of *secondary* causes, God himself being the primary cause of all things as he both created and governs them—is just what *providentialist* history is. A better name for the identification of supernatural intrusions would be *miraculist* history.

William Murchison, professor of journalism at Baylor University, recently published a brief appreciation of Christopher Lasch in *Touchstone* magazine. He titled his piece, tellingly, "Near Prophet." An Episcopalian himself, Murchison writes of "Lasch's Lacuna": "you can talk, but you can't talk adequately, about a culture of narcissism without proposing a religious cause for the present disturbance." The decline of the family, which Lasch charts so well, is due not only to economic changes that caused changes in the roles of fathers and mothers, but also to "an antecedent spiritual collapse within the hearts of family members" as parents no longer see themselves "as tenders of ancient responsibilities" that derive from responsibility to God. In urging us to build communities back up by cultivating "the not-yet-lost instinct to bend the knee before—as we Anglicans say—the 'Maker of all things' and 'Judge of all men,' to whom we 'acknowledge and bewail our manifold sins and wickedness,'" Murchison infuses the question once again with moral and religious force. He points us to the recognition that the common grace that enables secular scholars to teach us valuable moral lessons has to do with not only our common origin in the Creator of all good things, but our common end-point on the great and terrible day of Judgment.[19] I would add to Maker and Judge a third, intermediate title, appropriate to our present discussion: God is the Governor of this world, who directs even the actions of wicked people to serve his good purposes, and who, as the Heidelberg Catechism says, "so preserves me that without the will of my heavenly Father not a hair can fall from my head."[20] History is the mysterious working out of God's purposes, even in a sin-sick world and even through the free choices of his creatures. God is the source of all good and the end of all good. What goods we enjoy have purpose beyond self in community, and beyond community in the participation in the divine nature. Our use of these goods—including the insights we glean from the secular academy—will be judged.

God by his *common* grace empowers scholars of all kinds, Christians as well as non-Christians, not only to discover the facts of history, but to discern much of the moral vision of a good society. In confessional Lutheran and Calvinist terms, these are good works in the sense of "civil righteousness"—real goods, whose ultimate source in God is by no means diminished by the free activity of human minds.[21] I submit that in assimilating the moral agenda of the secular academy (selectively and discerningly, of course, for there are also a lot of *bad* moral agendas out there), we can be practitioners of properly providentialist history. And such providentialist history involves not only welcoming the insights of the secular academy as God's providing, but transmuting, the call to community into a call to know God in community—embracing (with due discernment) the place and people in which God has providentially placed us.

Notes

1. Benjamin Breckinridge Warfield, "The Present Status of the Doctrine of Evolution," *Presbyterian Messenger* 3:10 (December 5, 1895), 7–8.

2. Warfield's classic statement of this is "The Idea of Systematic Theology," *Presbyterian and Reformed Review* 7 (1896): 243–71, reprinted in his *Studies in Theology* (New York: Oxford University Press, 1932; vol. 9 of his collected *Works*), 49–87.

3. For example, Gary Scott Smith, *The Seeds of Secularization: Calvinism, Culture, and Pluralism in America, 1870–1915* (Grand Rapids, Mich.: Christian University Press, 1985).

4. I am referring to such works as: Christopher Lasch's *Haven in a Heartless World*, *The Culture of Narcissism*, *The Minimal Self*, *The True and Only Heaven*, and *The Revolt of the Elites*; Philip Rieff's *The Triumph of the Therapeutic*; Jackson Lears's *No Place of Grace*; Alasdair MacIntyre's *After Virtue*; and Robert Bellah's *Habits of the Heart*. I might also include with qualifications such works as Theodore Roszak's *The Making of a Counter Culture*. Notice the diversity of these authors, ranging from outright hostility to Christianity (Roszak) to a kind of fellow-traveler status (Lasch) to nonevangelical Christians who function within the secular mainstream and would probably never be seen at a meeting of the Conference on Faith and History (Bellah, MacIntyre).

5. Robert N. Bellah et al., *Habits of the Heart: Individualism and Commitment in American Life* (Berkeley: University of California Press, 1985), 6.

6. Ibid., 47.

7. Christopher Lasch, *The True and Only Heaven: Progress and Its Critics* (New York: W. W. Norton, 1991), 47.

8. Christopher Lasch, *The Revolt of the Elites and the Betrayal of Democracy* (New York: W. W. Norton, 1995), 226, 228.

9. Stewart Weaver, "Introduction," in *Plain Style: A Guide to Written English*, by Christopher Lasch (Philadelphia: University of Pennsylvania Press, 2002), 26–27.

10. Richard John Neuhaus, "While We're At It," *First Things* 44 (June/July 1994): 44, writes: "[Dale] Vree is very much a Catholic and thinks Lasch edged up to becoming one, but finally, says Vree, 'he is to be counted among "some of the best friends of the Church" who could not quite come in.' "

11. T. J. Jackson Lears, *No Place of Grace: Antimodernism and the Transformation of American Culture, 1880–1920* (New York: Pantheon Books, 1981), 305; cf. his classic essay, "From Salvation to Self-Realization: Advertising and the Therapeutic Roots of the Consumer Culture, 1880–1930," in *The Culture of Consumption: Critical Essays in American History, 1880–1980*, ed. Richard Wightman Fox and Lears (New York: Pantheon Books, 1983).

12. Eric Miller, "Alone in the Academy," *First Things* 40 (February 2004): 30–34.

13. Stephen Carter, "The Future of the Public Intellectual: A Forum," *The Nation* 272:6 (February 12, 2001), available online at http://www.thenation.com/doc/20010212/forum (last accessed March 13, 2010).

14. On givenness, embodiment, lament, and community I recommend Ken Myers's excellent Mars Hill Audio Journal. These are perennial themes of his interviews and commentary. They are available online at http://www.marshillaudio.org/.

15. Augustine of Hippo, *On Christian Doctrine*, book 1, chaps. 3–4.

16. I am harking back to Carl Becker's classic essay, "Everyman His Own Historian," his presidential address to the American Historical Association ca. 1932, reprinted in *The Historian as Detective: Essays on Evidence*, ed. Robin W. Winks, 5–23 (New York: Harper & Row, 1970).

17. Jan Shipps, "Remembering, Recovering, and Inventing What Being a People of God Means: Reflections on Method in the Scholarly Writing of Religious History," in her *Sojourner in the Promised Land: Forty Years Among the Mormons* (Urbana: University of Illinois Press, 2000), 187.

18. Lasch, *True and Only Heaven*, chaps. 1 and 9.

19. William Murchison, "Near Prophet: Christopher Lasch's *The Culture of Narcissism*," *Touchstone* 18:9 (November 2005): 13–15.

20. Heidelberg Catechism, Lord's Day #1.

21. Augsburg Confession, art. 18; Westminster Confession of Faith, chap. 16, section 7. Both confessions stress the *limited* goodness of acts of civil righteousness—that they have no salvific value—but the point holds that they are good in a relative sense, and that as such they come from God's directing hand.

Chapter Eight

AFTER MONOGRAPHS

A Critique of Christian Scholarship as Professional Practice

CHRISTOPHER SHANNON

IT HAS NOW BEEN MORE THAN TEN YEARS SINCE GEORGE Marsden first proposed the "outrageous idea" that personal Christian faith not only could, but perhaps should, make a difference in the research and writing of history.[1] After the countless conference panels and roundtables that greeted Marsden's provocative thesis, is there anything left to be said about the idea of Christian scholarship? My sense of the mood among contemporary historians interested in the issue is that the answer is both no and yes. First, the everlasting nay. At the level of theory, George Marsden's work seems to have settled the question for most of those concerned. The Marsden settlement goes something like this: Christian scholarship consists in Christian scholars infusing the relatively neutral, technical, procedural norms of the various academic professions with their distinctly Christian background faith commitments. These spiritual commitments inspire distinctly Christian questions and nurture a sensibility capable of producing distinctly Christian interpretive insights that may enrich the historical understanding of Christian and non-Christian alike—provided the Christian scholar achieves these insights with all due respect to secular professional standards of evidence and argument. Next, the everlasting yea. Marsden's theoretical justification of Christian scholarship raises the question of how Christian faith commitments affect the study of specific historical problems. The panel topics at any given conference on religious history are but the tip of the iceberg facing our scholarly Titanic. More work always needs to be done, and an army of Christian historians stands ready to be up and doing.

It is at this level of practice where the current consensus on Christian scholarship shows its true colors, colors indistinguishable from its secular counterpart. The "big table" at which Marsden wishes to secure for Christians a seat is less a forum for discussion than a factory for production. The price of admission is a deep commitment to the moral necessity of feeding the monograph machine. This commitment places Christian historians in one of two equally undesirable positions: either they follow the secular profession in its relentless strip mining of the past, so that the sacred people, places, and events of Christian history become fodder for historical revision; or they temper their criticism with sympathy, and write history that affirms, or at least remains silent on, the truth value of Christianity. Intellectually, the first position renders them rearguard Christians, the second, rearguard scholars.

I have elsewhere offered my critique of the Christian character of Marsden's idea of Christian scholarship.[2] In this essay, I would like to shift the focus of the debate from the adjective "Christian" to the noun "scholarship." The problem with so much of the debate is less that it has failed to offer a distinctly Christian historical practice, but that it assumes current secular historical practice to be, despite an undue secular bias, just fine, thank you very much. Through all the debates of the last decade, few if any commentators have questioned the basic moral and intellectual necessity of the standard academic history monograph. A kind of writing little more than a hundred years old, the monograph has somehow acquired the status of a self-evident truth, an unquestionable base from which all rational historical questioning must proceed. The monograph is the practical manifestation of a theoretical consensus on empiricism that unites historians across the range of background faith commitments. Any serious challenge to the current consensus on Christian history must show how, in terms of the monograph, more work decidedly does not need to be done. Christian history can do its greatest service to Christians and non-Christians alike by abandoning the futile effort to build a better monograph and shifting the focus of scholarly inquiry from writing back to reading.

The pieties expressed in the annual American Historical Association presidential address aside, a survey of recent trends in historical publishing and scholarship reveals the history monograph to be as much a relic of the nineteenth century as the railroad. Scholars, Christian or non-Christian, would be foolish to bank their intellectual future on it. Completely apart from the debate over Christian scholarship, a few brave secular thinkers have dared to say that the emperor has no clothes. Lindsay Waters, executive editor for the humanities at Harvard University Press, has for several years now been decrying "the tyranny of the monograph." Writing from inside the whale, he has charged that the publish-or-perish ethos of contemporary academia has inflated the currency of the monograph to the point where individual scholarly studies have lost all value as guides to assessing the progress in knowledge within various disciplines. Tenure review committees pressure scholars to produce more and more at ever earlier stages of their career, with a predictable decline in the quality of scholarship. Writing with a keen historical insight, Waters traces the rise of the monograph to the rise of the modern research university in the late nineteenth century. The university legitimated itself in terms of a broader commitment to the newly authoritative ideals of empirical science. Their own authority in decline, humanities scholars modeled their professional practice on that of the natural sciences: if scientists write monographs, then humanists must prove their rigor by also writing monographs. Still, Waters insists that the problem goes deeper than the simple need to temper scientism with humanism. The overproduction of monographs has worked to undermine any clear sense of humanism at the same time that it is driving many university presses into economic insolvency. Waters sees no solution short of a radical, fundamental reorientation of academia away from the tyranny of the monograph.[3]

Academics might sympathize with the economic plight of university presses, but most remain committed to the intellectual ideals that justify the mass production of monographs. Historians may have given up on what Peter Novick has called "that noble dream" of scientific objectivity, but this dream continues to structure the practice of the profession.[4]

Those uneasy with the disjunction between the dream and reality of objectivity take solace in the various formulations of objective relativism touted by the likes of Thomas Haskell and David Hollinger, but for most historians such theoretical justification is superfluous.[5] Again, the practice of producing monographs has assumed the standing of something like a self-evident truth. A universal solvent, the monograph has even proved capable of maintaining a deep professional peace beneath the surface of today's supposedly contentious culture wars. Those who fear postmodernism as a new wave of barbarism should look at what postmodern scholars do: they write monographs, lots of them, all with plenty of proper footnote citations. The jargon may be unfamiliar, but the long established process of revision has always brought with it new jargon.[6] With historical writing, the only constant is change, the only sin, sloth. Scholars left, right, and center are awash in a sea of productivity.

Waters's scathing critique of this productivity is lost on practicing historians. Those who concede that most of what is published should never have even been written still seem to take a certain pride in having the courage to confront the monographic wasteland. Several years ago I attended a retirement dinner for an eminent historian of American Catholicism. The after-dinner speaker, himself a leading historian of American religion, praised the guest of honor as one of the leading historians of religion of his generation. At the same time, he conceded that the work of even the best historian is hardly read outside of a small circle of professionals; even within that group, it rarely survives beyond the generation in which it was written. For the lesser lights the outlook is even bleaker. So many monographs, so little time. Most works will live and die in obscurity. Yet still, like Sisyphus, historians must roll their monographic boulder up that hill, again and again. Listening to that talk reminded me of a story, perhaps apocryphal, about the great German sociologist Max Weber. When asked once "Why do you do sociology?" Weber is reported to have replied, "To see how long I can stand it."

Why should Christians study history? I would hope for better reasons than Weber offered for his commitment to sociology. Before I suggest any reasons why Christians should do history, I would like to take a closer look at what history (as a professional practice) does to Christians. First, it deprives them of a Christian telos to history. Christian historians may think that the Holy Spirit caused the Great Awakening, but they cannot make that argument in their capacity as professional historians. This would be to raise the specter of the dreaded providentialism, surely the ghost that haunts much of the current debate on Christian history writing. Those who place themselves within the Marsden settlement insist there is no going back to providential history. Attributions of divine causality are empirically unverifiable and politically dangerous; providentialism is of a piece with the Crusades, the Inquisition, the Salem Witch trials, and all the other bogeys of a time when Christians tried to equate human with divine purposes. Responsible Christian historians must confine themselves to purely naturalistic causality.

It is my contention that in embracing naturalistic causality and the procedural norms of the historical profession, Christian historians merely trade one providentialism for another. Where Christian historians of old once looked for the hand of the Holy Spirit, the new-model Christian history follows the naturalist quest for historical agency. The modern secular monograph tells us, with pious, mind-numbing regularity, that human beings, as individuals and groups, make history, but not under conditions of their own making. Within the general framework of accommodation and resistance, secular historians remind us of the ironic disjunction between intended actions and unintended consequences, but insist on the primacy of action, whatever its consequences. Historical actors are those people who manipulate, negotiate, and reshape their relations with each other and with nature in the effort to maximize their individual or collective autonomy from imposed constraints. History, through a process of dialectical struggle, reveals the natural unfolding of a kind of instrumental individualism. The producer ethic of the middle-class professional historian is written into the narrative structures of history. It finds its most immediate material manifestation in the industrial production of history monographs.

At the level of ideas and institutions, modern academic history writing thus embodies what I would call a kind of providential professionalism. Those who acknowledge this conception of human agency as particular and far from neutral still argue that, while it is weighted with normative assumptions about the essential nature of the human person, these values, unlike Christian providentialism, can be proven through fact. I would argue that providential professionalism is no more empirically verifiable than Christian providentialism. The examples are legion, but I will take one from a popular, though perhaps now dated, monograph I feel to be representative of the empirical limitations of the quest for historical agency. The text is Kathy Peiss's *Cheap Amusements: Working Women and Leisure in Turn-of-the-Century New York*. With a triumphalism that would put a nineteenth-century evangelical to shame, Peiss celebrates the opportunities for the emancipation of women from traditional constraints offered by the popular amusements of the Gilded Age/Progressive Era American city. To take but one example, I would like to share with you Peiss's interpretation of the "tough girls" subculture of turn-of-the-century New York. Peiss cites a New York vice investigator's account of an incident involving one such girl, an Italian immigrant:

> The girl had no hat on and had probably just left her house to go on an errand when she met this man[.] I heard her say, my mother will think I got lost I was supposed to go to the drug store she wouldn't know what became of me. The man was under the influence of liquor and was trying to put his hands under her skirts, she resisted at first but afterwards let him go as far as he liked.[7]

Peiss's interpretation: "Although the investigator does not describe this incident and its participants in great detail, the vignette suggests the powerful allure of leisure as a realm of assertion, sexual experimentation, and escape from parental demands."[8] Hmm. . . . Says who? Maybe it is a symptom of a culture of rape. Maybe it is a sign of the triumph of the cultural hegemony of a libidinal anarchy that forces women into sexual experimentation they would not otherwise choose for themselves. Take your pick.

Inferring agency from action is about as empirically valid as claiming that the Holy Spirit caused the Great Awakening. Sources do not really help us much. Were the Italian girl that Peiss celebrates to have kept a diary revealing her innermost thoughts, would this really prove whether her decision to let a drunk feel her up was a free act? Any literary critic will tell you that diaries are notoriously unreliable as factual evidence and tend to reflect conventions of the literary genre as much as they do authentic experience; indeed, the very fact that someone would keep a diary already places them on the road to the kind of individuality privileged by historians.

Peiss's sexually adventurous immigrant women may seem a long way from the kind of questions that concern historians of religion, but her quest for agency has deeply religious historical roots. It is in many ways a modern secular equivalent of the old Puritan quest for the certainty of salvation. The question "are you really saved?" becomes "are you really a historical agent?" Individual diary-keeping and the rigorous, direct scrutiny of pastors could not answer the former question for Puritans in their own time; there is no reason to think that this question will be any more answerable with our vaunted historical distance. Psychohistory has a fairly low standing in a profession that prides itself on nontheoretical empiricism, but the quest for historical "experience"—an inherently subjective phenomenon—makes all history into a kind of psychohistory.

Historians do not direct themselves to the study of human agency because it is that about which the sources allow them to speak. They do so because it is a deeply held value that defines them as middle-class professionals. History monographs are not proofs of fact; they are reflections on value. Take for instance Nancy Cott's recent providential history of divorce—uh, I mean marriage—*Public Vows*.[9] Cott is widely recognized as one of the leading historians of her generation. I am not familiar with the sources she draws on in her study, but I have no reason to doubt that she uses them responsibly. Her argument, such as it is—that the last hundred and fifty years have seen a liberalization of divorce laws accompanied by an increase in the autonomy of women—is unobjectionable. Indeed, it is so unobjectionable as to raise the question of why she would feel the need to "prove" such a point in a heavily documented work of historical research. Aside from reflecting Cott's inability to shake the acquired professional habit of writing monographs, the book stands as a testament to the belief that the marshalling of empirical data to verify a certain development somehow invests this development with a kind of objectivity—and implicitly a kind of moral legitimacy. For this kind of Whig history, what is, is right.

The further back in time an historian goes in Western history, the more difficult it becomes to tell Cott's story of the triumph of autonomy, but even stories of failure confirm autonomy as a value. Historians of the medieval period may acknowledge the marginality of autonomy to the culture of medieval Europe, but then that very marginality becomes the focus of their study. In many ways the *locus classicus* for this kind of study has been the story of the rising middle class, generally told through developments in commerce, artistic innovation, or theological heresy. The more recent variations on this story include the search for the first socialist, the first feminist, the first critical race theorist, or the first libidinal anarchist. I do not doubt that the quest for autonomy has a genealogy stretching back even before the Renaissance. The monographic output of the last one hundred years has done a fairly thorough job of clarifying the material and cultural conditions under which the value of autonomy thrives or withers. If this is the purpose of professional history writing, I would say, mission accomplished. If the purpose of academic history is to chronicle the potentially infinite variety of conjunctures between a specific constellation of material conditions and a specific degree of autonomy, I do not see what distinguishes historians from antiquarians.

Secular historians pursue this research agenda with such vigor because they take autonomy for granted as something like an inalienable right. The first question for Christians in the historical profession should be: Is autonomy a Christian value? I would answer no. Those who would defend it as an orienting value for Christian historical inquiry would do well to look upon the consequences of autonomy in secular historical inquiry.

Looking at the cycles of revision over the last fifty years or so, we can see autonomy as a constant value with a maddeningly fluid and shifting social location. The great liberal historian Richard Hofstadter offered the most explicit association of the value of autonomy with the professional middle classes, in particular middle-class intellectuals. Hofstadter placed intellectuals at the vanguard of human freedom and located the forces of reaction in mass political movements, most famously in his attack on the Populists as protofascist anti-Semites. New Left historians attacked intellectuals as technocrats—the lap dogs of the corporate liberal order that produced the Vietnam War—and returned the torch of freedom to the people, perhaps most significantly in Lawrence Goodwyn's rehabilitation of agrarian populists as radical democrats. The economic or class-based radicalism celebrated by New Left historians soon came under attack for being blind or even hostile to issues of race and gender, so the vanguard of the march of human freedom shifted to women and minorities. Today, the wheels of revision grind on, with sexual orientation the current cutting edge of human liberation.[10] The interpretation produced by such revision are new only in the sense of being this year's model in an intellectual marketplace addicted to novelty.

This is the monographic practice of professional historians. Do Christians really want to subject their own history to this process?

To take one example close to the debates on Christian scholarship, let us look briefly at George Marsden's history of the American university, *The Soul of the University*. By highlighting the de-Christianization of American higher education, Marsden revises the older framework of professionalization. The story of communities of competence displacing gentry communities of inheritance becomes the story of rising secular elites displacing declining religious elites.[11] Marsden's sympathies clearly lie at one level with the displaced Christians; he would like to see believing Christians once again have a significant role in shaping the main currents of American intellectual life. Still, Marsden clearly rejects any notion that he is arguing for a return to the ethos of the antebellum college. The old Christian regime was just as oppressive as the current secular one. Through his notion of background faith commitments, Marsden would situate the Christian scholar between confessionalism and secularity. Such marginality would actually afford Christians the ability to claim the mantle of true intellectual freedom abdicated by secular elites in their exclusion of religious points of view from the academy.

I have no objection to Marsden's basic narrative of de-Christianization, but I do object to the intellectual position in which he locates Christian scholarship. His liminal space, between two worlds, is the privileged position of autonomy.[12] It is the classic position from which secular historians write. The history that proceeds from it will be secular history. Secular history is inherently corrosive of its subject matter. I do not question the personal faith or professional good intentions of George Marsden or any of those who accept his settlement. But as Marsden himself, along with James Turner and others, have shown, the road to secularity is paved with good intentions. In his *Without God, Without Creed*, Turner argues that unbelief came to dominate intellectual life in America not because confirmed atheists succeeded in disproving the existence of God but because believing Christians committed themselves to proving the existence of God through reason alone: if you do not need to believe in order to understand, you soon find yourself not having to believe at all.[13]

The current debate on Christian scholarship seems to be replaying the nineteenth-century debate on the historical-critical method in theology. Many of its original practitioners adopted the method out of a deep commitment to enriching their faith; many who continue to practice it today do so for the same reasons. This commitment, in the end, can be no more than personal. As a general intellectual orientation, it leads inevitably from theology to religious studies, precisely the position that has caused such unease among believing Christian scholars today.[14] To get beyond this deadlock, we have to think beyond (or perhaps behind) the nineteenth century, something that scholars trained in a nineteenth-century discipline like history are generally reluctant to do. The triumph of naturalistic explanation in modern secular history writing is the culmination of a long revolt against premodern interpretive traditions, a revolt rooted in the Protestant Reformation. *Sola fides* is a theological position I am not prepared to debate. *Sola scriptura* reflects a broader set of assumptions about the nature of interpretation that bear directly on the historian's craft

As Peter Harrison has argued in his great book, *The Bible, Protestantism, and the Rise of Natural Science*, *sola scriptura* has profoundly shaped the way we look at not only the Bible but all books, including the book of nature, the natural world.[15] Harrison examines the paradigm shift away from medieval interpretive traditions in ways that are particularly relevant to contemporary debates on the relation between faith and history. Historians have generally understood the rise of the historical-critical interpretation of the Bible in the nineteenth century as a consequence of the spread of Enlightenment rationalism into theological inquiry. Harrison provocatively argues that this method actually has its roots not in the scientific revolution of the seventeenth century but in the religious revolution of the sixteenth. The Protestant revolt against allegory cut short the endless chain of symbolic reference of the medieval Catholic interpretive tradition in favor of a new authority, the "literal" sense of scripture. According to Harrison, this new reading of the Bible changed the reading of the world, not vice versa, as is generally understood.[16] This is precisely the kind of causal argument that historians devote careers to attacking and defending; I doubt that it will hold up to the relentless revision demanded by the profession. The significance of Harrison's book lies more in the way that it links the rise of causal historical arguments to a new understanding of the biblical textual authority as rooted in a direct, literal correspondence to empirical reality. Modern history writing is in this sense a legacy of the Reformation.

Harrison's account of pre-Reformation interpretive traditions offers an important aid to reflecting on the place of this approach to the Bible within a broader Christian intellectual tradition shared by both Catholics and Protestants. David Lyle Jeffrey's recent work, *Houses of the Interpreter: Reading Scripture, Reading Culture*, shows the ecumenical potential of these ancient interpretive traditions.[17] The history of biblical interpretation in turn sheds light on the recent epistemological debates among secular historians. Were St. Augustine to be magically transported to a roundtable discussion on Peter Novick's *That Noble Dream*, he would likely find himself accused by academic historians of something akin to Nietzschean irrationalism. Anxieties concerning evidence and authorial intention were unknown to the late antique/early medieval reading of texts. The literal or factual meaning of scripture was but one of the four senses of scripture—*historia, allegoria, analogia,* and *aetiologia*—and by no means the most important. Augustine explicitly warned against a preoccupation with accuracy that came at the expense of reflection on the spiritual significance of texts.[18] The same interpretive standards applied to the world, which classical and medieval Christians understood as a repository of spiritual truths. Harrison writes that for these Christians, "To be concerned with natural objects alone was to be 'a slave to the sign': it was to engage in an idolatrous 'literalism' applied to objects."[19] Historians, *J'Accuse*.

The tradition of the four senses of scripture grew out of a recognition of the undeniably equivocal nature of biblical texts. The Reformation rejected this tradition. Luther attacked allegory as itself an idolatrous accretion that clouded the pure, simple meaning of scripture. If the Bible were to be the final authority, then it had to be deprived of ambiguity. As Harrison describes this change, reformers came to "deny the indeterminacy of meaning of canonical texts, and thus . . . insist that each passage of scripture had but a single, fixed meaning." The interpretation of the world again followed the interpretation of texts, but within the new nonsymbolic interpretive regime, "objects were related mathematically, mechanically, causally, or ordered and classified according to categories other than those of resemblance." Scripture was "no longer . . . to provide the key to the hidden religious meanings of the natural world—instead, discoveries in the book of nature were to shed light on the neglected scientific treasures of the sacred text." As a consequence, the interpretation of stories such as that of Noah and the flood shifted from "fruitful allegorising" to "mundane questions of science and logistics"; only "when the story of creation was divested of its symbolic elements could God's commands to Adam be related to worldly activity." Having removed God from space, the Reformers reserved a place for him in time. In the genre of providential history, typology survived the assault on symbol, but this too came under assault with the development of secular historical consciousness.[20]

This brings us to our present state of affairs. Despite the attacks of postmodern critics, modern science seems an insurmountable obstacle to those who would wish to rehabilitate premodern interpretive traditions. I am certainly not prepared to challenge science as an approach to the natural world. It conceives of nature as pure instrumentality. At a narrowly technical level, it has achieved a remarkable degree of control over these instrumentalities. I may question the value of a faster computer chip, but I cannot deny that computer scientists consistently meet their stated goal of making a faster microprocessor. Social scientists and historians are on much shakier ground. Originally conceived as progressive disciplines on the model of the natural sciences, the social sciences have failed to achieve progress at the level of textual interpretation, much less control over the social forces that are supposed to be their special area of expertise. The industrial production of history monographs has produced an orgy of information, all the while recycling a few basic narrative scenarios. Christian historians should read and teach the best of these monographs as reflections on the irony of human agency, but human agency cannot be at the center of Christian history. That privileged place belongs to God.

David Hollinger has challenged those promoting Christian scholarship to put their money where their mouth is and produce a new research agenda that would make an original, distinct contribution to scholarship along the lines of women's history or African American history.[21] As should be clear from my assessment of the state of the monograph, I think Christian historians would be foolish to build up yet another research fiefdom; beyond their empirical subject matter, histories of gender and race are not really all that distinct from their white male counterparts, and the current work that passes for Christian scholarship suggests that a Christian research agenda is not likely to change things much. The proper site for the return of God to history is the classroom, not the publishing house. The appropriate scholarly activity for this return is reading, not writing. Critics such as Hollinger may never be convinced of the value of Christian scholarship, but it would be nice if we could silence their legitimate skepticism as to the distinctiveness of Christian history. I suggest, as a place to start, a complete reorganization of the undergraduate history curriculum.

In our teaching, we need to separate the narrative dimension of history from whatever critical or analytic dimensions remain after abandoning that noble dream of objectivity. The narrative approach to Christian history would entail not much more than simply telling the Christian story. This "uncritical," narrative history would be of a survey variety, with an emphasis on, yes, that bogey of Progressive education, rote memorization. It would not be an introduction to historical methods. It would neither provide students with their first taste of the critical examination of primary sources nor prepare them for the upper division courses found in most colleges and universities in America. It would simply give them the names of the people, places, and events that make up the Christian story, a very partisan story whose telling would vary with the denominational context in which it is taught. This would be the setting where historians could freely make assertions regarding God's providence; this is where one could say the Holy Spirit caused the Great Awakening. Most of the monographic literature produced over the last one hundred years would be of little use in such a class, beyond providing information to crib for lectures.

I do believe, however, that the best of the monograph tradition does have an important place in a Christian approach to history. In teaching these books, Christian historians must detach them from their social scientific roots and return them to a philosophical setting where they can be read for what they really are: less accounts of fact than reflections on value. Modern history writing arose as an attempt to explain the rise of the modern world: the transition from the organic, hierarchical relations of the medieval *Gemeinschaft* to the mechanical, egalitarian relations of modern *Gesellschaft*. The historical profession has a moral and intellectual investment in *Gesellschaft*. It has also nurtured a small but vocal cohort of *Gemeinschaft* grousers (I count myself among them).

In her book *Natural Symbols*, the Catholic anthropologist Mary Douglas argues that cultural orientations such as *Gemeinschaft* and *Gesellschaft* should be seen less as stages in evolution than as enduring, opposed cosmological types.[22] She is specifically concerned to debunk the standard sociological notion, drawn from Weber and Durkheim, that religions naturally progress from a primitive emphasis on ritual to a modern, civilized emphasis on ethics. Though her bias (and mine) is clearly toward the primacy of ritual, Christianity has, in different ways at different times, proved capable of accommodating both ritual and ethics—in a sense, both *Gemeinschaft* and *Gesellschaft*. Jesus is priest, prophet, and king; he is also our brother.

Christian theologians have struggled for centuries with the tensions between hierarchy and radical egalitarianism in the Christian story. John Milbank has argued that sometime during that infamous seventeenth century, this problem and a whole range of related issues were detached from their theological moorings and reconstituted in a new field called social theory. For Milbank, the social sciences (I would include history in this) have been carrying on a quasi-theological discourse fatally flawed by the inability of its practitioners to recognize or acknowledge its theological roots.[23] Norman O. Brown made a similar argument in his classic study of Sigmund Freud, *Life Against Death: The Psychoanalytic Meaning of History*. Brown rejected Freud's own self-conception as a scientist and argued that Freud is better understood as a literary-philosophical thinker writing about old issues in a new way. For Brown, Freud does not explain *Oedipus Rex*, he rewrites it. Freud's linking of greed to the anal stage of psychosexual development is less a reflection of the evidence drawn from his clinical study of patients than an enduring literary association that goes back through Jonathan Swift to Martin Luther.[24]

Brown took Luther and Swift seriously enough to write about them, but argued that Freud's formulation of certain enduring problems spoke most powerfully to the needs of the historical moment in which he wrote. I take history monographs seriously enough to read them, but I do not think they speak most powerfully to our current historical moment. We should read them as Brown read Luther. Or perhaps to state my position more sharply, we should read the best of the monographic literature of the last hundred years the way Jefferson read the Bible: we need to separate out the magical, miraculous elements (causality, agency) and concentrate on the ethical, philosophical content (the information, the thick description of the world we have lost and the world we have found). Texts would be studied and taught not as more or less accurate accounts of particular historical periods, but as more or less true arguments illuminating aspects of Christian social philosophy.

Eamon Duffy's *The Stripping of the Altars* is an example of the kind of text no undergraduate should leave a Christian college without having read.[25] The value of Duffy's book lies not in his controversial argument that the Reformation was imposed by a rising elite on an unwilling populace still faithful to the teachings and practices of the Catholic Church, but in his rich though relatively unobjectionable rendering of the enchanted world of time and space in late medieval England. The causal argument is the stuff of historical revision, a losing game Christians must abandon if they are to develop any distinct tradition of historical thinking. The description is fully in line with a long tradition of scholarship dating back to the Victorian medievalists; its very lack of novelty commends it as worthy of study. Christian historians should engage the profession not by adopting partisan positions on the causes of the Reformation but by exposing the real stakes of this debate: the legitimation of the modern secular world.

Ideally, students would encounter Duffy's text not in a topics course on the history of religion or a period course on early modern Europe, but in a course on post–World War II history writing. History would be taught historiographically, with students introduced to history books as certain kinds of writing shaped by certain kinds of narrative. In this, Hayden White should be our guide—not for his romantic view of the historian as a kind of literary hero, but simply for his literary emphasis on the rather limited range of stories historians have been able to tell.[26] This historiographical curriculum would expose students to the best of history writing from Herodotus to our own time. Given the relatively late arrival of history as a significant genre, readings would be weighted toward this century. No undergraduate history major would be able to graduate without having read E. P. Thompson, Edmund Morgan, or Phillipe Ariés, to name but a few.[27] An undergraduate who has read these writers closely and carefully will have a better understanding of history than an Ivy League graduate with a personally designed tool belt of survey, period, and topics courses.

Approaching history books as morally charged narratives is at once a premodern and a postmodern turn. Despite Marsden's appeal to postmodern perspectivalism, his understanding of Christian scholarship remains firmly in the modernist idiom. Like Thomas Haskell, his defense of modernism is as much moral as epistemological. Both historians write as committed political liberals; both see professional, monographic history as the kind of history writing appropriate to a pluralistic, liberal democracy; and both see any kind of providentialism or confessional history as inviting a return to the barbarism of the Crusades and the Inquisition.

I have tried to argue for the inescapability of providentialism. I would like to conclude with a reminder of the inescapability of barbarism. Liberal history grew up with the nation state and has provided a kind of court history of secular modernity. In the name of civilization, the American version of modernity has condoned the enslavement of Africans and the near-extermination of Native Americans. It has waged perhaps the most destructive wars in human history, and has vaporized civilian populations with nuclear weapons. It currently condones the abortion of roughly a million and a half unborn children each year. Liberalism has no monopoly on violence, but it has developed the denial of violence into something like a new art form. Liberalism has made religion, either as cultural lag or return of the repressed, the scapegoat for the persistence of violence in the modern world. Without repeating the error and demonizing liberalism as the root of all evil, I think it is fair to say that liberalism's moral record is at best mixed; it is certainly not one to appeal to as a substitute for rigorous epistemological argument. Christian defenders of liberal history as an intellectual enterprise must point to reasons more substantial than its potential tolerance for the cage-rattling of our background faith commitments.

NOTES

1. George Marsden, *The Outrageous Idea of Christian Scholarship* (New York: Oxford University Press, 1997).

2. Christopher Shannon, "Between Outrage and Respectability: Taking Christian History Beyond the Logic of Modernization," *Fides et Historia* 34:1 (Winter/Spring 2002): 3–12.

3. Lindsay Waters, *Enemies of Promise: Publishing, Perishing, and the Eclipse of Scholarship* (Chicago: Prickly Paradigm Press, 2004).

4. Peter Novick, *That Noble Dream: The "Objectivity Question" and the American Historical Profession* (Cambridge: Cambridge University Press, 1988).

5. Thomas Haskell, *Objectivity is Not Neutrality: Explanatory Schemes in History* (Baltimore: Johns Hopkins University Press, 1998). David A. Hollinger, "The Return of the Prodigal: The Persistence of Historical Knowing," *American Historical Review* 94 (June 1989): 621.

6. Imagine the plight of a mid-century historian committed to the materialism of a Charles Beard when faced with Richard Hofstadter's notion of a "status anxiety"; see Richard Hofstadter, *The Age of Reform: From Bryan to F. D. R.* (New York: Vintage, 1960).

7. Kathy Peiss, *Cheap Amusements: Working Women and Leisure in Turn-of-the-Century New York* (Philadelphia: Temple University Press, 1987), 71.

8. Ibid.

9. Nancy F. Cott, *Public Vows: A History of Marriage and the Nation* (Cambridge, Mass.: Harvard University Press, 2002).

10. Lawrence Goodwyn, *The Populist Moment: A Short History of the Agrarian Revolt in America* (New York: Oxford University Press, 1978). Herbert G. Gutman, *Work, Culture and Society in Industrial America* (New York: Vintage, 1977). Nancy F. Cott, *Bonds of Womanhood: "Woman's Sphere" in New England, 1780–1835* (New Haven: Yale University Press, 1977). George Chauncey, *Gay New York: Gender, Urban Culture, and the Making of the Gay Male World, 1890–1940* (New York: Basic Books, 1995).

11. George Marsden, *The Soul of the American University: From Protestant Establishment to Established Nonbelief* (New York: Oxford University Press, 1994).

12. For an account of the privileging of this position across the broad range of American culture, see Werner Sollors, *Beyond Ethnicity: Consent and Descent in American Culture* (New York: Oxford University Press, 1986).

13. James Turner, *Without God, Without Creed: The Origins of Unbelief in America* (Baltimore: Johns Hopkins University Press, 1985).

14. On this problem, see D. G. Hart, *The University Gets Religion: Religious Studies in American Higher Education* (Baltimore: Johns Hopkins University Press, 2002).

15. Peter Harrison, *The Bible, Protestantism, and the Rise of Natural Science* (Cambridge: Cambridge University Press, 2001).

16. Ibid., 3, 4.

17. David Lyle Jeffreys, *Houses of the Interpreter: Reading Scripture, Reading Culture* (Waco, Tex.: Baylor University Press, 2004).

18. Harrison, *Bible*, 123, 31.

19. Ibid., 30.

20. Ibid., 111, 114–15, 137–38, 128, 207.

21. David Hollinger, "Enough Already: Universities Do Not Need More Christianity," in his *Cosmopolitanism and Solidarity: Studies in Ethnoracial, Religious, and Professional Affiliation in the United States* (Madison: University of Wisconsin Press, 2006).

22. Mary Douglas, *Natural Symbols: Explorations in Cosmology* (New York: Routledge, 2003).

23. John Milbank, *Theology and Social Theory: Beyond Secular Reason* (Cambridge, Mass.: Blackwell, 1993).

24. Norman O. Brown, *Life Against Death: The Psychoanalytic Meaning of History* (Middletown, Conn.: Wesleyan University Press, 1985).

25. Eamon Duffy, *The Stripping of the Altars: Traditional Religion in England, 1400–1580* (New Haven: Yale University Press,1992).

26. Hayden White, *Metahistory: The Historical Imagination in Nineteenth-Century Europe* (Baltimore: Johns Hopkins University Press, 1975).

27. E. P. Thompson, *The Making of the English Working Class* (New York: Vintage Books, 1963). Edmund Morgan, *American Slavery, American Freedom: The Ordeal of Colonial Virginia* (New York: W. W. Norton, 1975). Philippe Ariés, *Centuries of Childhood: A Social History of Family Life* (New York: Vintage Books, 1975).

Chapter Nine

THE PROBLEMS OF PREACHING
THROUGH HISTORY

JAMES B. LAGRAND

THOSE WHO HAVE TAUGHT HISTORY FOR A WHILE HAVE experienced both the good and the bad regarding how the public views their discipline. Positively, many people state that they enjoy at least certain topics or fields in history, which is regularly borne out by lists of best-selling books. And even those who don't view themselves as historians often have a hobby—whether music, art, science, cars, or sports—that itself has a history. Some fields of study are only truly appreciated and enjoyed by professionals, but not history. There's no human thought, word, or deed it does not touch. Yet there's another side of the public's relationship to the discipline of history, as well. At times, people become cool to history because it seems too academic and abstract. What they want, they sometimes say, is a history that's relevant, that teaches us lessons, that has an agenda, a history that in a sense preaches.

Historians have long wrestled with this issue as they've considered both the benefits and the costs to being more deliberately and self-consciously relevant. Recent years have seen greater numbers of both Christian historians and other Christian scholars whose work touches on history advocating scholarship that in various ways has a dominant moral agenda. Consider, for example, Charles Marsh. Marsh's experience growing up in the South within the white segregated church has

187

led to him to reflect on race relations, social ethics, and the civil rights movement in a number of works that combine autobiography, history, and lived theology. In *God's Long Summer: Stories of Faith and Civil Rights*, he examines a group of people active during Mississippi's Freedom Summer of 1964. All were shaped by their Christian faith, but in wildly divergent ways, he argues. Responding to their Christian faith, some were led to fight racial oppression, others to join the Klan that was terrorizing African Americans, and still others to sit on the sidelines during this pivotal time. Marsh notes that those in the last group knew their Bible and sometimes said the right things, but they didn't act out their Christian faith. They failed to commit themselves to the goal of reconciliation between the races and so were hypocrites. This group, like the more virulent racists, came to frustrate Marsh as he did his research. His hope, he says, is that his book will help readers "make sense of Christianity's complicity in racism and violence" and eventually help bring about true reconciliation, a "time when whites and black together will reckon with their common humanity."[1]

Marsh's subsequent book, *The Beloved Community: How Faith Shapes Social Justice from the Civil Rights Movement to Today*, also uses accounts of the movement to critique those he accuses of having trivialized Christianity both then and now. Believing that white Christians have grown complacent, he tells them they shouldn't feel too proud about the successes of the civil rights movement in ending legalized segregation. Beyond this, there's a greater, profound goal rooted in the movement that still remains unrealized. "The nation has experienced precious little of repentance, reconciliation, and costly discipleship," he writes. Marsh's message, which combines history and calls for transformation, has inspired many readers and listeners both in the general public and in the Christian community. Marsh is a popular speaker at Christian college campuses, seminaries, and divinity schools, and *Christianity Today* recently included his *The Beloved Community* as one of its top five books on the civil rights era.[2]

Richard Hughes also would like to have his scholarship help us learn lessons, in this case, within the nation. His book *Myths America Lives By* argues that the American people have been misled by five powerful myths about their identity and history. The problem with these myths,

Hughes suggests, is twofold. He argues that they have led to both moral blindness as well as a misunderstanding of America's past. He particularly hopes that readers would hear the voices of the oppressed in American history and, in response, bring about a "revolution of American values." Like Marsh's work, Hughes's book is in part a call to repentance for sins of the past, including Americans' assumptions about the goodness and fairness of their country's political economy. Picking up on this theme, one reviewer called *Myths America Lives By* "a wake-up call" that can "help Christians rethink their role and mission in American life."[3]

Marsh and Hughes work in the field of religious studies, in which history is combined with other disciplinary emphases, although their books are often listed under history. Moreover, some Christians whose central vocation is as historians—teachers, scholars, and writers—have also been asking recently whether history needs an agenda to make it a faithful and authentic vocation.[4] And to the degree that traditional norms of history might interfere with this goal, they've advocated a distancing from the profession. Michael Kugler, influenced by theologians John Howard Yoder and Stanley Hauerwas, has advocated a Christian history whose agenda would be to preach against idols prevalent today, what St. Paul in Ephesians refers to as the powers of this dark world. Christopher Shannon has suggested that Christian historians should refuse to adopt some of the standards of the mainstream academy, which he sees as capricious and restrictive, and rather try to make use of traditions and discourses distinct to Christianity. William Katerberg also calls Christian historians to reject disciplinary norms and habits, to be more forthrightly interdisciplinary, and to be resolutely activist in their work focused on critiquing the status quo.[5]

The Appeal of Preaching through History

All of the above represent an approach to history that sees it as a means to an end, the end of personal or collective transformation. This instrumentalist use of history has long had appeal because of the clear lessons and agendas it seems to offer. It appears to have a renewed appeal in recent years for Christian scholars. For them in particular, there are several attractions to a discourse that allows them to preach by focusing attention on application. For one thing, this practice has the ability to bring about spiritual or moral revival. If only we had the right moral exemplar (found someplace in the past), it's often suggested, we could shake up people today to live their lives differently. This tendency leads to the inclination to judge and to look for moral heroes and villains while studying history.

A second appeal to preaching through history is that it allows us to try to imitate Christ in our historical scholarship and professional lives, not only in our personal lives. For those troubled by a dichotomy between personal and professional, this idea can be quite enticing. Given Christ's frequent engagement with the outcasts and marginal people of his time, perhaps those historians who also strive to follow Christ when it comes time to choose research subjects might turn their attention to those on the margins, those far from political, economic, and social power.

A third appeal to preaching through history is that it allows us to identify and confront sin. When we look at the past (or the present) we're often overwhelmed at the actions contrary to God's will and destructive of the shalom God intended for his world: racism, greed, slavery, the lust for power and other idols, and on and on. The list of sins in history is truly endless. Some Christian scholars, as noted above, have followed in the footsteps of the Old Testament prophets who delivered God's message of judgment to Israel for her sin and idolatry. These contemporary Christian scholars have focused on sin in America's past, in what they also call a "prophetic" style or voice.

And a fourth appeal to the preaching discourse is that it allows Christians to acknowledge God's role in history. This understanding is central in the Christian faith. We worship a God who acts in history— not a capricious divinity who toys with people from time to time, not an absentee landlord or watchmaker god—but a God who acts. Scripture is full of actions attributed to God—from sparrows falling from heaven to mighty kings being overthrown. Psalm 136 contains a litany of just some of the acts of God: He made the heavens and the earth, divided the Red Sea in two, made Israel pass through the midst of it but overthrew Pharaoh and his host, remembered us in our low estate, and rescued us from our foes. More than this, in the fullness of time, God was made incarnate and entered human history.

I acknowledge, then, that for those of us who are Christians, preaching through history can be deeply satisfying. Indeed, at first glance, this seems to be an obvious way to do history as a Christian—full-throated and unapologetic. Although there are many attractive reasons to preach in this way while doing history, I will suggest in this essay that conflating historical understanding and preaching by focusing first and foremost on a political agenda poses significant problems. Indeed, it has the potential to limit our understanding of the past, a troubling prospect for historians. Ultimately, I'll argue that despite the personal and emotional satisfactions gained from preaching through history, it is an unsatisfactory model of Christian history.

THE PROBLEMS OF PREACHING—ROOTED IN HISTORY

Part of the problem with the type of instrumentalism I'm calling preaching through history lies in the nature of history itself. Here, it would be helpful to look briefly at the origins of what we know as history and to review some signal developments in Western historiography. Before the fifth century BC, there was not yet anything that we today would consider history. Rather, there were epics, works of "heroic history," such as the *Iliad* and the *Odyssey*. The differences between these epics and history are striking. In the epics, the gods were the leading figures and most ordinary human beings were absent. Both time and space were shrunk with no attempt to connect past, present, and future. The purpose of the epics was to teach timeless virtues, not to view human beings within time. But this began to change when Herodotus helped establish history as we now know it, thereby earning himself the name "the Father of History" in the Western tradition. History's characteristics now included a view of time as continuous or linked, a commitment to examining human activity in a human and not a timeless context, and a focus on causation—what future history students would come to describe as the notorious "why question." Following Herodotus, history became the story of the human and contingent world, far from the eternal, changeless essences of philosophers. History began to have its own methodological approaches and practices apart from other ways of thinking and understanding the world.[6]

Jumping ahead, two further developments germane to the consideration of preaching through history came in the nineteenth century. At this time, positivism dominated the natural and social sciences. Many great minds were focused on discovering the general laws that were thought to govern all natural and human phenomena. Some historians were swayed by this, believing that history could and should be a science. They thought that history, like other disciplines, could follow the scientific method down the pathway to "timeless truth." These "scientific historians" started with the timeless and totalizing theories created by social scientists and then used "history" to prove the theory. Most historians did not follow the positivist scientific path, however. They found "social laws" like those of Auguste Comte or "economic laws" such as Karl Marx's about the means of production to be wooden, overstated, and ultimately unconvincing when examined next to what we know about human history with all its complexity and ambiguity.[7]

Also in the nineteenth century came the spread of historicism, an intellectual movement that argued that the autonomy of the past should be respected and that the task of understanding the past should precede any attempts to apply its insights to the present. The problem with some efforts to immediately apply history to fulfill an agenda, historicists argued, is that our understanding of the past might become skewed and warped in the process. One long-popular example of the kind of instrumentalist history historicists have warned against is the use of history to try to prove either uniform progress or decline over time, what we might call a type of "secular preaching." And what I'm calling preaching through history in this essay is another example. Here, the primary purpose of history becomes confronting guilt or repenting for sins, rather than trying to understand the past. These and other instrumentalist uses of history can do violence to our understanding of the past. Still today, those influenced by historicism and appreciative of history's distinctive features continue to be helpful in reminding us of the frequent differences between present and past, differences that should not be blurred or obscured solely to meet some present-day need.[8]

This is not to say that historians, even those of us in part shaped by historicism, care nothing for morality or moral improvement. Indeed, we might argue convincingly that in addressing morality through a historical lens, the conclusions we reach become all the more valuable and more relevant. Peter Stearns makes this point in a short essay written for the American Historical Association on why students and others should study history. Among the six reasons he gives is that history contributes to moral understanding. He writes, "History . . . provides a terrain for moral contemplation. Studying the stories of individuals and situations in the past allows a student of history to test his or her own moral sense, to hone it against some of the real complexities individuals have faced in difficult settings. People who have weathered adversity not just in some work of fiction, but in real, historical circumstances can provide inspiration."[9]

The problem with preaching in history, then, is that it literally takes us outside of time and human history, outside of human life as it has been lived. In so doing, its results can produce a fleeting good feeling, but they're so disconnected to human history that they remain in an abstract limbo state. The messages that drive efforts to preach through history (for example, spiritual or behavioral improvement) are often admirable. But their timeless, ahistorical context makes them less relevant than they might appear at first glance.

Michael Kazin notes the pitfalls of radical instrumentalist history in particular in his review of Howard Zinn's best-selling *People's History of the United States*. Kazin shows that Zinn is more an "evangelist" than historian in that he explains little and dodges many questions of historical causation. Zinn practices a timeless and abstract approach to the past, using it as a grab bag for the stock villains and beaten-down but plucky heroes that fill his book. Thus, Kazin points out that not only is Zinn's book "bad history," it's not even good instrumentalism or secular-style preaching because it never provides a developed, coherent account grounded in history of how Zinn's virtuous losers might ever win some of their battles.[10]

But despite the many problems with agenda-driven history that preaches first rather than understanding and explaining the past, I've observed its pull over the course of my teaching career. When I published a book on Native Americans in twentieth-century Chicago, I had the opportunity to speak to a wide range of audiences.[11] At my talks, there were sometimes people who were a bit disappointed when they discovered that the book didn't tell a more powerful and guilt-inducing story of Indian victimization. Afterward, they suggested to me that's what my book should have done—in the light of such nineteenth-century atrocities as the Sand Creek and Wounded Knee massacres. I played the role of the historian in responding. I tried to explain that much changed for Native American people from the time of Wounded Knee to the upsurge of Native American urbanization half a century later. I supported my argument for a picture of at least partial success for Indian people in cities using a wide range of evidence. But this approach didn't always convince and certainly didn't emotionally satisfy everyone. For some readers, my failure to give the ritualistic moral sermon they expected was jarring. It deflated the instrumentalist use of the past they wanted. On another occasion, someone from another discipline working on a paper approached me looking for evidence of widespread germ warfare waged by soldiers and pioneers in the American West against Native Americans. He was disappointed when I could give him at best one possible and much-disputed case of this. This wouldn't help his sermon against American depravity he hoped to deliver in the midst of his academic paper. In his mind, instrumentalism or preaching trumped history.

At times, historians who subscribe to some degree of historicism in first trying to understand the past and only then moving to application are misunderstood as being politically motivated or cheerleaders for a particular cause. These accusations, though, are unfounded. In my experiences talking about Native American history with others, it's not that I wanted to let America off the hook for what are clearly legions of sins and injustices committed against Native American people over centuries. Rather, my role as an historian led me first to try to understand the past before applying its insights to the present.

Certainly there are many ways that history that follows the sequence of first understanding and then applying can still be edifying in moral, religious, or political ways. It needn't in any way be cold and "academic." But there is an important distinction to be recognized between this kind of edifying history and preaching through history which alters the traditional historian's sequence to apply first. In so doing, preaching through history can compromise history's great explanatory power.

THE PROBLEMS OF PREACHING—ROOTED IN CHRISTIAN THEOLOGY

Beyond disciplinary matters, there is another problem with preaching through history related particularly to the Christian faith. One tendency among some of those I'm characterizing as preachers is an inclination toward providential, or God's-eye, history. For example, Charles Marsh explains in *The Long Summer* that he "ask(s) questions about God" while exploring the history of the civil rights movement. Elsewhere in telling the story of the movement, he proposes moving past history "into a new way of seeing, into the world of God." Historian Steven Keillor, too, has recently advocated the validity of providential history. Others wouldn't go as far as Marsh and Keillor in reading the mind of God in history, but they might be described as anti-anti-providentialists because of their dissatisfaction with those who foreswear providential history.[12]

Christians have long struggled with the question of God's actions in history. It is clear that God acts, but what are his purposes in acting? Can we know what these are? Through much of the Old Testament, scripture seems clear about God's purposes in his treatment of his chosen people. The Israelites received blessings as a result of obedience and curses following disobedience and idolatry. But scripture also speaks of God sending rain on both the just and unjust, it criticizes Job's friends who thought they knew why Job was suffering, and it reminds us that we generally see through a glass darkly when it comes to discerning God's purposes here on earth.

Still the most helpful figure in the Christian tradition on the issue of God's purposes in history is St. Augustine of Hippo. This church father faced the question of what God was doing in history under the most trying of circumstances. After Rome was captured and sacked by Visigoth invaders in AD 410, there was widespread shock and outrage. It was thought that Rome would stand forever, and now it had been overrun. Many pagan Romans looked to the Christians living there as the culprit. They charged them with angering the gods and causing the sack of Rome because of their efforts to curtail pagan worship practices. Added to Roman Christians' anxieties was the fact that many had become influenced themselves by the idea of *Roma Aeterna* (Eternal Rome), and had come to associate the Roman Empire with the sacred story of the world taught by the Christian religion, which they understood as stable and orderly. Now this stability and order lay in ruins. In this context, Augustine began writing *The City of God*, which he completed in AD 426.

Augustine rejected the way in which the Roman Empire (or any earthly empire) had been associated with the divine. Countering this popular notion, he described two different fields or cities, the City of God and the Earthly City. These differed in their origin, their motivations, and their historical progression. Augustine writes, "Two cities, then, have been created by two loves: that is, the earthly by love of self extending even to contempt of God, and the heavenly by love of God extending to contempt of self. . . . In the Earthly City, princes are as much mastered by the lust for mastery as the nations which they subdue are by them; in the Heavenly, all serve one another in charity."[13]

The strikingly different natures of these two cities and the way in which they both overlapped and remained distinct made it difficult to figure out God's purposes in human, post-biblical history, Augustine suggested. He noted that by human standards, God appears inconsistent in his actions and judgments: "There are good men who suffer evils and evil men who enjoy good things, which seems unjust; and there are bad men who come to a bad end, and good men who arrive at a good one. Thus, the judgments of God are all the more inscrutable, and His ways past finding out." In the Earthly City or post-biblical human history, Augustine concluded, no overarching meaning or stability could necessarily be expected or discerned by human beings.[14]

Although Augustine has become enormously influential for many Christian historians, this was not his primary vocation. As a bishop of the church, Augustine was intent on instructing and preaching. Given our focus here on preaching in history, the exact nature of Augustine's preaching bears noting. On some issues he expressed certainty, but on others acknowledged uncertainty.

While Augustine acknowledged that the judgment of God was difficult to figure out in his time and in human history generally, it didn't follow that we should question or downplay the idea of God's judgment in the human experience altogether. Rather, Augustine pointed his readers past the chaotic and confusing events that understandably had consumed their recent attention to a time when God's purposes would be made clear, the final "day of judgment" or "day of the Lord." God's judgment is real, Augustine argued, but our understanding of its purposes now and in the hereafter is markedly different.

I'd suggest that centuries after his death, Augustine should continue to serve as a model for Christians both in his conviction to preach about the things of God and in his decision not to surpass the limited knowledge human beings have about God's purposes in this world in order to do so. Augustine reminds us to resist conflating the "things of God" with the "things of humans." We know that God acts, and we see examples of God's providence around us. But in looking at the sweep of human history wearing the lenses we have on this side of the final day of judgment, we should not try to do providential history.

Many have followed in this Augustinian tradition. Reinhold Niebuhr often addressed the limits of human understanding and vision in his writings. He applied this inexorable human characteristic also to attempts to read God in history. As a result, he particularly admired Abraham Lincoln's speeches given during the Civil War. Niebuhr believed these speeches were admirable both in their acknowledgement of the Almighty's purposes in history and in their skepticism about our ability to discern these purposes. Reflecting on Lincoln's legendary words, Niebuhr notes, "While the drama of history is shot through with moral meaning, the meaning is never exact. Sin and punishment, virtue and reward are never precisely proportioned."[15]

This Augustinian tradition was also influential at the time Christian historians in the academy organized in 1967 a professional organization named the Conference on Faith and History. By then, providential history was a distinctly minority position among Christian academics.

Frank Roberts and George Marsden, two early members, helped guide Christian historians between the two poles of "overassurance" associated with providential history and "overdiffidence," or a complete rejection of the idea of relating history and Christianity. Neither of these was an appropriate Christian response, they believed. Echoing Augustine, Niebuhr, and others, Roberts gently critiqued those overly assured historians who viewed a "Christian approach to history as essentially the unveiling of the divine plan within specific events of the past, and the pointing out of the good and evil forces within history."

This led Roberts to weigh in on a debate about Herman Dooyeweerd, the Dutch philosopher of history. Dooyeweerd had been the subject of intramural discussion in Reformed intellectual circles for some time. But in a broader sense, he represented another in a long line of philosophers of history wanting to tell historians how to go about their work. Dooyeweerd had established a whole new set of timeless laws and reductionist models, which he said explained all of human history. But because his work was distinctly and boldly Christian, some Christian historians were drawn to it. Roberts, though, warned his fellow Christian historians about the cost of adopting this. After Dooyeweerdianism's totalizing interpretative tools were trotted out to explain every aspect of the past, Roberts observed that "there remains very little ambiguity in history."[16] Here, then, was yet another theorist whose all-powerful categories had the potential to skew and warp our understanding of the past.

George Marsden, too, has weighed in on the topic of providential history. He has long argued for the legitimacy of Christian scholars in the academy against those who believe it should be a strictly secular domain for value-neutral knowledge. Christians, Marsden says, should be allowed to enter the academy with their identity intact—just as Marxists, feminists, postmodernists, and others do. But he's also said there's a requirement for Christian scholars in this arrangement. They're to observe the same set of common academic rules as their non-Christian colleagues. Both groups should do their evidence-based research or "detective work" in the same way. Both should subscribe to the norms and standards of history. These rules clearly place providential history or a special claim to knowledge of God's purposes in human history out of bounds. Arguments inspired by religious faith, what Marsden calls "background beliefs," can be put forward, but they should be argued on grounds that are accessible to all historians, not based on special private revelation.[17]

A second problem with preaching through history that emerges particularly in a Christian context has to do with sin. From the tone used by some recent Christian scholars, it seems that they are surprised to find sin in history. One wouldn't think that those with a Christian anthropology would be surprised by sin. But once again, our various purposes in studying the past—some instrumentalist and others historicist—explain this phenomenon. For those of us focused on trying to understand the past by examining history within a human context, sin comes as no surprise. For it's all too evident in the historical record—in addition to being taught by Christian theology.[18] But for those focused on confronting guilt, either individual or collective, and on bringing repentance using the Kingdom of God as the context, then sin becomes a more jarring presence—even sin in history.

Herbert Butterfield was among those historians in the former historicist group committed to doing history in a human, rather than a divine, context. This led him to warn historians against making moral judgments about such things as sin in *The Whig Interpretation of History*. Though this practice might be tempting, Butterfield argued that making moral judgments was not in the historian's purview and would lead to a vocational dead-end. Here is Butterfield's description of what historians do: "Historical explaining does not condemn; neither does it excuse; it does not even touch the realm in which words like these have meaning or relevance. . . . It is neither more nor less than the process of seeing things in their context. True, it is not for the historian to exonerate; but neither is it for him to condemn. It greatly clears his mind if he can forgive all sins without denying that there are sins to forgive; but remembering the problem of their sinfulness is not really a historical problem at all." Few have expressed this idea more starkly than Butterfield: sin might well be a personal or moral or pastoral problem, but it is not strictly speaking a historical problem.

Butterfield went so far as to state that if historians began to focus excessively on making moral judgments, they would lose their function as historians. No longer having a place to stand, they would only be able to deliver empty, abstract statements. "Moral judgments are useless unless they can be taken to imply a comparison of one man with another," he wrote. "Otherwise, the historian would have to fall flat with the commonplace that all men are sinners sometimes." For an historian shaped by historicism such as Butterfield, sin within history is no surprise; it hardly bears noting.[19]

Also struck by the ubiquity of human sin was Reinhold Niebuhr, whose exploration of this theme shook the intellectual world of mid-twentieth-century America. As a young man, Niebuhr was active in socialist and pacifist circles. But over time, his growing conviction about the stubborn "egoism" of human nature caused him to doubt the wisdom of philosophies or programs based on idealism. He started the process that would eventually see him become the foremost spokesman for "Christian realism" by the 1930s when he published *Moral Man and Immoral Society*. Niebuhr shocked many of his colleagues with this book, arguing that morality is impossible to achieve for collectives like the United States or any other nation. While it was obviously true that individuals exhibited self-interest, Niebuhr argued that collectives' "unrestrained egoism" was exponentially greater. Failing to realize this, Niebuhr said, would only result in "unrealistic and confused political thought."[20] Likewise, historians who share Niebuhr's view of human nature might suggest that a failure to see human nature accurately also leads to confused history.

Since the time of Butterfield and Niebuhr, historians, like any other group, have varied in their assessment of human nature and the potential of human endeavor. George Marsden has observed that in recent years many cultural critics and historians have failed to recognize the selfish, dark side of human nature. And it appears that many American Christians no longer have a classical Christian or Augustinian understanding of human nature, as evidenced by polls in which they state that human beings are "basically good."[21] But there have continued to be significant Christian voices since Butterfield's and Niebuhr's time reminding of the pervasiveness of sin. One is Kenneth Scott Latourette, the historian of Christian missions at Yale University during the middle of the twentieth century. Elected president of the American Historical Association in 1948, he decided to give his end-of-term presidential address on the topic "The Christian Understanding of History." Before a large group of his fellow historians listening in a Washington, D.C., hotel ballroom, Latourette talked among other things about how the Christian tradition he held to did not expect perfection within history, did not expect "the full conformation of mankind to the measure of the stature of the fullness of Christ" until the Second Coming.[22] Likewise, Wilfred McClay recently has written about the important task given to historians with a Christian worldview. They are particularly well equipped, he suggested, to navigate our way forward. "By relentlessly placing on display the pervasive crookedness of humanity's timber," McClay writes, "history brings us back to earth, equips us to resist the powerful lures of radical expectations, and reminds us of the grimmer possibilities of human nature—possibilities that, for most people living in most times, have not been the least bit imaginary. With such realizations firmly in hand, we are far better equipped to move forward in the right way."[23]

Thus, in addition to the disciplinary problems posed by agenda-driven preaching through history, there are particular problems here for Christian historians, problems it would be helpful for recent Christian instrumentalist historians to engage and confront. Instrumentalism, whether of the ancient, nineteenth-century, or contemporary variety still does not help us with one of history's central purposes: to try to understand the past. By advocating that we view things ontologically rather than historically, instrumentalism tends to rely on static ready-made models rather than evidence and historical detective work. This type of approach, whether taken by Christians or others, can't deal with the "messiness" of history, its unexpected twists and turns, the surprise of finding evil people doing good things and virtuous, moral people revealing a fatal flaw in some of their actions. Preaching through history unfortunately has no room for this.

A CASE STUDY OF THE PROBLEMS OF PREACHING THROUGH HISTORY

One example of the problem of preaching through history can be found in the study of American race relations, specifically the part of it that saw the rise and fall of *de jure* segregation (or "Jim Crow"). If any topic would seem to fit the preaching model, it's this one. The history of sit-ins and massive resistance, of Martin Luther King and Bull Connor, seems to cry out for preaching and some type of moralistic approach. Charles Marsh is among many writers who have followed this path. Yet even here, the preaching approach has run into problems, and the traditional historians' focus on understanding the past has yielded significant and valuable results.

Two of the most significant books on the history of segregation are C. Vann Woodward's *The Strange Career of Jim Crow* and David L. Chappell's *A Stone of Hope: Prophetic Religion and the Death of Jim Crow*.[24] These two much-praised books are united in their deceptively simple focus. Both start by asking the question: "Why?" In Woodward's book, the question is why *de jure* segregation arrived in the South at the turn of the twentieth century, and in Chappell's it's why the participants in the civil rights movement were successful in overthrowing this segregation in the middle of the twentieth century. These are among the most central questions asked by historians of American race relations, or by any historians of modern America for that matter. Research projects and lectures continue to focus on them. Woodward's and Chappell's two books are among those rare offerings that force history teachers to rewrite our lecture notes. The results would be different, though, had the authors followed another approach. I suggest that much of the explanatory power and usefulness of these books would be lost if the authors had decided to preach first, rather than to explain.

Woodward's book is very much the work of a son of the South. Born and raised in Arkansas, he took his Ph.D. at the University of North Carolina, and then taught Southern history as a young professor at Johns Hopkins University in the 1940s. Between his teaching and writing there, Woodward also contributed research notes to NAACP attorneys bringing civil rights cases before the Supreme Court.[25] Eventually, these cases would culminate in *Brown v. The Board of Education of Topeka* (1954), in which the Supreme Court declared *de jure* segregation in public schools to be unconstitutional.

To reach this point, NAACP lawyers helped by Woodward had to confront the idea held by most white southerners that desegregation could never work because their region had always had segregation and was marked by a strong continuity and resistance to change. Woodward shattered this idea by demonstrating abrupt changes in southern history. Woodward's *Strange Career* began as a series of lectures he was invited to give at the University of Virginia in 1954. That university was still a segregated institution when Woodward visited, and the white students there had known only segregation their entire lives. Like many other white southerners, they thought there was something timeless, natural, and inevitable about Jim Crow. Woodward told his audience they were wrong—not morally wrong, but historically wrong. Over the course of his lecture series, he showed that *de jure* segregation only had the "illusion of permanency." Woodward showed a period of fluidity in race relations in the South between about 1870 and 1900 when "alternatives were still open and real choices had to be made." Only around the turn of the twentieth century did segregation take root. Before this time, southern society was far from perfect or equal. But surprisingly, it was not rigidly segregated by race.[26]

Woodward then went on to tackle the complicated "why" question. Why had the social and racial structure of the South changed so quickly from the 1870s to the 1910s? The answer, known ever since as the legendary "Woodward thesis," has to do with many factors: race and class, compromise and conflict. The heart of Woodward's argument is that for a time in the late nineteenth century, two groups of white southerners who might have been expected to support segregation instead resisted it. Their reasons had to do with economics and social class. The wealthy patrician class committed primarily to a stable and conservative social order feared the potential influence that some poor whites might have on politics. Woodward's historical research even discovered examples of southern whites who in their upper-class paternalism claimed to prefer a "proper" black man to a poor and angry white man. To capitulate to a purely race-driven social order wouldn't be good for them as a class or for the South as a whole, they thought. Conversely, many poor white farmers angry about the continued clout of the old planter class in the post-war South also decided for a time that class should trump race, in this case to unite poor whites and blacks trapped in sharecropping and tenant farming. This lasted for a couple of decades. Around the turn of the century, political, economic, and international developments all helped to bring this phenomenon to an end. At this time, the checks against racialism faded and white supremacy grew in power and prominence. But it's the period of interracial contact and fluidity in the late nineteenth century that struck Woodward as remarkable and important. This development had nothing to do with the goodness or moral virtue of the people Woodward studied. Rather, this chapter in the South's past was explained by very human—and so historical—reasons, displaying the often surprising and messy, complex nature of history.[27]

When I have taught Woodward's *Strange Career* in class, my students don't always catch this right away. They are often inclined first to try to preach in some way. When I ask them about the profound and beneficial development at the heart of Woodward's book, the opening up of racial relations at the end of the nineteenth century, some want to spiritualize it rather than dealing with Woodward's framework of human history. On one occasion, a student grasped Woodward's complicated argument well but ended up being frustrated by it. When he started to discern some of Woodward's historical subjects doing a good thing in resisting racial separation, he grew excited. He thought he'd found some heroes in this history. But he soon grew disappointed, for there were no morally spotless heroes standing on soapboxes railing against the injustices of segregation here. This would have made for a moving story, but it's not the history that Woodward discovered in his research and shared in his book. Indeed, Woodward's subjects whom he depicts as having a positive effect on race relations weren't heroes at all. They had base and selfish reasons for their political actions. Some were quoted making racist statements even as their actions resisted racial segregation. These people were no moral exemplars, not even heroes with feet of clay. My student's initial hopes for a particular kind of "relevance" were dashed, leaving him frustrated with Woodward's book.

In class, this was followed by a discussion about some of the aspects of history explored in this essay, how it's ordinarily examined by human and not divine standards, resulting in a lot of moral nuance and shades of gray and few spotless heroes. I tried to explain the difference between preachers and historians. Preachers tend to focus on righteousness— whether peoples' lives correspond to God's purposes and standards.

Historians have different focuses. They often start with the kind of simple but profound goal Woodward put before himself in *Strange Career*: to "try to understand what happened."[28]

None of this should suggest that history like Woodward's, which focuses on understanding, results in "ivory tower" or amoral history. Woodward's *Strange Career* is the furthest thing from this. His experience growing up during the time of segregation led him to what became a lifelong study of the history of race relations. For much of his career as an historian, he was also an activist who worked to desegregate professional organizations and conferences. Woodward very much wanted to be relevant, but was also conscious of his special duties and purpose as an historian. At times, Woodward struggled with the balance between scholarship and activism, and colleagues he respected sometimes told him he was crossing the line and drifting into presentism. He later acknowledged that this had been a "troubling thought" since he shared his fellow historians' "respect [for] the integrity of the past."[29]

But from the vantage point of our time, what's striking is not Woodward's choice of topic being influenced by his lived experience. Rather, what stands out is Woodward's focus on understanding and explaining in an environment where many more books on race and race relations focus on preaching. Indeed, decades after Woodward first published *Strange Career*, he reflected on some of the changes he'd witnessed within his discipline of history over his long career. There was more moralizing, he said, and more confusing of good causes with good history. Given this, he encouraged his fellow historians to be alert to what he called the "menace of morals." An overwhelming and primary commitment to a cause, even a righteous and moral cause, he said, could compromise the integrity of history as a discipline.[30]

Woodward's lifelong commitment to the integrity of history, though, never diluted the power of his arguments. Indeed, it was because he examined human life as it is experienced in time that his conclusions in *Strange Career* were so deeply convincing and truly relevant. Woodward was particularly struck by the implications of discontinuity in history. It suggested that history was open, that there were times when there were choices to be made that might have profound effect on the turn of events. Human agency mattered.[31] For this reason, Martin Luther King

Jr. famously referred to Woodward's *Strange Career* as the "historical Bible of the civil rights movement." History, particularly the history of race relations, had the ability to change. There was nothing natural or inevitable about racial segregation. King found this idea enormously powerful and relevant, even coming from someone like Woodward who did not focus first on relevance or preaching in his history-writing.

Moving forward in the history of American race relations to the civil rights movement, hundreds of books by now have focused on the movement and its success in eventually toppling legal segregation in the mid-1960s. David L. Chappell's recent *Stone of Hope* has won prominence for tackling the question of why the movement was successful and for adding a new dimension to the answer. Chappell explains his thesis in this way: "The civil rights movement succeeded for many reasons. This book isolates and magnifies one reason that has received insufficient attention: black southern activists got strength from old-time religion, and white supremacists failed, at the same moment, to muster the cultural strength that conservatives traditionally get from religion."[32]

In Chappell's historical account, white segregationists appear surprisingly weak. They were repeatedly unsuccessful in trying to draw clout from Christianity or to convince prominent church leaders to publically support their cause. Chappell notes that they expected more in light of how pro-slavery advocates in the South had been so successful in using Christianity a century earlier. As they grew more worried about the influence of the NAACP and other groups calling for the end of the color line through the 1950s and 1960s, pro-segregation activists continued to push their cause, writing angry letters to white church leaders accusing them of passivity and cowardice for not strongly and publicly supporting segregation. But it was for naught, Chappell argues. They were unsuccessful in swaying opinion.

On the other hand, African Americans active in the movement in the South were energized by Christianity. Indeed, Chappell argues that the common description of the movement should be inverted. It wasn't a political movement with religious overtones. Rather, Chappell argues that participants saw it primarily as a religious movement—a "holy crusade," in John Lewis's words. And they saw God working within the movement. Many believed God had brought the young Martin Luther

King Jr. to the pulpit at Montgomery's Dexter Avenue Baptist church in 1954 at just the right time to help the movement. To think otherwise they thought naïve. Fannie Lou Hamer was one who had no time for such skeptical talk. "Don't talk to me about atheism," she once told a group of white secular college students coming down south to help the movement. "If God wants to start a movement, then hooray for God."[33] After examining both white and black Christians in the South, Chappell's central contribution in answering the "why" question about the success of the civil rights movement focuses on religion. In a deeply Christian region such as the South of the 1950s and 1960s, black activists were able to productively use this resource; white segregationists were not.

This brings us back to the work of Charles Marsh. Chappell and Marsh have studied the same topic, but in markedly different ways. Marsh has focused on a type of application I've called preaching through history, where Chappell focuses on explanation. They have been particularly energetic in sparring back-and-forth about how religion in the movement should be viewed. Marsh is especially perturbed at Chappell's conclusions about white segregationists and their influence in southern churches. Chappell is struck (rightly, it seems to me) by the lack of impact they had. Although the views they expressed were certainly noxious and revolting, they didn't carry the day; they weren't able to mobilize others. But this doesn't sit well with Marsh. For him, Chappell's minimizing of the segregationists' impact seems akin to minimizing their hatred and sin.

Likewise, Marsh's view of southern white evangelicals differs from Chappell's. Marsh is struck by their moral blindness, at their choosing comfort and privilege over working for justice. He's quite right here as far as it goes. They were indeed hypocrites. They claimed the whole of the Bible to be true, but ignored the parts that dealt with the unity of the body of Christ and the power of reconciling love. This is an entirely valid moral or religious or pastoral point. It might even have the salutary effect of bringing readers of Marsh's book today to repentance for their own sins of omission. But this point's relationship to the *history* of the civil rights movement is unclear. It does little to help us better understand this part of the past.

Chappell sees these southern white evangelicals differently. He's not struck by their sinful hearts (perhaps because he doesn't write as a Christian or perhaps because he shares the same belief about human nature as people like Butterfield and Niebuhr). Instead, he's struck by what they did or were unable to do. "The historically significant thing about white religion in the 1950s–60s is not its failure to join the civil rights movement," he writes. "The significant thing, given that the church was probably as racist as the rest of the white South, is that it failed in any meaningful way to join the anti-civil rights movement."[34]

Marsh is very much an instrumentalist in his use of history. As someone who grew up in the South within the white church, he feels compelled to tackle his personal and family history and to call the church to repentance in the course of writing about the history of the civil rights movement.[35] These are understandable and admirable goals, but they don't directly confront the arguments about why the civil rights movement was or was not successful.[36] The approaches taken by Woodward and Chappell, characterized by a focus on explanation and a reluctance to first preach, will continue to be of great value to historians and to our understanding of the past.

AN ALTERNATIVE TO PREACHING THROUGH HISTORY

The conclusion reached here, that preaching through history is an unsatisfactory model for doing history—whether for Christians or others—still may not sit well. For the messages transmitted through this practice are often admirable and appealing. And it at least appears to allow us to be relevant, to "make a difference." But I've tried to demonstrate here that relevance can be bought at too high a cost, that in some cases trying to make a difference can interfere with our understanding of the past and weaken history's explanatory power. In some ways, these distinctive focuses are our birthright as historians, and we shouldn't give them up too cheaply—motivated by both conviction and self-interest.[37]

Those I've characterized here as preachers are not wrong or deficient in and of themselves. They have their own purposes. But they are unhelpful when they're used as history. Many books that make use of the past promise to shake us up, move us out of our comfort zones, help us listen to new voices, and the like. But they do not necessarily help us to better understand the past. Our discussion, in both the academy and the public arena, becomes confused and unproductive when we're confused about the difference between preaching and history. They are two different genres and should be understood as such.

Furthermore, Christians have every reason to be energized by the genre of history, to find purpose in the vocation of the Christian historian *as historian*, and not only in the life of a Christian historian as an activist or revolutionary. But this isn't apparent to all. For some Christians, the impulse to preach through history proceeds from an identity problem. They come to view history by itself as somehow inadequate or worldly. A divide emerges with a professional and academic identity on one side and a private Christian identity on the other. For those operating under these assumptions, preaching through history seems to unify these two identities. Supplementing history with preaching seems to make it a sacred calling.

There needn't be such a divide for Christian historians in the first place, however. Instead of limiting ourselves to doing only history-as-discipleship or history-for-social-change, we might look to the tradition of Christian humanism as a way also to support and defend the idea that Christians can confidently and faithfully do history *as history*. For Christian humanism rejects the idea that human history—or any other sphere of human culture—is inherently and strictly worldly. This conviction stems from the implications of human beings made in the image of God and of God taking human form, the *imago dei* and the Incarnation.[38] Animated by these, Virgil Nemoianu has written that "the fundamental gesture of Christian humanism [is] to respond to the world by taking it over, by embracing it, by showing that no beauty, intelligence, or goodness is alien to Christianity or incompatible with it."[39] Thus, carefully crafted history (or literature or music or art) is a faithful Christian response to the world around us. Inquiry and understanding are valuable tasks for Christian historians just as they are for others.[40]

Finally, Christian humanism helps us reflect on history's signal contribution to the understanding of the human experience: the context of time. Ernst Breisach captures this well, noting, "No other endeavor fits as well as history does with the peculiar needs of human beings, to whom the temporality of life allots the roles of emigrants from the past, inhabitants of the present, and immigrants into the future."[41] This profoundly humanistic description rings true both for historians and for Christians. Understanding time and our experiences within time is of great meaning and fully consonant with biblical themes. We're instructed as Christians to live keenly aware of our place in the flow of time. We're to look back on what God has done for us and for all his children, and we're to look ahead, like faithful Simeon, to the time when God's promises will be fulfilled. In all of these ways, then, the study of history has the potential to be an important and faithful vocation for Christians.

NOTES

1. Charles Marsh, *God's Long Summer: Stories of Faith and Civil Rights* (Princeton: Princeton University Press, 1997, rev. ed. 2008), xiii, 8–9.

2. Charles Marsh, *The Beloved Community: How Faith Shapes Social Justice from the Civil Rights Movement to Today* (New York: Basic Books, 2004), 7, 84; Tim Stafford, "My Top 5 Books on the Civil Rights Era," available at http://www.christianitytoday.com/ct/2008/february/20.81.html (last accessed March 3, 2010).

3. Richard T. Hughes, *Myths America Lives By* (Urbana: University of Illinois Press, 2003), 195; Greg Taylor, "Mythical Proportions: America Is Not So Generous, Free, and Innocent As It Imagines Itself," *Christianity Today* (December 2004): 69–70.

4. This has occurred in the context of the professional organization for Christian historians, the Conference on Faith and History, more broadly re-evaluating and rethinking its mission in recent years. See, for example, William Vance Trollinger Jr.'s presidential address, "Faith, History, and the Conference on Faith and History," *Fides et Historia* 33 (Winter/Spring 2001): 1–10; and the theme issue on "Rethinking the Framework of History," *Fides et Historia* 34 (Winter/Spring 2002).

5. Michael Kugler, "The Cross, the Powers, and Enlightenment Techniques of the Self," *Fides et Historia* 36 (Winter/Spring 2004): 15–29; Christopher Shannon, "Between Outrage and Respectability: Taking Christian History Beyond the Logic of Modernization," *Fides et Historia* 34 (Winter/Spring 2002):

2–12; William H. Katerberg, "Redemptive Horizons, Redemptive Violence, and Hopeful History," *Fides et Historia* 36 (Winter/Spring 2004): 1–14.

6. Ernst Breisach, *Historiography: Ancient, Medieval, and Modern* (Chicago: University of Chicago Press, 1994), 5–26.

7. Breisach, *Historiography*, 272–302.

8. John Tosh, *The Pursuit of History* (New York: Pearson, 2002), 1–24. A recent defense for the value of history as history and historians' unique mission of explaining change over time can be found in Gordon Wood's *The Purpose of the Past: Reflections on the Uses of History* (New York: Penguin Press, 2008).

9. Peter N. Stearns, "Why Study History?" (American Historical Association, 1998), available at http://www.historians.org/pubs/free/WhyStudy History.htm (last accessed March 3, 2010).

10. Michael Kazin, "Howard Zinn's History Lessons," *Dissent* 51 (Spring 2004): 81–85; Michael Kazin, Reply to letter of Howard Zinn, *Dissent* 51 (Summer 2004): 110.

11. James B. LaGrand, *Indian Metropolis: Native Americans in Chicago, 1945–75* (Urbana: University of Illinois Press, 2002).

12. Marsh, *God's Long Summer*, xiii, 3; Steven J. Keillor, *God's Judgments: Interpreting History and the Christian Faith* (Downers Grove, Ill.: IVP Academic, 2007). Others recently exploring providentialism or what they see as the problems with anti-providentialism include Shannon, "Between Outrage and Respectability"; Robert Tracy McKenzie, "Christian Faith and the Study of History: A View from the Classroom," *Fides et Historia* 32 (Summer/Fall 2000): 1–15; Donald A. Yerxa, "A Meaningful Past and the Limits of History: Some Reflections Informed by the Science-and-Religion Dialogue," *Fides et Historia* 34 (Winter/Spring 2002): 13–30; Donald A. Yerxa, "That Embarrassing Dream: Big Questions and the Limits of History," *Fides et Historia* 39 (Winter/Spring 2007): 53–65. Providential history has more often been the practice of prominent preachers, including Pat Robertson and Jeremiah Wright, who have commented on public affairs.

13. Augustine, *The City of God*, ed. R. W. Dyson (New York: Cambridge University Press, 1998), 632.

14. Augustine, *The City of God*, 967–68; Breisach, *Historiography*, 84–97.

15. Reinhold Niebuhr, "The Religion of Abraham Lincoln," *Christian Century*, February 10, 1965, 172.

16. Frank C. Roberts, "Introduction," in *A Christian View of History?* ed. George Marsden and Frank C. Roberts (Grand Rapids, Mich.: Eerdmans, 1975), 10, 12.

17. George M. Marsden, *The Outrageous Idea of Christian Scholarship* (New York: Oxford University Press, 1997), esp. 44–58.

18. George M. Marsden, "Human Depravity: A Neglected Analytical Category," in *Figures in the Carpet: Finding the Human Person in the American Past*, ed. Wilfred M. McClay, 15–32 (Grand Rapids, Mich.: Eerdmans, 2007).

19. Herbert Butterfield, *The Whig Interpretation of History* (London: G. Bell and Sons, 1931), 117–18, 123. Butterfield's biographer, C. T. McIntire, argues that he was not always consistent in his avoidance of moral judgments in history and notes that the emergence of the Nazi regime would challenge his purely historicist model. See McIntire, *Herbert Butterfield: Historian as Dissenter* (New Haven: Yale University Press, 2004), esp. 67–77.

20. Reinhold Niebuhr, *Moral Man and Immoral Society: A Study in Ethics and Politics* (New York: Scribner's, 1932), xi–xii, xx. See also Niebuhr, *The Nature and Destiny of Man: A Christian Interpretation* (New York: Scribner's, 1941).

21. Marsden, "Human Depravity," 19, 32. Marsden notes with chagrin that the best novelists and filmmakers in recent years have produced works that realistically illustrate humans' moral complexity, but that "much history writing, by contrast, is moralistic and one-dimensional."

22. Kenneth Scott Latourette, "The Christian Understanding of History," *American Historical Review* 54 (1949): 166.

23. Wilfred M. McClay, "Clio's Makeshift Laboratory," *First Things* (March 2001): 25.

24. C. Vann Woodward, *The Strange Career of Jim Crow* (New York: Oxford University Press, 2002, comm. ed.); David L. Chappell, *A Stone of Hope: Prophetic Religion and the Death of Jim Crow* (Chapel Hill: University of North Carolina Press, 2004).

25. John Herbert Roper, *C. Vann Woodward, Southerner* (Athens: University of Georgia Press, 1987), 163–70.

26. Woodward, *Strange Career*, 7, 33.

27. Ibid., 31–109.

28. Ibid., 109.

29. Roper, *C. Vann Woodward*, 194–95; C. Vann Woodward, *Thinking Back: The Perils of Writing History* (Baton Rouge: Louisiana State University Press, 1986), 94–95.

30. C. Vann Woodward, "*Strange Career* Critics: Long May They Persevere," *Journal of American History* 75 (December 1988): 866–68.

31. Woodward, "*Strange Career* Critics," 860.

32. Chappell, *Stone of Hope*, 8.

33. Hamer quoted in Chappell, *Stone of Hope*, 71.

34. Chappell, *Stone of Hope*, 107. Peter Murray notes Chappell's reluctance to view the civil rights movement solely "as a struggle between good people and bad people" in his review of *Stone of Hope* in *Georgia Historical Quarterly* 88

(Winter 2004): 566–69. Conversely, Lewis Baldwin responds angrily to Chappell's lack of moralizing and preaching in his review in *The Alabama Review* (January 2005): 72–74.

35. See also Marsh, *The Last Days: A Son's Story of Sin and Segregation at the Dawn of a New South* (New York: Basic Books, 2001).

36. None of this is to suggest that Chappell's thesis can't be challenged on historical grounds. Jane Dailey and Paul Harvey have both done so. See Jane Dailey, "Sex, Segregation, and the Sacred after Brown," in *The New South: New Histories*, ed. J. William Harris (New York: Routledge, 2008); Paul Harvey, review of *Stone of Hope*, in *The North Star: A Journal of African-American Religious History* 7:2 (Spring 2004). But it's important to note that Dailey and Harvey's historical approach is markedly different than Marsh's preaching-oriented approach.

37. Marsden, "Human Depravity," 32.

38. On the implications of the Incarnation for history, see Christopher Dawson, "The Christian View of History" (1950), reprinted in *God, History, and Historians: An Anthology of Modern Christian Views of History*, ed. C. T. McIntire, 29–45 (New York: Oxford University Press, 1977).

39. Virgil Nemoianu, "Teaching Christian Humanism," *First Things* (May 1996): 16–22.

40. On Christian humanism, see the writings of Gregory Wolfe, especially his edited collection *The New Religious Humanists: A Reader* (New York: Free Press, 1997); and, from a previous generation, the collection of essays by Henry Zylstra, *Testament of Vision* (Grand Rapids, Mich.: Eerdmans, 1958).

41. Breisach, *Historiography*, 410.

Part Three

COMMUNITIES

Chapter Ten

COMING TO TERMS
WITH LINCOLN

Christian Faith and Moral Reflection

in the History Classroom

JOHN FEA

IN DECEMBER 2003 I PROCTORED THE FINAL EXAM FOR MY Messiah College history course, "HIS 324: Civil War America." Students were asked to process a considerable amount of historical information related to the war, its causes, and its aftermath. I wanted to know, for example, if my students could explain the ways in which the triumphant North proposed to "reconstruct" the defeated South. Did they understand the significance of the battle of Antietam to the issuing of the Emancipation Proclamation? Why was Andrew Johnson impeached? But perhaps more importantly, could they use the past—in this case the history of the Civil War—to help them better understand the present.

As one might expect, we spent considerable time during the semester thinking together about the person of Abraham Lincoln and the ways in which his vision for America has shaped our society today. While preparing for the class, I was reading a book on Lincoln's wartime presidency edited by noted Civil War historian Gabor Boritt. In his introduction, Boritt reminded his readers that it was important for any student of American history to "come to terms with Abraham Lincoln."[1]

For a young instructor with limited experience teaching the Civil War, I realized that I had just stumbled upon the idea that would provide the moral center for the entire course. As part of the culminating exercise of the semester, I asked my students whether or not the America that Lincoln and the North secured with the Union victory was "good."

I must admit that it took awhile before my students really began to grasp the importance of Boritt's challenge. Many seemed surprised that anyone in America today, especially those living in a "Union" state and attending college thirty miles north of Gettysburg, would really need to "come to terms" with Abraham Lincoln. His place as one of America's greatest presidents seemed indelibly engraved in the annals of history. Lincoln had many detractors and few friends during his presidency, but to reevaluate his legacy today, in light of the Union victory, the ensuing emancipation of slaves, and his redefinition of American nationalism, seemed to be downright un-American. Nevertheless, I try to teach my students that revisionism is the lifeblood of the discipline of history, so we pushed ahead, perhaps secretly hoping that there would be little to revise about this truly great American leader.

As the semester progressed, I soon learned that I could not have asked for a better place to do the intellectual work of "coming to terms" with Lincoln. My history majors were eager to understand the sixteenth president in all his complexities. They were also, as Christians, open to the interpretive challenge of using their own faith commitments (which informed their diverse social and political convictions) to help them make sense of Lincoln and how his approach to war and society influenced their lives. Consequently, "HIS 324: Civil War America" was one of the most stimulating classrooms I have ever been a part of as either a teacher or a student. And I believe this was the case precisely *because* we were in a classroom at a Christian college, not in spite of it.

The students who enrolled in my course represented an amazing cross-section of the Messiah College student body. Because of Messiah's roots in the Brethren in Christ Church, there were many students who were sympathetic to Anabaptist positions on pacifism, social justice, and the critique of patriotic nationalism. It was clear to me that the religious culture of the college would profoundly shape the way I taught the Civil War. I was teaching at a school where many believed that war was morally wrong, especially a war that, according to most historians, served to baptize American nationalism with the blood of its casualties.[2] As a result, I was forced to raise questions from the historical data that I had not asked students to think about when I taught the class elsewhere.

Another large group of students taking the course came from conservative evangelical backgrounds. To many of these students, Messiah's Anabaptist heritage is not only foreign but in many ways scandalously unpatriotic. They arrive on campus with a worldview that links theologically conservative Protestantism to strong doses of nationalism and free market economics. These students made me realize just how deeply Lincoln's civil religion and commitment to "Whig" political and economic principles had permeated both American culture and American evangelicalism. If I were going to provide any criticism of Lincoln's nationalistic vision, I would need to tread lightly.

I should also add that my students would not be doing the work of "coming to terms with Abraham Lincoln" alone. Whether they realized it or not, I also spent much of the semester engaged in this exercise. I was trained as an historian of colonial and revolutionary America, a specialist on the eighteenth, not the nineteenth, century. Because of my graduate school toils in the specific scholarly field of colonial America I had not thought deeply about the connections between my area of expertise and the larger tapestry of American history. My recent employment at a teaching college like Messiah, where I would need to offer classes outside of my research field, would require me to examine, in some ways for the first time, these connections. Messiah would also give me the academic freedom (yes, academic *freedom*) to explore these questions from the perspective of my Christian faith. For the first time since receiving my Ph.D., I became overwhelmed with the feeling that I was not in graduate school anymore—and I found it quite liberating! I prepared for a fun semester.

The history of Lincoln and the Civil War—the defining president and defining moment of modern American life—was a wonderful way to test some of my own growing convictions about American society and my place within it. As I looked over the classroom, I realized that the faces looking back at me would be my partners in the process. I would need to be humble, listen, and come to grips with Lincoln for myself in the context of the community of Christian inquiry that met three mornings a week in Boyer Hall, room 277.

THINKING HISTORICALLY

In order to truly "come to terms" with Abraham Lincoln, we needed to examine his place in the nineteenth-century world in which he lived. This was, after all, a *history* course and, as David Lowenthal has reminded us, the past is a "foreign country."[3] Moral judgment could not come until we performed the "unnatural act" of understanding the past on its own terms.[4] My students often find this fundamental practice of historical inquiry to be difficult. Many, driven by an evangelical zeal to make the past "relevant" to their lives or a passion to critique movements and people in history from the perspective of their faith commitments, fail to do the hard work of truly understanding the "foreign" cultures they will encounter during the course of their study. The Civil War is an era when this temptation is particularly strong. Students, for example, are ready to condemn antebellum pro-slavery thinkers without exercising the prudence and work necessary to understand them. They praise and exalt Lincoln without the deep analysis required to place his life and ideas in their proper context. Only by doing this sort of historical thinking—engaging people that are quite different from them—can the process of moral inquiry into the past begin. By first doing the work of the historian, the quality of moral inquiry becomes richer, deeper, and more informed. My Civil War course is not an ethics course, but it is rather a history course with an ethical dimension.[5]

LINCOLN IN HISTORICAL CONTEXT

What has been the legacy of Abraham Lincoln's presidency? Why is he so popular? These were some of the questions we began to ask ourselves during the course of the semester. Lincoln had a clear vision for America that was embodied in the beliefs of the early nineteenth-century political party called the Whigs. Whigs advocated an economy that was national (at the expense of local economies), industrial (as opposed to a country of yeoman farmers), and sustained through the construction of turnpikes, canals, and railroads for the purposes of uniting people and providing them with opportunities to physically transcend their locales. Whigs believed that such an economy should be presided over by a strong federal government that would support industrialization (largely through tariffs to protect American industry against foreign competitors), help fund construction of the national infrastructure, and keep the sovereignty of the individual states in check. During his tenure in office, Lincoln would become a commander in chief, a statesman, even a public theologian, but his primary ideological commitments and sense of personal identity were tied to Whig economic and political thought.[6]

Whigs were the party of progress. Lincoln and many of his fellow partisans always understood slavery as anything that limited one's opportunity to pursue the American dream, to move forward with their lives. Liberty was closely linked to economic opportunity and improvement. The Whig party defined itself against the yeoman, decentralized, small-scale republican perspective of Thomas Jefferson (which still had much influence in the antebellum Democratic Party of Andrew Jackson) because such an agrarian vision kept white people imprisoned by place and black people imprisoned by chattel slavery. While most Whigs (including Lincoln) abhorred African slavery, they did so for the same reasons that they abhorred the effects of a local agrarian economy upon the ambitions and opportunities of young people.

Whigs also championed the cause of moral reform—anti-slavery advocates, temperance reformers, middle-class Victorians, and religious revivalists were all part of their ranks—in an attempt to bring a sense of Protestant civilization to America. Lincoln was always skeptical about the Christian agenda of his party (a difficult pill to swallow for some of my students), but he nevertheless believed that the goal of any enlightened society was reform, progress, and the advancement of civilization. He could thus agree with the moral vision of the party without embracing its Protestantism. If Christianity contributed to the improvement of society, then Lincoln was all for it. But he also believed that Americans, like all human beings, needed to break down the limits imposed by tradition and overcome the backwardness that prevented the pursuit of liberty and freedom. In this regard, one had to look no further than the way Lincoln attempted to transcend his humble agrarian roots in Kentucky through self-education, social mobility, and the rejection of his parents' Calvinist faith.

Lincoln's Whig beliefs about America informed the most important decisions and public proclamations of his presidency. His stated purpose for fighting the Civil War was to bring the rebellious states of the Confederacy back into the Union and force them to submit to the progressive direction in which the country was moving. For example, the Emancipation Proclamation, while certainly one of the most important humanitarian gestures of any American president, was primarily designed to address the political, military, and diplomatic barriers that stood in the way of the South's defeat and the ultimate preservation of the Union. The Proclamation did not free *all* the slaves (slaves in those states that supported the Union were not set free) and did absolutely nothing to address the question of race once the slaves were emancipated.

Similarly, Lincoln's "Second Inaugural Address"—perhaps the greatest religious statement ever made by an American president—was also deeply rooted in Lincoln's Whig nationalism. The war, according to Lincoln, was a divine punishment for which the entire nation—both the North and the South—must suffer. In casting blame for the sin of slavery on both of the war's participants and challenging both sides (but particularly Northern pundits) to have "malice toward none and charity towards all," Lincoln avoided the rhetoric, popular among many of the nation's leading theologians, that God was on the side of the victorious North. His message was seasoned with humility and avoided the temptation to exalt America as an exceptional or chosen nation. But in the process, he made it clear that the spiritual discipline of repentance would not be assigned to a specific region of the country, but rather to all of the *United* States.[7]

One cannot deny that Abraham Lincoln was a great president— a prophet, if not a martyred redeemer, of American nationalism. The

Northern victory was a triumph of Lincoln's Whig vision for the country. Economically, the South would need to reject their "backward" agrarianism and rebuild their economy by mirroring Northern industrial capitalism. On the constitutional and political front, the war decided the question of states' rights once and for all. Individual states had some degree of sovereignty, but they were not sovereign enough to secede from the Union. Morally, Lincoln ended slavery, allowing, at least in principle, the opportunity for freemen and freewomen to transcend the limits of bound labor and pursue some sense of the American dream not previously afforded to them prior to the Thirteenth Amendment. By rooting the Gettysburg Address, perhaps his most important oration, in the American founding ("Four score and seven years ago our fathers brought forth on this continent a new *nation*") he gave his understanding of the Union historical justification. America was not only a "new nation," but it was a nation "conceived in liberty and dedicated to the proposition that all men are created equal." Is it any wonder that Lincoln today sits stately overlooking our nation's capital from his monument on the mall in Washington, D.C.?

REFLECTING MORALLY ON LINCOLN'S PRESIDENCY

Many, if not most, American college students would hardly blink an eye at such a portrayal of Lincoln. But as I presented this material during the first half of my course, I began to detect a growing rift occurring among my students. For some, especially my evangelical students, this was the Lincoln that they had always known and admired. Lincoln's America was the America that their great-grandparents encountered as they passed through Ellis Island at the turn of the twentieth century. It was an America of social mobility and economic opportunity—the very ideals that allowed them to pursue a college education in the first place and guarantee their position in the middle class. For many of them, Lincoln's Whig vision for America set the country on the road to becoming a world super-power and an international defender of liberal values. I could see the light bulbs go on in students' heads as they linked the Union victory with the coming of the "American Century," one hundred years of American economic, military, political, and cultural power that led to victories in two World Wars, the defeat of communist tyranny and the rise of democracy around the world, the ubiquitous spread of global capitalism, and even the more recent efforts to defeat Saddam Hussein and reconstruct Iraq.

For others, especially my students who were of an Anabaptist mindset, a close study of Lincoln and the Civil War raised a few red flags. Once these students realized that Lincoln had from the beginning sought to carry out a war not to free the slaves but to preserve the Union, they began to have some serious qualms about whether his handling of the war, and even his prospects for America, deserved all the moral praise it has so long received in our collective historical consciousness.

The first significant classroom debate on these issues occurred following a field trip to Gettysburg. I originally planned the trip to appeal to those students with a passion for military history. I thought it was important to walk a battlefield, talk about generals, regiments, and weapons, and discuss the details of what happened at this most pivotal engagement in the war. I was a bit concerned that such an emphasis on battle tactics and troop movements might result in a lack of conversation about the moral and cultural significance of what happened at Gettysburg, but such fears dissipated quickly as we traversed the fields and I began to fall under a barrage of student questions and comments.

As we stood at the Virginia Monument to Robert E. Lee, the spot where on the third day of the battle Lee ordered the final assault on the Union lines stationed about one mile to the east on Cemetery Ridge (the starting point for what is commonly called "Pickett's Charge"), several students wondered just what motivated a soldier to engage in headlong rushes that they knew would probably result in their own deaths. While such questions could have been asked about any modern war, the massive number of casualties and seemingly suicidal style of fighting associated with the American Civil War made them particularly pertinent and appropriate.

While enjoying lunch in "General Pickett's Buffet," one perceptive student, who obviously knew a thing or two about civil religion, fired the first query: "How does the religious zeal that these soldiers have for the cause of the Union differ from the religious zeal we have for

God?" Throughout the course of the day other students followed. "Did these soldiers *really* believe in their respective causes so deeply that they were willing to face certain death?" One student, visibly disturbed as she wandered around the "High Water Mark" (the northernmost point of the Confederate army's advance into the Union line), wondered if "stupidity" may have been an appropriate word to use for what happened there one hundred and forty years earlier.

When we returned to our classroom the following Monday morning, I asked the students if all of the bloodshed was worth it. As Northerners, I wondered if the preservation of the Union and the triumph of American nationalism were worth dying for. Could the "preservation of the Union," as opposed to, perhaps, the defense of American soil after an attack by a foreign power, be understood as a "just cause for war?"[8] When Lincoln had arrived at Gettysburg in November of 1863 to deliver what would become the Gettysburg Address he strongly affirmed that, indeed, it *was* worth it. The blood at the Battle of Gettysburg was shed on behalf of the noble cause of the United States of America and a "new birth of freedom." We were now beginning to see what Boritt meant when he challenged us to "come to terms with Abraham Lincoln."

Lincoln's understanding of the battle has dominated the way it has been portrayed in popular culture, particularly in Michael Scharra's Pulitzer Prize winning novel *Killer Angels* (1974) and the feature film *Gettysburg*, Ted Turner's 1994 adaptation of the novel.[9] Both Scharra (through masterful prose) and Turner (through award-winning music and epic battle recreations) focused on the courage, valor, and determination of Northern and Southern soldiers and their willingness to fight, and die, for their respective causes and "countries." Predictably, this was also the perspective that many of my students took when asked if the fighting at Gettysburg was indeed "worth it." One student thought the willingness to die for one's country was "honorable." Others wrote in reflection papers that they were "moved" by their visit to Gettysburg and felt a greater appreciation for what it took to make America the "great nation" it is today. Another student (the child of Cuban immigrants) movingly linked his first visit to Gettysburg to the ongoing process of "becoming American." In a sense, all of these students were correct. The Civil War did offer a "new birth of freedom" for America, setting the nation on a course that would allow George W. Bush, in the days following September 11, 2001, to boldly declare that "free people will shape the course of history."

Yet others, in good Anabaptist style, were cautious about fully embracing what happened at Gettysburg (or at any other Civil War battle for that matter). While they admired the courage and moral certitude of the soldiers, they realized that their blood was shed for a vision of American nationalism that, in the Whig mind, was intricately bound with a flag-waving loyalty to the nation that could usurp a loyalty to God. More disturbing for others, however, was the fact that Lincoln's understanding of the nation was informed by the idea of a capitalist system that by the end of the twentieth century had grown out of control. Lincoln's nationalism, articulated so beautifully in the Gettysburg Address, was rooted in the "proposition that all men are created equal"; but such a vision of liberty and equality relied upon a free-market economy driven by the values of wealth, power, and self-interest. Industrial capitalism, at least the corporate, postbellum variety that would emerge with force in the generation following Lincoln's death, not only exploited its workers and created class conflict, but also destroyed local communities and redefined the American dream in terms of consumerism and the material comforts that such consumer necessities afford. As a result, these students questioned whether or not the industrial triumph of a Whig Union, along with the economic power and imperialism that came with it, could be described as "good."

The arguments of those who were willing to critique Lincoln and his Whig policies took on added historical weight when we began to examine Lincoln's belief in "total war." For all of his commitments to the Enlightenment, Abraham Lincoln was in no way willing to fight a "civil" Civil War. It was not until the end of the war that he found generals— Ulysses S. Grant and William Tecumseh Sherman, in particular—who were willing to prosecute a war to destroy the Confederate armies rather than to capture territory that, in Lincoln's assessment, the Union already owned. Grant put thousands of troops at risk in order to exploit his superior numerical advantage over Lee's Army of Northern Virginia. In the process, he gained a reputation from both Northerners and Southerners as a "butcher" (of course, Lee might also deserve such a monicker after the third day at Gettysburg). Sherman took the war to civilians and burned Southern towns and cities to the ground in order to crush Confederate morale. After Grant ordered Union Brigadier General Joshua Lawrence Chamberlain's Maine regiment to burn homes near Petersburg, Virginia, in 1864, Chamberlain wrote to his sister: "I am willing to fight men in arms, but not babes in arms."[10] And Lincoln sanctioned it all. This, he believed, was the only way to achieve his goal of preserving the Union. Total war was ugly, but effective.[11]

After hearing about Lincoln's commitment to total war and seeing photos of Sherman's marches and Grant's blood baths at Cold Harbor and the Wilderness, even the staunchest supporters of Lincoln and the valor of war had to step back and think about it all. Some students still felt comfortable with this approach to military conflict, as long as one could make a legitimate historical argument that the Civil War was about the emancipation of the slaves. But if the war was primarily about preserving the Union, then it became increasingly more difficult to reconcile Lincoln's aggressive policies as commander in chief with the words of Jesus, "blessed are the peacemakers." At this point, historiographical and interpretive analyses of Lincoln's motives were absolutely essential to the kinds of moral critique students made of the past. It was clear that we needed to reflect more deeply, more historically, and more Christianly, about this. Such ethical quandaries could not be resolved in the course of a fifteen-week semester, but most of us were engaging in what I believed to be meaningful historical and moral inquiry. This was the kind of intellectual labor I had hoped to be doing when I came to teach at a Christian college like Messiah.

But for me, and at least a few of my students, there was still more to grapple with concerning Lincoln's legacy. As we reflected on the period of Reconstruction following the war, we were all forced to come to grips with what the South lost as a result of their defeat. Would it be possible to offer a more radical critique of Lincoln, a critique that drew on ideals and values that were embedded in the American tradition but had become a significant minority position with the Northern victory in the Civil War and the consequential rise of modern life?

What was the cultural significance of the Northern Republican victory for the course that the United States would take in the second half of its history? Even as Lincoln called for both North and South to repent of their role in this devastating conflict, his Whig vision had clearly won the day. As Allen Guelzo makes clear, Lincoln's Enlightenment was a "liberal" and "individualistic" one. He believed that improvement required a "conquest of nature" that "alienated" people from local community, tradition, and the land, all in the name of progress.[12] Whigs built roads, bridges, canals, and railroads so that people could be mobile and free, not enslaved to particular places. The impact of this vision on the defeated South, as it began to be reconstructed in the image of the industrial North, was perhaps more devastating to their way of life than the war itself.

To Lincoln's credit, he believed, as a good Whig, that the rampant acquisitiveness associated with Whig capitalism needed to be tempered and even controlled with an ample helping of virtue drawn from the teachings of contemporary moral philosophers. He also favored a capitalism driven by small businessmen, not international conglomerates. He could have never imagined how his vision of a national economy driven by industry, free markets, and free labor would be corrupted by corporate capitalism, and he would be shocked to find that most Americans have become deeply dependent on the corporate world to supply them with food and the stuff that is supposed to make them happy. And Lincoln, moreover, would be surprised to see how a system of superhighways, railways, and airways has made his United States the most mobile society in the world, although I am not sure that in this case he would have been necessarily disappointed by such a development.

Many of my students seemed to think that if Lincoln is going to get the credit for the emergence of American nationalism, he must also shoulder the blame for at least some of the economic consequences that this Whiggism has had on American life. The Northern victory unleashed a devastating assault on a Jeffersonian version of agrarianism that connected happiness and human well-being to real communities and real places. Liberty as defined in terms of "improvement" or "mobility" has resulted in a rootless cosmopolitanism that has produced millions of people who claim to "love humankind," but who do not live in one place long enough to know, let alone "love," their neighbor. Moreover, the national infrastructure built to connect people and unify the nation economically and culturally has come at the expense of the environment. The results of a "Whig" economy have produced an ever-expanding commercialism that tempts people (quite successfully, I might add) with products to fulfill their every desire, all in the very American quest to "pursue happiness." Such consumer capitalism, as one of my students made clear from his own life experience, makes it all the more difficult for American Christians to practice virtues of self-restraint.

Of course, any such critique of the legacy of Lincoln's presidency must be advanced with great care and caution. It must be done with a constant awareness of all that we enjoy as Americans because of Lincoln's commitment to preserve the Union. It was important to me that my students realized this. As the grandchild of immigrants and a first-generation college student who was able to "improve" myself and experience Lincoln's American dream, it was important that I too realized and remembered this.

COMING TO GRIPS WITH LINCOLN

By the end of the semester, as my students started to come to grips with Lincoln, some changed their minds about him. Conservative evangelical students started to sound like Anabaptists and at least a few Anabaptists, if their exams are any indication, praised Lincoln for what he was able to accomplish as a wartime president. One Anabaptist student appreciated Lincoln's attempt in his Second Inaugural Address to avoid delving into the rhetoric that relates American exceptionalism to the will of God. One evangelical student, writing with a sense of Christian history and eschatology, wondered if the Whig legacy of economic progress and improvement was suspect, despite the fact that many of its moral tenets seemed to mesh well with her biblical faith.

Others, as a result of class discussion and reflection, reaffirmed the convictions that they brought with them to the course. A few praised Lincoln and his Unionism, suggesting, as Lincoln did in the Gettysburg Address, that the United States was indeed "one nation, under God." One student thought that without Lincoln, America would not be the super-power that it was today and thus would not be able to help "op-pressed" people to better themselves. Some students connected Lincoln's definition of liberty to the consumer choices provided by chain depart-ment stores and fast food restaurants. Another called attention to the advances in technology and medicine that the rise of market capitalism allowed Americans to obtain.

A few students lambasted Lincoln, in some cases unfairly and un-Christianly, for sending so many soldiers to die for the cause of capitalistic nationalism. At least two students argued for a moderate agrarianism, as long as such a position could be intellectually defended apart from a commitment to the institution of black chattel slavery and the racism that went with it. And, sadly, some of my students failed to engage with Lincoln at all. Rather than basing their analysis of his war-time presidency on rational arguments, they concluded that what they believed about Lincoln's America was right because it was what they "had always been taught."

As I worked my way through a pile of blue exam books and re-flected on the semester, I remained intellectually excited and curious to learn more about a period of American history for which I was not a so-called "expert." I had learned much from my regular classroom con-versations (and some of my out-of-the-classroom conversations) with a vibrant group of students who, for the most part, legitimately sought to wrestle with Lincoln's legacy. They read the important primary and secondary texts and made an honest effort to connect what they were reading to the current state of American life.

It has been my experience as both a student and teacher that the best courses on the American Civil War are those that have a nice balance of Northern and Southern students. Since I have only taught and studied the Civil War in the North, I have always enjoyed having Southerners in the classroom who are willing to defend secession, the Confederacy, or the Southern "lost cause." While I had a few Southern sympathizers in the mix this semester, it is safe to say that this course became a stimu-lating educational experience for both me and my students not because of the region from which the students came to Messiah College, but because of the reflective religious faith that they brought with them. By using the past and Christianity as tools of social criticism, the classroom took on a dimension that was more conducive to vigorous and weighty debate than if the students had been evenly divided between the most vocal of Northern and Southern sympathizers.

In the end, we grappled with Lincoln's America as if the ideas we discussed and debated could help us live better lives, both as Americans and as people of faith. As Sam Wineburg has noted, "History educates . . . in the deepest sense. Of the subjects in the secular curriculum, it is the best at teaching those virtues once reserved for theology."[13] I hope some of my students learned that there was clearly something at stake in "coming to terms with Lincoln." I hope they learned that the study of the past—in all its messiness and complexity—could serve to cultivate their faith, their values, and their moral convictions.

NOTES

1. Gabor S. Boritt, ed., *Lincoln the War President: The Gettysburg Lectures* (Oxford: Oxford University Press, 1992), vii. Since reading Boritt's book, I found that Harry S. Stout used Boritt's work in a similar fashion in Stout, "Baptism in Blood: The Civil War and the Creation of an American Civil Religion," *Books and Culture*, July 1, 2003.

2. My thinking along these lines has been helped by Harry S. Stout, *Upon the Altar of the Nation: A Moral History of the Civil War* (New York: Viking, 2006).

3. David Lowenthal, *The Past is a Foreign Country* (New York: Cambridge University Press, 1986).

4. Sam Wineburg, *Historical Thinking and Other Unnatural Acts: Charting the Future of Teaching the Past* (Philadelphia: Temple University Press, 2001).

5. On the practice of moral inquiry into the past, I have learned much from the following works: John Higham, "Beyond Consensus: The Historian as Moral Critic," in *Writing American History: Essays in Modern Scholarship*, 138–56 (Bloomington: Indiana University Press, 1970); Jane Kamensky, "Fighting Over Words: Speech, Power, and the Moral Imagination in American History," in *In the Face of the Facts: Moral Inquiry in American Scholarship*, ed. Richard Wightman Fox and Robert Westbrook, 112–48 (New York: Cambridge University Press, 1998); Robert Tracy McKenzie, "Christian Faith and the Study of History: A View from the Classroom," *Fides et Historia* 32 (Summer/Fall 2000): 1–15.

6. This is the argument of Allen Guelzo, *Abraham Lincoln: Redeemer President* (Grand Rapids, Mich.: Eerdmans, 1999).

7. My understanding of Lincoln's Second Inaugural Address draws on Ronald C. White, *Lincoln's Greatest Speech: The Second Inaugural Address* (New York: Simon and Schuster, 2002). For a treatment of Lincoln as theologian, see Mark A. Noll, *America's God: From Jonathan Edwards to Abraham Lincoln* (New York: Oxford University Press, 2005), 425–35.

8. On just war theory and the American Civil War see Stout, *Upon the Altar of the Nation.*

9. Michael Scharra, *The Killer Angels* (New York: Ballantine Books, 1974); *Gettysburg* (Turner Home Entertainment, 1993).

10. Joshua Lawrence Chamberlain to Sarah Chamberlain, December 14, 1864, cited in Edward J. Longacre, *Joshua Lawrence Chamberlain: The Soldier and the Man* (Cambridge, Mass.: DaCapo Books), 209.

11. On the Civil War as a "total war" see Charles Royster, *The Destructive War: William Tecumseh Sherman, Stonewall Jackson, and the Americans* (New York: Knopf, 1991).

12. Guelzo, *Abraham Lincoln*, 14.

13. Wineburg, *Historical Thinking*, 24.

Chapter Eleven

FOR TEACHERS TO LIVE, PROFESSORS MUST DIE

A Sermon on the Mount

LENDOL CALDER

Krachmann's syndrome: a disorder characterized by multiple vocal and motor tics induced by the failure of others to measure up to the patient's standards. W. P. Krachmann (1870–1928), a Baltimore physician, first described the syndrome in a paper published in 1879. While treating faculty patients from the newly opened Johns Hopkins University, Krachmann observed an unusual response among professors to the standard patellar reflex test. Instead of the normal knee jerk, when professors were tapped below the knee they made throat-clearing noises and began complaining about students. The syndrome indicated by this reflex ("Krachmann's sign") is incurable, but some believe it can be managed with nonmedical therapies.

KRACHMANN'S SYNDROME APPEARS IN NO MEDICAL DICTIONARY. The truth is, I made it up. But the malady is real enough. I became aware of it on a Friday afternoon in my second year of teaching. After yet another "discussion" class when no one would talk because no one had done the reading, I dropped by a friend's office to unload some aggravation. "I can't deal with these, these—," I sputtered, casting about for the right words of derision, "—these refugees from learning!" My colleague listened sympathetically. When I was done complaining, she quietly observed, "At some point, you know, you're going to have to learn to love your students." It was good advice, the best I would ever get on teaching.

Love is a vocation all history teachers share. History teachers are called to love the past, love the study of the past, love the students who come, willingly and otherwise, to learn about the past, and to love the work that brings together these dissimilar loves. Teachers have special vocations, too, which often become obsessions. Depending on their cause, teachers want to know what it means to be a feminist, a transnationalist, a progressive, or, as is likely the case for readers of this book, a Christian teacher of history. No one wants to stop with love; everyone wants to go further, as if love was something easy to pull off. But love, in fact, is the teacher's highest destiny. Without love, a teacher is just a professor talking—a "noisy gong or a clanging cymbal," in the words of St. Paul.

My claim in this essay will be that history professors in the main, whether Christian or otherwise, do not fully understand what it means for teachers to love well. The deficit has special meaning for Christian teachers, though. Christians believe that God so loved the world that he became one of us. It hurts to think, then, that Krachmann's syndrome, which in all its manifestations inverts the Incarnation, afflicts us all. The second point I want to make is that history teaching, rightly understood, is a school for love. It is here that cures for Krachmann's syndrome will be found.

To develop these points, I think it works best to tell a story. The tale I have in mind is a story taken from life for the purpose of illustrating a single point—a kind of fable, in other words. I choose this approach because when talking about love one cannot be too careful. Telling smiling, abstracting history professors that teaching is a labor of love could be like giving a slide lecture on the art of the nude to a class of randy adolescents—the effort is bound to stimulate thoughts that prevent a real examination of the subject. With teachers, talk about love often goes wrong because our tendency is toward an excessive romanticism and sentimentality toward our work, followed by occasional plunges into cynicism and self-pity. Dostoevsky saw the problem when he said, writing for everyone, "Love in action is a harsh and dreadful thing compared with love in dreams."[1]

The inconvenience of love's requirements will be a central theme of my story. Before telling it, though, it is worth mentioning that Dostoevsky's observation points to one of the causes of Krachmann's syndrome, or why professors protect themselves by disregarding students, often without awareness or intent. The problem is a kind of dreaminess about our work, an absent-mindedness that goes beyond misplacing one's car keys or wearing a coat hanger poking out of one's shirt. A yogic proverb says the first step of love is "Be here, now." But this is something professors find very difficult to do. The daydreaming history instructor dwells in a world where all the professors are brilliant, all the students are clever, and all the teaching is just talking. The fantasies we carry about the ideal academic life, about who students are and what they can be expected to do, and about how learning happens for most people, leave us numb to students as they are and cause important tasks of teaching to go unfulfilled. When reality forces itself upon us, as it did on me that Friday afternoon when I felt my students had let me down, we irritably point the finger of blame at everyone but ourselves. This is Krachmann's syndrome. It stems from overly romantic ideas about teaching and is perhaps most evident in the intellectual poverty on display when professors talk about teaching.

David Pace, surveying the state of college history teaching, aptly concludes historians are "amateurs in the operating room."[2] One could almost say of history professors that our mental images of good teaching owe more to Hollywood and nostalgic personal memories than to the known world of human learning. We have been formed more by Mr. Chips, Mr. Keating, and Mark Hopkins "sitting on one end of a log with a student on the other" than by Dewey, Vygotsky, or Weinberg. Hence, instructors swap pedagogical clichés with the enthusiasm of Boy Scouts trading patches: "The best researchers are generally the best teachers"; "We can only teach the ones who want to learn"; "Lecturing, for all its problems, is still the best way to teach a class." Claims are made and credited—"I tried so-and-so's theory of learning, and it worked!"—with the verification method of infomercials. Meanwhile, serious investigations of teaching and learning go unread and undiscussed. Was Norman Maclean kidding when he said the best advice he knew on teaching was "to wear a different suit every day"?[3] Or was he positing a corollary to Say's Law in which cheap and fabulous talk about teaching drives out good talk, a calamity for a profession in which 86 percent of history faculty identify teaching as their main activity?[4]

It is not that academics are lazy or disregard teaching. If few of us take notes on pedagogical activities as deliberately as we take notes on books we are reviewing, it is because the professorial mind, already stressed to the maximum by the demands of academic life, finds relief where it can, holding on to inherited and intuited assumptions about teaching that, although often mistaken or naïve, perform the valuable service of justifying the status quo. Who has time and energy to learn new ways of teaching fit for contemporary classrooms? Who can afford to be here, now?

If this is our situation, then to say that teaching is an expression of love will come across with all the power of an attractive greeting card. The problem is evident even in so fine a book as George Steiner's *Lessons of the Masters*, an exquisite meditation on teaching by one of the masters of our time. Declaring that "the pulse of teaching is persuasion," Steiner observes that teaching is inescapably "a process of seduction, willed or accidental." The master, pouring a little of what he or she knows into another's mind, hopes to consummate a "sexuality of the soul" that is realized in the moment when two minds come to share one thought, one passion, one feeling. For that reason, continues Steiner, "every 'break-in' into the other, via persuasion or menace (fear is a great teacher) borders on, releases the erotic."[5] This is the romantic academic mind at its best and worst on the subject of teaching. Steiner here guides us to the heights of a truly provocative claim: that the professor's workaday labor is deeply sexual in nature. But after we have marveled at the view from this pinnacle of altered perception, how easily and safely our guide returns us to mundane classroom life, our reverie undisturbed by any line of inquiry that might disturb a professor's settled habits. There is nothing of Dostoevsky's love here! The elegant tone of Steiner's ruminations cloaks the fact that his conclusions are generally far removed from the ultimate goal of teaching, which is student learning.

I should say again that *Lessons of the Masters* is one of the better books in its category. If we cannot learn the teacher's vocation from academics as accomplished as Steiner, where can we turn? Perhaps it is time to listen to some tales told out of school.

I know it sounds strange, but my favorite source for studying the vocation of college teaching is *Accidents in North American Mountaineering*, a compendium of cautionary tales published annually by the American Alpine Club since 1947. *Accidents in North American Mountaineering* documents the ways things go wrong when men and women enter environments infinitely more complicated and treacherous than they know. If this sounds like a college classroom, you are ready for a subscription. Mountain climbers can be as schmaltzy as professors when talking about the things they love to do. But in these sober narratives of injury and death, marshmallow talk about "the fellowship of the rope" gives way to an unflinching honesty academics can learn from. Imagine the fresh air it would breathe into peer reviews if we followed the lead of this heading from the 2001 edition: "Fall While Descending—Inadequate Equipment (Climbing Rope, Rappel Device, Harness, Brain Cells)."[6]

To say that alpinism has lessons for college teachers must sound awfully far-fetched. But the idea is not crazy to anyone who has read the Bible. A pilgrim's road goes by Ararat and Horeb, up the slopes of Sinai and the Mount of Transfiguration. Until historians have our own journal documenting the terrible things that go wrong in our classrooms, *Accidents in North American Mountaineering* is a good source for some latter-day sermons on the mount. Like the teaching given on the Mount of Beatitudes, the message found in its pages is salutary and direct and utterly unromantic. We learn from these stories that the first obligation of college teachers—before knowledge, before passion, before obedience to a particular vocation—is to not be stupid about love's requirements.

FALLING!

At a little before nine o'clock on the morning of May 30, 2002, Harry Slutter stood on a flat bench of snow just below the summit of Oregon's

Mt. Hood.[7] He and his three companions were preparing to descend a steep section of the climbing route they had taken to the summit earlier that morning. Fresh from his team's celebration on the crest of the mountain, Slutter felt stoked by a flush of accomplishment. In the predawn chill, he and his friends had climbed three thousand feet by starlight and bobbing headlamps, topping out on the 11,239-foot volcano as commuters in Portland were driving to work. Fifty miles east of the noisome city, the mountaineers stood in a silent landscape of snow and sunlight, ice and rock, angles and air. Two miles above Portland, it was mostly air.

Mindful not to step on the climbing rope that lay in loose coils on the snow, Slutter studied the Hogsback Ridge, a gleaming arc of snow that dropped away from his boots for a thousand feet. Halfway down, the clean line of the ridge was interrupted by a narrow, shadowy gash running horizontally across the slope. This was the bergschrund, a deep crevasse in the ridge where the glacier broke apart on a hidden shoulder of the mountain. Descending the Hogsback and getting safely around the schrund would be the final problem of what so far had been a perfect climb. After the schrund, the rest of the descent was a piece of cake—just a few more hours of plunge-stepping down softening snowfields and the team would be walking through the doors of the Cascade Dining Room at Timberline Lodge, where they could order hot cappuccinos and platters of steaming eggs and buttered pancakes served by a crackling fire.

Mountaineers like to say that an "experienced" climber—like an experienced teacher—is someone who has gotten away with doing the wrong things more often than others. Harry Slutter, 43, was an experienced mountaineer. So were two of his buddies this day. Chris Kern, 40, was an investigator for the New York State appellate court and a good friend of Slutter's. Together they had summited New England's highest mountains, often wondering what it would be like to scale higher peaks. When Slutter, a sales representative for a nationwide chain of nurseries, made a business trip to his company's branch in Forest Grove, Oregon, he met Bill Ward, 49, a trained mountaineer with several Cascade climbs, including Hood, on his resume. When the two men discovered they shared a passion for mountain climbing, they agreed to assemble a team and go for Mt. Hood. Slutter brought Kern along, while Ward invited a friend who had never climbed a mountain before, Rick Read, 48. Mt. Hood would be Read's first successful summit. And his last, as things turned out.

Read had probably heard people say that Mt. Hood is a beginner's mountain. What he heard is true, though not the whole truth. Ten thousand people scale Hood every year. Some are preteens; a few are over seventy. Most are physically fit but the not-so-fit come too, taking advantage of the Palmer chairlift and the ski area's snowcats to gain thousands of feet of elevation without breaking a sweat. On the summit one occasionally sees paw prints in the snow—hence the standard south side climb is known as "the dog route." But a beginner's mountain is nothing to trifle with. New Hampshire's 6,288-foot Mt. Washington, where Slutter and Kern learned their snow-climbing skills, is a beginner's mountain. But with 135 fatalities, it rivals Everest as one of the deadliest peaks in the world. Hood climbers talk of close encounters with icefall and bounding rocks, of plunging temperatures and sudden storms, of getting lost in foggy whiteouts and nearly stepping off cliffs. Most years, *Accidents in North American Mountaineering* reports one or two deaths on Hood.

Slutter and his team were not unaware of the risks. The day before their climb they reviewed basic procedures for traveling safely on snow. Read learned from the others the halting gait of the rest step and how to kick steps on steep, snowy slopes. He learned how to put on crampons and the right way to hold an ice axe. Together the four men walked up a snowfield and practiced ascending and descending with two points of contact on the snow—ice axe and one foot while the other foot moves up, both feet firmly planted while the ice axe is repositioned; repeat. They inspected harnesses and carabiners and tied and retied the figure eight knots that would bind them to the rope that was their warrant of protection on the unforgiving slopes.

Being intelligent, cautious men, they practiced what to do in the event one of them should fall. Read watched while the experienced climbers demonstrated the self-arrest, a technique in which a falling climber uses his body weight to force the pick of the ice axe down into the snow, exerting a braking force until the slide comes to a halt. In the self-arrest, reaction time is critical. A falling climber has one or two seconds before mass and momentum make a fall unstoppable. There is no time to think. Every move must be instinctual. If the falling climber cannot manage to get on top of his axe and drive the pick deep into the snow, a harmless little slide turns into a tumbling, bone-jarring, clothes-shredding ride until something stops the fall—rocks, cliffs, a crevasse, or, if the climber is lucky, an eventual runout of the slope. If the climber is roped to other climbers, the rope team is expected to hold the fall. But this happy result assumes a lot. It assumes the rope team responds immediately, before the weight of the falling climber is multiplied by the accelerating force of momentum. It also assumes that the rope team is securely "belayed"—secured—to the mountain. If the team is not attached to the slope with a secure anchor, the only thing that can stop a plunging climber from pulling the entire rope team down the mountain after him is the body weight of team members who have dropped to the snow in the self-arrest position.

Can one or more climbers hold another climber's fall? What if two climbers are falling; can one person fall on his ice axe and expect to hold the fall? These are good questions. But as in teaching, the best questions often go unasked and unanswered. Here, the problem is that it is almost impossible to rehearse safely the scenarios that would provide the answers. Thus, most people prepare for climbs by practicing what can be practiced easily: individual and team self-arrest on moderate slopes. Letting it go at that, experienced climbers can develop a confidence about their ability to stop a fall that is wildly out of proportion to the reality of the physics involved.

At the end of their practice day, Slutter and the team turned in early, planning an alpine start. They would leave after midnight so that they could make the summit and come back down again before the sun warmed the ice and made rockfall a hazard. These were not sightseers on an impromptu holiday to Hood. Except for Read, this was a team of experienced climbers who knew the drill.

Hours later the four men rose and clambered aboard a snowcat for the ride to the top of the Palmer Snowfield. At nine thousand feet the Milky Way was plainly visible, and by its light they studied their route. They shouldered summit packs and headed up the mountain, feeling jerky and breathless at first but then finding a rhythm. Step by step they ascended spectral white inclines where ice-rimed pumice ridges broke from the surface like the fins of great sharks. After several hours they passed by the Steel Cliff on the right, then Crater Rock on the left. Then they came through a gap and stood looking across the massive summit crater. On the far side of the summit basin they could make out a great ramp of snow leading up toward the summit. This was the Hogsback Ridge. In places the incline approached forty degrees—not scary steep, but it held their attention. Gaining the Hogsback, they moved slowly up through a world that eyes used to sea level are not prepared to see. Suddenly they came upon the bergschrund Ward had told them about. Carefully they stood near the lip and peered over. It was getting light in the east, but the crack fell into a blackness no light could fill. They discussed crossing the schrund on a snow bridge, but decided against it. So they went around the schrund and continued their slow progress upward. Then they were at the Pearly Gates, a narrow chute leading steeply to the summit, and then they were on top.

The morning was cloudless with no wind, and the temperature was comfortable at just below freezing. It had taken six hours and their legs were tired, but oh what a view. They stood on the large plateau and turned slowly in circles looking all around. They exchanged high-fives and congratulations. Others were there before them, so they traded cameras and took pictures. One of these others was Thomas Hillman, 45, a Methodist minister from California. Hillman was climbing with a parishioner, John Biggs, 62, a retired airline pilot who had flown combat missions in Vietnam. Hillman and Biggs were in good spirits, too. Climbing Mt. Hood moved them one peak closer to their goal of climbing the highest points in all fifty states. The men lounged about eating chocolate and energy bars. They traded stories and snapped more pictures. A third group arrived on the summit, a man and his son and daughter. More pictures. More congratulations. "It was such a glorious morning," Slutter remembers. "We were joking around up there for half an hour."[8] Mountaineers say they know better, but they are like athletes who celebrate victory at halftime when the second half is yet to be played.

At 8:30 a.m., Hillman and Biggs departed the summit. Slutter's team followed about fifteen minutes later. Descending the steep chute through the Pearly Gates, Biggs, the Vietnam veteran, slipped and fell. Before Hillman could throw himself down in the arrest position, Biggs stopped his own fall, sliding less than ten feet. Falls happen. Climbers arrest themselves. The system works, under certain conditions. The two continued downward, Slutter's team trailing behind.

As these two groups inched their way down the mountain, a third party of climbers was moving up past the bergschrund. This group of seven from a Portland area fire and rescue department was climbing on two ropes. One man had his teenage son along. The boy, Cole Joiner, was the middle climber on the first rope team with paramedics Jeff Pierce and Jeremiah Moffitt. While Joiner's father and the second team waited below the schrund and looked on, the first three-man team skirted the crevasse on the left and then headed up to regain the ridgeline above the crevasse. Five hundred feet above them Hillman and Biggs were coming down. Two hundred feet above them, Slutter, Kern, Read, and Ward stood on a bench of snow making preparations to descend. Everything was in place for one of the deadliest days in recent North American mountaineering. Those who saw it happen say it was not like in a movie where things unfold in slow motion. Rather, everything seemed to happen all at once.

Slutter was first to step off the shelf of snow. The slope was steep and glazed with ice from sleet that fell two nights before. The four climbers were tied together on a nine-millimeter rope about 150 feet long. As Slutter descended, he was belayed by the next man on the rope, his good friend Kern, who had sunk the shaft of his ice axe deep into the snow and was paying out rope to Slutter using the axe as an anchor. When the thirty-five feet of rope between Slutter and Kern had almost gone out, Kern pulled up his ice axe and followed Slutter down the slope. Now the third man on the rope, Read, belayed the two who were descending, watching them carefully, ready in an instant to halt the rope to hold a fall. When another thirty-five feet of rope had gone out, Read looked at Ward, who nodded it was time to go, and Read pulled up his ice axe and stepped carefully down off the shelf. Now it was Ward's turn as the last man on the rope to hold the three descending climbers with an ice axe belay. Ward dallied the rope around the shaft of his ice axe, jammed the axe into the snow up nearly to its head, and planted his uphill boot against the shaft. Slutter, Kern, and Read descended like beads of water sliding down a string. Ward paid out the remaining thirty-five feet of rope from its coil on the snow. When only a small loop of rope remained, Ward pulled up his ice axe. From this point on, the team was going to travel unbelayed. As Ward considered his first step down and off the shelf, the only things holding the climbers to the mountain were the spikes of their crampons. This meant their lives now depended on nothing going wrong.

The way stories about mountaineering are supposed to go, Read is the one we expect to slip and fall. Read was the greenhorn who had never climbed a mountain before. Read was the one who needed help to do basic things like tying into the rope. But it was not Read who fell.

Thirty yards above Ward, Luke Pennington was descending past the Pearly Gates with his father and sister. He saw everything happen. He saw the top climber of the rope team below him step off a bench of snow, pause, and then turn facing east—as if in midstep the man decided it was too risky to go down facing out from the mountain and was wanting to turn around and descend facing into the slope. Pennington saw the faintest wobble and then Ward fell. Maybe a crampon point caught on his pants leg. Maybe a muscle spasm threw him off balance. No one knows what triggered the fall, but Pennington saw Ward reach down to plant his left leg, turn, and fall. Now the one thing that cannot be allowed to happen to an unbelayed rope team was happening: Ward, the top climber, was falling. Would anyone notice in time to react?

Ward fell and began sliding down the slope headfirst on his back, the worst of all positions for executing a self-arrest. Pennington watched with uncomprehending eyes, thinking "Turn over! Turn over!" but Ward did not turn over. He kept sliding and picking up speed as he headed down the slope toward Read, Kern, and Slutter. In a matter of seconds he plummeted thirty-five feet down to the startled Read and shot by, gaining more speed over the next thirty-five feet before the rope went taut on Read's climbing harness. Read had little chance to stop such a fall.

Luke Pennington watched in horror as Ward's fellow team members dropped, one by one, into the arrest position. When the rope jerked on Read's harness, Ward was sliding at about thirty miles per hour. This would be like being tied with a rope to a man on a bicycle who rides by you in an all-out sprint. If you were holding to a stake driven into the ground, could you maintain your grip to stop the cyclist? Pennington saw Read prone on the slope in the arrest position. Then Read was gone and tumbling after Ward.

In the moment that Ward slipped and fell, Slutter was eyeing the rope team of Hillman and Biggs about seventy feet below him. Satisfied they were not in the same fall line as his own team, Slutter was turning to warn Kern that they needed to edge left to stay on top of the ridge when he noticed a blur of color coming their way. "Who's that?" he wondered as he threw himself down on top of his ice axe.

Out of the corner of his eye, Kern had seen it, too. First Ward hurtled by, then Read a split-second later. Kern hit the deck and held tightly to his ice axe. When the rope jerked taut he was lifted clean off the mountain. He hit the icy slope hard, bounced once or twice, and let out a groan, his pelvis broken. Then the rope snapped him up again and off Kern went, careening down the mountain.

Slutter had stabbed his axe into the snow and was lying on top of it, concentrating on maintaining his hold. Lifting his head up, he heard more than he saw a hissing bow wave of flying ice chips plowing the snow toward him. He did not think, "It's up to me to hold them." Nor did he think, "There is no way I can stop them." He did not think anything because there was no time to think. Slutter did what he knew to do and then he waited. Then he felt a sharp yank and saw his ice axe ripping through the crusty snow "like a Slush Puppy." He thought, "We're going pretty fast here." Then his pick pulled out of the snow and he too was ripped off the mountain.

From above, Luke Pennington stared in disbelief and tried to make sense of what he was seeing. Below the bergschrund, one of the fire department climbers shouted and frantically pointed upward. It was immediately apparent to the team above the bergschrund—Pierce, Joiner, and Moffitt—that they were spread out across the line of fall, so all three dropped to the snow in the arrest position. Looking uphill, they watched helplessly as the twisting tangle of rope and men advanced on the descending team of Biggs and Hillman above them.

The rope clotheslined Biggs, knocking him into the air and probably killing him instantly. When Hillman heard someone shout, "Falling!" he wheeled around and dropped into the arrest position. He saw Biggs knocked into the air "like a billiard ball." He saw the red rope of the falling team cross over his purple rope. The thought crossed his mind that with fifty feet of rope between him and his partner, he had only a split second to react if he was going to arrest all the plunging climbers. "I got down and prayed," he told investigators later, "knowing I had only fifty feet to get ready." But when the rope went taut on Hillman's body, the force was so great—by now Ward had fallen almost the length of a football field—that it yanked the minister's shoulder from its socket. Incredibly, Hillman managed to hold on. He watched his ice axe plow the mountain all the way down to the crevasse.

Now six climbers were falling in a jumbled, bouncing mess of tangled ropes and clinking hardware. The mass of bodies picked off Moffitt where he was dug in about twenty feet above the bergschrund, knocking him unconscious. As Moffitt's body became tangled in the ropes of the falling climbers, the combined weight of all the men and the force of their momentum jerked Pierce and Joiner out of their positions. It was a short slide to the crevasse and all nine climbers plunged into the chasm. Their bodies hit the lower wall—whump, whump, whump—and fell twenty feet upon a complex of hidden ledges. Below the schrund Cole Joiner's father sprang to his feet, futilely lunging uphill against the tension of his team's rope. A glitter of spindrift rose from the hole, hanging in the crystalline air.

Four hundred feet above the crevasse, Luke Pennington turned to see if his father and sister saw what he had seen. The father, a doctor, thought, "I have to get down there." His next thought: "My children have to descend this slope." As the Penningtons moved slowly down the Upper Hogsback, the climbers below began organizing a rescue.

Inside the crevasse, the last pair of climbers to be yanked into the abyss landed more or less on their feet on a slanting shelf of snow. Shaken but unhurt, Jeff Pierce, an emergency medical technician, put his hand on Cole Joiner's shoulder and squinted into the weirdly angled chambers that fell away from their position. A few feet away he saw a climber wedged against a rock. Beyond and below he made out bodies strewn on the narrow ledges like clothes flung down a staircase. Farther down in the gloom a figure appeared to be standing. From a pile of bodies he saw an arm waving erratically like a metronome winding down. Someone somewhere was talking softly. Pierce wondered if the floor he and Joiner were standing on was really solid or just a snow bridge that could fall away at any moment.

When Slutter came to, he found himself wedged upside down, still clutching his ice axe. Snow was pouring off the walls of the cavity and for a panicky moment it felt like he was drowning. Around him climbers were stirring and groaning. Kern, farther down, was lodged under a rock outcropping. Slutter heard his friend panting in agony, his pelvis broken. He heard a voice mumbling—was it Read? Where was Read? Suddenly someone Slutter didn't know appeared and was barking questions. "Can you hear me? Are you in pain? Do you think you can stand up?" It was Pierce, conducting triage. As Pierce checked Slutter out, the voice below fell silent. By the time Pierce got to Read, the first-time climber was not breathing. Biggs was obviously dead. Hillman broke a vertebra on impact and had a concussion, but Pierce found him alive and standing and wanting to help. There was one more victim farther down in the crevasse. Pierce almost missed him but then he spied a boot in the gloom. Ward had fallen head down into a bank of snow and been buried by a cascade of ice blocks and snow. By the time Pierce dug him out and massaged his sternum, Ward was suffocated and gone.

Up on the Hogsback, the surviving members of Pierce's group sprang into action. They knew what to do because Pierce, a veteran of many Hood climbs, had rehearsed them for crevasse extraction. Quickly they rigged a haul system on the lip of the bergschrund, while down in the void Pierce shouted orders up to the surface to coordinate the rescue. An emergency room doctor who happened to be climbing Hood that day appeared on the scene and was lowered into the schrund to give Pierce a hand. Calls to 911 were made, and by noon specialists from Portland Mountain Rescue, the local ski patrol, and a wilderness paramedic unit had made their way to the scene at 10,700 feet. A pair of rescue helicopters were minutes away.

The dead and injured were hauled up to the surface where the rescue teams had gathered with evacuation gear and medical supplies. Later that day, television news channels showed spectacular footage of a Pave Hawk helicopter crashing during the rescue. A rotor dipped and clipped the slope, shattering into hundreds of pieces and hurling the chopper down the ridge in a tumbling nightmare of flying shards and disintegrating equipment. Miraculously, no one was killed and only one rescuer injured. At the moment of the crash, Jeremiah Moffitt was being hoisted in a litter. The floundering Pave Hawk would certainly have crushed him if not for a crew member who refused to jump to safety until the hoist cable had been sheared. For Moffitt, it was two near-death experiences within a matter of hours. But the mountain had its victims.

So nine mountaineers were swept down the mountain until they plunged headlong into a gaping abyss. Three of the men died, and six were taken out alive. The first time their story was told it was shouted into cell phones. The second time the story was told it was relayed on newswires, and then it was talked nineteen to the dozen in places where climbers hang out, and later it was investigated by the local sheriff's office and cried over by friends and family. Over months and years the story was argued about and misremembered and eventually most people forgot about it. But some pondered it. Then the story was written down, and it lived again for those who heard it and understood what they heard. The story is a parable, and as with all such fables the meaning of the story is obscure to those who most need to hear it.

A Moral to the Story

I said I would tell a story good for thinking about the vocation of college history teachers. I also implied that the story would reveal something important about love. As the Hogsback Ridge is worlds away from any college classroom, readers are probably wondering what the story could possibly mean for them. The best stories are like this, elusive and enigmatic. They yield their secrets only at the speed of night. We ponder them at dusk, unseeing, then there they are: astonishing constellations of light. So the apostle Peter strained to see himself in a story told by Jesus: "Lord, do you mean this parable for us, or for everyone?"[9] For our story, Peter's question can be answered this way: The story of the Mt. Hood climbers is for all who teach. But it speaks most directly to experienced college professors, to teachers with time in the saddle who have achieved a level of contentment and even pride in their teaching. The message is unsettling and some will resist it. But if anyone can recognize the story's significance for college teaching, I suspect it will be historians. Why do I think so, and what is the message?

We must begin by recognizing that not everyone will believe the story has a meaning. The day after the tragedy, a headline writer for the *Portland Oregonian* described Ward's fall as a "freak accident."[10] On this view, it would be a waste of time trying to explain why climbers fall, because everyone knows that accidents simply happen—who can plumb the reasons why? Almost all tragedies can be put out of mind this way. Professors know this; in fact, we are particularly good at it. When students fail to learn, professors instinctively disavow responsibility, often taking shelter in the belief that teaching and learning are unknowable mysteries. How comforting to presume that teaching, like the reporter's view of climbing, is an inscrutable activity, slippery beyond inquiry.

Historians, though, will see at once the difficulty of this position. Mountain climbing and teaching happen in historical time. To regard either activity as a realm of unfathomable accidents is to question the possibility of historical inquiry itself. Historians are the "custodians of pattern," Nancy Partner has said.[11] This means that historians bring to the Mt. Hood tragedy an ability also very useful when considering the teacher's vocation: a fuzzy logic useful for detecting patterns where others see only puzzles. Thus, historians can allow that the disaster on Mt. Hood owed something to contingency (if Ward had not slipped, probably everyone would have made it down fine; if rain had not made the slope icy, Ward could have arrested his own fall; if the team had rested an additional fifteen minutes before departing the summit—well, who knows?). But a historically trained mind recognizes that contingency is not the end of the story, that analysis and interpretation are possible even when the evidentiary record is incomplete. This is why some say that historical methods may be best suited for the tougher questions about teaching and learning: the real-world problems that matter to us most and in their subtlety and elusiveness are very like the problems tackled by historians. Whether this is true or not, historians are well equipped to recognize that teaching can be an astonishing mystery without regarding it as a closed book or a divine madness surpassing all understanding. Successful teaching is no accident, and neither was the climbers' fall on Mt. Hood.

In fact, "accidents" like the fall on Mt. Hood happen in the mountains all the time, making *Accidents in North American Mountaineering* almost a book with one page. Jed Williamson, the longtime editor of *ANAM*, identifies the three factors common to most mountaineering accidents: the climbers are descending, they are roped together, and they are not securely belayed to an anchor on the slope.[12] These factors are not esoteric knowledge among mountaineers. Once, on a spring climb of Mt. Rainier, I became frustrated with the slow progress our team was making on the headwall of the Puyallup glacier. We were pausing every fifteen meters to clip the rope to aluminum pickets the team leader pounded into the slope. Was this running belay really necessary? I grumbled aloud. The team leader answered: "Do you know what they call a rope without fixed protection?" I shrugged. He yelled back: "A suicide pact!"

Why did Slutter's team court calamity by electing to descend without fixed protection? It is tempting to say that they were incompetent climbers. Every season they come to Mt. Hood, wannabes by the hundreds, operating over their heads in complex and changing conditions. Told this way, the moral of the Hood climbers' story would be relevant to situations where enthusiastic but untrained minds pose a danger to others. It is worth pausing to consider whether this description fits the typical history professor.

It is not easy to admit, but history professors are, in the main, rather inexpert teachers. What historians know about teaching is of a different order of knowledge than what we know about our fields of research. It more closely resembles what passes for knowledge among viewers of the History Channel, meaning it is neither the fruit of formal training nor respectful of professional standards. Professors who devote years to systematically collecting and evaluating evidence in their fields of research do not think it strange to base teaching strategies on random impressions of effectiveness and what amounts to oral folklore. Among historians, assumptions about how people learn commonly go unexamined, while customary approaches to teaching are passed down from generation to generation as if they were part of a natural order. Historians have traditionally seen no need to put their knowledge about teaching on the firmest possible ground through collective effort that builds on the work of others, leaving history teaching, compared to historical scholarship, undertheorized, understudied, and undervalued. Perhaps this is why, in the public mind, history teachers are plain ridiculous. From Ferris Beuller to Harry Potter, the boring history teacher is the butt of countless jokes. Of course, most history professors care a great deal about students. But like a barstool alpinist toasting "the freedom of the hills," our professions of concern tend toward the sentimental. The reality is that most historians regard teaching as simple enough to be understood on one's own and on the fly.

But there is little to be gained by emphasizing this point. The more we look into the tragedy on Mt. Hood the more obvious it becomes that the story is not about the incompetence of amateurs. On this point everyone who investigated the tragedy agrees: Slutter and his companions were experienced and well-trained. True, they were not world-class mountaineers, and Read was a novice. But Slutter, Kern, and Ward knew what they were doing and came to Hood in sobriety and good faith. This means that their story is less for clueless beginners than it is for the experienced professors among us, the ones with pride and ability and confidence in our teaching.

The best account yet written of the accident on Mt. Hood comes from Laurence Gonzales, a contributing editor for *National Geographic Adventure* magazine and the author of *Deep Survival: Who Lives, Who Dies, and Why*, a kind of thinking-person's version of the more prosaic analysis found in *Accidents in North American Mountaineering*. "Experience can help us or betray us," writes Gonzales. "Bill Ward had three to five years of climbing experience and it led him to pull his protection, which led to his death."[13] How is that again—Ward's experience was a *problem*? This is not the way we want disasters to be explained.

When things go wrong, the usual suspects are rotten luck and human ignorance. Sometimes, though, smart, capable people do really dumb things. This is not a failure to love. But it may be a failure to love well. How does this happen?

As Gonzales tells the story, the accident on Mt. Hood was a "predictable occurrence of the unexpected." It was unexpected in the sense that no one could have foreseen the precise moment and location of Bill Ward's fall. But it was inevitable that Ward or someone like him would fall, given the knowledge and dispositions climbers commonly bring to their pursuits. Gonzales suggests that we look for the cause of the accident in two interlocking elements: the climbers' faulty mental model of the world in which they operated, and a psychology that produced overconfidence in their flawed model.[14]

Academics are familiar with the concept of mental models or "engravings," the deeply held beliefs people use to explain and predict how people and things work.[15] Everyone uses conceptual models to navigate their way through the world. In this respect, the college student who signs up for a history class thinking, "I should do well in this class—I am good at remembering things," is no different than the history teachers who aided and abetted the students' misconception about historical study as they acted upon mental models of their own ("Students must memorize facts because you can't think without facts").

The mental model Slutter and his friends brought to the mountain was based on years of training and experience, which had inscribed in their minds a set of beliefs about climbing as basic to their functioning as the ice axes they leaned on when ascending steep, snowy slopes. At the center of their model was the belief that while falls were inevitable, the rope would always hold them. Additionally, they believed that self arrest is reliable. They believed that team arrest is possible. They believed that the top man on the rope—a position always taken by the strongest climber—cannot allow himself to fall, and therefore, on this mountain, on this day, he would not fall. Each element of the model was confirmed by long habit, reason, and experience.

So, when the climbers came to Mt. Hood, they came not as tourists but as mountaineers in full. They respected alpinism's best practices and took care to ensure that the various parts of the system they were familiar with were connected and working properly. They inspected the rope for nicks and abrasions. They checked their harnesses to see that the buckles were threaded the way they should be. They tied and retied their knots. They remembered to keep the rope straight and not to step on it with their crampons. They reminded each other to keep two points of contact on the slope at all times. They continually rehearsed in their minds how they would fall on their ice axes if a self arrest became necessary. All of these rituals are good things to do. Yet they were not enough to prevent the disaster that befell them.

If we could have been with Slutter's team on the day before their ascent, their pre-climb preparations might have reminded us of ourselves. A conscientious professor gets ready to teach a class. She reviews her notes from the last time she gave the lecture. She smiles, or winces, to see how a changing world has changed her angle of vision. She ponders her hastily scrawled annotations, indicating moments of difficulty when students stumbled. She stares at the ceiling. She reaches for a book. She updates a figure. She rearranges the narrative. She adds things she didn't know before, deletes things that seem less necessary now. She looks for a better analogy, inserts a funnier anecdote, she makes a PowerPoint slide show. In the last minutes before going to class, she commits to memory key passages. All of these things are good things to do. Yet as Gonzales points out, formal procedures like these often substitute for a thorough analysis of the entire mental model with which one is operating. The result is ironic and sometimes, as in the case of the Hood climbers, deadly: the very care the climbers took to reduce risk encouraged faith in a faulty model.

If the faults of mental models were obvious, then *Accidents in North American Mountaineering* would be a much shorter series of volumes. But the flaws in mental models can be anything but obvious. Consider the climbing rope, which appears to be such a simple technology. As Gonzales points out, its simplicity masks a deceptive system. Everyone thinks they know how a rope works because everyone has handled cords since the day they first tied their shoes. But a rope's apparent simplicity masks hidden factors, forces, and interactions capable of producing surprisingly complex behaviors. The outcomes of these behaviors are difficult to imagine beforehand. This is how the outcomes of team arrest are explained in mountaineering schools: Can you catch a brick if it were dropped from a height of six inches? Most people would say yes. But could you catch the same brick if were tossed from a third-story window? The problem with the Hood climbers was that they were operating with a mental model suited for catching bricks at six inches.

Yet with their own eyes they had seen parts of the system work. They had seen climbers fall and arrest themselves, like Biggs at the Pearly Gates. In their rehearsals they had practiced team arrest, with one climber falling and the rest dropping on their ice axes to hold the fall, and it worked. In their minds, the system was backed up and nearly fail-safe. But what their faulty model did not recognize is that when the top climber on a rope team slips and falls, he will slide seventy feet before the slack in the rope is gone. During a long fall of this type tremendous forces of energy are built up that eventually get transmitted to the rope. Slutter's team was oblivious to the hidden energies of such a fall. So they did what their training and experience told them to do. Put the most experienced climber at the top. Check your knots. Step wide of the rope. Be ready in an instant to fall on your ice axe. The rituals built their confidence. When Hillman told investigators that he thought he had a chance to stop the five falling climbers, it indicates how little he knew of the hidden energies in the system.

On any given day on Mt. Hood—or on Rainier, or Denali, or any high mountain on earth—climbers can be seen roped up and descending without fixed protection. They do it all the time and get away with it, bolstering their confidence in a mental model that is more romantic— "the fellowship of the rope"—than reasonable for every situation. Descending without protection was a dumb decision for Slutter and his team. But this does not mean they were inept beginners. As experienced climbers, Slutter's team had a good idea of how ropes behaved, but only under certain conditions. As much as they knew, there was so much more that they did not know. It was their experience that hid this from them. "The human condition," Gonzales reminds us, "makes it easy for us to conceal the obvious from ourselves, especially under strain and pressure. The Bhopal disaster in India, the space shuttle *Challenger* explosion, the Chernobyl nuclear meltdown, and countless airliner crashes, all happened in part while people were denying the clear warnings before them, trying to land the model instead of the plane."[16]

Laurence Gonzales is right: the climbers on Mt Hood were set up for disaster not by their inexperience but by their experience. There is an obvious message here for midcareer history professors.

But what does any of this have to do with the vocation of college history professors, which some pages ago I said is a call to love? The climbers on Mt. Hood loved each other and they loved the alpine arts. Their bonds of affection for each other were real. Their passion for mountaineering speaks for itself. But the truth revealed by their story is that it is possible to love with sincerity and warmth while faulty mental models prevent us from loving well.

What might be said of the mental models—one could also say, the vocational vision—traditionally governing the teaching of undergraduates? Like mountaineering, college teaching takes place in marvelously complex environments with assumptions and procedures that are rarely adapted for the specific situation at hand. Faulty models are handed down without fear and almost without thought. I recall a moment just before leaving graduate school when I expressed doubts to an advisor about my ability to teach. "It's a lot easier than you think," said my advisor, hoping to buck me up. "Just take a deep breath and tell the students what you know." The advice may have been what I needed at the time. But as a complete model for teaching it got me into trouble right away.

Six months later I was teaching at a state university. For fifty minutes a day, five days a week, I told what I knew to 150 students taking a U.S. history survey course. A morning came when I wanted to deepen students' understanding of the philosophy of nonviolence as practiced in the early civil rights movement. My plan was to give a lecture on Reinhold Niebuhr's concept of "a spiritual discipline against resentment." This attitude or bearing, which Niebuhr had seen in Ghandi, is not the easiest moral outlook to describe. I prepared my lecture carefully, then went to class resolved to tell the students what I knew. As I approached the climax of what felt to me like a stirring tribute to the brave activists of the 1965 Selma campaign, I felt tears welling into my eyes. Pausing to get a grip, I heard the stillness of the lecture hall broken by a wave of muffled titters. Disoriented, I scanned the hall looking for the source of the interruption. Giggles became guffaws and then the whole class seemed to be laughing. It seems that the whole time I had been marching from Selma to Montgomery, some of the students had been marching in a different direction, passing around bawdy photographs taken at a recent fraternity party. Mortified, and forgetting for the moment all about a spiritual discipline against resentment, I walked out midlecture, seething with righteous anger. Krachmann's syndrome followed, with its debilitating effects. Years later, recognizing that a part of me never returned to that, or any, classroom, I would describe my Selma moment as "the day the professor died."

Today, I feel grateful for the day the professor died, because the experience punched a hole in a faulty mental model for teaching I might otherwise never have questioned. The callow students deserved my anger, but it is also true that they opened my eyes to a truth about teaching that in graduate school went unmentioned. I like to call this truth Auerbach's Law, in honor of the late Celtics coach Red Auerbach who, when asked the secret of how he produced so many NBA superstars, replied, "I figured out early on it's not what you say; it's what they hear."[17] As a mental model for teaching, Auerbach's Law improves on the standard-issue model I was using the day the professor died. The standard model could be summarized this way: "If I mention it, that means they have learned it."

Professors share at least this much with climbers: our faulty mental models go undetected in most situations. But the false confidence we gain from our apparent successes in the classroom merely sets the stage for inevitable, ongoing catastrophes. Unlike in the mountains, failures in the classroom are not often spectacular. Classes never end with rescue helicopters transporting the injured to the hospital or morgue. But there is plenty of reason to believe that college classrooms can be disaster zones for learning. If this sounds overstated, one can either believe the research or believe the professors who, eager for promotion and advancement, boast about their effectiveness with claims ranging from wishful thinking to the utterly fantastic.[18]

As a young teacher suffering from Krachmann's syndrome, I blamed my classroom difficulties on the cluelessness of undergraduates. Defending myself by blaming others is what I was doing the day I received the best advice I would ever get on teaching, that I needed to learn to love my students. Later that year, the lesson was driven home in an unexpected way while on a climbing trip in the White Mountains of New Hampshire. Intending to climb Mt. Jefferson, our team was driven back from the summit by a fierce November storm that sent us retreating to a climbers' hut we had passed just below the tree line. Tumbling through the door of the hut we found an older man sitting in the dark. A hush fell over our group as we recognized who we would be spending the night with. It was Guy Waterman, the one locals called "the real Old Man of the Mountain," a former speechwriter for Eisenhower, Nixon, and Ford, who became a New England climbing legend and peerless advocate for wilderness preservation, and whose son's tragic death on Denali in Alaska would later be related in Jon Krakauer's *Into the Wild*. Waterman welcomed us to his hut, and as the wind moaned and shrieked and rattled the wooden storm windows, we sat by the wood stove swapping tales and stories, some of them true. Waterman held us in thrall with endless stories. He was charming and witty and prone to oracular statements that made perfect sense at the time. Late in the evening, I asked Waterman if he had any advice for a young academic who felt at home only in the mountains. I must have expressed regret for not summiting Jefferson that day, because after thinking for a moment he said, "The thing you have to remember is, for a mountaineer to live, the climber must die."[19]

"The climber must die." Even today, I am not exactly sure what Waterman meant. But in my sleeping bag that night I understood his koan-like pronouncement to mean that being a climber is not enough because, if mountaineers want to live, they have to think about being good descenders too. It was truly a radical thought. Nobody ever says, "I'm going to *descend* Mt. Hood next week." Moreover, Waterman seemed to be saying that people who narrow their focus to bagging peak after peak with little regard for anything else are a danger to themselves, to others, and to wilderness itself.

Thinking about this on the drive home the next day, it occurred to me that if the challenge of descending is difficult for summit-hungry climbers, it is not easy for professors, either. "You have to learn to love your students," my colleague had said. What had kept me from loving them? Mountaineers are not the only ones who climb. Professors climb the ladder of advancement, and we climb to search for truth. We climb on our high horses, too. But teaching, it suddenly occurred to me, is more about descending. Informed by love, it traces a pattern drawn by Jesus, "who, though he was in the form of God, did not count equality with God a thing to be grasped, but emptied himself, taking the form of a servant, being born in the likeness of men."[20] "God is love," wrote John the apostle. The truth of God's love is humility. This means love requires a commitment to descending. Waterman's advice was good for professors, too.

Professors profess, which is to say, professors talk—a lot. We talk when we have something important to say and we talk when we do not. We talk when people are listening and we talk when people are not. Professors can be so busy talking that they do not know whether anyone is listening at all. This is why for teachers to live, it is necessary for professors to die. Certain kinds of professors, anyway. The professors who talk too much. The professors with Krachmann's syndrome. The drive-by professors who fire bursts of information into a crowd of students and then speed away to do their "own work." The professors who love students but not enough to join a social order that shares verified knowledge about teaching and learning as community property. The professors who love teaching—that is, talking—more than they care about learning. For the teacher within us to live, these kinds of professors must die. That is what it means to answer the history teacher's calling, which is a call to love.

Practical Steps to Love Well

To make my points, I have departed from the conventions of the academic essay and told a story instead. Now, I will break with custom another way. Having exposed a significant problem and drawn attention to its harms, a common move at this point is to apologize for running out of steam and then to call it a day. "I've done my part; the reader can take it from here," authors will say. I prefer the style of the Old Testament prophets (though I am nothing like a prophet). In biblical prophecy, criticism ("Stop doing wrong! Learn to do right!") is always joined with specific ideas for reform ("Share your food with the hungry! Provide the poor wanderer with shelter!"). If the history teachers' problem is a lack of discernment about what it means to love well, then what do I think history teachers should do about it?

First of all, we must make the so-called move from teaching to learning. Professors love teaching; they love to talk about how much they love teaching; they love to spout theories and opinions about good teaching. All these loves are self-referential. What professors traditionally do not do is descend to the level of struggling, greenhorn students to see the world of ideas and argument as they see it, as something opaque and incomprehensible, in order to inquire how student learning might be improved. The books to read here are three: Gerald Graff's *Clueless in Academia: How Schooling Obscures the Life of the Mind*; the National Research Council's *How People Learn: Brain, Mind, Experience, and School*; and Ernest Boyer's *Scholarship Reconsidered: Priorities of the Professoriate.*[21] The word on the street is that Boyer, who was chancellor of State University of New York before he took the helm of the Carnegie Foundation for the Advancement of Teaching, was inspired to call for a "scholarship of teaching and learning" by his meditations on the meaning of the Incarnation for academics. If true, then Boyer is a supreme example of a Christian academic responding to the teacher's vocation, which is a call to love.

Second, significant time must be given to rethinking the design of college courses. It is certainly the case that what college teachers can do is often limited by institutional constraints. But too often this becomes an excuse for not trying to do better with the resources that we have. The books to read here are Grant Wiggins and Jay McTighe's *Understanding By Design* and Dee Fink's *Creating Significant Learning Experiences: An Integrated Approach to Designing College Courses.*[22]

Finally, readers who are in positions of power, such as department chairs, should rethink program curricula to take advantage of the latest discoveries in history teaching and learning. The book to begin with is Sam Wineburg's *Historical Thinking and Other Unnatural Acts: Charting the Future of Teaching the Past.*[23] It is a cliché to say it takes a village to raise a child. But it remains true that single teachers and single courses are not enough to educate students for lives of discernment. The call to love is a communal project, too; history programs should reflect this.

For teachers to live, professors must die. The nature of this death to self is that teachers must descend to the level of students to inquire what they know, to see as they see, discarding the mental models that make such activities seem unnecessary or beneath a professor's dignity. This will not be easy. "I have decided to stick with love," Martin Luther King Jr. was fond of saying toward the end of his life. "I'm not talking about emotional bosh when I talk about love; I'm talking about a strong, demanding love."[24]

The vocation of the college history teacher demands that history professors sacrifice a great deal. But the rewards are great, ultimately appearing in the lives of our students. George Steiner, whom I criticized earlier, says it beautifully: "To awaken in another human being powers, dreams beyond one's own; to induce in others a love for that which one loves; to make of one's inward present their future: this is a threefold adventure like no other."[25] Teaching is an adventure like no other? Steiner, it is safe to say, never climbed Mt. Hood.

Notes

1. Fyodor Dostoevsky, *The Brothers Karamazov*, trans. Constance Garnett (Garden City, N.Y.: International Collectors Library, 1949), 50.

2. David Pace, "The Amateur in the Operating Room: History and the Scholarship of Teaching and Learning," *The American Historical Review* 109 (October 2004): 1171–92.

3. Norman Maclean, "On Changing Neckties: A Few Remarks on the Art of Teaching," in *Norman Maclean*, ed. Ron MacFarland and Hugh Nichols (Lewiston, Idaho: Confluence Press, 1988), 58–59.

4. Robert B. Townsend, "Historians Teach More and Larger Classes, Make Less Use of Technology," *AHA Perspectives* (April 2006): 18.

5. George Steiner, *Lessons of the Masters* (Cambridge, Mass.: Harvard University Press, 2003), 26–27.

6. *Accidents in North American Mountaineering* 56 (2003): 67.

7. To tell this story, I have drawn from the following sources: Steve Rollins and Tim Bailey, "Fall Into Crevasse: Unable to Self-Arrest, Inadequate Protection, Poor Position," *Accidents in North American Mountaineering* 56

(2003): 80–82; Tim Bailey, "Final Report on Mt. Hood Climbing Accident; Clackamas County Sheriff," *Traditional Mountaineering*, available at http://www.traditionalmountaineering.org/Report_Hood_Bergschrund.htm (last accessed March 3, 2010); Laurence Gonzales, "The Slipping Point: Heroes of Mt. Hood," *National Geographic Adventure* (September 2002): 56–65; James Vlahos, "Lives on the Line," *National Geographic Adventure* (August 2002): 33–35; Laurence Gonzales, *Deep Survival: Who Lives, Who Dies, and Why* (New York: Norton, 2005), 97–114.

8. Gonzales, "The Slipping Point," 56.

9. Luke 13:41.

10. Eric Mortenson and Harry Esteve, "Just a Freak Accident," *Portland Oregonian*, May 30, 2002.

11. Nancy F. Partner, "Making Up Lost Time: Writing on the Writing of History," *Speculum* 61 (January 1986): 90–117.

12. Cited in Gonzales, *Deep Survival*, 118.

13. Ibid., 117. Gonzales analyzes the Hood tragedy in chapters 6 and 7.

14. Ibid., 106.

15. Howard Gardner, "Educating the Unschooled Mind," *The Science and Public Policy Seminar Series*, American Educational Research Association, May 14, 1993, 5–10. Gardner's larger works on this subject include *The Unschooled Mind* (New York: Basic Books, 1991).

16. Gonzales, *Deep Survival*, 126.

17. "Red Auerbach: True Stories and NBA Legends," *Morning Edition*, National Public Radio, November 2, 2004.

18. For summaries of research on this subject, see John D. Bransford, Ann L. Brown, and Rodney R. Cocking, eds., *How People Learn: Brain, Mind, Experience, and School* (Washington, D.C.: National Academy Press, 1999), 8–16, 30, 147–51, 225–26; Cameron Fincher, "Learning Theory and Research," in *Teaching and Learning in the College Classroom*, 2nd ed., ed. Kenneth A. Feldman and Michael B. Paulsen, 57–80 (Needham Heights, Mass.: Simon & Schuster, 1998); and L. Dee Fink, *Creating Significant Learning Experiences: An Integrated Approach to Designing College Courses* (San Francisco: Jossey-Bass, 2003), 2–6.

19. Four years after our night together at the Randolph Hut, Waterman hiked up Mt. Lafayette on a cold February afternoon and ended his life by laying down on an exposed ridge to die of exposure. For more on Waterman's life and death, see Rob Buchanan, "A Natural Death," *Outside*, June 2000.

20. Philippians 2:6–7.

21. Gerald Graff, *Clueless in Academia: How Schooling Obscures the Life of the Mind* (New Haven: Yale University Press, 2003); Bransford, Brown, and

Cocking, *How People Learn*; Ernest Boyer, *Scholarship Reconsidered: Priorities of the Professoriate* (Princeton: The Carnegie Foundation for the Advancement of Education, 1990).

22. Grant Wiggins and Jay McTighe, *Understanding by Design*, 2nd ed. (Alexandria, Va.: Association for Supervision and Curriculum Development, 2005); Dee Fink, *Creating Significant Learning Experiences: An Integrated Approach to Designing College Courses* (San Francisco: Jossey-Bass, 2003).

23. Sam Wineburg, *Historical Thinking and Other Unnatural Acts: Charting the Future of Teaching the Past* (Philadelphia: Temple University Press, 2001).

24. Speech delivered at the Eleventh Annual Convention of the Southern Christian Leadership Conference, Atlanta, 16 August 1967, in *A Call to Conscience: The Landmark Speeches of Dr. Martin Luther King Jr.*, ed. Clayborne Carson and Kris Shephard, 171–99 (New York: Warner Books, 2001).

25. Steiner, *Lessons of the Masters*, 183–84.

Chapter Twelve

PUBLIC REASONING BY
HISTORICAL ANALOGY

Some Christian Reflections

JAY GREEN

THE CONVERSATION BETWEEN CHRISTIAN CONVICTION AND historical study is today as lively and contested as ever. But I sometimes wonder if this good conversation too narrowly confines itself to questions of historical theory, method, and pedagogy, giving precious little attention to history as a *cultural force* whose significance and implications extend well beyond (and often have little regard for) the halls of academe.[1] Popular understandings and uses of the past do far more to shape how we see the world than have all the scholarly monographs and articles ever written, a fact that historians find painful to admit. The historical misinformation and half-truths generated in common discourse have played a definitive role in crafting the narrative plotlines of modern social memory, justifying consequential policy decisions and supplying countless blunt weapons for use in cultural warfare. If these charges are true, the historian's task must go beyond writing more and "more relevant" monographs. Public-minded engagement with our world demands that historians consider the problems and consequences of this informal pop-historiography every bit as much as we do the books published by respected university presses.

Such a reexamination of the historian's task only makes sense if we conceive of history as a varied and multilayered calling; and, for the Christian, a calling of a very peculiar kind. Christian ethicist John Howard Yoder has argued that the "church's calling is to be the conscience and the servant within human society." He adds focus to this claim by charging Christians "to contribute to the creation of structures more worthy of human society."[2] The noble task of "truth telling" that stands somewhere near the heart of the historian's vocation certainly has the potential of encouraging the creation of such structures. And while I do not question the prophetic value of writing accurate and often highly critical narrative reconstructions of the past, I believe that the Christian calling of historical study must reach further. In addition to the normal and important work of writing meaningful accounts of the past, William Katerberg suggests that the Christian historian is called "to contribute to the relevance of history for life."[3] Since Christian historians are also Christian citizens with moral responsibilities to "the city of man," I submit that we bear a unique responsibility to critique and reform unreflective modes of civic discourse about the past, and I would further argue that we must do so by bringing some of the tools of modern historical study to bear on contemporary public uses of history. The following discussion intends to explore popular uses of the past that appeal to historical analogy, and suggests some ways that Christian historians might especially respond to these public renderings of history in a manner that befits our dual callings as conscience and servant of human society.

This broadened vision of the historian's vocation is becoming more fully realized among a growing cadre of historians willing to describe their craft as a method of moral inquiry.[4] Although the intended meanings of moral and inquiry here are often less than clear, those who comfortably use the terminology widely believe that historical study supplies needed resources for living thoughtful, reflective, responsible lives. In this vein, as regards education, Sam Wineburg states that "history holds the potential, only partly realized, of humanizing us in ways offered by few other areas in the school curriculum."[5] In the human endeavor of mapping moral pathways of personal and social behavior, so the argument goes, a conscious and critical relationship with the past is essential.

For some, this goal is achieved as we come to understand how our present realities owe their existence to deeply embedded historical impulses that we neither control nor even perceive. In a remarkable confession, journalist George Packer illustrates the power of the past in confronting his own identity.

> At twenty I thought I was the author of my own life and could go on willing it into any shape I wanted—being myself had nothing to do with being my father's son. In my thirties I discovered how much had been fixed by the accidents of birth. Not just the twisting chains of nucleic acids that gave me the broad mouth of a long-dead Jewish grandmother, the freckles of southern cousins, my mother's temper and flair for rhetoric, the listening gesture of cupping chin in hand that came from my father along with high cholesterol and a tendency toward depression. Along with these, I also inherited a history that went in one direction back to the Jews who came to New York City around 1900, and in another down into the defeated and impoverished South. I was born, like everyone, into the legacy of a genetic makeup, a family tree, a historical moment—even a worldview.[6]

The use of history as moral inquiry here might be described (quite literally for Packer) as genetic, in that it seeks to relate present to past by tracing lines of historical descent that are discernibly connected in a narrative plot of cause and effect.

Another approach to history as moral inquiry is older and, generally speaking, out of vogue in academic historiography. It seeks to understand present realities by comparing them to past personalities, events, and institutions that have allegedly similar characteristics. No formal attempt here is made to define the present as the cumulative outcome of the past (though neither is this possibility necessarily denied). It suggests instead that historical study provides an occasion for examining the past to find what one historian has called "an inventory of alternatives," making sense of the present by situating it against what others have thought and accomplished.[7] This use of history as moral inquiry might be described as analogical, in that it seeks to relate present to past by means of comparing one with the other.

While both of these approaches offer up "usable" pasts, only the former has had much currency among professional historians sympathetic to the task of moral inquiry.[8] Since the advent of historicism in the nineteenth century, academically trained historians have had little stomach for what has been derisively labeled "exemplarism," or the study of history in pursuit of commendable characters, states, and eras. Pushing such "lessons of history" smacks of moral philosophy, whereby the past seems reduced to a mere reservoir of good and bad types for the historian to recommend or caution against: philosophy teaching by examples.

But moving out of academe and onto the street, the analogical approach dominates public statements about the past and its relevance for the present. Contemporary media and political cultures are awash with attempts to understand pressing issues of the day by tapping into a widely shared social memory. Witness efforts among television pundits and congressmen to understand the American military presence in Iraq: it is difficult to observe this debate for long before stumbling on an explicit appeal to a past analog. We are invited to think of Iraq as Vietnam, circa 1966. The Iraqi people as European Jews, circa 1941. Abu Ghraib as My Lai. Western European powers as Munich "appeasers." The American "Empire" as the Roman Empire. September 11 as Pearl Harbor. Although historical analogies in the American experience have had the greatest salience in matters of foreign policy, their uses are hardly limited to these. (Note the number of political scandals over the past generation that have had the suffix "-gate" attached to them.)

The appeal to historical analogy is and long has been a dominant mode of public discourse. In fact, I would suggest that the most common way modern people relate to the past is by appeals to historical analogy. As self-described custodians of the past, historians are uniquely positioned to assess this social phenomenon and to evaluate its significance for historical understanding and moral reflection. Historians rightly devote most of their energies to reconstructing and evaluating the past in the interest of promoting sharpened historical awareness. But the task of doing so requires that we also consider the social settings into which we speak, accounting for what cognitive sociologist Eviatar Zerubavel calls "the unmistakably social maplike structures in which history is typically organized in our minds."[9] Rather than simply dismissing these "lessons of history" as distortions or abuses of the past, historians should enter this already vital public conversation, adding the clarity, caution, and nuance that are hallmarks of their academic training.

The online *Dictionary of the Philosophy of Mind* defines analogy as a "systematic comparison between structures that uses properties of and relations between objects of a source to infer properties of and relations between objects of a target structure."[10] It functions as a conceptual bridge between two sets of data, one familiar and the other new. The familiar data, or source analog, provides a frame of reference capable of rendering the new data, or target analog, clearer or more understandable. For instance, the early nineteenth-century philosopher William Paley famously sought to make complexity in the natural world (target analog) plain by likening it to a watch (source analog). Taking what was widely known and understood about the intricate working of a watch, he reasoned that sophisticated design likewise stood behind the natural world. He further argued that the obvious existence of a designer in the watch signified the necessity of an intelligent creator for the natural world.

Psychologists and philosophers of mind describe this reasoning process as "cognitive mapping," and, as Keith Holyoak and Paul Thagard note, the impulse to construct such cognitive maps is foundational to creative thought and a natural part of all human development from the earliest stages of childhood.[11] More specifically, the use of past analogs to map conceptions of present and future is basic to the functions of the human mind. Human conduct is unthinkable without some conscious or unconscious daily reckoning with the past. The most personal form this relationship takes is individual memory, which is necessary for anyone to navigate her way through life, moment by moment. As I awaken each morning, I must (sometimes rather slowly) reconnect to whom I was and what I was doing the previous night, week, year, and so on, in order to function appropriately and rationally in the day ahead. Without the skillful capacity to remember these details—a capacity that most of us take for granted—I am helpless.

In somewhat less intimate but equally intuitive ways, we also appeal to the past in crafting our personal identities by observing and incorporating our knowledge of past others who have traveled paths we are either now walking or aspire to walk. Much of what I have incorporated into my own practice of being a man, for instance, I have learned from past experiences, images, and notions of manhood that have been socialized into my consciousness. My personal sense of manhood has been shaped by an enormous host of prototypical men in my lived and imagined past. These models mined from my remembered and received memories inform every thought I have and decision I make about my life as a man.

In a social-structural sense, human understanding likewise relies on collective memory to erect structures of meaning for social and civic engagement.[12] Personalities, events, and institutions become understandable only after their origins, developments, and *implications* have been disclosed and examined. By definition, present realities and, even more, future developments can never be elucidated in anything like a comprehensive fashion until they become part of the past. With this in mind, Neil Postman wryly notes his suspicion "of people who want to be forward-looking. I literally do not know what they mean when they say, 'We must look ahead to see where we are going.' What is it that they wish us to look at? There is nothing yet to see in the future."[13] Postman rightly concludes that the only way we discover anything true about the future, or the present for that matter, is by reference to something previously said or done in the past.

It's not surprising that historical analogies are attractive, because they provide us with tools to understand, anticipate, and control the shape of the present and the course of the future. As we have seen, they are natural, necessary, even inevitable elements in our personal and social lives. But these same otherwise helpful tools regularly warp, obfuscate, and undermine honest examinations of history, doing severe damage to the integrity of the past. Visions of the present and future that we desperately want to believe too often urge us to remember the past quite selectively, and to use it narrowly to the strategic advantage of our own party, cause, and a priori convictions.[14] When this happens, appeals to historical analogy ironically impoverish public discourse by creating conceptual barriers between genuine historical awareness and moral inquiry about present realities. So we are left with the difficult challenge of handling the powerful instrument of historical analogy in ways that both promote a genuine understanding of the past and shed needed light on the present, while resisting the urge to turn them into dangerous forms of propaganda.

To this end, I think we must divide historical analogies as used in personal, popular, and political discourse into two overlapping categories. The first is historical analogy as rhetorical strategy: when rigidly fixed notions about a past person, event, or institution (the source analog) are chosen to justify and benefit one's position in relationship to a present person, event, or institution (the target analog). The second is historical analogy as a critical exercise of the historical imagination: when a past person, event, or institution (the source analog) is carefully explored to identify the comparable features it might hold for understanding a present person, event, or institution (the target analog). It is my hope that clarifying and taking care to distinguish between these two kinds of analogy will result in a more thoughtful public understanding of the past and, in turn, a greater capacity for clear moral thinking about the present and the future.[15]

The use of historical analogy as a rhetorical strategy is a common, even integral component of Western culture and language. In this tradition of public discourse, elements of the past are transformed into cultural symbols that function as a kind of linguistic shorthand to signify practices deemed good or evil, noble or scandalous, heroic or cowardly. Such analogies sometimes become so fundamentally embedded in our language that we scarcely think of them as ever having been authentic flesh-and-blood realities. An attempt to convict parties using spurious evidence and trumped up charges is described as a "witch hunt," alluding to the 1692 trials in Salem, Massachusetts. An individual who makes a high-risk, decisive, and unalterable resolution has "crossed the Rubicon," a reference to Julius Caesar's defiance of the Roman Senate. Any traitor is a "Benedict Arnold," the disaffected American general who attempted to betray his post to the British in the American War of Independence. A court of law whose judgments are deemed tyrannical or arbitrary is a "Star Chamber," the royal court that acted accordingly during the Stuart era of English history.

A more recent example of an historical-figure-cum-symbolic-idiom is Rosa Parks. The African American seamstress renowned for refusing to give up her seat to a white man on a Montgomery, Alabama, bus in 1955 is credited with sparking the grass-roots bus boycott that energized the subsequent civil rights movement. Her solitary act has come to signify all acts of individual defiance—especially by women—against large-scale structures of injustice, corruption, and encultured prejudice. A cursory web search turned up several hundred "Rosa Parks of" varied spheres where comparable acts inspired movements of social change. Terri Schiavo was hailed as the "Rosa Parks of the disabled" movement amid an intense national debate about whether her husband should allow her to die by removing her feeding tube. The mother of a slain U.S. soldier, Cindy Sheehan, was called the "Rosa Parks of the antiwar movement" after she sought an audience with President George W. Bush to decry America's war in Iraq. Margie Richard, a retired schoolteacher from rural Louisiana, was tagged "the Rosa Parks of the Environmental Justice Movement"; Libby Chernoff, "the Rosa Parks of the Jewish Deaf World"; Michi Nishiura Weglyn, "the Rosa Parks of the Japanese American Redress Movement"; Charlene Teeters, "the Rosa Parks of American Indians"; and, not least, Markus Bestin, "the Rosa Parks of male prostitution."[16]

I do not mean to disparage or disavow present uses of cultural symbols drawn from history. They are indispensable to our linguistic lives and natural functions of our collective memory. But the value these almost poetic nods to the past hold for promoting historical understanding is another thing altogether. Such analogies are constructed and used wholly independent of the particular times and places they reference, and thereby tend to take on lives of their own. When such analogies, like other "metaphors we live by," become a part of our ordinary language, they assume fixed and final meanings with no regard for the nuances of the past from which they came.[17] They may help to perpetuate a certain kind of social memory, but, ironically, they lessen the likelihood of revisiting the past afresh with new questions or challenging perspectives.

An even greater danger these rhetorical devises pose to historical awareness is their tendency to whitewash the past by reappropriating its personalities and events to fit them more comfortably into the standing order. Francesca Polletta's thoughtful study of how Martin Luther King Jr. has been remembered on the floors of both houses of Congress illustrates this problem. Polletta examined each instance that "Martin Luther King" or "Dr. King" was recorded in the *Congressional Record* over a four year period, exploring the question of how states commemorate their own histories of social protest. She notes that, at least among white speakers, the "congressional representations of King assimilate him into a pluralist framework by representing community service and institutional politics as the proper legacy of his activism."[18] She suggests that King's memory has been typically raised to demonstrate the legitimacy of whatever agenda a public speech sets forth, and to identify a given speaker with some semblance of King's legacy, regardless of his or her message. Little that was truly subversive or prophetic in King's life is evident in these public pronouncements as they make the memory of his more insubordinate words and actions safe by domestication and cooptation.

The deceptive potential of historical rhetoric is not lost in even the most populist form of public discourse: the internet "comment" culture. Observers of weblog (or blog) and usenet forums have long understood how appeals to historical analogy can cheapen public discussion and obscure historical understanding. Already in 1990, famed usenet pioneer Mike Godwin had begun to note how the then-infant form of public discussion was susceptible to what he labeled the "Nazi-comparison meme." He observed that on almost every topic imaginable, the heat of debate would eventually lead one participant or another to compare her opponent's ideas to those of Nazism. In response, he developed the now widely accepted Godwin's Law of Nazi Analogies: "As an online discussion grows longer, the probability of a comparison involving Nazis or Hitler approaches one." By highlighting this tendency, Godwin hoped to chasten online discourse and forestall patterns that depreciated realities of the past. "It was trivialization," writes Godwin, "I found both illogical (Michael Dukakis as a Nazi? Please!) and offensive (the millions of concentration-camp victims did not die to give some net.blowhard a handy trope)."[19]

The fact that historical analogies are inclined to mislead and distort is merely symptomatic of the more basic problem attending their rhetorical use. Such analogies are dubious because they exist for reasons other than understanding the past or responsibly informing the present. They serve a purely instrumentalist function that justifies—never challenges—the preconceived purposes of those who use them. While I agree with Christopher Hemmer that not all historical analogies fit within this "rationalist explanatory framework," I would submit that, when used in this way, the "actor's interests are unaffected by the process of analogical reasoning and are simply deducible from the actor's position in a given material structure."[20]

In political discourse, historical analogies are most often employed to advance an existing cause or policy decision. Here, the past is invoked as a brand of rigid precedent that lawmakers and other government officials hold up to demonstrate that identical decisions were made in the past with positive results, or that the negative legacy of past inaction will certainly have the same detrimental consequences if repeated. These patterns are rooted in an unflinching certainty that "history repeats itself." Unfolding situations and emerging personalities may well become "another Bay of Pigs," "another Reformation," "another Abraham Lincoln," or "another Pol Pot."

In an August 2005 speech summarizing the American "War on Terrorism," George W. Bush stated that, "In the Cold War, freedom defeated the ideology of communism and led to a Europe that is whole, free, and at peace. Now, once again, freedom is confronting the followers of a murderous ideology, and like the hate-filled ideologies that came before it, the darkness of terror will be defeated, and the forces of freedom and moderation will prevail throughout the Muslim world."[21] In typical fashion, Bush establishes a one-to-one relationship between a very complex historical event and an equally complex present situation, and, in doing so, gives the past the task of predicting the future. The practical effect is an appreciation of neither past nor present, and an unwarranted set of expectations about the future. The only ways to make the past truly helpful for the present is to insist that historical investigation include elements of critical analysis and allow for ample complexity. And these elements are present in historical analogies only when they have been made to exercise and enrich the historical imagination.

Alun Munslow describes the historical imagination as "the mental power of rehearsing possible past cause and effect relationships, connections and situations . . . [and] the application of the general capacity of the human mind for comparison, connection, analogy, and difference to the study of the past and its sources."[22] It is a cognitive awareness that carefully attends to the contexts, complexities, and contingencies of the past. This awareness is "exercised" through any process that brings about a sharpened, mature grasp of these contexts, complexities, and contingencies. The historian's craft since the age of Leopold von Ranke has upheld several principles that guide historians in achieving these goals, and John Tosh in *The Pursuit of History* identifies three of them that I believe will attend any appeal to historical analogy that successfully exercises the historical imagination.

The first principle Tosh lists is that of historical difference or strangeness, "recognition of the gulf which separates our own age from all previous ages."[23] As David Lowenthal has reminded us, "the past is a foreign country, where they do things differently."[24] Those who lived in the past did not necessarily share our outlook, our values, our fears, our goals, and our definitions of success. The natural temptation to bend everything in the past to accommodate our present sensibilities helps explain why historical analogies are so naturally drawn and so often ring true. Historical analogies only work as easily manipulated rhetorical tools when we willfully remain in the prison of the present and when the only voices we allow ourselves to hear in the past are ones that sound a lot like our own or those of our present nemeses.

The historical imagination thus requires a measure of self-doubt about the way we see the world past, present, and future. The neatly packaged order of things we often carry in our minds require scrutiny. We must prepare ourselves to be surprised, even shocked at how the familiar assumptions we make about the past are altered when inspected more closely. Such questioning may admittedly lead to a cynical view of the world, and academically minded people too often gravitate in this direction. But Sam Wineburg suggests that the principle of historical strangeness may instead cultivate a healthy attitude of intellectual charity.

> It is an understanding that counters narcissism. For the narcissist sees the world—both the past and the present—in his own image. Mature historical knowledge teaches us to do the opposite; to go beyond our own image, to go beyond our brief life, and to go beyond the fleeting moment in human history into which we have been born.[25]

One of the great values of studying history is that it forces us to look beyond our own times, refreshing us by what C. S. Lewis called "the clean sea-breeze of the centuries," a relationship with the past that makes a person "in some degree immune from the great cataract of nonsense that pours from the press and microphone" of our present era.[26] Recognizing historical difference insures that it can do just this.

We derive these benefits from historical study only when we are conscious of the contexts of the past, the second attribute of historical awareness. "The underlying principle of all historical work," Tosh writes, "is that the subject of our enquiry must not be wrenched from its setting."[27] All human developments emerge from within uniquely complex matrices of material and ideological conditions that make them singular moments in time. When historical analogies are used for rhetorical purposes, they violate this principle in a fundamental way. Past and present analogs can at best be described as similar, and it is proper to identify factors they share in common. But the often profound structural differences that always exist between such analogs necessarily militate against the simplistic formula that "history repeats itself."

Professor Gary Daynes helpfully observes that, although historical analogies can be valuable, they are always inexact. "There will never be 'another Vietnam' (even if the United States goes to war in Vietnam again) and no dictator, however brutal or megalomaniacal, will be 'another Hitler.'" For this reason, any "who would use historical analogies as the basis for present behavior need to consider both the conditions in the past that created a particular historical situation and how those conditions have changed since."[28] Daynes illustrates why analysis must be a component part of any responsible appeal to historical analogy. Engaging in comparison is a legitimate aspect of any search for a usable past, but must always be understood against the numerous peculiar circumstances that make past and present quite distinct from one another.

Historians make sense of the gulf that stands between divergent contexts of one era and another by tracking changes along Tosh's third principle, historical *process*. The so-called historicity of human reality is found in recognizing that "every aspect of our culture, behavior, and beliefs is the outcome of processes [of growth, decay, and change] over time."[29] This historicist sensibility, as previously mentioned, sees a genetic interconnectedness to all human development. To put the matter succinctly, every element of the present is causally rooted in the past and can be explained by examining the trends of social change that brought it into existence. The nuanced understanding of the past that contextual awareness introduces to the evaluation of historical analogies is compounded when one considers the complexity brought about by the forces of social, political, economic, and intellectual change.

As a traditional Christian believer, I find this principle especially challenging because it seems to have the implication of negating all notions of moral and philosophical fixity by rendering the substance of every norm in each age of human development relative to its times and entirely subject to the historicizing winds of change. A religious belief, a theological proposition, or an ethical injunction in the historicist's hands become mere historical artifacts, socially constructed and "true" only in the most limited, temporal sense. I, differing from this conception, do not recognize history as a totalizing or ultimate force. I believe in the existence of some significant and fixed norms, grounded in that which is outside of time and space: the living God. Historical process, itself, cannot adequately account for the definitive origins of human value and moral law. When historical study attempts to locate within the historical process the original construction of every human norm, it begins to lose its usefulness as a means of assessing the human condition and becomes, instead, a religious dogma unto itself.

Nevertheless, all humans do in fact encounter ethical, theological, and philosophical norms within thickly embedded contexts and amid the flux of changing times and circumstances. Humans at every stage of historical development have received and appropriated these ideals in ways that reflect their own personal psychologies (even pathologies) and social situations. Human understanding and uses of these fixed norms of God's creation have always been embedded within and colored by the social constructions of human culture. The norms themselves are not thereby reducible to the historical process, nor are people incapable of understanding the general meaning of these norms simply because they receive them within the parameters of space and time. But when understood as factors in social development, it is legitimate to think of human uses of moral and philosophical norms as functions of social context and change. And so, with the above caveat in mind, I believe Tosh's emphasis on historical process stands as a significant principle in exercising the historical imagination, and must be a basic element in any appeal to historical analogy.

Our failure to contemplate historical difference, context, and process has resulted in a distorted awareness of the past and a morally stunted sense of the present and the future. The health of our public discourse and institutions depends upon a revitalized historical imagination, equipped to engage the wellspring of resources in our past with thoughtful reflection and nuanced perspectives. If historical analogies are to play a role in informing a morally responsible public discourse, and ultimately creating structures more worthy of human society, they must be carefully imagined, cautiously reasoned, and always tentative. And those who use them must overcome the temptation to conceive of past events as simple morality tales whose stories and players exist as fixed archetypes of good and evil rather than actual people and events rooted in the vagaries of time and space. Rather than drawing analogies for purely rhetorical purposes, the Christian calling of historical study demands we act as a conscience amid the warp and woof of public discourse by cultivating a thoughtful historical awareness that has the prophetic potential to alter our sense of ourselves and the world we are called to serve.

Notes

1. A number of very helpful books have come out in recent years seeking to understand history in these terms. See especially Roy Rosenzweig and David Thelen, *The Presence of the Past: Popular Uses of History in American Life* (New York: Columbia University Press, 1998); and David Glassberg, *The Sense of History: The Place of the Past in American Life* (Amherst: The University of Massachusetts Press, 2001).

2. John Howard Yoder, *The Politics of Jesus* (Grand Rapids, Mich.: Eerdmans, 1994), 155.

3. William Katerberg, "Is There Any Such Thing as 'Christian' History?" *Fides et Historia* 34:1 (2002): 64.

4. See Richard Wightman Fox, Robert B. Westbrook, and Lee H. Hamilton, eds., *In Face of Facts: Moral Inquiry in American Scholarship* (New York: Cambridge University Press, 2002); David Harlan, *The Degradation of American History* (Chicago: University of Chicago Press, 1997); Samantha Power, *A Problem from Hell: America in the Age of Genocide* (New York: Harper Perennial, 2003).

5. Sam Wineburg, *Historical Thinking and Other Unnatural Acts* (Philadelphia: Temple University Press, 2001), 5.

6. George Packer, *Blood of the Liberals* (New York: Farrar, Straus, and Giroux, 2000), 6–7.

7. John Tosh, *The Pursuit of History*, 3rd ed. (London: Longman, 2002), 31.

8. George Frederickson's comparative history project is an interesting possible exception. His systematic exploration of parallel historical movements provides a somewhat sophisticated amalgam of genetic and analogical history. The project is not adequately described using the past for moral reflection, but it does make use of analogical reasoning in ways that depart from much mainstream historical writing. See George Frederickson *The Comparative Imagination: On the History of Racism, Nationalism, and Social Movements* (Berkeley: University of California Press, 1997), and *White Supremacy: A Comparative Study of American and South African History* (New York: Oxford University Press, 1982).

9. Eviatar Zerubavel, *Time Maps: Memory and the Social Shape of the Past* (Chicago: University of Chicago Press, 2003), 1.

10. Paul Thagard, "Analogy," *Dictionary of the Philosophy of Mind*, available at http://philosophy.uwaterloo.ca/MindDict/A.html (last accessed March 3, 2010).

11. Keith Holyoak and Paul Thagard, *Mental Leaps: Analogy in Creative Thought* (Cambridge, Mass.: MIT Press, 1996), 1–17.

12. An important corollary to this argument that I will not explore in this essay involves the lack of historical knowledge in modern culture and its debilitating impact on social self-understanding. Robert C. Bartlett aptly describes this problem. "Unburdened by knowledge of the past, my students are crippled by an amazingly constricted frame of reference. They know nothing of Pericles and little of Churchill and so cannot compare the utterances of our democratic statesmen with those of the ancient Athenians or even of modern British leaders. Pyrrhic victories, Quixotic undertakings, and Socratic irony are lost on them. They wouldn't recognize a Shylock or a Jezabel if they stumbled over one, and if some day they meet their Waterloo, it will all be over before they know what hits them." See his "Souls Without Longing," *Public Interest* Winter 2003, available at http://www.findarticles.com/p/articles/mi_m0377/is_2003_Wntr/ai_95965975 (last accessed March 3, 2010).

13. Neil Postman, *Building a Bridge to the Eighteenth Century: How the Past Can Improve our Future* (New York: Alfred A. Knopf, 1999), 13.

14. These distortions of the past in the service of the present are typically rooted in commitments either to progress or nostalgia. Christopher Lasch helpfully describes progress as that "willingness to submit every advance to the risk of supersession," and nostalgia as "feelings that the past offered delights no longer obtainable." See his *The True and Only Heaven: Progress and its Critics* (New York: W. W. Norton, 1991), 48, 83.

15. My description of these approaches as "overlapping" deserves comment. The qualification is important because, in reality, even the most manipulative form of historical-analogy-as-propaganda can, at least theoretically, exercise the historical imagination. And all appeals to historical analogy that exercise the historical imagination, in the end, can function as rhetorical strategies that advance a peculiar ideological or political cause. In other words, while some historical analogies are best described as one or the other, they also share a lot in common. So I do not mean to present these alternatives as mutually exclusive, and do not submit this method as a way of placing appeals to historical analogy in one "camp" or the other. The framework instead provides a general guide for evaluating public discourse in an effort to encourage a more careful handing of the past in shedding light on the present.

16. "View from the Front of the Bus," *Hog on Ice* blog, 21 March 2005, no longer available online, but quoted at http://physicsgeek.mu.nu/archives/2005_03.php; Angela K. Brown, "Grieving Mother's War Protest Draws Notice," available at http://www.countermilitary.org/Articles/WarProtests/General/GrievingMotherNotice.html; Steve Lerner, "The Rosa Parks of the Environmental Justice Movement: Margie Richard," *Common Ground*, March 2005, available at http://commongroundmag.com; "Jewish 'Rosa Parks' Helps Break the Sound Barrier," *Orthodox Union*, 15 April 1999, available at http://www.ou.org/oupr/1999/

jewishrosa.htm; Phil Tajitsu Nash, "Michi Weglyn, Rosa Parks of the Japanese American Redress Movement, dies at 72," *Conscience and the Constitution,* April 26, 1999, available at http://www.resisters.com/news/Michi_obit.htm; Terri Jean, "10 American Indians You Should Know," *Manataka: The American Indian Council,*" available at http://www.manataka.org/page136.html; "Markus Bestin Claims to Be the Rosa Parks of Male Prostitution," *Openfreedom.info,* February 3, 2010, available at http://openfreedom.info/item/1088462?hl=nevada (all URLs last accessed April 7, 2010).

17. George Lakoff and Mark Johnson, *Metaphors We Live By* (Chicago: University of Chicago Press), 3.

18. Francesca Polletta, "Legacies and Liabilities of an Insurgent Past: Remembering Martin Luther King, Jr., on the House and Senate Floor," in *States of Memory: Continuities, Conflicts, and Transformations in National Retrospection,* ed. Jeffrey K. Olick (Durham, N.C.: Duke University Press, 2003), 197.

19. Mike Godwin, "Meme, Counter-Meme," *Wired* 2:10, October 1994, available at http://wired-vig.wired.com/wired/archive/2.10/godwin.if_pr.html (last accessed March 3, 2010).

20. Christopher Hemmer, "Historical Analogies and the Definition of Interests: The Iranian Hostage Crisis and Ronald Reagan's Policy Toward the Hostages in Lebanon," *Political Psychology* 20:2 (1999): 267.

21. George W. Bush, "President Addresses Military Families, Discusses War on Terror," August 24, 2004, available at http://www.globalsecurity.org/wmd/library/news/iraq/2005/08/iraq-050824-whitehouse01.htm (last accessed April 7, 2010). I should note that there is nothing partisan about the use and appeals of these analogies. See these comments by former Senator Ernest F. Hollings (D-South Carolina): "Now we have another Vietnam. Just as President Johnson misled us into Vietnam, President Bush has misled us into Iraq. As in Vietnam, they have not met us in the streets hailing democracy. Thousands of miles away, we are once again 'fighting for the hearts and minds.' Again, we are trying to build and destroy. Again, we are bogged down in a guerrilla war. Again, we are not allowing our troops to fight and win—we do not have enough troops. Again, we can't get in, can't get out"; see his *Making Government Work* (Columbia: University of South Carolina Press, 2008), 125–26.

22. Alun Munslow, *The Routledge Companion to Historical Studies* (New York: Routledge Press, 2000), 124.

23. Tosh, *Pursuit of History,* 9.

24. David Lowenthal, *The Past is a Foreign Country* (New York: Cambridge University Press, 1985), 191.

25. Wineburg, *Historical Thinking,* 24.

26. C. S. Lewis, "On the Reading of Old Books," in *God in the Dock: Essays on Theology and Ethics* (Grand Rapids, Mich.: Eerdmans, 1970), 202; "Learning in Wartime," in *The Weight of Glory* (New York: Touchstone Books, 1996), 49.

27. Tosh, *Pursuit of History*, 10–11.

28. Gary Daynes, "The Use of History in the Movement for the Civic Engagement of Higher Education," *The Journal for Civic Commitment* 1:1 (2003), available at http://www.mc.maricopa.edu/other/ engagement/Journal/Issue1/ Daynes.shtml (last accessed March 3, 2010).

29. Tosh, *Pursuit of History*, 12.

Chapter Thirteen

DON'T FORGET THE CHURCH

Reflections on the Forgotten Dimension of

Our Dual Calling

ROBERT TRACY MCKENZIE

"WHAT DOES IT MEAN TO SERVE GOD FAITHFULLY IN THE specific circumstances in which He has placed me?"[1] Every Christian should ask this question regularly, and to their credit, in recent years a number of Christian professional historians have done so publicly. The result has been a small but burgeoning literature on the relationship of religious faith to the study of the past.[2] As a Christian historian myself— one still trying to understand his calling after nearly two decades in the profession—I am grateful for this public discussion and have learned much from it. Yet in my opinion the participants have typically framed the conversation too narrowly. My goal in this essay is to broaden the discussion by calling other Christian historians' attention to an often overlooked aspect of our calling. Implicitly, at least, we have typically asked, "What does it mean to be faithful to our callings as Christian historians *as we labor within the academy*?" The qualifier, unfortunately, allows us to ignore the tension between our responsibilities to the academic community, on the one hand, and to our communities of faith, on the other. I have come to believe that, as a Christian historian, I am called not only to labor within the academy as a Christian, but also to labor within the church as an historian. Because historians have paid considerable attention to the former, the reflections that follow concentrate on the latter: why I believe that Christian historians are called to serve the church, why I think we so often overlook this dimension of our calling, and, above all, what taking it more seriously might require of us, practically and specifically.

A Dual Calling

I take as my starting point two verses from Christian scripture, one an exhortation, the other a warning. The exhortation is found in Paul's letter to the Christians at Rome. After explaining that the church, like the human body, has many members with different functions, the apostle concludes, "Having then gifts differing according to the grace that is given to us, let us use them" (Romans 12:6a). The warning comes from the words of Jesus in the Sermon on the Mount: "No one can serve two masters; for either he will hate the one and love the other, or else he will be loyal to the one and despise the other" (Matthew 6:24). How do these verses speak to the matter of vocation? Embedded in Paul's exhortation to the Romans is the principle that God gives us gifts with service in mind, especially (though not exclusively) service to His church. Surely then, part of the vocation of the Christian scholar is to serve not only the academy but the church as well—as a scholar. I would not argue that every Christian historian is called to share equally in this task, much less to fulfill it in the same way—our circumstances and opportunities will vary greatly—but I think that the basic principle stands: part of the calling of the Christian historian is to be an historian *for* Christians, not only to have a voice in the academy but also to speak in, to, and on behalf of the church. If we take this aspect of our calling seriously, however, we will likely run head on against the values of an academic culture that is skeptical of overtly Christian reflection about the past, is dismissive of questions that tend to interest our faith communities, and is reflexively suspicious of scholarship geared toward a popular audience. Here Christ's warning in the Sermon on the Mount speaks to us. To pursue our dual calling faithfully, we must be prepared to do so in submission to *one* master.

Based on their written works, it would appear that Christian historians in the United States have not spent much time thinking about their responsibilities to the church. The most pointed allusion that I have come across is now three decades old. In the introduction to an essay on approaches to the study of early American history, Mark Noll presented Christian historians with the following challenge: to speak *in* the profession as well as *to* the profession, to speak *to* the church as well as *in* the church.[3] Noll devoted only two paragraphs to developing this ideal, however, and few believing scholars appear to have responded to his exhortation. Certainly, there have been exceptions, and one could quickly construct a short list of Christian scholars who write from time to time intentionally *for* or *to* the church.[4] When we turn to the large and still growing literature on the concept of Christian scholarship, however—Christian historians' most public ruminations about the nature of their calling—we find a conversation driven almost entirely by concerns regarding our place within the walls of academe.[5]

Not surprisingly, historical circumstances help to explain this. As late as the 1960s, a broad public conversation among Christian historians on *any* topic was well nigh impossible. Few Christian historians at secular institutions were open about their faith, while those laboring at Christian colleges felt isolated from the mainstream academy by a vast and unbridgeable chasm. John W. Snyder, the first president of the Conference on Faith and History, noted that when that organization was founded in 1967 most Christian scholars "felt strangely alone and slightly illicit in confessing both to serious pretensions as a historian and to faith in Jesus Christ." Another member similarly recalled that "most of us had only a limited expectation that committed Christians could be distinguished historians." Fearing to be viewed as mere "teachers of history," they exhorted one another to pursue the highest standards of scholarship, and they stressed to their own students that "a Christian who wants to be a Christian historian can do no less than go to the best graduate school that will accept him."[6] Insecurity was rampant, and it is not surprising that, in this context, lonely scholars may have been concerned more with their uncertain status within the academy than with their potential ministry to the church.

Much has changed since that time, though. To their credit, numerous Christian historians labored tirelessly both to *gain* and to *deserve* a larger voice within the academy—and they succeeded. The last third of the twentieth century witnessed an outpouring of scholarly writing about religion in history, as well as the emergence of a number of highly accomplished, openly Christian scholars who have made a substantive impact on the wider profession. The result has been a much greater sense of optimism among Christian historians, who now appear to feel a lot more "comfortable walking down the corridors of the academy."[7] They encourage one another to reflect openly about how their faith informs their approach to the past, and they have no qualms about exhorting one another to model excellence in "Christian scholarship." And yet, as D. G. Hart has rightly observed, the call for more "Christian" scholarship still typically means one thing: a call for greater professional accomplishment and recognition *within the academic community*.[8] What about our communities of faith? The absence of any extensive discussion of the question would seem to speak volumes about the degree to which Christian historians have incorporated the agenda of the secular academy.

"Speak for yourself," I can hear teachers at Christian colleges interject. "Aren't those of us laboring at Christian institutions already serving the broader church through our on-campus teaching?" Absolutely that is true—and I do not want for a moment to minimize the importance of such labors—but forgive me for pointing out what a small proportion of Christians in the United States ever cross the threshold of a Christian college or university. Christian higher education may be booming, but it is still the case that Christian colleges and universities account for only about 10 percent of total enrollments in two- and four-year schools.[9] And although the trend is ever upward, it is still the case that barely half of U.S. adults have received any post-secondary education at all. The bottom line, then, is that while roughly two-thirds of U.S. adults are members of Christian churches, and approximately 40 percent attend church at least twice a month, no more than 5 to 6 percent have ever enrolled in a Christian college or university.[10] To serve the remainder—that is to say, to serve the overwhelming majority of American Christians—requires that we reach beyond the boundaries of the Christian college campus, indeed beyond the boundaries of the academy entirely.

Anecdotal evidence, at least, suggests that we are doing a pretty poor job at this, as a brief walk through a typical Christian bookstore will make clear. As part of my "field research" for this essay I toured a couple, both large stores in major nationwide chains, and I looked for titles pertaining to U.S. history, my own field of concentration. In the first I found no works at all. In the second I found only one, an anthology of brief historical sketches titled *Under God—Triumph and Tragedy: Stories of America's Spiritual Battle*. The editors, at least according to the claims of the book jacket, were Toby Mac and Michael Tait, "scholars" you may know better as two-thirds of the "pioneering" Christian rap group, *dc Talk*, a Grammy-winning trio famous for albums such as *Nu Thang* and *Jesus Freak*. Although I left that second bookstore pretty depressed, I know it exaggerated the bleakness of our current situation. Magazines like *Christian History* and *Books and Culture*, for instance, and presses such as Eerdmans do labor admirably to bring substantive Christian scholarship to popular audiences. Yet even their efforts are limited disproportionately to topics in church history. As William Trollinger observed in his presidential address to the Conference on Faith and History a few years ago, Christian historians still seem to think that "to have a Christian perspective on history . . . means that one chooses religious history for one's topic."[11]

But while Christian academics focus on the realm of religion *in* history, the stimulus for religious discussion *about* history is coming almost entirely from outside the academy, from individuals (for U.S. history) like the Reverend Peter Marshall Jr., author of the fabulously popular *Light and the Glory* series; Pastor Gary DeMar, president of American Vision; and, yes, from Christian rappers Toby Mac and Michael Tait. Such individuals have at least two characteristics in common, it seems to me: (1) they have minimal historical training and little grasp of the complexity of the American past; and (2) they do a much better job than most Christian academics in communicating with the church. Here I cannot help but recall Carl Becker's observation that the only historical knowledge that really does any work in the world is the knowledge that human beings actually carry around with them in their brains.[12] To the degree that Christians in the United States have a "faith-informed" understanding of American history, they are acquiring it primarily from Christian pastors and musicians, not from trained Christian historians. While we hold learned discussions among ourselves about whether such a thing as "Christian scholarship" even exists, Marshall's triumphalist celebration of God's role in the American founding goes into its twenty-fourth printing, and DeMar, author of *America's Christian History: The Untold Story*, gives interviews to *Time* magazine, CNN, Fox News, and the BBC. Our temptation, I suspect, is to shrug our shoulders when faced with such realities and dismiss the popularity of such nonscholars as simply one more reflection of the rampant anti-intellectualism that besets the modern evangelical church. It *is* that of course, but as Christians and scholars, how are we not complicit in that anti-intellectualism unless we are doing all within our power to combat it?

To take even the most modest step in that direction will test both our *loyalty* and our *judgment*. Here I think the passage that I quoted earlier from the Sermon on the Mount is particularly relevant, although I want to take great care in using it. Christ's admonition against serving two masters can easily be misapplied, serving as a rhetorical weapon with which to question the commitment of Christian scholars deemed overly accommodating to the rules of the academy.[13] That is the last thing that I want to do in this essay, yet I do think it is healthy—I know it is for me, at least—to return to this verse regularly, for it reminds us that our questions and conversations about the nature of Christian scholarship are never wholly "academic." There is a moral dimension inescapably present in the way that we define our vocations, for surely part of pursuing our callings faithfully is striving to understand them rightly.

To glean maximum insight from this verse, however, we must understand it in the larger context of Jesus's teaching. If Christ warns us about trying to serve God and mammon—thus teaching us that our ultimate allegiance cannot be divided—he also instructs us to "render . . . to Caesar the things that are Caesar's" (Matthew 22:21), suggesting that there are circumstances in which we may freely give a limited allegiance to multiple institutions as part of a larger act of obedience to God. This, I think, is exactly where we will find ourselves as Christian historians trying to speak both to the academy and to the church. As we strive to pursue our twofold calling in faithful obedience to one master, we will often be pulled in contradictory directions. We must be prepared to make difficult judgment calls about the degree to which either community should be allowed to shape our public voices. The line between accommodation and compromise will often be murky, and sincere Christian scholars can and will disagree. If we are going to take seriously the dual calling of the Christian scholar, however, we should "count the cost" at the outset and identify some of the challenges that lie ahead.

Many of those challenges will originate within the academy, of course. Depending on our surroundings, we may find ourselves working in institutions committed to a "diversity" that leaves little room for Christian perspectives, possibly teaching alongside colleagues who equate traditional Christian beliefs with superstition and ignorance. In such settings, historians who seek to reach a popular Christian audience will invite the skepticism of their co-workers and may even jeopardize their careers. Indeed, prudence may dictate that untenured faculty in such circumstances postpone efforts to fashion their scholarship with a Christian audience in mind. I am convinced, however, that for many of us the greatest obstacle we will face is not intrinsically antireligious at all: it is the daunting task of overcoming years of acculturation in an elitist academic establishment that produces historians increasingly aloof from the society they claim to serve.

In this sense, the challenge that Christian historians face in speaking to the church reflects a more general challenge facing the discipline as a whole. Within the last decade, presidents of both the American Historical Association (AHA) and the Organization of American Historians have called on the profession to do more to "make an intellectual connection with our audiences" and to make "history accessible to the public in a form that it will accept and use." Summarizing trends in the latter half of the twentieth century, a recent survey of the discipline decries "professional historians' unwillingness to credit the legitimacy of the public desire for a history that ordinary people can understand."[14] These words of admonition have largely fallen on deaf ears, however, and most academic historians still write primarily for other academic historians about questions that academic historians have decided are important.

The reasons for the estrangement between academic historians and the general public are complex and controversial, and an exhaustive explanation would go well beyond the scope of this essay. Suffice it to say that the trend is an old one, emerging simultaneously with the emergence of history as a professional discipline toward the close of the nineteenth century. Fully sixty years ago a distinguished president of the AHA felt constrained to chide the profession for its elitism and to remind his colleagues that "in the long run the teaching of history has to justify itself . . . in terms demonstrably significant to the average citizen."[15] Since that time the chasm between professional historians and "the average citizen" has only widened. The drive for ever greater specialization is surely part of the story, as is the "publish or perish" climate that places a premium on innovation and propels young scholars to ever more esoteric and inconsequential projects in search of an "original contribution to the literature." Other culprits might include the fashionable use of social-science theory (and the pretentious conceptualizing and jargon-ridden prose that often accompanies it), as well as a widespread ideological bias that produces contempt for the "dead white male" history that is so popular outside the academy.

Whatever its causes, the effects of such elitism are undeniably debilitating. We come to take it for granted, to see it as natural, indeed, not to *see* it at all. As Christian historians seeking to breach the walls of the academy and speak to our communities of faith, it is imperative that we recognize and repudiate the pervasive presumption that *the only scholarship that matters is the scholarship for other scholars.* This will be no easy task, for I suspect that most of us have been unconsciously internalizing this dogma since our earliest introduction to the profession. I know this was true in my case. Indeed, I sometimes joke that, if I ever write my autobiography as a Christian scholar, I'll play off of Robert Fulghum's *All I Really Need to Know I Learned in Kindergarten* and entitle the first chapter "Most of the Ideas that Really Messed Me up I Acquired in Graduate School." In reality, that's a cheap shot. The faculty with whom I worked were competent and kind, and I learned a great deal of value from them. It was in graduate school that I really mastered the building blocks of historical thinking: attention to change over time, understanding of causality, awareness of contingency, sensitivity to context and complexity.[16] There I saw modeled the scholarly virtues of prudence and humility and their integral connection to sound historical judgment. If I am equipped at all to serve the church as an historian, it is in large part because of the training I received in my secular graduate program.

And yet I learned other lessons in graduate school that discouraged me from thinking about the church at all. It was in graduate school that I first really encountered what Jean Bethke Elshtain has called "the by-far most common form of indoctrination" in today's academy, an indoctrination that, as Elshtain describes it, is neither "political nor religious" but "methodological and epistemological."[17] In countless ways, Elstain explains, she was taught as a graduate student that only certain questions mattered, only certain perspectives were acceptable, only certain kinds of evidence were valid. My experience was similar in many respects, although I would expand on Elshtain's list of debilitating lessons. It was in graduate school that I first began to internalize the advantages of specialization, oblivious to the dangers of what Irving Babbitt called the "maiming and mutilation of the mind that comes from over-absorption in one subject."[18] It was there that I came to accept as normal the rage for *innovation* that minimizes the importance of *communication*. It was in graduate school that I first came to see the academy as a self-contained world, and it was there, above all, that I was trained to write for other Ph.D.s rather than for the general public.

My first several years at the University of Washington—a large, characteristically secular research institution—simply reinforced the lessons of graduate school. As I turned my sights beyond the Ph.D. toward promotion and tenure, I picked up on the skepticism and condescension in my department directed toward any scholar devoted to writing "popular" history, and I discovered that job candidates who eschewed the latest trends were dismissed as "intellectually uninteresting." I soon learned to preface every prospective journal article with a lengthy acknowledgment of all the other academics who had already read the manuscript, always making clear my membership in good standing in the society of scholars. I figured out the importance of procuring the most prestigious press possible to publish my book, even if the book would be too expensive for anyone to afford. In short, I passively allowed the academy to shape my priorities and to define what would pass for excellence and success—in effect, to define my calling. Ill prepared to think critically about what Parker Palmer calls the "invisible curriculum" of the university, I had unwittingly conformed to the predominant values of my profession.[19]

I remember distinctly the time in my life when I first really saw this—*felt* this—clearly. It came at the moment that I achieved the professional goals for which I had long been laboring. In the very same month in the spring of 1994 two awful things happened to me: I obtained an advance copy of my first book, a study of post–Civil War agricultural reorganization soon to be published by Cambridge University Press, and I received a letter from the president of the university informing me that I had been promoted and granted tenure. Ultimately, these experiences profoundly disturbed me. I weighed these twin "successes," and the more I thought about it the more I was troubled by what my university was choosing to value and reward. Humanly speaking, I owed the perpetuation of my career to a slender volume to which I had devoted more than eight years of my life. Deeply researched but narrowly focused, it was of keen interest to a handful of specialists and of little interest to anyone else. Worse, there were no eternal issues therein, no "permanent things," no questions of importance to my local church or to the broader community of faith. As that truth sank in, a single unshakable resolve soon followed: Never Again.

The post-tenure letdown is so common that it has become a cliché, so I do not pretend for a moment that my experience was unique.[20] But God used this time of discouragement and searching to help me think critically and deeply—really for the first time—about my calling as a Christian scholar. It has been a slow process. My initial reaction, I see from hindsight, was an overreaction, coming perilously close to a Manichaean pietism that rejected all scholarship intended for the academy as intrinsically "evil" (or at best, a waste of time) and viewed only scholarship intended for the church as potentially "righteous." More clearheaded now, I see plainly the perniciousness of this simplistic view. There is definitely a place for careful, scrupulously researched monographs on narrowly focused topics, and Christian historians who feel called to labor on such projects can do so "heartily, as unto the Lord."

At the same time, it should give us pause to remember that such contributions to knowledge are most fruitful when the community of scholars uses them to build coherent reflections on life's deepest questions—a task utterly beyond the modern fragmented academy. And it should still trouble us that so little of our labors are undertaken with the church in mind. Our concentration on scholarship for other scholars is not offensive in and of itself, but paired alongside a contemporary church that learns its history from rap musicians, it becomes so. The problem, in sum, is one of proportion, and I know of no better way to rectify it than for Christian historians to reassess the relative emphasis of their individual labors. The quest to craft a *single* scholarly project (whether monograph, article, lecture, or class) that will speak *simultaneously* both to the academy and to the rank and file in our churches is probably futile. Their questions, concerns, and objectives are just too dissimilar. On the other hand, the obstacles to addressing those two communities *alternately*, though still daunting, are far from insuperable.

History in the Church

The challenges to pursuing our dual calling do not originate solely within the academy, however. Indeed, there is little evidence that the church is eager to hear from us. We will occasionally encounter Christians both interested in and open to our teaching, but I suspect that, initially at least, we will more frequently meet with either indifference or resistance—indifference from those who do not care about history, resistance from those who do. The indifference we are probably used to, although since we cannot use grades as an inducement we will need to find some other way to create a demand for the services we hope to provide. The resistance will be more foreign to us; it is the resistance of those already deeply invested in a particular understanding of the past and suspicious of any who would challenge it. The result, as Douglas and Rhonda Jacobsen rightly observe, is that "the terrain Christian scholars must negotiate within [their] churches is perhaps even more challenging" than what they face within the academy.[21] I have no magic formula for how to negotiate this terrain successfully, but I do have several suggestions, most of which I have arrived at after a good deal of trial and error (especially the latter).

First, I think we must *begin with our local churches.* This is partly a matter of principle. It is in our local churches that we encounter the "body of Christ" incarnate; it is there that we can most concretely model our calling to serve a body with many members but different gifts. There are also numerous practical benefits to such an approach. To begin with, not all of us will have the time, opportunity, and skills required to speak effectively to the broader church, but if we are prepared to look for them, we can find numerous opportunities to engage our own congregations. For example, in the last few years I have been able to address various members of my church about the "civil religion" of eighteenth- and nineteenth-century America, the causes of the Civil War, the defining principles of "Christian historical scholarship," the evolution of the Thanksgiving holiday, and, most delicately, the very serious flaws in the public teaching on American history from a prominent pastor in our denomination. Also, in two of the last three years I have had the privilege of teaching a weekly seminar on U.S. history to home-schooled students drawn from a half-dozen area churches. There are a variety of other ways that you might begin to engage your local church if you have not already done so. Season your casual conversations with historical "salt." Recommend books that will whet others' appetite for high-quality history. Offer to lead an informal book group. Write and circulate short historical essays on the background of particular American holidays such as the Fourth of July, Labor Day, Memorial Day, Presidents' Day, or Martin Luther King Day. Even if your ultimate goal is to write books or articles for the broader church, it is in engaging your local congregation that you will best learn how to communicate with your prospective audience.

Second, we should *be prepared to make a positive case for the importance of history.* Adopting our own variation of 1 Peter 3:15, we must "always be ready to give a defense to everyone who asks" us why we care about the past. Our reply should be concrete, concise, and tailored with Christians in mind. My own standard response includes five key points: (1) History is integral to Christianity, for the latter "presents us with religious doctrines which are at the same time historical events or historical interpretations."[22] (2) God is the Author and Lord of human history, and when we decline to study the past we ignore a "sphere created by God and sustained for his own glory."[23] (3) The study of history helps us to see our own day with new eyes and offers a perspective that transcends the brevity of our own brief sojourn on earth. The student of history, as C. S. Lewis observed, has figuratively "lived in many times and is therefore in some degree immune from the great cataract of nonsense that pours from the press and the microphone of his own age."[24] (4) Attention to history enables us to sift wisdom from our ancestors. The student of history, in the words of G. K. Chesterton, refuses to "submit to the small and arrogant oligarchy of those who merely happen to be" alive.[25] Respect for the past is respect for tradition and a logical extension of the biblical precept to honor age. (5) Most pragmatically, in a free society such as the United States, public debates over governmental policy frequently include essentially historical arguments. This is true of debates concerning immigration and its effects, the consequences of affirmative action, and the meaning of the first amendment, to list but a few examples. Ignorance is not our ally.

Third, we should strive to *eliminate unnecessary barriers*. A significant part of our audience may be reflexively suspicious of intellectual elites and skeptical of finding allies within the academy. Especially as we move beyond our own specific congregations, we need to take every opportunity to *identify ourselves as believers to our Christian audiences*. As professional historians we have been trained to hide our personal commitments and convictions in the interest of "disinterested scholarship." Much good may come of showing our audiences that we are "on the same side." We must still pursue truth with the utmost integrity, of course, but why not openly acknowledge that we strive to do so as an act of service to God and of love for His church? Similarly, we would be well advised to abandon the dry, laborious, scholarly prose that is the bane of academic history. We should bear in mind that Christians willing to read history or attend a historical lecture are often more in search of entertainment and inspiration than of education. To make these propensities work in our favor, we need to *refine our abilities as storytellers*—a talent that the academy sometimes discourages—and look for ways to integrate complex truths into compelling narratives. Dull pedantry will undo us, no matter how brilliant our insights.

Fourth, we need to *learn the interests of our target audience and educate ourselves accordingly.* A little knowledge of local history may offer a more natural bridge to our congregations than, say, our erudite mastery of European feudalism. Likewise, even minimal reading in recent Middle Eastern history could pay rich dividends in casual conversations about contemporary events. Pulitzer Prize–winning historian Gordon Wood holds that it is not primarily their "jargon-ridden" prose or obsession with fashionable theories "that prevents most academic historians from becoming popular"—although he laments the prevalence of both. Rather, Wood maintains, it is "the questions that they ask about the past, and the subjects that they write about."[26] In the congregations of which I have been a part, the historical topics of greatest interest have involved war (anywhere, anytime) and the dead white European males who helped to found the country. Shall we shun such topics—as the academy has generally—or shall we use them as entry points to engage our churches more generally?

Fifth, we can *learn the objectives of our target audience and take them seriously.* In conversations about American history with members of my church, for instance, I have found that those who are interested in history for more than personal entertainment want to plumb the past in search of life lessons and larger meanings. Although they may have never heard the maxim, many intuitively accept the view of history as "philosophy teaching by example," and they assume that a primary function of history is to generate moral lessons for our edification. Others are more interested in questions that pertain to God's providential work in the American past, wanting to know exactly when and how God has intervened and for what purposes. Such agendas may make us wince, but I believe that we err in simply dismissing them. In the first place, and most pragmatically, when we ignore the cherished agendas of our prospective audiences we simply invite them to ignore us in return. More importantly, I am convinced that such questions about larger meaning bespeak a very natural, human longing for something more than the detached perspective of the technical expert, and to ignore them entirely may actually violate the law of love.[27] Taking such longing seriously does not necessarily mean that we can satisfy it, of course. When our audiences demand certainty concerning God's providential work, for example, we may instead remind them that "the secret things belong to the Lord" (Deuteronomy 29:29), caution them about presumption, and show them how difficult it is to "prove" God's intentions with regard to any specific historical event. At the same time, the mere act of acknowledging such yearning for deeper meaning may help us see more clearly the academy's own version of anti-intellectualism to which we may be inclined: the temptation to hoard innumerable discrete facts without ever linking them to larger questions about human existence.

Sixth, we should *search proactively for common ground with our audience*, affirming the historical truths that they hold dear whenever we can, in good conscience, do so. Whether we are speaking to our local churches or to the broader church, we would be well advised to bear in mind William McNeill's dictum from a quarter-century ago. In his 1980 presidential address to the AHA, McNeill observed that, to be *useful* to society, historians must "tell the people some things they are reluctant to hear," but if they expect to be *heard* by society, they must also tell the people some things that they want to hear.[28] Let me hasten to make clear what I am not suggesting: I am not recommending that we pander to our audiences or adopt the mentality that "the customer is always right." I do believe, however, that unless we are careful we will define our call to speak to the church wholly in negative terms. Of course part of our task is to correct—at times even to rebuke. Much of what passes for "Christian history" is abysmal, and it is often disseminated in arrogance by combatants in the culture wars who approach the past not in a quest for understanding but in a search for ammunition. Love often requires hard words, and we must not shrink from delivering them. My point is simply that our Christian audiences will likely be more receptive to hard words when they are not the only kind that they hear from us.

I have learned this by experience. In my own first stumbling efforts to serve my local church, I engaged the congregation almost exclusively on questions in which—in my judgment—they were in error. Employing a sledgehammer where a scalpel was called for, I overwhelmed the majority and offended more than a few. For example, shortly before

Thanksgiving a few years ago, I crafted a brief essay to share with my church that focused on how American Christians have mythologized the "First Thanksgiving." My goal was to use the commemoration of the holiday as a context for thinking about the dangers of conflating our national and religious heritage, but I offered my congregation nothing positive or encouraging to offset my unsettling challenge to their understanding. I simply "debunked" much of what they thought was true and then wished them a "Happy Thanksgiving." To his credit, my pastor discouraged me from circulating this less than edifying piece. Two years later I had a go at the topic a second time in the form of a public lecture sponsored by my church, but on this occasion I balanced the debunking with positive (and historically accurate) portrayals of the pilgrims' commitment to faith and family. I think this portion of my remarks served as an indispensable bridge to my audience, and the lecture as a whole was a success.

My final suggestion, and by far the most important, is that *we strive to love our churches with the love that "bears all things . . . hopes all things, endures all things."* If we love them enough to tell them what they are reluctant to hear, we can count on our share of awkward and stressful moments. When I challenged some of the historical assertions of a leading pastor in my denomination, for example, my own pastor questioned my motives, and a member of the congregation interrupted a church lecture I was giving in order to accuse me publicly of sin. In such moments our temptation will be to throw up our hands and walk away, but love requires that we persevere. And as we persevere in loving our churches—not only as historians but in the myriad of mundane ways that God calls His children to love one another—we may gradually win an ever greater hearing for our historical teaching otherwise foreclosed to us and in the process learn experientially what it means to pursue the often forgotten dimension of our dual calling.

Notes

1. This essay originated, in somewhat different form, as a paper delivered to a session sponsored by the Conference on Faith and History at the 2005

meeting of the American Historical Association in Seattle, Washington. At that time I benefited from prepared remarks from commentators Douglas Jacobsen and Sandra Yokum Mize. Since then I have been further aided by extremely helpful feedback from the editors of this anthology.

2. Most notably, see George M. Marsden, *The Outrageous Idea of Christian Scholarship* (New York: Oxford University Press, 1997); Bruce Kuklick and D. G. Hart, eds., *Religious Advocacy and American History* (Grand Rapids, Mich.: Eerdmans, 1997); and Ronald A. Wells, ed., *History and the Christian Historian* (Grand Rapids, Mich.: Eerdmans, 1998). Broader explorations still of relevance to historians include, among many, Mark R. Schwehn, *Exiles from Eden: Religion and the Academic Vocation in America* (New York: Oxford University Press, 1993); Andrea Sterk, ed., *Religion, Scholarship, Higher Education: Perspectives, Models, and Future Prospects* (Notre Dame, Ind.: University of Notre Dame Press, 2001); and Douglas Jacobsen and Rhonda Hustedt Jacobsen, eds., *Scholarship and Christian Faith: Enlarging the Conversation* (New York: Oxford University Press, 2004). No single essay has stimulated my thought more than Alvin Plantinga, "Advice to Christian Philosophers," *Faith and Philosophy: Journal of the Society of Christian Philosophers* 1 (1984): 253–71.

3. Mark A. Noll, "The Conference on Faith and History and the Study of Early American History," *Fides et Historia* 11 (1978): 8.

4. A range of examples would include Noll's own *The Scandal of the Evangelical Mind* (1994), Steven J. Keillor's *This Rebellious House* (1996), any number of titles in the "Library of Religious Biography" series published by Eerdmans, and the efforts of the contributors to *Christian History, Books and Culture,* and *First Things.*

5. Jacobsen and Jacobsen offer a thoughtful discussion of "Christian Scholarship in the Context of the Church" but do not discuss the role of historians specifically. See *Scholarship and Christian Faith,* 162–66. I must stress again that I am not suggesting that there have been no efforts by Christian historians to write for the church, but rather that the large and growing literature on the nature of "Christian scholarship" has been driven almost entirely by questions concerning Christian historians' role within the academy.

6. John W. Snyder, "Open Letter from the President," *Fides et Historia* 1 (1968): 3; Charles J. Miller, "The Conference on Faith and History: Reminiscences about Origins and Identity," *Fides et Historia* 9 (1977): 59. See also D. G. Hart, "History in Search of Meaning: The Conference on Faith and History," in *History and the Christian Historian,* ed. Ronald A. Wells, 68–87 (Grand Rapids, Mich.: Eerdmans, 1998).

7. D. G. Hart, "What's So Special about the University, Anyway?" in *Religious Advocacy and American History,* ed. Bruce Kuklick and D. G. Hart (Grand Rapids, Mich.: Eerdmans, 1997), 137. See also Wells, *History and the Christian*

Historian, 3–4; and Tim Stafford, "Whatever Happened to Christian History?" *Christianity Today*, April 2, 2001, 42.

8. D.G. Hart, "Christian Scholars, Secular Universities, and the Problem with the Antithesis," *Christian Scholar's Review* 30 (2001): 383–402.

9. National Center for Education Statistics, *Digest of Education Statistics, 2003*, chap. 3, available at http://nces.ed.gov/programs/digest/d03/tables/dt182 .asp (last accessed March 3, 2010).

10. U.S. Census Bureau, American Community Survey 2003 Data Profile, table 2, available at http://www.census.gov/acs/www/Products/Profiles/ Single/2003/ACS/Tabular/010/01000US2.htm (last accessed March 3, 2010); George Gallup Jr. and D. Michael Lindsay, *Surveying the Religious Landscape: Trends in Religious Beliefs* (Harrisburg, Pa.: Morehouse Publishing, 1999), 12–15.

11. Quoted in Stafford, "Whatever Happened to Christian History?" 47.

12. Carl L. Becker, "What Are Historical Facts?" *Western Historical Quarterly* 8 (1955): 327–40.

13. George M. Marsden, *The Outrageous Idea of Christian Scholarship* (New York: Oxford University Press, 1997), esp. p. 11 and chap. 3.

14. Joyce Appleby, "The Power of History," *American Historical Review* 103 (1998): 2; James Oliver Horton, *Journal of American History* 92 (2005): 802; Peter Charles Hoffer, *Past Imperfect: Facts, Fictions, Fraud—American History from Bancroft and Parkman to Ambrose, Bellesiles, Ellis, and Goodwin* (New York: Public Affairs, 2004), 231.

15. Conyers Read, "The Social Responsibilities of the Historian," *American Historical Review* 55 (1950): 279.

16. The categories are from Thomas Andrews and Flannery Burke, "What Does It Mean to Think Historically?" *Perspectives* 45:1 (January 2007): 32–35.

17. Jean Bethke Elshtain, "Does, or Should, Teaching Reflect the Religious Perspective of the Teacher?" in Sterk, *Religion, Scholarship, Higher Education*, 193.

18. Irving Babbitt, *Literature and the American College: Essays in the Defense of the Humanities* (Washington, D.C.: National Humanities Institute, 1907), 128.

19. Parker J. Palmer, *To Know as We Are Known: Education as a Spiritual Journey* (San Francisco: Harper & Row, 1983), 34.

20. Lawrence Douglas and Alexander George, "Treating Post-Tenure Depression," *Chronicle of Higher Education*, February 21, 2003, B20.

21. Jacobsen and Jacobsen, *Scholarship and Christian Faith*, 166.

22. Herbert Butterfield, *Christianity and History* (New York: Charles Scribner's Sons, 1949), 3; C.S. Lewis, *The Discarded Image* (Cambridge: Cambridge University Press, 1964), 174.

23. Mark A. Noll, *The Scandal of the Evangelical Mind* (Grand Rapids, Mich.: Eerdmans, 1994), 23.

24. C. S. Lewis, "Learning in War-Time," in *The Weight of Glory and Other Addresses* (New York: Macmillan Co., 1949), 28–29.

25. Gilbert K. Chesterton, *Orthodoxy* (New York: Image Books, 1990), 49.

26. Gordon S. Wood, "The Man Who Would Not be King," *New Republic*, December 20, 2004, 33.

27. Ronald H. Nash, *The Meaning of History* (Nashville: Broadman & Holman, 1998), 7.

28. William H. McNeill, "Mythistory, or Truth, Myth, History, and Historians," *American Historical Review* 91 (1986): 10, emphasis added.

Chapter Fourteen

ON THE VOCATION OF
HISTORIANS TO THE
PRIESTHOOD OF BELIEVERS

A Plea to Christians in the Academy

DOUGLAS A. SWEENEY

*Come to him, a living stone, though rejected by mortals yet chosen
and precious in God's sight, and like living stones, let yourselves be
built into a spiritual house, to be a holy priesthood, to offer spiritual
sacrifices acceptable to God through Jesus Christ.*

—1 Peter 2:4–5

DURING THE PAST FEW DECADES, CHRISTIAN HISTORY HAS
been reborn as Christian scholars have labored diligently on the relationship of Christian faith and historical understanding.[1] As recently
as the 1960s, Christians languished on the margins of the historical
profession, still waxing in some divinity schools but waning in history
departments. Today, the reverse is true. Divinity schools no longer feature many distinguished historians. The American Academy of Religion
is often the butt of historians' jokes. However, in history departments

and conferences all over North America, Christians are thriving as their scholarship is gaining a wider hearing.

Some suggest that this success has begun to obviate the enclaves in which Christians meet together for mutual aid and strategic planning. Christian historians, they contend, no longer need separate mechanisms for scholarly promotion. Nor do we need to seclude ourselves before we speak from Christian perspectives. We have earned the right to partici-pate in secular conversation at the late modern, multicultural, academic table. To isolate ourselves within an academic ghetto would be to forfeit all the gains that we have won in recent years.

Such statements deserve a hearing. It is true that our senior col-leagues have made broad strides within the academy, blazing a trail for those among us who want to work in secular settings. It is true that some have ascended to the top tier of the profession and no longer need sectarian networks of support and encouragement. But it is also true that even the most proficient of our leaders have just begun to scratch the surface of the field of faithful history.[2] Moreover, many Christian historians work in Christian college settings, where administrators and students expect a deeper and more explicit brand of Christian scholar-ship than is appropriate in secular institutions. Most importantly, per-haps, this way of thinking is far too selfish—especially for those who follow Jesus. Too much talk of self-promotion, scholarly rights, and secular privileges can distract us from the task of self-sacrificial, schol-arly service.

I would like to speak in this chapter about a part of our vocation often neglected in conversations about our task as Christian scholars. I want to address the theme of vocation to the priesthood of believers (or the priesthood of the baptized, as we Lutherans often phrase it). In so doing, I hope to goad us to further reflection upon our labors, filling out our conversation about the work we do as scholars with an emphasis on our roles as priestly ministers in the guild. I want to stress the fact that we are called to lives of service—to our students as well as our peers— service funded by God's grace and shaped by scripture and tradition. We are called, I will argue, to a form of Christian ministry, to practices in support of which ecclesial aid is needed (whether sectarian or not).

LUTHER AND OTHERS ON VOCATION AND THE
PRIESTHOOD OF THE BAPTIZED

The English notion of "calling" comes in part from the Greek word *klesis*, which appears frequently in the New Testament as an "invitation to [an] experience of special privilege and responsibility."[3] Perhaps the best-known use of this term is found in a prison epistle of Paul, Ephesians 4:1–6, in which he begs his friends in Ephesus to

> lead a life worthy of the calling to which you have been called, with all humility and gentleness, with patience, bearing with one another in love, making every effort to maintain the unity of the Spirit in the bond of peace. There is one body and one Spirit, just as you were called to the one hope of your calling, one Lord, one faith, one baptism, one God and Father of all, who is above all and through all and in all.

The Western church translated *klesis* with the Latin word *vocatio*, from which we derive our English word "vocation."[4] Latin churchmen spoke of *vocatio* before the Reformation. But the theologian who pioneered the doctrine of vocation as the calling of believers to priestly ministry in the world was Martin Luther, who wrote of *vocatio* and, in German, *der Beruf*. Many others followed his lead, both Protestants and, in recent decades, Roman Catholics too.[5] As I will remind us in what follows, the priestly functions of the laity received extensive and authoritative treatment at Vatican II.

André Lacocque contends that, even in the Hebrew Old Testament, God's people were called to live as a *nation* of priests. A representative system was formed for practical, ceremonial purposes. Firstborn sons stood in for their families (Ex 13:2, 13; 22:29). Levites ran the tabernacle and, later, the temple worship (Nm 3:12). Not everyone was appointed to the *office* of the priesthood, but all were called to sacrificial lives of divine service.[6] In the New Testament, of course, this priestly calling was expanded. Gentiles were included, the Holy Spirit dwelled in the hearts of all who came to faith in Christ, and the mystical bride of Christ was now "built into a spiritual house, to be a holy priesthood, to offer spiritual sacrifices acceptable to God through Jesus Christ" (1 Pt 2:4–5).[7]

At least as Luther saw things, Christians were given the keys of the kingdom, with which they could loose the chains that bound their fellow sinners in despair (Mt 16:19, 18:18; Jn 20:23). Ordained ministers bore special responsibility for these keys. Whenever possible, they should be set apart to administer word and sacrament. But all true Christians were priests, called to mediate the love, grace, and mercy of their Lord to a world still plagued by the evils of sin, death, and the devil (Ex 19:6; 1 Pt 2:5, 9; Rv 1:6, 5:10).[8]

Beginning in 1520 with his *Treatise on the New Testament, Freedom of a Christian*, and address *To the Christian Nobility*, and continuing through most of the rest of his own priestly ministry, Luther developed a radical doctrine of the priesthood of the baptized. He wrote in *Treatise on the New Testament*, "faith alone is the true priestly office. . . . Therefore all Christian men are priests, all women priestesses, be they young or old, master or servant, mistress or maid, learned or unlearned. Here there is no difference, unless faith be unequal."[9] He expanded upon this notion in his *Freedom of a Christian*,

> Not only are we the freest of kings, we are also priests forever, which is far more excellent than being kings, for as priests we are worthy to appear before God to pray for others and to teach one another divine things. These are the functions of priests, and they cannot be granted to any unbeliever. Thus Christ has made it possible for us, provided we believe in him, to be not only his brethren, co-heirs, and fellow-kings, but also his fellow-priests.[10]

In his *Commentary on Psalm 110*, first preached in 1535, Luther summarized this point succinctly: "every baptized Christian is a priest already, not by appointment or ordination . . . but because Christ Himself has begotten him as a priest and has given birth to him in Baptism."[11]

Especially as he grew older, Luther proved careful to distinguish between the priesthood of believers and the priesthood of the pastors. Indeed, despite the misperception common today among evangelicals (and even many Lutherans), Luther did not intend to democratize the governance of the church. Nor did he think that all could preach, teach, and administer the sacraments. "Although we are all equally priests," he wrote, "we cannot all publicly minister and teach." Moreover, "we ought not do so even if we could."[12] Luther denied that ordination conferred an indelible character (*character indelebilis*), a spiritual mark that sets a priest apart from the laity. But he affirmed that God supplies the ordinand with special grace, and he insisted that ordination be restricted to those who are called and trained to preach the Word and administer the sacraments. "Every Christian," he proclaimed, "has the right and the duty to teach, instruct, admonish, comfort, and rebuke his neighbor with the Word of God at every opportunity and whenever necessary." Nonetheless, "out of the multitude of Christians some must be selected who shall lead the others by virtue of the special gifts and aptitude which God gives them for the office. . . . For although we are all priests, this does not mean that all of us can preach, teach, and rule. Certain ones of the multitude must be selected and separated for such an office."[13]

Reformed Protestants, as well, affirmed the priesthood of believers, appropriating the doctrine for their own territories. As John Calvin codified it in the leaves of his *Institutes*, Christ counts all true Christians "companions" in his priesthood. "For we who are defiled in ourselves," Calvin wrote, "yet are priests in him, offer ourselves and our all to God, and freely enter the heavenly sanctuary that the sacrifices of prayers and praise that we bring may be acceptable and sweet-smelling before God." Indeed, "every member of the church is charged with the responsibility of public edification according to the measure of his grace, provided he perform it decently and in order." Again, "In [Christ] we are all priests" who are called "to offer praises and thanksgiving, in short, to offer ourselves . . . to God."[14]

Of course, Protestants have differed over the doctrine of the ministry ever since the Reformation. The Council of Trent, furthermore, resisted the pan-Protestant move away from the earlier, sacramental understanding of ordination.[15] Indeed, as William Placher has noted in his reader on vocation, Christians have lived by *multiple* meanings of the biblical notion of *klesis*, not to mention the calling to clerical ministry. "One lesson to be learned," he avers, "from the history of Christian ideas of vocation is that there is not just one account of what vocation means."

In fact, some late-modern thinkers, in response to industrial capitalism and "alienated labor," have begun to divorce jobs, or the work we do for money—even the work of ordained clergy—from the biblical notion of calling, reserving the latter for use in explaining our general call to live for God. Jacques Ellul, James Holloway, and Miroslav Volf, for instance, have argued, in Volf's words, "that the dead hand of 'vocation' needed to be lifted from the Christian idea of work. It is both inapplicable to modern societies and theologically inadequate."[16]

Christian views of calling and vocation are complex. Believers have rarely spoken univocally about them. However, especially in recent years, Christians all around the world—Catholic, Protestant, and Orthodox—*have* concurred in stressing the priestly work of the laity. It is simply no longer credible, if it ever really was, to claim the priesthood of believers only for Lutherans or Protestants. All Christians now agree *at least* that those who follow Jesus share in their Lord's priestly ministry and play an important role in spreading his love and grace in the world.

At Vatican II, Catholic leaders emphasized this point most clearly. In the *Dogmatic Constitution on the Church,* or *Lumen Gentium,* they declared in terms so helpful that I quote them here at length: The laity are,

> in their own way made sharers in Christ's priestly, prophetic and royal office, play their own part in the mission of the whole christian people in the church and in the world. . . . They live in the world, that is to say, in each and all of the world's occupations and affairs, and in the ordinary circumstances of family and social life; these are the things that form the context of their life. And it is here that God calls them to work for the sanctification of the world as it were from the inside, like leaven, through carrying out their own task in the spirit of the gospel, and in this way revealing Christ to others principally through the witness of their lives, resplendent in faith, hope and charity. It is, therefore, their special task to shed light upon and order all temporal matters, in which they are closely involved, in such a way that these are always carried out and developed in Christ's way and to the praise of the creator and redeemer.[17]

Somewhat later in the council the Catholic Church went even further, declaring that God has called the laity "to the apostolate." In the *Decree on the Apostolate of the Laity*, in fact, the council declared that "laypeople, sharing in the priestly, prophetic and kingly offices of Christ, play their part in the mission of the whole people of God in the church and in the world. They truly exercise their apostolate by labours for evangelizing and sanctifying people, and by permeating the temporal order with the spirit of the gospel."[18]

In short, today more than ever, Christians all across the globe are coming together in support of the priestly ministries of the laity. It is only fitting that Christian historians, few of whom are ordained, reflect at length upon their own priestly potential.

Priesthood in Our Guild

As Karl Hertz reminded us nearly half a century ago, "As priest I must act on behalf of my neighbor who is in need." In fact, "the heart of the Christian priesthood is just this intercessory action on behalf of others."[19] A few years later, Gerhard Ebeling wrote that a calling to the priesthood was a calling to "be for others." In his essay on "The Protestant Idea of the Priesthood," he insisted famously that "all" believers are "by faith, through Christ, priests united in being for others." Of course, as Ebeling knew well, his was a modern, existential way of making the older Lutheran claim that Christians are called to become "Christ for another," to live as the body of Christ in the world, to flesh out the work of redemption, applying our lips, limbs, hands, and feet to the gospel.[20] Such an incarnational witness accompanies all genuine faith. However, as Christians have long affirmed, its most robust expression requires intentionality and sacrifice, a cruciform existence oriented toward the other, a humble life of charity in service of God and neighbor.

Nowhere is this sacrifice more necessary today than in the academy, which is so full of fragile egos, insecurities, uncertainties, and fears, to say nothing of most of the ordinary forms of human suffering. Our guild is full of sinners standing in need of grace and mercy, people plagued by doubts and debts but still expected to perform as confident masters of their subjects and magnanimous public figures. These pressures breed anxiety and chronic self-absorption, yielding a morally repugnant blend of obsequiousness toward those whom we assume can ease our burden and obliviousness, or outright disrespect, toward those who cannot. We spend an inordinate amount of time in making a name for ourselves. We do what we must to stay employed and advance in rank within our departments. But all too often we find ways to take the intellectual high ground for behavior that is frankly self-promoting.

In the midst of this situation, Christian historians share a special calling to worldly ministry, to live as priests among our partners in the guild. We share a mandate from the scriptures to serve in the manner of our Lord, whose life was spent for people like us in humble, self-defeating love. As depicted by St. Paul in his epistle to the Philippians (2:3–8), this mandate reads as follows:

> Do nothing from selfish ambition or conceit, but in humility regard others as better than yourselves. Let each of you look not to your own interests, but to the interests of others. Let the same mind be in you that was in Christ Jesus, who, though he was in the form of God, did not regard equality with God as something to be exploited, but emptied himself, taking the form of a slave, being born in human likeness. And being found in human form, he humbled himself and became obedient to the point of death—even death on a cross.

Without confusing our secular roles with those of officially ordained priests, or assuming the weighty mantle of ecclesial authority, we are nonetheless to engage in acts of sacrificial service to our students, colleagues, and others who come in contact with our work. We are to make time for others, put their needs before our own, support their academic labors, and rejoice in their success. More importantly, perhaps, we are to help them personally, demonstrating compassion for their welfare in the world, encouraging them as they struggle with the pressures of the academy, and praying for them and their loved ones without ceasing.

In an era characterized by academic acquisitiveness, we are called to model a counter-cultural style of scholarship.[21] Rather than spending so much time attracting attention to ourselves, trying desperately to impress, and practicing scholarly one-upmanship, we are called to build up others, valorizing their achievements. Rather than trying quite so hard to be known as players in the academy, to win respect at the Ivies, and to demonstrate to colleagues that Christians are not as dumb as they seem, we are called to be "poor in spirit," to "hunger and thirst for righteousness," to be "pure in heart," and "salt" and "light" in the world (Mt 5:1–16). We are also called to witness to the "foolishness" of history (1 Cor 1–2)—calling things as we see them through the spectacles of faith—and to submit, yes submit, our minds to the sovereignty of Christ, even as we pursue historiographical excellence.[22]

ECCLESIAL SOURCES OF ENCOURAGEMENT FOR PRIESTS WHO REALLY MEAN IT

This is a very tall order, much too tall for someone like me. But this is precisely why I need the help of fellow Christian historians. I do not need this kind of help to gain a platform for my work. You do not need this kind of help to gain a seat at the scholarly table. But all of us need this kind of help as we pursue the call of God to serve each other in the guild with academic generosity.

In the words of Richard Hughes, "if we hope to serve as effective teachers and scholars, then our work must proceed from a profound sense of vocation."[23] This sense of vocation, one might add, requires nurture in community if it is ever going to flourish. Christian life is difficult, especially amidst the secular city. It was never intended for expression in terms of modern individualism. Christians need communities of support and encouragement. We are called to walk the way of the cross—to find our lives by losing them—and we live in a world that tempts us to avoid this narrow road. Hughes recounts the words of a Dutch Reformed Christian, Gerrit tenZythoff, who survived Nazi torture near the end of World War II: "Good *will* triumph over evil," he proclaimed. "All that you and I must do is suffer."[24] To be sure, suffering is essential to the history of redemption, though none of us should have to bear it alone. For as St. Paul informed the church in Corinth regarding the body of Christ, "If one member suffers, all suffer together with it" (1 Cor 12:26).

Richard Goode has exhorted us recently to what he calls "radical scholarship," work that is *driven* by human suffering and should scandalize the powers that be in our guild. Advocating an Anabaptist view of Christian history, Goode contends that "scandalous" history, or radically Christian scholarship, should "inspire Christians not to take power, but to volunteer for poverty." He continues in a voice intended to rattle conventional scholars: "Because we have a faith that calls us to die," he declares, "we need a historiography that can teach us how to get killed." We need methods of practicing history that promote peace and justice, especially among the oppressed, and these will never be perfected if we restrict ourselves as Christians to the oft-cited "canons of the profession." Radical scholarship requires a humble willingness to work along the margins of academe—away from the corridors of power—with means and ends not always suited to those who play by the rules of the game, control the purse strings of the profession, and tend to favor historiographical consensus.[25]

Although I am not an Anabaptist, I applaud Goode's argument. It *is* time for us to move beyond the kind of status anxiety that keeps us from faithful service in our guild and in our world. During the mid-twentieth century, Christian scholars had to work hard to earn the respect of secular colleagues. We devoted a great deal of energy to impressing them with our work. We sought to acquire places of honor at the academic banquet. But now that we have done this, a different agenda may be in order.

I hope you will not misread me. I am certainly *not* calling for a return to shoddy scholarship—not even the kind that is animated by pietistic passion. We must maintain, and even improve, our levels of academic excellence if we hope to make a difference *as historians* in our guild. But rather than operate as other-directed, status conscious scholars, I hope we will finish the task of moving beyond our need for recognition and engage a bit more freely in public service that is fueled by Christian faith.

Too many of us today continue to imitate our colleagues in the corridors of power, conforming to their canons (even their personal preferences) and failing to share with them those things that make us different. I am *not* suggesting that we should now exaggerate our uniqueness, calling attention to ourselves like adolescents in rebellion. In the main, I think we should knuckle down and practice history well, taking pains to help our colleagues with careful teaching, research, and writing. However, I also think that we should practice scholarship as ministry, a form of priestly service intended to bless the larger world. Rather than holding back for fear that other scholars will reject us, it is time for us to reach out and face the consequences of faith, hope, and love within the academy.

It is time to shower attention on those who have no power over us, meeting the needs of junior colleagues before we tend to our CVs, and looking for ways to treat others—especially "the least" of those among us—as though they were better, more important, than ourselves. It is time to tell the truth—the whole truth—about our materials, "outing" ourselves as Christians when the occasion calls for it. We need not drive away our colleagues with annoying, artificial attempts to make a Christian difference, substituting spiritual chatter or religious moralism for painstaking scholarship. But we *do* need to resist the many professional enticements, institutional incentives, and pecuniary tugs to live as scholarly Nicodemites, practicing Christian faith by night but afraid to show ourselves, or be ourselves, by day.

I am not calling for revolution. Most of us try to do these things. We pray for the grace to honor God and serve the needs of those around us as we do our historical work. Further, many of us are blessed by association with teachers and colleagues who exemplify the priestly traits I am advocating. *I* have been so blessed. In fact, I would not be writing these words today, or even practicing history, if not for the example and the academic *ministry* of one whose humility and earnest desire to put his colleagues first keeps me from mentioning his name. This former teacher is widely known for his scholarly acumen and excellence. I must admit that this is what drew me to his classes in the first place. But the thing that kept me there and made me want to practice history was his humble, loving example of scholarly service: his willingness to work on behalf of projects and for people whom he knew could not boost his own career; his habit of deflecting the many kudos that came his way, making sure that others received their due for toiling in his vineyards; his tireless support for junior colleagues in need of help; and his practice of responding to malformed questions from his students and aspersions from opponents with a spirit of genuine charity and an eagerness to learn. I am sure that many of you could testify to such experiences with others who have blessed you in these ways.

Still, I think that we can do better within the guild of Christian historians to fortify and exemplify the priesthood of believers. We can encourage a deeper *faith* in God's vocation on our lives, strengthen one another in our common, priestly service and—precisely in so doing— help each other become much better Christian scholars. *Crede, ut intelligas*, say the Augustinians. Let us help each other believe *in order that* we may understand.[26]

As Kenneth Hagen has written of Luther's doctrine of vocation, "The vocation of love, serving the neighbor, is not optional. The whole structure of God's world is ordered so that the neighbor is served in and by vocation."[27] I need to order *my* work in this way—and I need your help to do so. May God help us all as we seek to serve our neighbors with faithful history.

NOTES

This chapter has been adapted (lightly) from a presidential address to the Conference on Faith and History, delivered on September 22, 2006, at Oklahoma Baptist University, Shawnee, Oklahoma. Thanks go to Andrew Finstuen, who inadvertantly inspired it, and John Fea, Jay Green, Will Katerberg, Scott Manetsch, Mickey Mattox, Eric Miller, Ben Peays, Hayden Thornburg, and my colleagues in the Deerfield Dialogue Group, who helped me to improve it. All scripture quotations are taken from the New Revised Standard Version (NRSV) Bible.

1. The best place to track the progress of this Christian historiography is in *Fides et Historia*, the journal of the Conference on Faith and History. See also the programmatic works of longtime members of the conference, such as George M. Marsden, *The Outrageous Idea of Christian Scholarship* (New York: Oxford University Press, 1997); Mark A. Noll, *The Scandal of the Evangelical Mind* (Grand Rapids, Mich.: Eerdmans, 1994); Ronald A. Wells, *History through the Eyes of Faith* (San Francisco: Harper & Row, 1989); and those whose

thoughts have been collected in a series of edited volumes, most recently Ronald A. Wells, ed., *History and the Christian Historian* (Grand Rapids, Mich.: Eerdmans, 1998). For a critical history of the conference, see D. G. Hart, "History in Search of Meaning: The Conference on Faith and History," in Wells, *History and the Christian Historian*, 68–87.

2. For a provocative set of essays calling historians to dig deeper in the field of faithful history, see "Rethinking the Framework of History," a symposium that originated in meetings at Calvin College and was published the following year in *Fides et Historia* 34 (Winter/Spring 2002): 1–40. Contributors include Wilfred M. McClay, Christopher Shannon, Donald A. Yerxa, Jay D. Green, and Eric Miller.

3. Frederick William Danker, ed., *A Greek-English Lexicon of the New Testament and Other Early Christian Literature*, 3rd ed., based on Walter Bauer's *Griechisch-deutsches Wörterbuch zu den Schriften des Neuen Testaments und der frühchristlichen Literatur*, 6th ed., ed. Kurt Aland and Barbara Aland, with Viktor Reichmann, and on previous English editions by W. F. Arndt, F. W. Gingrich, and F. W. Danker (Chicago: University of Chicago Press, 2000), 549.

4. On the theological uses of the Latin word *vocatio*, see Richard A. Muller, *Dictionary of Latin and Greek Theological Terms, Drawn Principally from Protestant Scholastic Theology* (Grand Rapids, Mich.: Baker, 1985), 329–30.

5. Paul A. Marshall, *A Kind of Life Imposed on Man: Vocation and Social Order from Tyndale to Locke* (Toronto: University of Toronto Press, 1996), is unusually insightful on subsequent Protestant work on the doctrine of Christian vocation, especially in Great Britain. On recent Roman Catholic developments, see Aurelie A. Hagstrom, *The Concepts of the Vocation and the Mission of the Laity* (San Francisco: Catholic Scholars Press, 1994).

6. André Lacocque, *But As for Me: The Question of Election in the Life of God's People Today* (Atlanta: John Knox Press, 1979). On Old Testament priesthood, cf. Philip Jenson's entry and extensive bibliography on *kōhēn* in Willem A. VanGemeren, ed., *New International Dictionary of Old Testament Theology and Exegesis* (Grand Rapids, Mich.: Zondervan, 1997), 2:600–605. Jenson confirms (600) that in the Old Testament "priestly language is occasionally used of the nation of Israel. In Exod. 19:6 Israel is called 'a kingdom of priests and a holy nation.' The priestly people are to mediate the knowledge and the blessing of the holy God to other peoples (cf. 15:11–17; 19:5–6; Lev. 20:22–26)."

7. The English word "priest" derives from the Greek word *presbyteros*, meaning "elder." After the time of the New Testament, *presbyteros* came gradually to refer to people and practices involved in priestly ministry. Over the course of the Middle Ages, *presbyteros* and the Latin terms *sacerdos* and *presbyter* came to be used interchangeably. On *presbyteros*, consult Danker, *A Greek-English Lexicon*, 862.

8. A brief but reliable English summary of Luther's doctrine of the priesthood may be found in B. A. Gerrish, "Priesthood and Ministry in the Theology of Luther," *Church History* 34 (December 1965): 404–22. The classic source on Luther's doctrine of the vocation of believers is Gustaf Wingren's Swedish book, *Luthers Lära om Kallelsen; Akademisk Avhandling* (Lund: C. W. K. Gleerups Förlag, 1942), the standard English translation of which is by Carl C. Rasmussen, *Luther on Vocation* (Philadelphia: Muhlenberg Press, 1957). Cf. Kenneth Hagen, "A Critique of Wingren on Luther on Vocation," *Lutheran Quarterly* 16 (2002): 249–73. For a shorter and more lucid introduction to this doctrine, see the essay by Karlfried Froehlich, "Luther on Vocation," *Lutheran Quarterly* 13 (1999): 195–207.

9. Martin Luther, *Treatise on the New Testament, That Is, The Holy Mass* (1520), trans. Jeremiah J. Schindel, *Luther's Works*, vol. 35, *Word and Sacrament I*, ed. E. Theodore Bachmann (Philadelphia: Muhlenberg Press, 1960), 101. For the German original, see *D. Martin Luthers Werke: Kritische Gesamtausgabe*, 69 vols. bound as 88 (Weimar: Hermann Böhlaus Nachfolger, 1883–2002, hereafter WA), 6:362. In every case, I have used the translations of the American edition of *Luther's Works* (hereafter *LW*), but have also cited the original sources as found in the *Weimar Ausgabe*.

10. Martin Luther, *The Freedom of a Christian* (1520), trans. W. A. Lambert, *LW*, vol. 31, *Career of the Reformer I*, ed. Harold J. Grimm (Philadelphia: Fortress Press, 1957), 355. For the Latin original, see *WA* 7:57.

11. Martin Luther, *Commentary on Psalm 110*, trans. H. Richard Klann, *LW*, vol. 13, *Selected Psalms II*, ed. Jaroslav Pelikan (St. Louis: Concordia Publishing House, 1956), 329 (comment on Ps 110:4). *WA* 41:205b. For other places in Luther's corpus where this doctrine is developed, see *The Babylonian Captivity of the Church* (1520), trans. A. T. W. Steinhäuser, *LW*, vol. 36, ed. Abdel Ross Wentz (Philadelphia: Muhlenberg Press, 1959), 112–13; *To the Christian Nobility of the German Nation Concerning the Reform of the Christian State* (1520), trans. Charles M. Jacobs, *LW*, vol. 44, *The Christian in Society I*, ed. James Atkinson (Philadelphia: Fortress Press, 1966), 129; *The Misuse of the Mass* (1521), trans. Frederick C. Ahrens, *LW*, vol. 36, 138–42; *Lectures on Isaiah* (1527–30), trans. Herbert J. A. Bouman, *LW*, vol. 17, *Lectures on Isaiah, Chapters 40–66*, ed. Hilton C. Oswald (St. Louis: Concordia Publishing House, 1972), 415 (in a comment on Is. 66:22); and Luther's *Sermons on the Gospel of St. John, Chapters 14–16* (1537), *LW*, vol. 24, ed. Jaroslav Pelikan (St. Louis: Concordia Publishing House, 1961), 242–43 (in a comment on John 15:8).

12. Luther, *Freedom of a Christian*, 356. *WA* 7:58.

13. Luther, *Commentary on Psalm 110*, 332–33. *WA* 41:210b–211b. On Luther's development of this doctrine, see Lowell C. Green, "Change in Luther's Doctrine of the Ministry," *Lutheran Quarterly* 18 (May 1966): 173–83. For a

helpful, brief summary of the doctrine of ordination during the time of the Reformation, see Wolfgang Klausnitzer, "Ordination," in *The Oxford Encyclopedia of the Reformation*, ed. Hans J. Hillerbrand (New York: Oxford University Press, 1996), 3:177–79.

14. See Calvin's *Institutio Christianae religionis* (1559), II, xv, 6; IV, i, 12; and IV, xix, 28. English translations are those of Ford Lewis Battles, taken from John Calvin, *Institutes of the Christian Religion*, 2 vols., ed. John T. McNeill, The Library of Christian Classics (Louisville: Westminster John Knox Press, 1960), 1:502; 2:1026, 2:1476. Cf. Calvin's comments on 1 Peter 2:9–10, published originally in his *Commentarii in Epistolas Canonicas, unam Petri, unam Ioannis, unam Iacobi, Petri alteram, Iudae unam. Ad Eduardum VI, Angliae Regem* (Geneva: Ioannis Crispini, 1551), and available in English in John Calvin, *The Epistle of Paul The Apostle to the Hebrews and The First and Second Epistles of St. Peter*, trans. William B. Johnston, ed. David W. Torrance and Thomas F. Torrance, Calvin's Commentaries (Grand Rapids, Mich.: Eerdmans, 1963), 265–67.

15. See especially the canons and decrees of the Council of Trent, Session 23 (July 15, 1563), in Norman P. Tanner S.J., ed., *Decrees of the Ecumenical Councils*, vol. 2, *Trent to Vatican II* (London: Sheed & Ward, 1990), 742–53.

16. William C. Placher, ed., *Callings: Twenty Centuries of Christian Wisdom on Vocation* (Grand Rapids, Mich.: Eerdmans, 2005), 328–30; and Miroslav Volf, *Work in the Spirit: Toward a Theology of Work* (New York: Oxford University Press, 1991), vii. Scholars like Volf, it should be noted, have gone on to develop alternative theologies of work, in Volf's case one based on the biblical conception of *charisma*, less conducive, he contends, than the Lutheran doctrine of *klesis* to ideological misuse by those who equate even the most dehumanizing forms of labor with God's will regarding one's occupational status. See Volf's *Work in the Spirit*, esp. 106–201. Perhaps this goes without saying, but in response to Volf and others I should point out that I do not maintain a medieval notion of calling nor an inflexibly hierarchical conception of society. Mine is not an attempt to defend Luther's doctrine in detail—especially not his assumptions regarding one's "external call" (*vocatio externa*) and its relation to one's station (*Stand*), on which see Volf, 105–6. Rather, I seek to appropriate Luther's doctrine of the sanctity of nonreligious vocations (that is, nonordained and nonmonastic vocations) for the daily lives and work of Christian historians. I side with Douglas J. Schuurman on the issues raised by Volf: "Clearly, the doctrine of vocation faces many pitfalls, and it can be and has been misused to exploitative and oppressive ends. But it remains a vital source of wisdom about faithful Christian living in the modern world. To recover that wisdom, we need to think again about vocation in the tradition of Luther and Calvin"; Douglas J. Schuurman, *Vocation: Discerning Our Callings in Life* (Grand Rapids,

Mich.: Eerdmans, 2004), 15. Cf. the exchange between Volf and Schuurman on the theology of work: Miroslav Volf, "Eschaton, Creation, and Social Ethics," *Calvin Theological Journal* 30 (April 1995): 130–43; and Douglas J. Schuurman, "Creation, Eschaton, and Social Ethics: A Response to Volf," *Calvin Theological Journal* 30 (April 1995): 144–58.

17. *Dogmatic Constitution on the Church* (*Lumen Gentium*—November 21, 1964), 4.31, as found in Tanner, *Decrees of the Ecumenical Councils*, 2:875 (cf. 4.34 in *Decrees* 2:877).

18. *Decree on the Apostolate of the Laity* (*Apostolicam Actuositatem*—November 18, 1965), 1.2, as found in Tanner, *Decrees of the Ecumenical Councils*, 2:982.

19. Karl H. Hertz, *Everyman a Priest* (Philadelphia: Muhlenberg Press, 1960), 19.

20. Gerhard Ebeling, "The Protestant Idea of the Priesthood," in *The Word of God and Tradition: Historical Studies Interpreting the Divisions of Christianity*, trans. S. H. Hooke (Philadelphia: Fortress Press, 1968; orig. pub. *Wort Gottes und Tradition* [Göttingen: Vandenhoeck und Ruprecht, 1964]), 203.

21. Sadly, non-Christian historians such as the radical Howard Zinn have often outpaced Christian historians in the arena of counter-cultural, self-sacrificial, scholarly service. For Zinn's scholarly program, see *The Politics of History*, 2d ed. (Urbana: University of Illinois Press, 1990).

22. After reading a draft of this essay, a philosopher friend reported that it reminded him of a well-known piece by Alvin Plantinga, "Advice to Christian Philosphers," *Faith and Philosophy* 1 (July 1984): 253–71, which originated as Plantinga's inaugural address as the John A. O'Brien Professor of Philosophy at the University of Notre Dame. I was pleased. For though I know well that I am no Alvin Plantinga, and though our essays differ somewhat in the advice they offer to colleagues, I applaud Plantinga's counsel: "My counsel can be summed up on two connected suggestions, along with a codicil. First, Christian philosophers and Christian intellectuals generally must display more autonomy—more independence of the rest of the philosophical world. Second, Christian philosophers must display more integrity—integrity in the sense of integral wholeness, or oneness, or unity, being all of one piece. Perhaps 'integrality' would be the better word here. And necessary to these two is a third: Christian courage, or boldness, or strength, or perhaps Christian self-confidence. We Christian philosophers must display more faith, more trust in the Lord; we must put on the whole armor of God" (254).

23. Richard T. Hughes, *The Vocation of a Christian Scholar: How Christian Faith Can Sustain the Life of the Mind*, rev. ed. (Grand Rapids, Mich.: Eerdmans, 2005), xxxi.

24. Hughes, *The Vocation of a Christian Scholar*, 134.

25. Richard C. Goode, "The Radical Idea of Christian Scholarship: Plea for a Scandalous Historiography," in *Restoring the First-Century Church in the Twenty-First Century: Essays on the Stone-Campbell Restoration Movement in Honor of Don Haymes*, ed. Warren Lewis and Hans Rollmann, Studies in the History and Culture of World Christianities (Eugene, Ore.: Wipf & Stock, 2005), 238–39. Another helpful, recent Anabaptist view of Christian scholarship may be found in a couple of articles by historian Perry Bush: "Economic Justice and the Evangelical Historian," *Fides et Historia* 33 (Winter/Spring 2001): 11–27; and "What Would History Look Like If 'Peace and Justice' Really Mattered?" *Fides et Historia* 34 (Winter/Spring 2002): 49–55.

26. For Augustine's use of this phrase, see his *Sermo*, 43.7, 9. Cf. Muller, *Dictionary of Latin and Greek Theological Terms*, 85, 117.

27. Hagen, "A Critique of Wingren on Luther on Vocation," 267.

The Christian Historian and the Idea of Progress

WILFRED M. MCCLAY

ONE THING THAT CHRISTIAN AND NON-CHRISTIAN HISTORIANS seem to share in the current dispensation is a profound unease with the very concept of progress. Of course, we are not prepared to give it up entirely. That would be nearly inconceivable. And in practice our skittishness about the idea of progress is a good deal more notional and superficial than it seems.

But the inertia of our culture's rooted belief in progress is being challenged constantly by the honesty of our questions. Hence when we speak of progress, it is so often "progress" that we speak of. The use of "sneer" quotes is often a way of pretending to be superior to the concept being invoked, and to those who would be so naïve or mendacious as to use the words without critical distance. But their use may also be a way of frankly confessing one's inability to get beyond straddling an issue. Or even a way of evading the law of noncontradiction, by both asserting and not asserting something at the same time. A way of saying tacitly what was once said biblically: "Lord I believe; help thou my unbelief" (Mk 9:24).

The idea of progress in history—the liberating song of the Enlightenment, the grand choral ode of the nineteenth century, the marching music central to the rise and dominance of the modern West—has gradually become problematic to us all. The skepticism runs deep. Not only is it our faith in the *inevitability* of progress that we question, but the very idea that we would have any sure means of judging what progress *is*, if it indeed does occur. Some of this can be attributable to intellectual fashion, or cultural boredom, or the occasional metastasizing of the Western self-critical impulse into a raging self-hatred.

But the nub of the problem arises not out of psychology, but out of historical reality. The idea of progress, after all, received its first, and perhaps profoundest, shock in the response to the First World War. That conflict's unprecedented, cataclysmic scale of destruction, its having arisen for the most obscure reasons and then having been carried along, seemingly unstoppably, by its own horrifying momentum, made a mockery of the great progressive assumption: that the growth of knowledge, social organization, and human control over forces of nature would lead steadily and inevitably to greater harmony, prosperity, rationality, and well-being.

The idea of progress has been on shaky ground ever since, and its detractors have found no want of additional evidence in support of their case. It sometimes seems as if progress has, all along, been accompanied by a doppelgänger, a shadow side, a reversal of Hegel's famous "cunning of reason," which has sought to make the works of reason all conduce to the benefit of unreason, and to make all that we had thought to be progress into something regressive. Such sweeping pessimism is, in a sense, far too easy, and regards too lightly such triumphs as the abolition of the African slave trade whose two-hundredth anniversary we have just observed, or the many material improvements, such as manifold advances in medicine and nutrition that have brought longer and fuller lives to countless persons all over the globe.

Yet it is plausible to argue that what we call "progress in history" has not brought moral progress along with material progress. It is plausible to assert that what progress we have made in freeing humankind from the constraints of material necessity has also increased the possibilities for human transgressiveness and wanton cruelty and destructiveness on larger and larger scales. In addition, it has estranged us further from nature, and perhaps also inhibited the development of resilient individuals who are also capable of sustaining love, empathy, and self-giving. In this starker view, what would appear to be steady progress has actually, in human terms, been steady degradation.

This last statement probably goes too far. But at the very least, one can say that the expansion of human agency, of the growing ability to master the material terms of our existence, has been an ambivalent achievement, one that does not necessarily bring moral improvement or human happiness. Far from bringing inevitable moral improvement, it may even severely impede the moral life, which derives not from a sense of mastery but rather from the acceptance of a life encircled by limitations and interdictions.[1] Far from bringing inevitable happiness, it may even bring on a kind of bottomless despair from which there is no exit, because there is no remaining excuse for one's failings, and no escape from one's putative mastery into the absolving fog of irresponsibility, let alone forgiveness. The more we are exclusively in control, the more we are exclusively to blame. The less willing we are to be judged, the less able we are to be forgiven.

If the idea of Progress is a big idea that we cannot do without, we can ill afford to hold it in disdain. But we need to find better ways of talking about it and thinking about it, ways of chastening it, restraining it, and protecting it against its excesses. It can survive as a big idea, but perhaps only if it is not *too* big. What this may mean is that progress needs to be liberated from being Progress, from the kind of nineteenth-century faith in Progress that posited it as a substitute for religion, with a secular and immanent eschatology.

Here is the first of several points at which the perspective of a Christian historian may offer epistemological advantages, and may have something particularly valuable to convey to the general practice of the discipline, at a time when it badly needs to hear it. Indeed, I would like to suggest that recent efforts to reclaim a "place at the table" for Christian scholarship, admirable and necessary as they have been, have understated what a historiography grounded in Christian assumptions and perspectives might contribute.

The need to sustain the idea of progress, in the face of all its problems, was also the underlying theme of sociologist Robert Nisbet's grand

and gloomy book, published at the tail end of the gloomy 1970s, entitled *History of the Idea of Progress*.² The chief innovation of Nisbet's book was its argument that the idea of progress is not exclusively modern, but that it had ample antecedents in many ancient and medieval authors and texts. But it is perhaps more noteworthy for my purposes to point out that Nisbet strongly connected the health of the idea of progress with the health of the Western religious tradition. "Any answer," Nisbet wrote, to the question of "the future of the idea of progress in the West" is going to require an answer to a prior question: "what is the future of Judeo-Christianity in the West?" It was, he argued, a prior belief in the dimension of the sacred in human existence that gave authority to "ideas of time, history, development, and either progress or regress." Only on the basis of such confidence in the existence of such divine patterning could the West come to be confident that there was also such patterning in the history of the world.³

Nisbet was not himself a conventional religious believer, but he is hardly the only one to have come to similar conclusions about the role of religion in forming many of the most crucially important secular ideas. The German philosopher Jürgen Habermas has said similar things in recent years. "For the normative self-understanding of modernity," he said in a recent interview, reported by Richard Wolin, "Christianity has functioned as more than just a precursor or a catalyst. Universalistic egalitarianism, from which sprang the ideals of freedom and a collective life in solidarity, the autonomous conduct of life and emancipation, the individual morality of conscience, human rights, and democracy, is the direct legacy of the Judaic ethic of justice and the Christian ethic of love."⁴

Although it is important to note that Habermas's focus here is on equality rather than "progress," and that he remains firmly committed to strictly secular standards of discourse and judgment, the features he names as byproducts of the belief in universalistic egalitarianism are the very same features that a robust Western belief in the idea of progress would wish to claim for itself. It is also worth noting that, according to Wolin, Habermas's perspective on these matters has been crucially informed by his dialogues with Joseph Cardinal Ratzinger, now Pope

Benedict XVI, and by his growing concern over the moral implications of unconstrained biological engineering and human cloning—problematic fruits of an uncritical idea of scientific or technological progress, and one in which the formulation of strictly secular grounds for the imposition of limits has been slow and uncertain in coming.[5]

So the question arises whether the perspective offered by the traditional biblical religious heritage of the West, by what Nisbet called "Judeo-Christianity," has not only been an originating source for the idea of progress, but is and remains a source for the critique of that idea's hypertrophy. Does a reconsideration of the idea of progress from that standpoint hold the prospect of giving us resources for a better understanding of that idea?

To begin exploring this problem I have in what follows selected for examination three important English-language books published at roughly the same time, during the middle interwar years: Herbert Butterfield's *The Whig Interpretation of History* (1931), Christopher Dawson's *Progress and Religion: An Historical Inquiry* (1929), and Reinhold Niebuhr's *Moral Man and Immoral Society* (1932). These were arguably the most important works produced by their authors, men whose work was centrally concerned with discovering the reasons why the idea of progress in history had become so problematic and what was to be done about it. Each author operated in such a way as to permit the examination of history on a very large scale. Each understood the calamity of the First World War as a mortal challenge to the once-regnant metanarratives regarding progress in history. But each one understood the challenge in a different way, with different conclusions and different implications for the future of the idea of progress. And each author came to the subject grounded in religious commitments which would be brought to bear, directly or indirectly, on the subject at hand. In some sense, the relationship between the Christian cultural legacy and the idea of progress was the subject each of them was engaging. Yet the uses to which they put Christianity varied strikingly, as did their answers to the questions posed above. The epistemological advantages of Christian commitment, though real, did not yield a single definitive answer, but rather a web of discourse that is highly relevant to our own condition today.

BUTTERFIELD'S MODESTY

Herbert Butterfield was one of the most eminent figures of British academic life in the early and middle parts of the twentieth century, teaching for over fifty years on the faculty at Cambridge (1928–79), where he was Master of Peterhouse, Vice-Chancellor of the University (1959–61), and Regius Professor of Modern History (1963–68).[6] He was a scholar of remarkably wide-ranging interests, and published influential books in such fields as the history of science, eighteenth-century constitutional history, and international politics, among other subjects. But his small book on the "Whig interpretation" of history is probably his most enduring contribution and one of the handful of truly influential books in the field of Anglo-American historiography.[7]

In *The Whig Interpretation of History* Butterfield defined "Whig" history (using the term somewhat idiosyncratically) precisely in terms of its alignment of the story of the past strictly in line with the dictates of the idea of progress and the present's imperious need to understand itself as a progressive advance upon the past. What he called "Whig history" referred to "the tendency of so many historians to write on the side of Protestants and Whigs, to praise revolutions provided they have been successful, to emphasize certain principles of progress in the past and to produce a story which is the ratification if not the glorification of the present."[8] Butterfield stood firmly against such tendencies, which seemed to him gross oversimplications of the past and betrayals of the rightful task of the historian. The historian should prescind from making such arguments, he thought, and choose for himself a more modest role, answerable to a different set of canons. No mere mortal historian had a right, or had sufficient knowledge, to be making the kind of final moral judgments about historical actors and movements that Butterfield saw and criticized in, for example, the writings of Lord Acton.

Instead, Butterfield sought a historiography that would take losers just as seriously as winners and, instead of tracing a line of triumphant truths culminating in the dominant conventional wisdom of the present, would seek deliberately to distance itself from Acton's smug view that "history is the arbiter of controversy," and firmly reject the self-satisfied idea that the way things have turned out is, in some sense, the

way they *should* have. The historian played a different kind of role, trying to study the past without insisting upon its reference to the present
and without playing the arbiter, the "avenging judge" who is engaged
in dispensing "verdicts." Instead, the historian had a broader civilizing
task. He should be trying to cultivate the intellectual and moral discipline required to "enter into minds that are unlike our own," to make
sympathetic contact with the full range of human experience and cognition, to "see all lives as part of the one web of life," and to take "men
and their quarrels into a world where everything is understood and all
sins are forgiven." It was a kind of God's eye view to which he aspired,
one in which a deliberate attempt was made to set aside the dominant
moral claims and sympathies of one's own era—not out of a misplaced
relativism, but out of a carefully thought-out set of judgments about the
limits of what historians can do, and the peculiar set of virtues to which
they should aspire.[9]

Such a view was, in a way, a precursor to the great flowering of
social history and history "from the bottom up" that has transformed
American historical writing over the past four decades. It also clearly
reflects the influence of Butterfield's active Methodist religious faith,
with its insistence upon respecting equally the historical experience of
all persons, and not merely those who were granted fortunate outcomes
and fortunate alignments in their lives. All were equally creations of
God; all fell equally within His providential reach; all had an intrinsic
importance and value; all would be judged by God alone. We should not
presume that the events and outcomes that we find to be of note are, in
fact, noteworthy *sub specie aeternitatis*. To cultivate such inclusiveness
of vision is a kind of spiritual discipline; to achieve it, even in only small
and intermittent measure, a kind of godliness.

One might have guessed that his strong Christian convictions would
have caused Butterfield to seek eagerly for the traces of God's hand in
history. Yet that was not the case at all. Butterfield was quite severe in
denouncing the idea that historians had it in their power to acquaint
themselves with the operations of Providence. That was stepping over
the line, from being god-ly to being god-like. Such was precisely the
error committed by the Whig historians, who were too confident that
they knew where "history" was "going," and that their judgments about

questions of importance and nonimportance corresponded with those of the Deity. Butterfield thought it a massive arrogation for the historian to think that he had even the remotest capacity for such high-level teleological judgments. That was simply not his job. More, it was beyond his ken, or that of any mere mortal. Paradoxically, then, it was not out of programmatic skepticism, but precisely out of Butterfield's robust religious beliefs, including his eschatological confidence in God's providence, that he was able so easily to insist that the historian has to forswear any attempt to make final moral claims about the deeds and the consequences of human history. Comprehensive providential understanding, just like vengeance, should be yielded up unto the Lord, and for exactly the same reasons. The best that the mortal historian can hope for, or aspire to, is an impartial record of what happened, with all its complexities and ambivalences. History is not an oracle. Instead, Butterfield thought that it had to be regarded with suspicion, as an ambitious upstart always willing to give itself over as a hireling or harlot, beholden to unsavory worldly alliances. Hence its judgments are never to be trusted as final or ultimate. "In other words," he said in his deceptively simple concluding words, "the truth of history is no simple matter . . . and the understanding of the past is not so easy as it is sometimes made to appear." The idea of progress, particularly as the Whig historians employed it, was in his view a terrible and dangerous simplifier, which puffed up ordinary men into prophets, and dispatched other men, particularly those who had the misfortunte to be history's losers, to oblivion.[10]

There is much to be said for the generosity and epistemological modesty of Butterfield's position, which sought, quite simply, to exclude the idea of progress from having any decisive influence upon the proper practice of historiography. It corresponds very well with the general stated ethos of the historical profession as it exists today (if not always necessarily the profession's actual practice). Yet this position, which for taxonomic purposes I will call the *exclusionary* stance, does not really do justice to the seriousness of the problem. In the end, it treats the idea of progress as dispensable, even as it relies upon the continued existence of the idea, as embodied in Whig historiography, as an antagonist, and hence an organizing principle. So accustomed is it to the rock-solid existence of the Whig hegemony against which it rebels, that it does not take seriously the possibility that, in the absence of such an ordering principle, Western history might have no good way to reorganize itself.

In addition, it seems to leave out of account one of the chief culture-forming distinctives of Judeo-Christianity: its understanding of divine history and human history as intersecting stories, and not merely parallel or disparate ones. It would be wonderfully simplifying if one did not have to take account of this complexity, and secular historians, of course, do not have to. But the Judaism and Christianity of the Bible are faiths whose God takes a very strong and active interest in doings of nations and the outcomes of historical events, and occasionally intervenes in them, sometimes quite dramatically. This Deity is also a God that delights in reversals and overturnings, making the first last, the last first, in ways that often entirely subvert the world's paradigms. But He does not *always* or *invariably* do these things. Sometimes He does the opposite. Hence, although Christians can have no expectation that there will be a sure correspondence between worldly success and metaphysical success, neither can they expect that the two will always be at odds.

What, then, was one to do with such a quirky, unpredictable, uncategorizable Providence? It seems that Butterfield did something rather similar to what the analytic philosophers of his day were doing: asserting that because nothing can be said with clarity and precision about God's activity in history, nothing should be said at all.[11] It was a perfectly reasonable move for any secular academic to make, and while a less obvious one for an avowedly Christian academic, nevertheless one that made considerable intellectual and moral sense, with an admirably ascetic integrity to it.

To be fair, it should be pointed out that Butterfield showed a keen awareness that there was some kind of necessary intersection, for Christians, of divine and human history, and laid that proposition out with clarity and eloquence in his impressively civilized 1950 study *Christianity and History*, a work now long out of print and sadly almost unavailable.[12] It is a work well worth reading, by Christians and non-Christians alike, as a classic statement of the civilizing effects of the historical imagination, and a glimpse into the mind of a great and humane scholar. Yet it has to be said that *Christianity and History* did almost nothing to show its readers how the Christian scholar might understand and explain the specific aspects of that intersection. Instead, the most powerful statements in the book tended to reinforce the separation of the two realms, rather than encourage their mingling, and to make the Christian view of history something highly individual, even subjective, in character. Approvingly citing Ranke's statement that "every generation is equidistant from eternity," Butterfield expands on the point:

> So the purpose of life is not in the far future, nor, as we so often imagine, around the next corner, but the whole of it is here and now, as fully as ever it will be on this planet. It is always a "Now" that is in direct relation to eternity—not a far future; always immediate experience of life that matters in the last resort—not historical constructions based on abridged text-books or imagined visions of some posterity that is going to be the heir of all the ages. . . . If there is a meaning in history, therefore, it lies not in the systems and organizations that are built over long periods, but in something more essentially human, something in each personality considered for mundane purposes as an end in himself.[13]

Even more powerful, but also perhaps more unsettling to some, are his concluding words:

> I have nothing to say at the finish except that if one wants a permanent rock in life and goes deep enough for it, it is difficult for historical events to shake it. There are times when we can never meet the future with sufficient elasticity of mind, especially if we are locked in the contemporary systems of thought. We can do worse than remember a principle which both gives us a firm Rock and leaves us the maximum elasticity for our minds: the principle: Hold to Christ, and for the rest be totally uncommitted.[14]

In other words, in place of Progress with a capital P, one should instead embrace the Rock with a capital R. Which is perhaps another way of saying that ultimate truth is, finally, outside of the reach of historical inquiry.

As I have already said, there is a great deal to be said for Butterfield's formulation. And in today's environment, many mainstream academics with religious commitments, perhaps even most of them, find that a choice to prescind from genre-mixing inquiries still makes a great deal of professional and personal sense. But such a stance does not give us any help in the task with which we began, namely, seeing whether there is a way that the perspectives provided by the great Western religious traditions might play a role in helping us to better understand, and perhaps reinvigorate or reappropriate, the idea of progress in history. On the contrary, Butterfield's position merely reinforces our distance from the very idea of progress in history. It does not merely problematize the relation between the two, but rules the question of their connection permanently out of bounds, a knowledge too noumenal for phenomenal beings.

DAWSON'S AMBITION

Christopher Dawson offers a very different kind of example, as an Oxford-educated independent scholar who had converted to Roman Catholicism in his twenties, and who never enjoyed the comforts of a regular academic appointment.[15] He was, then, something of an outsider compared to the ultra-insider Butterfield. But not entirely so, for he managed to cut his own impressive swath across the intellectual history of his time. He was widely respected for the broad learning and profound synthetic insight of his many books, as was amply evidenced by his selection to present the prestigious Gifford Lectures in 1947–49, from which his important book *Religion and the Rise of Western Culture* was derived, as well as his election as a Fellow of the British Academy, and his appointment as the Charles Chauncey Stillman Chair of Roman Catholic Studies at Harvard Divinity School from 1958 to 1962.[16] In addition, he was an important (and warmly avowed) influence on T. S. Eliot, among others, and a member in good standing of some of the same Anglo-Catholic intellectual circles in which Eliot ran. He had many admirers, and his bold and imaginative syntheses displayed the kind of expansive range and interpretive flair that one associates with such "big thinking" contemporaries as Arnold Toynbee and Oswald Spengler.

Progress and Religion: A Historical Inquiry appeared in 1929, and was explicitly composed as a response to the confidence-shattered aftermath of the Great War.[17] That conflict had, he remarked, led many people to "despair of the future of Europe," and to adopt "fatalistic theories of the inevitability of cultural decline"—again, the very inverse of the idea of progress.[18] Dawson agreed that the idea of progress was deeply imperiled, and felt the full weight of that fact. But he attributed that imperilment not to the *bouleversement* wrought by the war, but to a wrong turn that modernity had made much earlier, in believing that it was possible to detach the idea of progress from its religious roots and make the idea of progress itself into the focal point of a *secular* religious or quasi-religious faith.

Religion was, for Dawson, the core institution of any and every culture. That something like an active religion had to be present at the center of a functioning culture was amply demonstrated, he thought, by the history of comparative religions. The existence of a culture itself demanded it. "Every living culture," Dawson argued, "must possess some spiritual dynamic, which provides the energy necessary for that sustained social effort which is civilization." In other words, every vital society must possess that organizing core, and the characteristic religion of a society "determines to a great extent its cultural form." Therefore the entire process of studying social and cultural development has to begin and end, not with a treatment of economic or political factors, but with a consideration of the animating faith, the *cultus* around which the culture was organized, since that is the source and destination of everything else that transpires in it.[19]

Such concerns informed his understanding of the current crises, including the diminished condition of the idea of progress. The West as we know it was for Dawson the product of the confluence of two factors: the religious tradition deriving from Judeo-Christianity and the scientific tradition which derived (ultimately) from ancient Greece. Dawson saw the two factors as entirely complementary, when properly understood. The second had proven to be enormously powerful and pervasive in its influence, not only in the realms of science proper but also in the development of Western philosophy, law, and modern political and social organization. Yet for Dawson it was the first, the religious factor, that constituted the truly "dynamic" force in Western civilization, the organizing spark and propulsive engine that supplied the energy and direction for the West. Hence the "Religion of Progress," an understanding of progress that had removed progress from its relationship to religion and established it as a strictly secular force, would continue to have vitality only so long as it was able to draw on the religious tradition that it had, explicitly or implicitly, rejected. But in the end it had no independent force of its own, and was doomed to fail when the inertial momentum had faded.[20]

By shunting aside its religious basis and making Progress itself into a false object of worship, the modern West had cut itself off from the chief sources of nourishment for its very roots, and made Progress into something potentially monstrous and uncontrollable. It is important to stress that this harsh judgment was not born of hostility to science on Dawson's part nor a desire to seek its repudiation. On the contrary, he saw modern science as an extraordinary human achievement and grasped the mutually beneficial relationship that could, and should, exist between religion and science. But that relationship ceases to exist when one force succeeds in overwhelming the other and the essential benefits of complementarity are lost. "Without religion," he observed, "science becomes a neutral force which lends itself to the service of militarism and economic exploitation as readily as to the service of humanity." But "without science," on the other hand, "society becomes fixed in an immobile, unprogressive order." Both are necessary, for it is "only through the cooperation of both these forces that Europe can realize its latent potentialities and enter on a new phase of civilization."[21]

As those rather upbeat final words should imply, Dawson was (unlike Butterfield) actually a quite enthusiastic believer in the career of the idea of progress, so long as the idea could once again become rightly understood, as it had *not* been over the past two centuries. "The religious impulse must express itself openly through religious channels," he insisted, rather than "seeking a furtive, illegitimate expression in scientific and political theories." There should be no disguises and no tacit premises. The West must acknowledge that "our faith in progress and in the unique value of human experience rests on religious foundations, and that they cannot be severed from historical religion and used as a substitute for it, as men have attempted to do during the last two centuries."[22]

But when properly understood again, the idea of progress would face few intrinsic limits to the levels of development that might be hoped for from it. Indeed, there were passages in *Progress and Religion* that sounded positively giddy and utopian, imbued with a kind of high Hegelian optimism that was as far as could be imagined from the sober limits imposed by a religion historically grounded in the doctrine of original sin. For example, consider these two sentences, near the book's conclusion: "The progressive intellectualization of the material world which is the work of European science is analogous and complementary to the progressive spiritualization of human nature which is the function of the Christian religion. The future of humanity depends on the harmony and co-ordination of these two processes."[23]

The Europe of the future would be something dramatically new, dramatically different, he thought, from both the immobility of the East and the sterile materialism of the current West. It would promise an elevation of the human being to a more and more purely spiritual level of being, which would pave the way for a more and more durable international unity, as "the spiritual element," rather than the political or economic ones, became "the mainspring of our whole social activity."[24] Like many other postwar observers, Dawson was convinced of the need for a European union. But he was convinced that only the Christian tradition could provide the foundation for "the social unification that [Europe] so urgently needs." We can well imagine what Dawson would have thought about the much-controverted question of whether the European Union's draft constitution should have included mention of Christianity. But in fact, his vision of European union was not political at all. It would not be a "theocratic state," but rather "a spiritual community," whose centripetal energy "transcends the economic and political orders."[25]

The thrust of Dawson's work, then, could hardly have been more different from that of Butterfield's. Where the latter stressed the inappropriateness of imposing ideas of progress upon accounts of political and social events, the former sought to insist on the impossibility of properly understanding political and social events *without* reference to precisely such ideas. Where Butterfield saw little or no position of culture-forming influence for the historian, Dawson saw instead an enormous task and a vital role. Where Butterfield wanted to keep the eternal and the temporal separate, Dawson saw the West as precisely that part of the world, and the Western story as precisely that part of human history, in which those realms had been shown to intersect, and in which the possibility of such separation had been decisively refuted. The Christian worship of the God-man, of "the Divine Humanity" expressed in the person of Christ, held the key to the reconciliation of opposites. "The Christian," said Dawson, "and he alone, can find a solution to the paradox of the inherence of eternity in time, and of the absolute in the finite, which does not empty human life and the material world of their religious significance and value."[26]

There is an undeniable richness and suggestive depth to this analysis, even for the non-Christian historian. Dawson saw Christianity not merely as a set of doctrines or theological assertions, or a set of private individual desiderata, but even more as the foundational principle of a whole society, the organizing force of an entire way of life. We might classify his, then, as a *foundational* understanding of the relationship between religion and historical practice, and between religion and a society's view of the idea of progress.

But even if it could be demonstrated with Euclidean precision that all of human history so far had afforded not a single example of a vital culture that was not built around a religion—well then, who was to say that the time had not come when such an innovation would at last *be* possible, just as heart transplants and transatlantic flights and instantaneous global communications and other formerly unimaginable things were now possible? Why should historical precedent be taken to overmaster historical possibility? Secular modernity had never claimed to be able to justify itself by pointing to its long line of historical antecedents. Instead, it was precisely its departure from that long line of antecedents that constituted its most powerful appeal. Why could not the overcoming of the need for religion be itself taken as a profound evidence of progress?

And was not Dawson's appeal to the functional role of religion, like all such arguments, subject to the complaint that it traded in the social *usefulness* of religion rather than its *truth*? Let us think of Christianity not principally as a potentially effective agent of cultural formation and a good way to organize and manage a culture, but more narrowly as a set of assertions about the nature of God and the nature of the world we live in. What was there in Dawson's argument as I have described it above that would suggest reasons why historic Christianity would be deserving of a fresh look from the secular world and another chance to be culturally dominant within it? It is one thing to argue that the Christian faith is socially beneficial and even intellectual and morally plausible, but quite another to argue that it is true. But unless men and women are convinced of the truth of the Christian faith, how can it have the culture-forming role that Dawson describes—how can it even be a "religion" in Dawson's sense, that organizing force that constitutes a social world? For to argue for the resurrection of religion *because* it is the dynamic core of the culture of the West, and the proper partner for (and opposite number to) science is, at bottom, to make an argument from utility, from the standpoint of consequences rather than truth.

It is possible, then, that if the exclusionary stance claims too little, the foundational stance seeks too much—too much in the way it wishes to conjoin religion with the idea of progress (which of course for Dawson means progress *rightly* understood). Instead of allowing us to draw freely upon religious perspectives for purposes of clarification and discernment, it insists that the idea of progress can never again be understood properly unless it is once again seen through the eyes of the historical Christian faith—which for Dawson is inevitably the Roman Catholic faith, Protestantism having been, for him, ultimately a cause and symptom of the secularism of the present moment. To survive, the idea of progress would have to be reincorporated into a fundamentally religious worldview, and a particular one with a particular institutional grounding. This may well be the case. But it transposes the problem of the idea of progress into an entirely different key from the one with which we began. A problem of insight has been turned into a problem of faith.

Finally, like all declension narratives (which are, so to speak, the black sheep of the Whig narrative family), Dawson's account suffers from its tendentiousness, its tendency to preordain results and to interpret decline as a result of a mistaken judgment or an intellectual or moral lapse, rather than as the result of an historical dynamic that may itself have an important place—even if only a provisional one, like a structure of temporary scaffolding—in the larger unfolding historical narrative. History is not just an unfolding Logos. It also is full of serendipities and contingencies and trivialities and unexpected finds, which often turn out to be matters of enormous consequence. It is in precisely such matters that Butterfield's epistemological modesty would seem likely to serve us better, and equip us for fresh understanding. "Either Europe must abandon the Christian tradition and with it the faith in progress and humanity," Dawson sternly declares in the concluding pages of *Progress and Religion*, "or it must return consciously to the religious foundation on which these ideas were based." And this foundation, he further insists, "cannot be severed from historical religion and used as a substitute for it, as men have attempted to do during the last two centuries."[27] But this challenging formulation, while undeniably powerful and thought provoking, also begs the question of exactly what the "tradition" and the "historical religion" are, and what it would mean to "return consciously" to them—matters about which there is notoriously little agreement even among Christians.

Niebuhr's Reflexivity

A third, and rather different, perspective on the subject comes from the man who was arguably the most prominent American public theologian of the twentieth century, Reinhold Niebuhr. He enjoyed an unusually long and productive career, churning out innumerable books, articles, reviews, sermons, speeches, pamphlets, and other writings in the years between the First World War and the Vietnam War. He was not merely a theologian and scholar of distinction, but a public intellectual of the first order, who addressed himself to the full range of contemporary concerns. He had a mind of enormous scope and ambition, and there is hardly an issue of importance—political, social, economic, cultural, or spiritual—that he did not discuss in his many works.[28]

His early formation was as a liberal Protestant of strongly progressive sympathies. Yet his explosive 1932 book *Moral Man and Immoral Society* was a salvo directed at progressivism's central belief in the malleability and perfectibility of human nature.[29] In so doing, he established himself as one of America's most notable internal critics of American progressive thought, breaking thereby not only with such distinguished contemporaries as John Dewey but with a long line of predecessors stretching back to the likes of Herbert Croly and Edward Bellamy. It became the burden of his career to present the Christian faith not merely as the carrier of progressive ideals but also as a tough-minded but essential corrective to them.

Born in 1891 in rural Missouri, he was the son of a German immigrant pastor affiliated with a tiny Protestant denomination known as the German Evangelical Synod. He inherited from his father not only a strong sense of theological vocation but a keen interest in social and political concerns. As a consequence of that influence, as well as his two years at Yale Divinity School, Niebuhr began his career as a devotee of the social gospel: the movement within liberal Protestantism that located the gospel's meaning in its promise as a blueprint for progressive social reform, rather than in its assertions about the nature of supernatural reality. Social gospelers were modernists who played down the authority of the Bible and the historical creeds, insisting that the heart of the Christian gospel should be understood symbolically and expressed in the language and practice of social reform. In Walter Rauschenbusch's words, "we have the possibility of so directing religious energy by scientific knowledge that a comprehensive and continuous reconstruction of social life in the name of God is within the bounds of human possibility." The Kingdom of God was not reserved for the beyond, but could be created in the here and now, by social scientists and ministers working hand in hand.[30]

This sounded like the makings of an organizing spark, but Niebuhr soon grew impatient with it. He found the progressive optimism undergirding the social gospel to be naïve about the intractable fallenness of human nature, and therefore inadequate to the task of explaining the nature of power relations in the real world. What Christianity called "sin" was not merely a byproduct of bad but correctible social institutions. "Sin" identified something inherent in the human condition, some deep and uncorrectable disorder in the structure of the human soul, something social institutions could never completely reform. The doctrine of original sin was, at bottom, empirically valid, simply because it reflected the observable truth about human behavior as it actually was, and did so far better than any of the alternatives on offer. It required an enormous leap of faith to conclude that men are perfectible, while it requires only open eyes to conclude that they are perverse.

Nor did Niebuhr accept the belief of so many American progressives that the individual was improved and morally uplifted by being "socialized," by being incorporated into the moral solidarity of social groups and thereby lifted out of the moral anomie of individual self-seeking. In *Moral Man and Immoral Society*, Niebuhr turned the social gospelers' emphasis on its head, arguing that there was an inescapable disjuncture between the morality of individuals and the morality of groups, and that the latter was generally *inferior* to the former. Individuals could transcend their self-interest only rarely, but groups of individuals, especially groups as large as nation-states, almost never.

In a word, he argued that groups generally made individuals morally worse rather than better, for the real glue that held human groups together was something more complicated than shared ideals. The larger the group, the greater the hypocrisy, the less genuine the altruism, and less humane the moral outlook. This became particularly complicated in questions of the nation, where some of the most admirable sentiments may feed the most unworthy goals. "Patriotism," he observed, "transmutes individual unselfishness into national egoism," and grants the nation moral *carte blanche* to do as it wishes. "The unselfishness of individuals," he mused, "makes for the selfishness of nations." That is why the idea of solving the social problems of the world "merely by extending the social sympathies of individuals" was so completely vain.[31]

Thus, Niebuhr dismissed as mere sentimentality the progressive hope that the sources of individual sin could be overcome through intelligent social reform, and that America could be transformed in time

into a loving fellowship of like-minded comrades, holding hands beside
the national campfire. Such a dismissive view of his progressive contemporaries was, to be sure, something of a caricature and unfair exaggeration, made for polemical effect. But it served to provide an effective
contrast to Niebuhr's own approach, which insisted relentlessly upon
the harsh and inescapable facts of fallen life. These harsh facts, however,
did not mean that Niebuhr gave up on the possibility of social reform
and the possibility of progress. On the contrary. Christians were obliged
to work actively for progressive causes and for the realization of social
ideals of justice and righteousness. This aspect of Niebuhr cannot be emphasized enough. Fatalism and complacency were not allowed. But in
doing so Christians had to abandon their illusions, not least in the way
they thought about themselves. The pursuit of good ends in the arena of
national and international politics had to take full and realistic account
of the unloveliness of human nature, as well as the unlovely nature of
power. Christians who claimed to want to do good in those arenas could
count on getting their hands soiled, for the pursuit of social righteousness would inexorably involve them in acts of sin and imperfection, not
because the end justifies the means but because the fallenness of the
world militates against the moral purity of any purposive action. Even
the most surgical action creates collateral damage, the responsibility for
which cannot be waved away.

But the Christian faith just as inexorably called its adherents to a
life of perfect righteousness, a calling that gives no ultimate moral quar-
ter to dirty hands. The result would seem to be a stark contradiction, a
call to do the impossible. Niebuhr insisted, though, that the Christian
understanding of life embraced both parts of that formulation. Man is a
sinner in his deepest nature. But man is also a splendidly endowed creature formed in God's image, still capable of acts of wisdom, generosity,
and truth, and still able to advance the cause of social improvement. All
these assertions were true, in his view. All had an equivalent claim on
the Christian mind and heart. In insisting upon such a tense, complex
formulation, Niebuhr was correcting the idea of progress, but he was by
no means abandoning it.

These ideas would continue to be developed in subsequent years.
In his own Gifford Lectures of 1939, later published as *The Nature and*

Destiny of Man, Niebuhr offered a magisterial *tour d'horizon* of the entire intellectual and spiritual history of the West, and in the process addressed himself more directly to the idea of progress itself.[32] His vision there incorporated insights that were highly reminiscent of both Butterfield's and Dawson's perspectives but enmeshed in a tensive and self-critical view that was very much Niebuhr's own, and that we here will call the *reflexive* stance.

As Niebuhr saw it, the Christian worldview had always understood history to be meaningful, but with its meaning sometimes discovered inside the crosscurrents of history and sometimes entirely outside them, a fact that, for him, made the interpretation of history a hazardous but necessary undertaking. The secularized idea of progress, however, had as its guiding principle belief in an immanent Logos that was no longer regarded as transcendent but was thought of as operating in history, bringing its disorder gradually under the dominion of reason, making chaos into "cosmos." Like Dawson, he understood this idea of progress as something that had originated under the wing of Christian theology and eschatology; the very language was the biblical language of creation, in Genesis and in the Gospel according to John. But the idea had been transformed and "liberated" during the Renaissance by two crucial post-Christian innovations, each of which discloses the emergence of a characteristic Niebuhrian theme. First, this new understanding of progress presumed that "the fulfillment of life" could occur without the supernatural interventions of "grace," and that the laws of reason and nature would serve as "surrogates for providence," giving "meaning to all of history." As for the questions of power that were at the heart of *Moral Man and Immoral Society*, the new view simply did not take those questions to be very important, precisely because it assumed that the Logos would "inevitably bring the vitalities of history under its dominion." Over against the idea that the Fall had rendered all of reality, and particularly human reality, out of joint with itself and beyond the reach of natural or human rescue, the new understanding sought to render all of reality as one potentially harmonizable continuum.[33]

A second and related point was that the thinkers of the Renaissance, while coming to regard history as dynamic, failed to see that the dynamism of history was *twofold* in character, and double-edged. They assumed, Niebuhr wrote, that "all development means the advancement of the good." But in so assuming, they failed to recognize that "every heightened potency of human existence may also represent a possibility of evil." Here we return to one of the concerns with which we began, the sense that even a very great progressive advance may contain within itself the potential for bringing about an equally great calamity. As Niebuhr explained it, everything that has its being within history is "involved, on every level of achievement, in contradiction to the eternal." This contradiction reflects the inevitable tendency of every comprehensive understanding of the meaning of history "to complete the system of meaning falsely," in a way that makes either the individual or the group "the premature centre, source, or end of the system."[34]

All modern interpretations of history, Niebuhr thought, show this tendency. Here his words are strongly reminiscent of Butterfield's: "They identify their own age or culture, or even their own philosophy, with the final fulfillment of life and truth and history. This is the very error which they have not taken into account or discounted in their basic principle of interpretation." But Niebuhr then goes on to add his characteristic reflexive dimension: "It is not possible for any philosophy to escape this error completely. But it is possible to have a philosophy, or at least a theology, grounded in faith, which understands that the error will be committed and that it is analogous to all those presumptions of history which defy the majesty of God."[35]

In short, for Niebuhr, modern interpretations of historical progress have been right in conceiving history dynamically and in taking a broader and more generous view of history's fertile and various possibilities. But they have conceived the dynamic aspects of history too simply. "They hope for an ever increasing dominance of 'form' and 'order' over all historical vitalities," he charged, "and refuse to acknowledge that history cannot move forward towards increasing cosmos without developing possibilities of chaos by the very potencies which have enhanced cosmos."[36] In other words, we are never out of the woods, so to speak, and the danger only increases as we progress. Man's capacity for evil advances apace with his progress toward the good; hence the greater the progress, the greater the need for vigilance, and the greater the need for some metaphysical check upon human pride.

In *The Irony of American History* (1952), Niebuhr explored how this same tension manifested itself in a consideration of America's role in the world.[37] Published at the height of the Cold War, *The Irony of American History* was a stinging attack on communism—and at the same time, a stinging indictment of American moral complacency and a warning against the moral failings to which that complacency made America vulnerable. Once again, Niebuhr was fighting on two fronts at once. Indeed, despite his passionate and unyielding opposition to the communist cause, Niebuhr also believed that the United States resembled its antagonist more than it cared to imagine, and much of the book is devoted to making that case. Americans rightly complained of the communists' dogmatic commitment to "philosophical materialism," the notion that mind is the fruit of matter and culture the fruit of economics. But, as Niebuhr pointed out, Americans could be said to be equally committed to materialism in practice. Here is a statement that rings even truer today than in 1952: "Despite the constant emphasis upon 'the dignity of man' in our own liberal culture," Niebuhr contended, "its predominant naturalistic bias frequently results in views of human nature in which the dignity of man is not very clear."[38]

So, he believed, the nation needed to be more rigorously self-critical in its exercise of its power. But he said something more. He added that America also had to act in the world, and do so effectively. Indeed, it had no choice but to do so. Just as the sinful and imperfect Christian is obliged to work intently for the cause of good, despite his incapacities and imperfections, so a morally imperfect America was and is obliged to employ its power in the world. Opting out is not an option; or rather, it is an option that is just as morally perilous as the alternatives it would avoid. Niebuhr puts it this way:

> Our culture knows little of the use and abuse of power; but we [now] have to use power in global terms. Our idealists are divided between those who would renounce the responsibilities of power for the sake of preserving the purity of our soul and those who are ready to cover every ambiguity of good and evil in our actions by the frantic insistence that any measure taken in a good cause must be unequivocally virtuous.[39]

Needless to say, Niebuhr rejected both of these options, which correspond roughly to attitudes of moralistic isolationism and amoral *Realpolitik*. He continued thus:

> We take, and must continue to take, morally hazardous actions to preserve our civilization. We must exercise our power. But we ought neither to believe that a nation is capable of perfect disinterestedness in its exercise, nor become complacent about particular degrees of interest and passion which corrupt the justice whereby the exercise of power is legitimatized.[40]

Niebuhr concluded *The Irony of American History* by invoking the example of Abraham Lincoln, whose Second Inaugural Address near the end of the Civil War exemplifies the doubleness of vision for which a Niebuhrian statesman should strive. Lincoln's great speech was notable for its unwillingness to demonize or diminish the soon-to-be-defeated enemy, and for its tempering of moral resoluteness by a broadly religious sense of a larger, imponderable dimension to the struggle. "Both sides," Lincoln famously declared, "read the same Bible, and pray to the same God. . . . The prayers of both could not be answered; that of neither has been answered fully. The Almighty has His own purposes." The vantage-point of a God who loves all his creatures was vastly greater than that envisioned by any fallible human cause.[41]

Again, one is reminded of the humanitas and humble restraint underlying the exclusionary historiographical stance of Herbert Butterfield. But it is also important to recognize that nothing in Lincoln's words suggested even a hint of faltering in the ultimate goal of destroying the Confederacy and reuniting the nation. Lincoln's awareness of the broader perspective invoked in his speech did not prevent him from taking strong action in the world, based on his own ideas of what constituted progress. And yet, the speech suggests not only Lincoln's great charity for the enemy but also his keen awareness of the arrogance, blindness, or triumphalism to which his own side was susceptible, flaws that might beget precisely the ironic effects that Niebuhr feared and deplored. This reflexiveness carries a price. Lincoln himself may not have been entirely innocent of such flaws, and the fact that his conduct of the war necessarily involved him in inflicting wounds that would be painfully slow to heal, only underscores the truth of his words. The combination of moral resoluteness about the immediate issues with a religious awareness of another dimension of meaning and judgment must be regarded as almost a perfect model of the difficult but not impossible task of remaining loyal and responsible toward the moral treasures of a free civilization on the one hand while yet having some religious vantage point over the struggle.[42]

There was no better example, Niebuhr thought, of the "dual aspect" to history's dynamism than the United States, where so many manifest strengths could also become dangerous weaknesses. America's "quest for happiness," he wrote, is suffused in irony, precisely because it has been so triumphant. The United States "succeeded more obviously than any other nation in making life 'comfortable.'" But it has "tried too simply to make sense out of life, striving for harmonies between man and nature and man and society and man and his ultimate destiny, which have provisional but no ultimate validity." This has had an ironic result. "Our very success in this enterprise," he observed, "has hastened the exposure of its final limits."[43] The "naturalistic bias" that has produced a condition in which even the very genetic foundations of human personhood are increasingly viewed as malleable on the deepest level has indeed led to a view of human nature "in which the dignity of man is not very clear."

Niebuhr understood the doctrine of original sin—which he believed to be at the core of the Christian understanding of human nature, with its dualities and tensions—as central to American democracy. As he often said, in various places and ways, man's capacity for goodness and justice makes democracy possible—and his susceptibility to sin and injustice makes democracy necessary. The tension between the two should be regarded as perpetual and mutually necessary, a perfect embodiment of the tense and necessary relationship between an optimistic idea of progress and a pessimistic view of human nature. The doctrine of original sin, while surely an enemy of Progress, is the best guarantor of the possibility of the marginal improvement of the human race, that is, progress rightly understood, since it offers us a truthful and realistic view of the crooked timber of humanity and prepares us rightly to live with a disjunction between the idea and the act, with the fact that we must strive, however imperfectly, for objectives whose fulfillment we may never see. "Nothing which is true or beautiful or good makes complete sense in any immediate context of history," wrote Niebuhr, in *The Irony of American History*, "therefore we must be saved by faith."[44]

DUAL ASPECTS

Of the three writers here under consideration, I suspect that Niebuhr may well be the one with the most to offer us in thinking about how a religious perspective can shed light on the present condition and future prospects of the idea of progress. His "reflexive" outlook takes account of the virtues of both Dawson's and Butterfield's works, by acknowledging that the idea of progress is deeply rooted in the Christian *Weltanschauung* and in Christian culture, but also by insisting that the misuses of the idea, including the overconfident identification of man's purposes with God's, are paradigmatic examples of sin at work—and moreover by insisting that the dynamic of progress in history, while genuine, is also *by its very nature* full of moral peril for us, precisely because of the kind of beings we are.

It also evades some of the defects in the other two authors' views. The exclusion of all moral or progressive criteria from the study of history, as Butterfield would seem to advocate, may be enormously enriching in the short term; but in the longer run it robs us of the uses of history as a source of moral orientation, since God's intentions, which are the only sure source of ultimate truth, are seen to operate entirely outside of the patterns of historical perception and validation. Yet Dawson's identification of the dynamic of progress entirely with the vantage point of "historical and traditional Christianity," and his imagined telos of "spiritualization" that envisions the eventual transformation of man *within* history, perhaps renders history's meanings too immanent, and thereby asks far too much of history, even as it fails to face up to the sheer incorrigibility of human nature. It perhaps fails to reverse the immanentizing of the eschaton that progressive secularism presumed.

What original sin is for the individual, the "duality of history's dynamic" is for the idea of progress in history; the second is merely the amplification of the first. What the nineteenth century lacked was a sense of the perilousness of progress. We now understand the peril. We have "progressed" this far, to such a level of self-understanding. But now we risk being overwhelmed by that sense of peril. Having discovered that Progress is not a god, we are now inclined to deny its existence entirely. This seems both unwise and unserious. What we need is a chastened but strengthened understanding of the idea of progress and of the possibility of a genuine human altruism that has the capacity to hold together a strong sense of both the promise and the peril that our efforts in the world inevitably entail.

Progress in history has turned from a complacent march into a tense tightrope walk. We can see now that every step we take not only carries us further along, which makes us determined, but also makes a possible fall more calamitous, which makes us terrified. We cannot afford to stop, but we also cannot afford to fall. So we must be very careful where we step, and how we step, and must consider where we are going. And to do so, with the right set of expectations, it would help greatly to have a clearer and more realistic idea of just what kinds of strange and willful, but also noble and imaginative, creatures we humans are. That the portrait supplied by the Christian faith is the best and truest on offer suggests just how crucially important the outlook of faithful historians could be in the revival of their own discipline.

Notes

1. A consistent theme of Philip Rieff, *The Triumph of the Therapeutic: Uses of Faith after Freud* (Chicago: University of Chicago Press, 1966); and *My Life Among the Deathworks: Illustrations of the Aesthetics of Authority* (Charlottesville: University of Virginia Press, 2006).

2. Robert Nisbet, *History of the Idea of Progress* (New York: Basic Books, 1980).

3. Ibid., 352–57.

4. Quoted in Richard Wolin, "Jürgen Habermas and Post-Secular Societies," *Chronicle of Higher Education*, September 23, 2005, B16.

5. Ibid., and Joseph Cardinal Ratzinger and Jürgen Habermas, *Dialectics of Secularization: On Reason and Religion* (San Francisco: Ignatius Press, 2006).

6. For biographical and other insights, see C. T. McIntire, *Herbert Butterfield: Historian as Dissenter* (New Haven: Yale University Press, 2004). Also extraordinarily valuable, particularly as a thorough meditation on Butterfield's view of Providence, is Keith C. Sewell, *Providence and Method: Herbert Butterfield and the Intepretation of History* (Sioux Center, Iowa: Self-published, 2001).

7. The most readily available edition in the United States is Herbert Butterfield, *The Whig Interpretation of History* (New York: W. W. Norton, 1965), which follows pagination of the 1931 British edition exactly.

8. Ibid., v.

9. Ibid., 1–8.

10. Ibid., 129–32.

11. I am thinking here, for example, of A. J. Ayer's famous statement in *Language, Truth, and Logic* (London: Victor Gollancz, 1936), 114: "Theism is so confused and the sentences in which 'God' appears so incoherent and so incapable of verifiability or falsifiability that to speak of belief or unbelief, faith or unfaith, is logically impossible."

12. Herbert Butterfield, *Christianity and History* (New York: Scribner's, 1950). See, for example, his insightful discussion of the relationship between religion and history on 1–8.

13. Ibid., 66–67.

14. Ibid., 145–46.

15. Biographical details are in Cristina Scott, *A Historian and His World : A Life of Christopher Dawson* (New Brunswick, N.J.: Transaction, 1991).

16. Christopher Dawson, *Religion and the Rise of Western Culture* (London: Sheed & Ward, 1950).

17. Christopher Dawson, *Progress and Religion: An Historical Enquiry* (London: Sheed & Ward, 1929; new Amer. ed., Washington, D.C.: Catholic University of America Press, 2001).

18. Ibid., 3.

19. Ibid., 3–4.

20. Ibid., 140–58.

21. Ibid., 191.

22. Ibid., 188.

23. Ibid., 190.

24. Ibid., 192.

25. Ibid., 191–92.

26. Ibid., 189.

27. Ibid., 188.

28. For biographical details, see Richard Wightman Fox, *Reinhold Niebuhr: A Biography* (New York: Harper and Row, 1987), and Charles C. Brown, *Niebuhr*

and His Age: Reinhold Niebuhr's Prophetic Role and Legacy (Harrisburg, Pa.: Trinity Press International, 2002). My own interpretation of Niebuhr's work, and particularly his book *The Irony of American History*, draws heavily on my essay "The Continuing Irony of American History," which appeared in *First Things*, February 2002, 20–25, also available at http://www.firstthings.com /article.php3?id_article=1975&var_recherche=mcclay+continuing+irony (last accessed March 3, 2010).

29. Reinhold Niebuhr, *Moral Man and Immoral Society: A Study in Ethics and Politics* (New York: Scribner's, 1932).

30. Walter Rauschenbusch, *Christianity and the Social Crisis* (New York: Macmillan, 1907).

31. Niebuhr, *Moral Man and Immoral Society*, 91.

32. Reinhold Niebuhr, *The Nature and Destiny of Man*, 2 vols. (New York: Scribner's, 1941–43).

33. Ibid., 165–66.

34. Ibid., 166–67.

35. Ibid., 167.

36. Ibid., 168–69.

37. Reinhold Niebuhr, *The Irony of American History* (New York: Scribner's, 1952).

38. Ibid., 6.

39. Ibid., 5.

40. Ibid.

41. Ibid., 171.

42. Ibid., 172.

43. Ibid., 63.

44. Ibid.

Contributors

Beth Barton Schweiger
Beth Barton Schweiger teaches the history of the early United States at the University of Arkansas. Her first book was a social history of religion in the nineteenth-century South. She has also co-edited, with Donald G. Mathews, a collection of essays on religion in the South. She is completing a study of reading and writing in the early nineteenth century.

Una M. Cadegan
Una M. Cadegan is an associate professor at the University of Dayton, teaching courses in U.S. culture and cultural history in the department of history and the American studies program. She holds a Ph.D. in American civilization from the University of Pennsylvania. Her research and publications explore the history of U.S. Catholic literary culture in the twentieth century.

Lendol Calder
Lendol Calder is professor of history at Augustana College in Illinois. A Carnegie Scholar, he works with others in the emergent field of the scholarship of teaching and learning to invent and share new models for teaching and learning at the post-secondary level. Currently he represents the Organization of American Historians on the board of the National Council for History Education.

John Fea
John Fea teaches American history at Messiah College in Grantham, Pennsylvania. He is the author of *The Way of Improvement Leads Home: Philip Vickers Fithian and the Rural Enlightenment in Early America* and *Was America Founded as a Christian Nation? A Historical Primer* (forthcoming).

Jay Green

Jay Green is in his twelfth year teaching history at Covenant College atop Lookout Mountain, Georgia. He and his wife have three school-aged children, and together make their home in Chattanooga, Tennessee. He is working on a book about Christian faith and public remembrance in American culture.

Bradley J. Gundlach

Bradley J. Gundlach is associate professor of history at Trinity International University in Deerfield, Illinois. He specializes in American intellectual, cultural, and religious history and also enjoys teaching broadly in world civilization, church history, and the philosophy and methods of history. He has made extensive study of the history of the evangelical engagement with evolutionary thought and is currently at work on a biography of Princeton theologian B. B. Warfield.

Thomas Albert Howard

Thomas Albert "Tal" Howard is associate professor of history and director of the Jerusalem and Athens Forum at Gordon College in Wenham, Massachusetts. He is the author of several publications, including *Protestant Theology and the Making of the Modern German University*, winner of the Lilly Fellows Program Book Award for 2007, and *God and the Atlantic: America, Europe, and the Religious Divide* (forthcoming).

William Katerberg

William Katerberg is associate professor of history and director of the Western American Studies Program at Calvin College in Grand Rapids, Michigan. He is also editor of *Fides et Historia*, the journal of the Conference on Faith and History. His most recent publications are *Conquests and Consequences: The American West from Frontier to Region* (co-written with Carol L. Higham) and *Future West: Utopia and Apocalypse in Frontier Science Fiction*.

Michael Kugler

Michael Kugler teaches European history at Northwestern College in Orange City, Iowa. His recent work focuses on Enlightenment debates about the theater, theological debates in the Enlightenment, and scholarly debates about the character of the Enlightenment era.

James B. LaGrand
James B. LaGrand is professor of history at Messiah College. He is the author of *Indian Metropolis: Native Americans in Chicago, 1945–75* and several articles on modern American history.

Wilfred M. McClay
Wilfred M. McClay holds the SunTrust Chair of Excellence in Humanities at the University of Tennessee at Chattanooga, and is the author of *The Masterless: Self and Society in Modern America*, which won the Merle Curti Award of the Organization of American Historians.

Robert Tracy McKenzie
Robert Tracy McKenzie is associate professor of history at the University of Washington. He is the author of *One South or Many? Plantation Belt and Upcountry in Civil War–Era Tennessee*, which received awards from the American Historical Association's Pacific Coast Branch and the Agricultural History Society.

Eric Miller
Eric Miller is associate professor of American history at Geneva College, in Beaver Falls, Pennsylvania. He is the author of *Hope in a Scattering Time: A Life of Christopher Lasch*. His essays have appeared in a range of publications, including *Christianity Today*, *The Cresset*, *First Things*, and *Books and Culture*.

Mark R. Schwehn
Mark R. Schwehn is Provost and Executive Vice President for Academic Affairs at Valparaiso University. He also serves as the project director for the Lilly Fellows Program in Humanities and the Arts, based at Valparaiso, and he holds an appointment in Christ College, the honors college of Valparaiso, as professor of humanities. In 1993, Oxford University Press published *Exiles from Eden: Religion and the Academic Vocation in America*, which is, among his publications, the one that relates

most closely to the subject of the present volume and to his own essay within it.

Christopher Shannon

Christopher Shannon is associate professor of history at Christendom College in Front Royal, Virginia. An historian of American intellectual life, he has written three books. *Conspicuous Criticism* and *A World Made Safe for Differences* examine the rise of the anthropological notion of culture as a secular substitute for a premodern, Catholic notion of tradition. He has recently published *Bowery to Broadway: The Irish City in Classic Hollywood Cinema*, a study of Catholic narratives of community in American popular culture.

Douglas A. Sweeney

Douglas A. Sweeney is professor of church history and the history of Christian thought and director of the Carl F. H. Henry Center for Theological Understanding at Trinity Evangelical Divinity School. He has written numerous books and articles on the history of Christianity.

Index